CONFLICTING WORLDS:
NEW DIMENSIONS OF THE AMERICAN CIVIL WAR

T. Michael Parrish, Series Editor

LINCOLN'S MERCENARIES

LINCOLN'S MERCENARIES

ECONOMIC MOTIVATION AMONG UNION SOLDIERS DURING THE CIVIL WAR

WILLIAM MARVEL

Louisiana State University Press
Baton Rouge

Published with the assistance of the V. Ray Cardozier Fund

Published by Louisiana State University Press

Manufactured in the United States of America
First printing

DESIGNER: Michelle A. Neustrom
TYPEFACE: Minion Pro
PRINTER AND BINDER: Sheridan Books, Inc.

LIBRARY OF CONGRESS CATALOGING-IN-PUBLICATION DATA

Names: Marvel, William, author.
Title: Lincoln's mercenaries : economic motivation among Union soldiers during the Civil War / William Marvel.
Description: Baton Rouge, LA : Louisiana State University Press, [2018] | Series: Conflicting worlds: new dimensions of the American Civil War | Includes bibliographical references and index.
Identifiers: LCCN 2018007292 | ISBN 9780807169520 (cloth : alk. paper)
Subjects: LCSH: United States. Army—Recruiting, enlistment, etc.—Civil War, 1861-1865. | United States. Army—History—Civil War, 1861-1865. | United States—History—Civil War, 1861-1865.
Classification: LCC E491 .M145 2018 | DDC 973.7/4—dc23
LC record available at https://lccn.loc.gov/2018007292

The paper in this book meets the guidelines for permanence and durability of the Committee on Production Guidelines for Book Longevity of the Council on Library Resources. ♾

FOR

James G. Smart,
my college advisor
AND
friend these forty years

CONTENTS

PREFACE

Thirty years ago I undertook a study of enlistment patterns among the Civil War soldiers from the New Hampshire town where I grew up, wondering whether the wealthier citizens of my community had let their poorer neighbors bear the burden of that conflict. Based on personal knowledge of generations of economic exploitation by local barons, I came to the question with a suspicion that this may have been the case, and most of the evidence I collected appeared to support that hunch. The finished article was published in 1988 under the now-cliché title "A Poor Man's Fight" in *Historical New Hampshire.*

James McPherson's Pulitzer Prize–winning *Battle Cry of Freedom* appeared that same year. Judging primarily on the basis of conscription loopholes, he concluded that the characterization of the war as a "poor man's fight" was not really accurate. In *For Cause and Comrades,* a 1997 book more specifically devoted to motivation, McPherson did not give much weight to the influence of money except in the case of men who accepted the largest bounties during the final twenty months of the war. Instead, as his book's title suggested, he emphasized the influence of patriotism—national pride, devotion to the Union, or love of liberty—as the primary initial and sustaining motivation for both Union and Confederate soldiers. We later corresponded about my contradictory local findings, and for a long time I concurred in his impression that my community posed an aberration, perhaps because so much of its population had been opposed to the war.[1]

Further research nevertheless resurrected my skepticism. Men enlisted with mixed motives to be sure, including a wish to prove their manhood or escape dull or obnoxious surroundings. Patriotism is also presumed to have been more pervasive in that day than in this, although claims of patriotic motivation warrant some scrutiny because of the tendency to glorify actions that were essentially pragmatic. Yet the direct comments or underlying circumstances of too many soldiers suggested obvious economic incentive.

The chance to earn some cash appears to have driven a great many men into uniform long before the advent of conscription and hefty bounties. The Union armies raised at the very outset of the war may, in fact, have fielded the largest proportion of financially motivated men. Those who "rallied 'round the flag" in 1861 have long been regarded as the most patriotic of all, yet they appear to have been at least as financially desperate as any who later enlisted for exorbitant bounties. Decades after the war, they may have forgotten facing unemployment or pressing debts when they enlisted, and that consideration has eluded most historians.

Civil War veterans' testimony about why they enlisted now dominates the narrative, as is illustrated by such incidental observations as Matthew Gallman's synopsis of what impelled the 1861 volunteers. "In the days after Fort Sumter," Gallman wrote in 1994, "the motivations for young men to enlist on both sides seemed wrapped up in the excitement of the moment: patriotic enthusiasm, the lure of adventure, and urge for vengeance." In his 1988 book on both armies, Reid Mitchell focused on Northern soldiers' devotion to Union and liberty.[2] McPherson's 1997 study reinforced that belief in altruistic inspiration. Most of what I wrote during that period reflected the same impression—despite nagging hints from my own community that more men of limited resources enlisted because they had greater need for the money it would bring.

As another historian has observed, concentrated examination of the voluminous contemporary manuscript material was only beginning when those books appeared.[3] The earliest studies of motivation during that research renaissance naturally reflected the most obvious of that evidence, which includes myriad direct statements of patriotic purpose, often expressed in soaring prose. That seemed to be the most prevalent motive because so many men insisted it was—believing it, or perhaps trying to convince others of it. Somewhat subtler manuscript evidence hinted at numerous other political, personal, or sociological reasons for military service, and those have been widely considered. Economic incentives attracted little scholarly attention because of the paucity of direct anecdotal evidence. It was understandably rare, after all, for a man to admit that he had enlisted because he needed the money (despite the numerous examples cited in these pages). Questioning economic motive therefore requires specific curiosity spawned by something other than direct testimony; examining that question involves extensive statistical research and concentrated study of individual circumstances.

A dozen years ago, during research for the first volume of what would become a four-volume series on Mr. Lincoln's war, I noticed conspicuous concentrations of shoemakers among early Union recruits. Then I stumbled on a monograph depicting the extreme economic distress afflicting those shoemakers as the war began. That prompted further research into the crippling recession of 1860 and 1861, which is seldom mentioned by historians of the war. Contemporary correspondence, diaries, and newspapers provided some direct evidence and much inferential evidence that this recession contributed heavily to Union recruiting during the first year of the conflict. Correlation of those and other sources also shows that other economic factors played a prominent role in filling Lincoln's armies throughout the war.

A panoply of economic studies of the Civil War have appeared since Charles Beard broached the subject more than a century ago. Those studies have compared slave and free labor or examined the economic causes of the conflict, the creation of the national banks, or the effect of wartime developments on the rise of capitalism. My focus is altogether different. I intend to show that most Union soldiers were drawn from the poorer echelons of American society, and to argue that economic influences had a great deal to do with bringing them into the army.

The most striking of the evidence is derived from a statistical analysis only recently made possible by the University of Minnesota's Integrated Public Use Microdata Series (IPUMS). Previously, efforts to settle questions such as the poor-man's-fight argument had to rely mainly on anecdotal evidence. Economic data from the census was not very useful in shedding light on such issues because it forced a reliance on mean (or average) wealth, which can be easily skewed. With its 1-percent sample of the 1860 census, the IPUMS project made it feasible to establish median wealth for every state based on census reporting—which, for all its flaws, is the best information available for so broad a study of individual economic circumstances.

Every man from a family below median wealth was not necessarily poor, but median wealth is more statistically meaningful than average wealth because it separates the poorer half of any population from the richer half. I did that with the equivalent of an army division of Civil War soldiers, running the names of every man in ninety-four sample companies from the Northern states through the 1860 census. In deference to the popular belief that the men who enlisted earliest did so from unbridled patriotism (which might infect rich and poor more equally), I focused on the first company mustered into service from each state during each recruiting period. When no roster was available for the first company, I went to the earliest for which I could find one. A winter of census research produced Table 1, which appears in chapter 2 and constitutes the core of this work. With surprising consistency, that data revealed that the earliest units were composed overwhelmingly of men from families claiming less than median wealth. The preponderance of poorer men was almost as significant among those who enlisted later in the war, except in some of the nine-month militia regiments of 1862 and especially the hundred-day volunteers of 1864.

Direct testimony and examples of individual economic condition augment that data, yielding an inference that is difficult to avoid. Patriotic ardor, an adventuresome spirit, and visions of derring-do surely did lure many Union recruits, but the desire for economic relief, an employment opportunity, or a financial windfall often provided the initial impetus or the overriding motive. Lest I be accused of unintended superlatives that cannot be proven, I contend only that economic incentives exerted greater stimulus on Union enlistments than has been acknowledged, and that ideology consequently may have exerted less influence than is currently believed.

Abundant and varied evidence reveals hundreds of thousands of unemployed, destitute men scattered across the United States early in 1861. A quarter of a century ago Robert A. Margo observed that, despite long-term growth in real wages during the first half of the nineteenth century, those real wages dipped significantly between 1850 and 1856; then came the Panic of 1857. Margo further noted that recovery from such a shock required as much as half a decade, but secession followed only three years after the panic, creating a deep recession in the industrialized Northeast and causing both market disruptions and a widespread currency crisis. As newspapers all over the country reported by the end of winter in 1861, huge numbers of men were thrown out of work or were not receiving their pay for what work they did. Such economic downturns usually create vast armies of migrant jobseekers, yet Eric Monkkonen's anthological study of tramps in the United States from 1790 to 1935 includes no reference to any instance of that phenomenon during the Civil War: one contributor concluded that the war "drew many wanderers off the roads and into army camps," which may have been a notable understatement.[4]

There is a touch of hyperbole in the choice of title for this book, which carries a tone of unintended insinuation but encapsulates the subject matter more concisely than anything the diligent pondering of several vocabularians could devise. Union soldiers did technically exercise mercenary behavior if they enlisted because they had no better options for obtaining money or sustenance; so did professionals in medicine or the ministry who joined the army because they could earn more there than as civilians. Few of those soldiers fit the popular connotation of someone who will defend any cause for money, and many of them felt patriotic enough, but students of the phenomenon do not always consider patriotism incompatible with mercenary service. Founding Father Robert Morris even thought, early in 1777, that Continental soldiers had become "the most mercenary beings" because of high enlistment bounties. No other single word except "mercenary" conveys the sense of someone who takes up arms for monetary reasons, even when that is not the exclusive motive.[5]

The financial inducements offered to recruits after the middle of 1863 grew so seductive that few historians have disputed the influence of that money on the decision to enlist, and consequently that period will receive somewhat less attention here.[6] Union soldiers were subject to mercenary motivation throughout the conflict, but the historiography of the war has almost universally presented the volunteers of 1861, and to a great extent those of 1862, as the purest of patriots. For all the recent inquiry into motive, no book has closely examined whether those earliest Union recruits might have been attracted by economic need, if not by the actual avarice that later enticed so many of the bounty men. It should not be terribly surprising to any believer in the constancy of human nature to find that this was often the case, despite the widespread presumption of greater patriotism then than now. The twenty-first-century soldier is also regarded as at least somewhat patriotic, but unemployment and economic disadvantage are still recognized as key factors in recruiting for the American military.

"An important predictor to military service in the general population is family income," Amy Lutz wrote in 2008 in a study of today's all-volunteer armed forces. "Class differences in military enlistment likely reflect differences in the non-military occupational opportunity, structured along class lines." Military service poses "fewer incentives for upper class participation," Lutz concluded. Despite other cultural differences, such observations are equally apt to the Civil War, which erupted in an era shaken by tremendous cultural ferment and economic transformation.[7]

While the source material for this book was drawn from all the loyal states, the statistical analysis of soldiers' financial circumstances is limited to the sixteen contiguous Northern states and Kansas. Border States are not included because they present political complications that could easily be mistaken for economic motivation. My scrutiny is also necessarily confined to white troops. The antebellum financial status of most black soldiers cannot be reliably documented, and much of that population would have been actuated by other obvious reasons that could not necessarily be attributed to their white counterparts.[8]

Some will inevitably wonder if Confederate recruiting followed a similar economic demography. Joseph Glatthaar's recent work indicates that Southern soldiers responded to different circumstances and incentives. Wealth did convey a measure of immunity from service in the Confederacy, though not to the extent seen in the North. As the profusion of soldiers from slaveholding households suggests, Southern troops were more likely to perceive their own interests in the war effort unrelated to Confederate scrip. Even if rebel armies had been disproportionately composed of the poor, any effort to determine why would be complicated by such factors as more comprehensive conscription, worse inflation, and the inclination to defend one's homeland from invasion.[9]

In an essay that appeared a few years ago, Adam Rothman remarked that "military historians are losing the battle for Civil War historiography" to those more interested in social and cultural history—citing in particular Chandra Manning's *What This Cruel War Was Over* and its theme of antislavery sentiment among Union soldiers. I see no battle between two types of history, although I do perceive a struggle for interpretive dominance. Some of the same sources that led Manning to a conclusion of soldier support for emancipation, or persuaded other historians of certain soldiers' patriotism, also provided me with evidence of men who enlisted for the money they could earn.[10]

No matter how many personal accounts may sustain a particular hypothesis, they cannot reveal the extent to which poor men carried the burden of the Civil War. The statistical analysis used here provides more reliably proportional evidence, even from a relatively small sample. Still, those personal accounts remain relevant to the narrative. Dry numbers may outweigh individual testimony as evidence toward a logical conclusion, but they will never replace diaries and letters as an expression of human experience. For that reason I include the words of the participants to support—and season—the statistical evidence.

ACKNOWLEDGMENTS

The first recipient of my thanks related to this book must be Jeff Wieand of Concord, Massachusetts, who is really responsible for its existence. Jeff read all four manuscripts in my series on the Civil War from the Northern perspective, and in the first volume, *Mr. Lincoln Goes to War,* I discovered extensive evidence for economic motivation among early Union volunteers. Research for *Lincoln's Darkest Year* produced similar evidence among Union soldiers who enlisted in 1862, before the period in which historians generally recognize the influence of financial incentives. With more of the same in the last two volumes, Jeff suggested that my next book ought to examine economic motivation among Union soldiers in general. A biography of Edwin Stanton distracted me for several years, but a census project at the University of Minnesota provided the data to test my economic theory with statistical analysis, and the results proved too consistent to ignore. So, Jeff, here's your book, albeit with a title you did not like.

Next comes Jim Smart, my college advisor, who volunteered to serve as a reader for this manuscript. His critical comments on the first two drafts convinced me to abandon much of my storytelling impulse and forced a fair amount of reorganization. My devotion to chronological narration precluded the wholesale topical rearrangement he would have preferred, but he nevertheless illuminated numerous areas in which shifting passages made obvious sense. Against determined resistance, he also had some success in abbreviating my Faulknerian prose. I may regret not following every particle of advice from someone so familiar with the idiosyncrasies of the academy (which may be the primary audience for this book), but I suffer from a nagging sense of loyalty to the general reader. The future of the past, after all, lies beside the armchair.

Mike Parrish, editor of the Conflicting Worlds series for Louisiana State University Press, aided me on past projects out of collegial generosity, sending long lists of relevant secondary works. As a slow reader who is always a few years behind in the current literature, I found that immensely helpful. For this book he inundated me with a blizzard of relevant secondary works on the subject, almost all of which proved useful. In him the press has a valuable ambassador, and its authors an attentive collaborator.

Joe Glatthaar, of the University of North Carolina, introduced me to the University of Minnesota's Integrated Public Use Microdata Series, which provided the census-based data on median wealth that formed the statistical foundation for this book. With the Northern focus of my research since 2004 and my perennial reading lag, I had not yet read Joe's latest census-based work when I attended the 2015 Fortenbaugh Lecture at Gettysburg, where he spoke on the results of that statistical research. A lack of reliable median-wealth data had previously stymied me from reentering the poor-man's-war debate, in which I could only have hoped that victory would go to the side with the heaviest bibliographies. In a barroom exchange after his lecture, Joe enlightened me about IPUMS, and the rest is history. But then, isn't everything?

George Rable, now "retired" from the University of Alabama and working as diligently as ever, shared the customary heavy volume of useful material that he encountered during his own research. I look forward to the day—I hope soon to come—when I undertake a project that will avail me a chance to reciprocate.

Will Greene has been more instrumental than he may realize in the production of this and recent books. His perusal of my manuscripts has saved me from many a factual and historiographical blunder. Much of my research for the past quarter century has also benefited from his and Maggie's hospitality at Casa Verde and Mesa Verde (which I think of instead as Casa de Vertigo). Periodic seminars at Petersburg's Pamplin Park—a treasure emanating almost entirely from Will's vision and vigor—have provided valuable opportunities for a reclusive historian to associate with peers. Will's wide circle of friends and colleagues has precipitated many an introduction to historians I previously knew only by reputation. It was also his endorsement that appears to have yielded my highly prized honorary admission to the "LSU mafia," which makes it all the more gratifying to have my name on an LSU Press book.

I must thank Leigh E. Cummings Jr. of the Aroostook County Historical and

Art Museum in Houlton, Maine, for permission to use the image of a wartime recruiting poster owned by that institution. I am also indebted to Sofia Yalouris of the Maine Historical Society for providing me with a usable version of that image.

As usual, I have been the beneficiary of much help from a legion of archivists and curators from around the country. The following are those whom I have pestered the most over the past dozen years: Jeff Flannery, Bruce Kirby, Patrick Kerwin, and Joseph Jackson at the Library of Congress; Richard Baker, Steve Bye, Tom Buffenbarger, Rodney Foytik, and Shannon Schwaller at the Army Heritage and Education Center, as well as Chief Historian Dick Sommers and David Keough, both since retired, and the late Art Bergeron; Peter Drummey's invariably helpful staff at the Massachusetts Historical Society; Eric Frazier at the Boston Public Library; Malia Ebel and the now-retired Bill Copeley and Peter Wallner at the New Hampshire Historical Society; Bill Ross, in Special Collections at the University of New Hampshire; retired New Hampshire state archivist Frank Mevers; Sarah Hartwell and her several successors at Dartmouth College's Rauner Library; Nick Noyes, Bill Barry, and Jamie Kingman Rice at the Maine Historical Society; Paul Carnahan and Marjorie Strong of the Vermont Historical Society; Jeff Marshall, of the Special Collections Department at the University of Vermont; Mary Huth, retired now from Special Collections at the University of Rochester; Janet Bloom at the University of Michigan's Clements Library, along with Malgosia Myc and Marilyn McNitt at Michigan's Bentley Historical Library; Nan Card at the Rutherford B. Hayes Presidential Library; Thomas Hamm at Earlham College; George Rugg, in Special Collections at Notre Dame; Steve Nielsen at the Minnesota Historical Society; Dennis Northcutt at the Missouri Historical Society; and Lin Fredericksen and Darrell Garwood at the Kansas State Historical Society. Accommodating staff members also served me at the American Antiquarian Society; the Southern Historical Collection at the University of North Carolina; Yale's Beinecke and Sterling Libraries; state historical societies of Rhode Island, Connecticut, Ohio, Indiana, Wisconsin, Iowa, and Nebraska; and the special collections departments of Indiana University and the Universities of Iowa, Missouri, and Kansas.

Last as always (and as always not least) is the gratitude I owe Ellen Schwindt. Her musical preoccupation not only allows me long days of concentrated study and writing but also entertains me with the muted echoes of Bach, Beethoven, Martinů, and Schwindt drifting up the stairway and heat registers. To her busy days of composing and cooking she often adds service as a typical, well-educated general reader, proposing a host of explanatory revisions to my manuscripts. She also provides me with a daily reminder of the importance of making time for play. Had I not begun one research trip to Washington early enough to attend the Glen Echo contra dance, my manuscripts might still be badly marred with esoteric prose and the drippings from toasted peanut-butter-and-jelly sandwiches.

LINCOLN'S MERCENARIES

INTRODUCTION

The historiography of the economic status of Civil War veterans is long, but it is neither deep nor conclusive. Since Fred Shannon's limited investigation of mercenary motivation among Union soldiers in 1926, the topic has been considered only through local studies in journal articles and dissertations. Some concluded that the poor bore the greater burden of military service, some argued that it was more equitably distributed (even while presenting statistics that hinted otherwise), and some left the issue unresolved.

Most of those studies necessarily relied on average wealth or on wealth thresholds chosen arbitrarily. Average wealth as claimed on the 1860 census was always easy to determine, since total wealth and total population are known. Yet average wealth serves little comparative purpose because a single wealthy individual can—and usually does—distort any company-sized sample. Median wealth instead divides a population precisely in half. Previously, determining median wealth was extremely laborious: one began by recording the amount of property claimed on the census by every person in a given community, in every dollar increment from nothing to the largest fortune, ranking those individual amounts from zero upward, tallying the number who claimed each of those amounts, and finding the dollar amount that divided the population into numerically equal halves. It was a feasible exercise in a town-sized sample and was still often possible at the county level, but beyond that it became too onerous to consider. The survey of median-wealth statistics derived from the 1860 census by the University of Minnesota's Integrated Public Use Microdata Series (IPUMS) now allows for easy computation of median-wealth figures in every state. Such figures provide the boundaries separating the less-affluent half of the population from the more affluent, making it possible at last to determine which bore the greater part of the military burden.

Close studies of enlistment patterns in individual communities usually confirm that those who entered the army were primarily young or middle-aged men with little or no property. In his study of York County, Pennsylvania, Mark Snell found that 14 percent of those who owned no property enlisted in 1861, but only 5 percent of men who owned any property did so—and he described even those men as "relatively poor." The same or worse seemed true after establishment of the draft, as Snell also noted, because legal provisions favored wealthier citizens with avenues for avoiding service.[1]

Studying the towns of Claremont and Newport, New Hampshire, before it was possible to establish median wealth, Thomas Kemp rejected the idea of the war as a poor man's fight, yet he cited evidence supporting that very conclusion. He calculated that only 7 percent of the men in Claremont who owned more than $1,000 in property ever enlisted, and only 8 percent in Newport, while 38 and 40 percent of the respective towns' overall population of military age enlisted. New Hampshire's median wealth in 1860 turned out to be $1,100, so Kemp's figures imply that all but a small fraction of those two towns' soldiers came from the lower half of the economic spectrum.[2] His figures inevitably would have been a little more moderate had Kemp been able to measure median family wealth.

Without realizing it, John Hoptak demonstrated in his dissertation that well over two-thirds of the men in his study group, the 48th Pennsylvania, came from the economically disadvantaged half of the state's population. Median-wealth statistics were not then available to Hoptak either, but in comparing relative wealth among members of that regiment he chose to divide them at the threshold of five hundred dollars in real and personal property. By coincidence, that turned out to be exactly the median household wealth in Pennsylvania in 1860. Of the 657 soldiers Hoptak was able to find on that census, only 207, or 31.5 percent, came from families holding more than five hundred dollars in property.[3]

Paul Ledman's study of volunteers from Cape Elizabeth and South Portland, Maine, also preceded any practical determination of statewide median wealth. He discovered that a significant majority of poorer men enlisted for the three-year term of service, while wealthier volunteers formed a majority in the nine-month militia service of 1862. Comparing the levels of wealth he selected against the state median wealth reinforces his observation that the men who did the actual fighting tended to be poorer. He also argued that because of the bounties offered later in the war, the nonresident volunteers credited to those towns were drawn heavily from the state's poorer people.[4]

In a 2012 article on early motivation among soldiers from northern Illinois, Wayne Duerkes conceded that money "was a motivator," noting the importance of bounties and family support. He also deduced that some men found the pay alone sufficient but identified "young men just leaving home" as the most susceptible to that incentive. Duerkes made no reference to the disastrous economic climate during the first year of the war.[5]

Stephen J. Buck's examination of soldiers who enlisted from DuPage County, Illinois, included a breakdown of their wealth that showed a different trend. Dividing the population into deciles of family wealth based on a random sampling, he concluded that families in the top five deciles supplied a significant majority of both the officers and the enlisted men from that county. The threshold between the fifth and sixth deciles would theoretically mark the median wealth of the county, which made Buck the first to apply any semblance of median-wealth statistics to the subject. DuPage County showed a slightly higher per-capita wealth in 1860 than the state of Illinois—$558.08 against $528.16—but that may not parallel how the county's family median wealth compared to the statewide median of $815. As a test, I chose forty enlisted men at random from four DuPage County companies of the 105th Illinois, and 72 percent of those found on the census came from families holding more than the median Illinois wealth. That exceeded even the proportion of wealthier soldiers detected by Buck, whose sample yielded 63 percent in the upper five deciles. Those results suggested that DuPage County, bordering booming Cook County, was richer than the average Illinois county, but nearly half of my forty soldiers did not appear on the census, indicating heavy immigration that might have sharply increased the ratio of poorer men. A majority of the missing men bore thoroughly German names, further suggesting subsequent migration as an explanation for their absence.[6]

Maris A. Vinovskis also doubted the poor-man's-fight theory, despite evidence for it in his survey of those who did and did not volunteer from Newburyport, Massachusetts. He concluded that the sons of high-status, white-collar employees and skilled artisans enlisted "at much higher rates" than the sons of unskilled workers, while skilled artisans of adult age were more likely to serve than the unskilled. He noted, not surprisingly, that those who themselves held high-status, white-collar jobs "were particularly averse to serving and enlisted at a very low rate." The sons of the poorest residents enlisted at a slightly higher rate than those of the richest, he conceded, and poorer volunteers suffered higher mortality. He differentiated between enlistments in the army and the navy but made no distinction between those who entered three-year regiments and those who selected safer short-term service. The length of term they chose gave volunteers some control over their destiny, especially in Massachusetts, where evidence points to some of the nine-month regiments as a military haven for the upper class.[7]

Vinovskis reported that "servicemen from disadvantaged backgrounds were more likely to be killed or wounded," suspecting that they may have been discriminated against by being assigned to more dangerous tasks. That reasoning is somewhat undermined by the nature of Civil War duty, in which an entire unit usually embarked on the same assignment, whether it entailed relative safety or great danger. Except for a few staff positions, every man in a particular regiment theoretically endured equal risk on the battlefield.[8]

Chulhee Lee considered economics in developing his "efficiency" theory as an alternative to the discrimination articulated by Vinovskis. Rather than poorer men being chosen for dangerous duty, Lee suggested that "superior recruits in terms of skills or abilities" were selected for higher rank, which might have improved their chances for survival. That amounted to the reverse of the discrimination theory, and it suffers from the same flaw: few positions within a regiment were more secure than any other. Poorer men more often became casualties because economic constriction limited their options for choosing a unit in which they could expect less danger.[9]

In an article devoted to memory rather than economics, Teresa Thomas's study of volunteers from Lancaster, Massachusetts, concluded that "the ranks were filled not by the poorest men but by the farming and mechanic classes." Based on the soldiers from that town, she also noted that "leadership was supplied in the main by the elite classes and the university-educated."[10] Her first observation is contradicted by the broader survey for this book, which shows that poorer men did dominate the Union army, especially in the enlisted ranks. In the army at large, officers less often rose from the "elite class and the university-educated," but on average they did tend to share more comfortable financial backgrounds.

W. J. Rorabaugh touched on economic motivation and the relative wealth of Union volunteers in a brief 1986 article on soldiers from Concord, Massachusetts. Comparing the enlistment rates of men with different occupations, Rorabaugh postulated long-term economic motivation—that is, career opportunity—among Union soldiers, particularly among clerks, farmhands, and skilled workers who enlisted. With no evidentiary support, he assumed that "patriotic sentiment was no doubt paramount" as the first hordes of volunteers swarmed the recruiting offices, although he hypothesized that these men also blamed the South for Northern economic stagnation. Rorabaugh reasoned that years of stalled wages and blighted opportunities had driven farm laborers, artisans, and clerks to support reform movements aimed at successive scapegoats: first alcohol, followed by immigrants (particularly Irish Catholics), and finally the slave power. That portion of his argument has since been expanded by others to ornament such economic hostility to slavery with an unconvincing veneer of abolitionist zeal. Meanwhile, the theoretical economic antagonism he outlined was eclipsed by the more immediate economic imperative of unemployment, often aggravated by existing or impending penury.[11]

One of the earliest treatments of mercenary motivation appeared in 1926, with Fred Shannon's overt examination of the subject, although his scope was confined to the obvious issue of bounty payments. That limitation long hobbled the broader discussion, pushing it into the last twenty months of the war. Only relatively recently was any attention given to the bounties of 1862, and the assumption persisted that patriotic impulse still drove enlistments at that stage of the war. Bill Blair wrote in 2002 that Pennsylvanians hung back for bigger bounties "not necessarily because of a lack of patriotism but because they hoped to secure as much money as possible to protect their families." It would, however, have been equally logical and perhaps equally accurate to attribute the recruiting delay to men waiting for some community to make an offer too generous to refuse.[12]

Clayne Pope noted decades ago that even the complete absence of wealth does not necessarily indicate poverty, since wealth often fluctuates through the stages of life, but that observation applies mainly to the individual.[13] The figures used to gauge the relative wealth of soldiers in the calculations for Table 1 represent median family wealth, which compensates for variables such as extreme average youth among recruits, and they are biased toward findings of above-median wealth. I let the worldly estate claimed by the head of a family stand for that of every person in that household: if a father's wealth exceeded the median even slightly, he and all his soldier-sons were counted above the median. Young farmhands posed a common potential error when they were enumerated with their employers but actually lived with their parents, whose wealth should have been counted, but that was usually statistically harmless: it was boys from humble families with below-median wealth who hired out for much-needed cash, while the sons of wealthier farmers usually worked at home. Other flaws include unreported wealth and inaccurate reporting, but median-wealth statistics derived from the 1860 census represent the best broad measure of the relative economic status of Civil War soldiers ever likely to appear.

If a soldier was enumerated with his parents on the 1860 census, the total wealth of that family determined whether I listed him above or below the state median. If he lived alone or with a family of no apparent relation to him, the wealth he claimed decided that question. If he had started a family of his own, I counted only his family's wealth unless he lived in the same household headed by an older relative, in which case the wealth of every member went into the calculation. I varied from this method only when a brother appeared to be living as a hired hand with a married sibling, since he could not be presumed to share ownership. Occasionally a young man appeared twice on the census, once in his parental household and once as a boarder, and in such a case his parental family wealth counted along with any personal property of the young man. Rather than lumping those whose family wealth fell precisely at the median with those above or below the median, I removed them entirely from the calculation.

The most time-consuming and frustrating facet of the census work involved searching for men with common names or complicated, misspelled names, especially when the roster source failed to indicate age or residence. Postwar collections of state adjutant generals' records provided a majority of the roster sources. In the absence of state registers, regimental histories occasionally served; the earlier those books were published, the more unreliable the spelling of names tended to be, but the National Archives pension index often helped correct those errors. Some Kansas muster rolls and descriptive lists are available online and provided much identifying detail. Sometimes two (or more) men of the same name, age, and birthplace appeared on the census of one community: if they all fell on the same side of the median wealth, I counted my soldier as identified; if one of them fell on the other side, I marked him "not found."

The ninety-four company rosters in my survey yielded a total of 8,518 soldiers, of whom I was able to "link" 5,881, or 69 percent, to individuals on the census. The advantage of computer-based census indexing probably accounts for such an improvement over the 55-percent success rate Vinovskis reported in Newburyport and the 35.3 percent Hoptak achieved in his examination of the 48th Pennsylvania.[14] Inaccuracy in the transcription of handwritten names for the indices of different census search engines nevertheless left me unable to track down many men, and the quality of the indices varies. The online version of the 1860 census produced for the National Archives seems to be the most unreliable, sometimes leaving a majority of name searches unavailing. Results from Ancestry.com's HeritageQuest database were generally far better, but in one memorable instance the National Archives version provided a crucial name that the HeritageQuest index had missed through misinterpretation of the spelling. While my census search was exhausting, it was undoubtedly not exhaustive, and in going back over the rosters after several months I detected a few names here and there that could be shifted to the "found" column.

A lack of distinguishing information on unit rosters often made it more difficult to locate recruits on the census, but it was in the West that the largest proportions of soldiers could not be found on the population schedules. So many men from such states as Minnesota and Kansas showed signs of having just arrived there that the large proportion who eluded the census marshals may reflect 1860 transiency—which has a tendency to reduce wealth, especially for recent immigrants. Below-median wealth may therefore have been higher than it appeared in samples where smaller ratios of men could be found on the census.[15]

To err conservatively once again in estimating the relative poverty of individuals and families, I calculated median family wealth based solely on the property claimed by the head of household. According to IPUMS estimates, about 2 percent of families on the 1860 census added the property of members other than the head of household, but I did not include that calculation in determining median wealth for each state. I did, however, include the wealth reported by all family members when determining whether an individual soldier or his family should be counted above or below the median. Median wealth in each state would have been higher had I calculated it with the property of all family members, and the proportion of men in each sample who fell below the median would therefore have been higher. As it was, the percentages of poorer soldiers stood impressively high even with the median wealth of each state deliberately set a little low.

I divide the chaotic and confusing progress of Union recruiting into seven basic periods. First came the president's call of April 15, 1861, for ninety-day militia, most of which took the field by late May. The second period includes both Lincoln's May 3 appeal for forty regiments of three-year volunteers and his request, authorized by Congress in July, to raise half a million three-year volunteers. Recruiting for those men ended with Secretary of War Edwin Stanton's order of April 3, 1862, to shut down all recruiting stations. Embarrassed by that blunder, Stanton quietly asked state governors for more troops in May, but few men responded until the president formally issued another proclamation on July 2 for 300,000 more three-year volunteers. That initiated the third recruiting epoch, and the fourth began when, after revisions to the militia law, Stanton ordered the mobilization of 300,000 nine-month militia on August 4, threatening to supply any deficiencies by draft.

Passage of the Enrollment Act early in 1863 enabled the first direct conscription of citizens into federal service. That resulted in several different draft calls between July, 1863, and December, 1864. For the statistical analysis in this study, the three-year draft levies of 1863 and early 1864 are combined in a fifth recruiting period. Then came the president's proclamation for 100-day volunteers in April, 1864, which I regarded as a sixth period. The draft calls in July and December of 1864, which were essentially for one-year troops, together constitute the seventh and last period. Stanton also issued an unauthorized call for ninety-day militia in May, 1862, and the president requested six-month troops in June of 1863, but neither raised enough men to merit separate statistical analysis.

These recruiting drives were conducted under fluctuating economic conditions. The three-month call of 1861 and the three-year mobilization that followed coincided with severe and widespread economic distress resulting primarily from the Southern trade embargo and debt repudiation. This recession lasted well into the autumn of 1861, and for some regions even later. Then the production of war matériel improved employment opportunities, and the circulation of new federal currency circumvented the collapse of local bank notes. The ensuing economic upturn reduced the appeal of military service, requiring the introduction of routine, substantial enlistment bounties in 1862.

Prices rose faster than wages throughout the war, and the bounties themselves aggravated inflation, which—in conjunction with the increasing brutality of the conflict—necessitated still-higher bounties. Oscillating confidence in the Union war effort often exacerbated that depression in real wages by reducing the value of currency against the price of gold. The inflation cycle peaked in 1864, by which time the inability to maintain one's farm or family was leading men who would not have been considered poor in 1861 to enlist for seemingly generous bounties. Prices only began to recede toward the spring of 1865.

The three-month troops of 1861 showed the highest cumulative average of men from families with below-median wealth, at 71 percent. Individual samples ranged from 62 percent in the 1st Wisconsin to 89 percent in the 1st New Jersey

Militia, reflecting the widespread unemployment that followed the secession winter. The long-term regiments raised from May of 1861 fielded a slightly lower percentage of poor men, although in eight of the seventeen states the proportion was higher than it had been among the ninety-day troops. The cumulative average of poor men in the two- and three-year 1861 regiments came to 70 percent. Two-thirds of the three-year volunteers of 1862 also fell below median wealth, at 67 percent, but the proportion dropped sharply, to 57 percent, for the nine-month regiments of that year: four of those nine-month regiments yielded the first majorities of men from the wealthier half of their states' populations.

The three-year regiments recruited in late 1863 and early 1864 revealed a noticeable rise in the proportion of poorer men—back to 70 percent—which is probably directly attributable to bounties they often found irresistible. Ten states raised hundred-day regiments in 1864, and the brief commitment (combined with assurances of noncombat duty) attracted so many wealthier men that those above the median composed a sizable majority in seven of the ten samples. The hundred-day regiments produced the only cumulative average with a solid majority of richer men, at 55 percent: in Massachusetts, New York, and Indiana, more than two-thirds of the sampled hundred-day soldiers came from the wealthier class. The one-year enlistments of 1864, recruited while full-scale battles still raged, raised the proportion of poor recruits back to 62 percent, with a low of 50 percent in the Indiana sample and a high of 73 percent in that from Minnesota. By then the price of everything, including substitutes, had risen so high that men of slightly more moderate wealth increasingly deemed it worth the risk of enlisting for the war's biggest bounties rather than buying their way out of the draft.

This book will, I hope, provoke further study by historians better versed in statistical analysis than I am (and toward that end, the data will be posted on Harvard's Dataverse site). Inferences drawn from the specific economic status of 5,881 soldiers are hardly going to be definitive, considering that overall Union forces were calculated at 2,656,553 soldiers, sailors, and Marines.[16] Even after accounting for upward of a million reenlistments, enough individuals wore Union blue at one time or another to reduce my sample to something between 0.25 and 0.33 percent of all Union servicemen. The sample sizes for some portions of Table 1 are higher: the first column, for instance, represents a 1-percent sample of the ninety-day militia call, and several of the percentages in that column reflect 10 percent of each state's three-month contribution. Because the number of men examined in each state for each recruiting period was roughly the same, the sample sizes vary widely by state—from less than 0.2 percent for New York, Pennsylvania, and Ohio to about 1.5 percent for Rhode Island, New Hampshire, and Kansas (adjusting for reenlistments).

My sample is nevertheless several times the size of the largest previous study of the same nature, but more importantly the trends revealed here are persuasively consistent. Even without anecdotal corroboration, the statistics in Table 1 indicate that the fighting regiments were filled primarily from the ranks of the poor, while wealthier recruits leaned toward short-term units that at least implied safer service.

This makes it much more difficult to deny that the Civil War was a poor man's fight, although the bottom has fallen out of the favorite argument for that claim. The commutation clause in the 1863 draft law, which allowed a conscript to pay three hundred dollars to be excused from that draft levy, was long regarded as the foremost evidence of economic discrimination in military service, but in fact it worked to the benefit of poorer men. As became evident once it was repealed, the provision for commutation limited the cost of hiring another man to serve permanently as one's substitute in the army, enabling many conscripts of modest means to stay home. The reduced price meant that a poor man would earn less by selling himself as a substitute, but if he wanted to avoid service he could more easily do so with commutation than without it. Once commutation was eliminated, the cost of substitutes rose precipitously.

Economic circumstances were ultimately more responsible for filling the army with poorer men than the draft was. The recruiting frenzy of 1861 drained off those who were desperate enough to enlist for nothing more than monthly pay and family subsidies, and by the summer of 1862, bounties had to be paid in advance to coax enough recruits. As the brutality of the war increased and recruiting depleted the next-most-desperate stratum of the population, bounties had to rise gradually to remain effective, although they never reached a level that wealthy men found seductive. The affluent always had the option of hiring poor men as substitutes, and when they were drafted almost all of them did just that—at whatever cost. In the first national draft levy, in 1863, only one drafted man in thirty went into uniform: in Massachusetts the ratio came to one in forty, in Maryland one in fifty, and in Connecticut one in sixty-three. Unless a man was unable to simultaneously support his family and hire a substitute or pay the commutation fee, it was easy to avoid going into the Union army, and the overwhelming majority of those who were called to serve did avoid it.

Except for the hundred-day regiments of 1864, which offered token, risk-free service for would-be warriors, two-thirds of the soldiers sampled for this study hailed from the lower economic strata of their communities. Twice as many "poor" men served as "rich" men did, yet the poor were probably not twice as susceptible to patriotic impulses as their richer neighbors. Those heavy majorities of poor men, along with contemporary comment from all economic backgrounds, testify that financial inducements, temporary employment, or career opportunities swayed a significant percentage of Union recruits. Epistemologically speaking, it would not be possible to prove that such economic attractions were the most common or most powerful incentive for Union enlistments, and I do not claim that they were. Neither would it be possible to conclusively prove the opposite. It does, however, seem quite safe to say that economic incentive is the most conspicuously overlooked major factor in the search for enlistment motive among Union soldiers.

1

HARD TIMES

Financial panic swept New York City on Sunday, October 11, 1857. The only day of rest that workmen usually enjoyed had been spoiled for many by the news that they would have no jobs to return to on Monday. On Saturday the men working on the Erie Railroad's Bergen Tunnel in New Jersey had also been told that there was no money for them, prompting several hundred of them to gather in angry protest. They threatened to destroy all the company equipment, and a makeshift battalion of hastily mustered militia had held them off long enough for the railroad to come up with sufficient cash to cover the wages they were due.[1]

Dyspepsia afflicted Sunday diners in more genteel surroundings, too. Banks had begun to topple as depositors withdrew their money and demanded specie for their bank notes, and businesses of sterling repute had suspended payment of their debts when they could obtain neither cash nor further credit. Sitting in his comfortable home opposite Gramercy Park, Wall Street lawyer George Templeton Strong dreaded Monday morning, when he expected to see a general run on the banks. "This week may be epochal," he noted in his diary, and indeed it was.[2]

Sidney George Fisher, a gentleman of leisure living on the outskirts of Philadelphia, knew the panic from both sides. As a passenger on a Philadelphia streetcar, he had lately seen runs on the Farmers & Mechanics and City Banks, and through his brother he knew of numerous wealthy businessmen forced into suspension because they could not liquidate any of their property to pay off loans the banks had called in. On that same October Sunday, two men of "very wretched" aspect stopped at Fisher's house and asked for food, telling him they could find no work. A third vagabond made the same request while Fisher was visiting his brother. With virtually all production at a standstill and so many thousands out of work on the brink of winter, Fisher felt a mixture of pity for the poor and fear for his own class as he and his neighbors anticipated the possibility of indigents resorting to burglary and highway robbery.[3]

New York Herald editor James Gordon Bennett expended little sympathy on the distress of the upper class. "The tailor or the seamstress may perish of starvation," he observed with bitter irony, "but what is that to the misery of being compelled to wear for another six months one's Raglan or silk gown?" With the traditional hard-money stance of Jacksonian Democrats, Bennett attributed the crisis to the very existence of paper money backed by little or nothing, which required the confidence of all parties to maintain its value. Strong, a Republican, blamed it on the distrust of men like Bennett, predicting that the solution would have to be "psychological rather than financial." Republican editor Horace Greeley agreed. "The worst thing we have to fear in this city is a panic," he wrote in the Monday issue of his *New York Tribune*.[4]

Yet the Panic of 1857 had begun. The origin of the crisis lay in Europe, where for more than two years the Crimean War had deprived Britain and France of Russian wheat and created a vast new market for farmers in the western United States. That war ended early in 1856, and with normalized relations Russia was able to resume wheat sales without the expense of transatlantic shipping, cutting off the new market and depressing prices in the American West, where land speculation had created a precarious economy based on a complicated network of credit. The sudden trade imbalance, or rebalance, threatened to reduce the flow of specie into the United States. Most American currency consisted of bank notes theoretically backed by specie, so a shortage of gold could damage public confidence in it.

In August of 1857, when corruption and unsafe lending practices forced the highly regarded Ohio Life Insurance and Trust Company to admit that it could not back its notes, a more general mistrust in banks took hold. Banking houses called in loans and tightened credit until mercantile trade and then industry virtually stopped. Depositor demands for gold coin closed the major banks of Philadelphia and Baltimore, and bank failures initiated uneasiness among stock-market investors. As the price of bloated railroad shares fell, banks and creditors everywhere began demanding payment on loans and other debts, and more depositors tried to convert their bank notes into gold. Those ripples eventually converged on New York's financial district as a tidal wave, and in mid-October all the banks there suspended specie payments, which precipitated a nationwide suspension.[5]

The panic interrupted a long period of general if erratic prosperity, but it exposed how vulnerable a growing proportion of the population was to the vagaries of the economy. On three separate occasions during the first week of November, thousands of unemployed workmen gathered in New York's Tompkins Square to demand either work or bread. On November 11 the New York Board of Emigration heard that immigrants were in a "starving condition" for lack of work, but it established a schedule of severely reduced wages they would have to accept if they were to avail themselves of the agency's benefits.[6] Immigration from abroad and from the countryside into the cities and industrialized areas of the Northeast had created a new, frangible society in which the labor force depended on the punctual payment of weekly wages for food and housing. Urban workers thrown out of employment lacked the option of home production of food and other necessities that their rural counterparts enjoyed, and any economic shock threw them face to face with serious want. Urbanization and industrialization explained why the incidence of pauperism rose by more than three-quarters between 1850 and 1860.[7]

Henry Carey, a monomaniacal political economist of considerable influence in the nineteenth century, had predicted increasing contentment and class harmony with industrial development, in which the capitalist and the employee essentially worked as partners. His utopian vision never materialized, and the reverse seemed increasingly to be the case, especially when the economy dipped. Employers found it profitable to pay subsistence wages or less, and those exploited workers were left at the mercy of an assortment of interruptions and disruptions to their employment. Newspapers espousing Carey's employer-friendly theory ignored the plight of workmen who had lost their jobs or had their wages cut, claiming that this would build capital and lay the foundation for better wages in the future. With the cupboard bare, the rent overdue, and no work in sight, the only options consisted of public relief or the poorhouse. Town relief often consisted of auctioning off the poor to act as household laborers; even in its more benevolent incarnations, public generosity waned in proportion to the demand.[8]

A decline in real wages—how much a wage earner's pay could buy compared to the value of that money at an earlier time—helped trigger the increased demand for public relief. Wages and productivity both improved for the first half of the nineteenth century: in the opinion of economic historian Robert Margo, real wages rose substantially between 1820 and 1860 but peaked in the early 1840s. The buying power of those wages began to drop in the late 1840s, continued dropping halfway through 1855, and only began to reverse in 1856 before the panic threw multitudes out of work.[9]

Robert Fogel described what he called a "'hidden' economic depression" from about 1848 until 1855, at least for laborers and tradesmen outside of agriculture and especially among native-born males. Heavy immigration, largely a result of famine in Ireland and political unrest in Europe, provided a stream of potential new workers on which capitalists could rely for cheaper labor. Nearly three million immigrants arrived in the 1850s, increasing the number of nonfarm laborers in the Northern states by nearly a third just in the first half of that decade. That influx of generally poor, eager people removed any incentive to increase wages—and actually encouraged them downward—while the flood of immigrants strained the housing market and drove up rents. Then the immigrants, who were usually desperate enough to work for less money, began replacing the native-born workers, first in less-skilled jobs and later in the trades. Sharp declines in the demand for materials production, construction, and railroad expansion in the early 1850s cost tens of thousands of native workmen their jobs and also cast like numbers of immigrant laborers out of work. The broadcast publication of a two-column parable called "The One-Acre Farm: A Cure for Hard Times" over the course of 1855 hinted at the geographical extent of economic hardship by that year. The West, then considered to be the region from Ohio to Iowa and Minnesota, endured particularly significant unemployment for at least two years before the Panic of 1857.[10]

Rising food prices and stagnant or declining wages may have precipitated nutritional deficiencies in the 1850s. The movement away from farms and into industrialized urban environments seemed to sharply reduce life expectancy between 1850 and 1860, particularly among the poorest elements of society, and the earlier death of breadwinners increased the poverty of many a family. The financial collapse in the autumn of 1857 fell on a society burdened by heavy proportions of its population hovering on the brink of indigence. It thus created a more personal panic within households, helping fuel another of the religious revivals that so often follow in the wake of terrifying events, and the revival itself may have become a subject of financial exploitation by desperate businessmen.[11]

The economy began to recover in the early months of 1858, but another year passed before the armies of unemployed laborers either found work or joined the westward migration. Suddenly laborers could not be found in many parts of the country, and real wages surged back to where they had been a decade earlier.[12]

Efforts to organize labor had failed consistently when teeming masses of idle workmen supplied abundant competition for any wages at all. Printers and textile workers who tried it had been forced to go elsewhere for jobs when they were simply replaced. The sudden tightening of the labor market in 1859 lent considerable encouragement to the more militant reformers among those classes of industrial workers whose situation remained fragile, and the shoemakers of Massachusetts surely fit that description.[13]

As the decade came to an end, more residents of the Bay State pursued shoemaking than any other manufacturing activity. From a population of 1,231,066, about 60,000 people worked in one aspect or another of this ever-more-specialized field, and a significant number of those employees were women.[14] The industry had recently completed a long transition from the tradesman's shop to factory production, leaving the state's boot and shoe workers increasingly vulnerable to volatile market fluctuations. Despite the longer hours they spent in artificially lighted, unventilated shops that ruined their eyesight and health, their real wages and in some cases their actual earnings had declined over the previous decade, and many lived on the brink of poverty. Operatives complained of earning as little as $2.75 per week when the rent for an average house ranged as high as $150 a year, the cost of weekly board averaged $2.51, and seasonal unemployment strained their budgets even further. Their plight led the shoemakers of Lynn, Massachusetts, to walk away from their machines in February of 1860, demanding higher wages and union recognition. Their strike spread rapidly through the state, and some 20,000 employees ultimately participated in what became the nation's largest antebellum labor action, but in their marginal economic circumstances they lacked the resources to sustain the walkout. Within little more than a month, the impoverished strikers' leaders effectively surrendered.[15]

Inevitably many of those who returned to work after several weeks without wages found themselves further behind financially than they had been when the year began, and 1860 ended with another economic blow to their sorely pressed class. With the election of Abraham Lincoln, Deep South states almost immediately began debating their separation from the Union, adopting a non-intercourse policy that included boycotts of products from Northern states and the repudiation of debts to Northern banks, bondholders, and manufacturers. So many Southerners chose to forego the traditional winter order of shoes from Massachusetts companies, and the radiating financial tremors sufficiently hamstrung Northern markets, that the shoe industry quickly stagnated. Democratic newspapers highlighted the bad economic and political news as a consequence of the election of Lincoln, while Republican papers tended to downplay the recession, but those editors closest to the shoe factories could hardly deny the blow. An industry journal reported that 1860 closed with "another very quiet week in the shoe market," noting that manufacturers had received far fewer wholesale orders than usual—and dared produce only a fraction of those, lest their customers find themselves unable to pay. "The workmen in the shoe towns are generally without employment," the editor lamented, "and there seems for them a gloomy prospect for the remainder of the winter."[16]

Late in February, 1861, shipments of shoes picked up somewhat thanks in part to orders from California, though not at the seasonal volume known before the secession crisis. In March even that began to subside. Cobblers who had made shoes as independent craftsmen until mechanization forced them into factories had to fall back on other skills to support their families. Younger cordwainers who had never developed any expertise beyond stitching shoes could only resort to daily labor, for which there was less call than usual because of the general recession precipitated by the secession crisis.[17]

Merchants whose clientele consisted primarily of an impecunious laboring class shared in its economic woes. Attachments emanating from myriad lawsuits between merchants and their debtor-patrons or creditor-suppliers littered newspapers long after the worst of the 1857 panic. Commerce depended on an intricate web of credit between different stages of supply, and failures anywhere along the chain radiated up and down the network. Congress discussed citizen petitions and a presidential recommendation for a national bankruptcy law in the wake of the panic, but produced no bill, leaving state legislatures to take whatever action they chose in the way of debtor relief. The chances for business failure ran fairly high even outside the periods of regional or national depression because inexperienced innocents so often entered commerce ignorant of accounting practices, naively anticipating an elusive promise of instant and inevitable wealth. Visions of ease and independence lured them too hastily into commerce, where an inability to distinguish between the relative value of assets or to foresee impending financial crises brought them to grief more often than not.[18]

Thanks to secession in general and Southern reluctance to pay Northern creditors in particular, a scarcity of trustworthy cash belabored all businesses that winter in every state bordering the Ohio or upper Mississippi Rivers. Too many banks in that watershed had secured the currency they issued with bonds on Southern commodities, and secession now severed the economic umbilical between Chicago and New Orleans, seriously eroding confidence in those bonds. Merchants began shunning bills from banks with such securities, leading would-be managers of Western credit like the state auditors of Illinois to discount and depreciate the money circulated by those institutions. The hammer fell soon enough after the election of 1860 that farmers, most of whom had raised bumper crops and had paid handsomely to harvest them, found their market had fallen flat; those who had held on to their grain for higher prices soon regretted it. If they managed to sell anything at all, it was often for money that was worth less, or entirely worthless, by the time they reached home. All this preceded a brutal winter that one Iowa tenant farmer said "would make any body weep," with deep cold, high winds, and heavy snow that threatened vulnerable cattle and delayed the next planting season.[19]

From Pennsylvania to Missouri and upriver to Minneapolis, those who needed cash could not get it, and those who had it would not spend it. Sensitive to the implication that their candidate's election had precipitated a financial crisis, Republican newspaper editors tried to dismiss the economic decline that followed Lincoln's victory, but the escalating frequency and intensity of their denials backhandedly recorded the collapse. As early as November 28, 1860, the *Republican* of Fort Dodge, Iowa, had referred to the depreciation of credit as "temporary," quoting the assurances of New York businessmen that the panic could not continue. Barely a week later the *Cedar Valley Times* reported that the crisis was already abating, hinting that it was all the mischief of charlatans trying to manipulate local currencies. A paper in St. Cloud, Minnesota, expressed similar confidence, supposing that the discredited banks would be reinstated within a few days. Instead of abating, the panic worsened.[20]

The Western wheat crop had been plentiful again. Still, six weeks after the election, the Democratic *Red Wing Sentinel,* just downstream from Minneapolis, complained how wheat that had been selling readily at seventy-five cents a bushel could hardly be sold any longer at forty-five cents. Few would pay cash for it at any price, and the Red Wing editor predicted that the blow would fall hardest on those with mortgaged farms or other debt. Low demand and lower prices kept all grain and pork out of most Minnesota markets, and by February,

1861, every edition of most newspapers there carried notices of forced property sales and mortgage foreclosures that sometimes filled an entire page. The pork market also grew "dull" in central Illinois and in the packing center of Cincinnati. Bank failures began to dominate the headlines, especially in Illinois, and it was probably no coincidence that counterfeit bills started turning up in that state about then.[21]

Surviving banks in St. Louis and elsewhere stopped lending money, so construction and commerce came to a halt. A month into spring, work of any kind could hardly be had. Retail marketers offered tempting bargains but refused any credit or terms, like the bootier in Quincy, Illinois, who was so anxious to be rid of his stock that he advertised ruinous prices but warned that no goods would be delivered without the money. A lack of demand made prospects for the immediate future of the Great Lakes lumber market "lugubrious." The bills of more banks were added weekly to the lists of discredited currency. Wisconsin money that was taken at par at the end of March was discounted 20 percent a week later and 25 percent a few days after that. On April 15 a student at the state university in Madison sold his local money for less than two-thirds of its face value, while ten days later no stores or banks would take any Wisconsin money.[22]

The political crisis had blossomed into open warfare by the time that Wisconsin student converted his money. The focus of political tension had shifted to Charleston, South Carolina, where a skeleton garrison held Fort Sumter—the least defensible but most conspicuous of the remaining U.S. installations inside the new Confederacy. During the first five weeks of his administration, President Lincoln hoped as fervently to hold Sumter as a symbol of his government's authority as Confederates wished to see it evacuated, and his decision to resupply the fort provoked a decisive confrontation. Rebel guns opened fire, and after a day and a half of constant bombardment the garrison surrendered. The next day, April 15, Lincoln exercised his authority under the Militia Act of 1795, calling on the states to supply 75,000 militia for the maximum three months allowed under the law. Upon receiving that order, four states in the Upper South refused, instead seceding with the other seven, and with that the Civil War had begun.

2

NINETY-DAY WAR

LINCOLN'S MILITIA CALL

Legions of men without work or money found employment with President Lincoln's call for militia. Only three states were able to respond on short notice with troops already organized, uniformed, and equipped for the field. A few companies of Pennsylvania militia slipped into Washington on April 18, garbed in frayed and variegated uniforms but unarmed, and the 6th Massachusetts arrived the next day after a bloody fracas with a Baltimore mob. The 7th New York had already departed for Washington by then, and several other New York regiments embarked soon afterward. In most states the three-month troops had to be raised from nothing or recruited around vestigial companies, and it was in the raising of those regiments that the unemployed first found relief. In the romanticized memoir he fashioned around a wartime diary, Josiah Favill alleged that "men in all conditions of life" vied with him for a place, including "rich men, scholars, professional men, and young fellows from college and school." Actually, those flocking volunteers were dominated by the humblest classes of society; Favill failed to mention that he himself had just arrived from England—a teenager in search of opportunity.[1]

What may have been the largest gathering of people to that date in American history filled Union Square in New York City on the Saturday after Lincoln's proclamation, spilling into the intersecting avenues to hear speeches and appeals for volunteers; the *New York Herald* called it "a national ovation." The convocation brought hundreds if not thousands of men to the recruiting offices, including heavy proportions of the unemployed. By early April, advertisements from people seeking work had filled nearly eight columns of the *New*

York Times—one-eighth of that daily broadsheet. After that massive recruiting rally, the "positions wanted" section nearly disappeared: none was published the following day, a Sunday, and that Monday such ads had been reduced to less than two columns, all but seventeen of them placed by women. The *Herald* accompanied its story on the rally with one about the liberality accorded the volunteers and their families, crediting reports that some twenty-five million dollars had already been pledged nationally for their aid.[2]

The same scene played out on smaller scales in towns and cities from Bangor, Maine, to Council Bluffs, Iowa. Bradley Mahana, a fifty-five-year-old painter and captain of a small Iowa militia organization, set about raising the first volunteer company in Iowa City. A crowd packed the courthouse there on the night of April 18, and after the customary paroxysm of patriotic music and rhetoric the managers of the meeting got down to the business of raising money and men. In a fever of generosity, different citizens pledged several thousand dollars to help support the families of those residents who answered the call. When Mahana announced that he wanted to complete his company, men all over the hall said they would go with him, and at least forty of them put their names on his roll that evening. A couple of nights later another meeting in Iowa City more than doubled the subscription fund for soldiers' families. There was also some vague talk about granting 160 acres in bounty lands to the ninety-day men—in echo of both ongoing land-warrant assignments for Mexican War service and the 1860 Republican campaign pledge to enact a homestead bill; destitute men cherished that dream, if only for the chance to claim land they could sell. With those alluring incentives, enough volunteers came forward to bring Captain Mahana's company to its full complement of three officers, two musicians, and one hundred enlisted men.[3]

For all the rousing speeches, waving banners, and national airs bleated by brass bands, Mahana's company enlisted in an economic atmosphere that the Dickensian reading public would have unequivocally characterized as "hard times." Out-of-work or underemployed carpenters, bricklayers, plasterers, painters, general laborers, and at least one man who specialized in roofing volunteered from Iowa's once-booming, now-inert former capital, accompanied by clerks without positions and farmhands who had not yet arranged for the next agricultural season. One impulsive farm laborer who enlisted with Captain Mahana opened a vacancy that was instantly filled by another youth who had just arrived in Iowa from New York. Even those who still had work nevertheless wondered when they might be paid and whether the money would be negotiable if and when they did get it; government wages and the stockpiles of community cash seemed a more certain prospect.[4]

A newspaper in another Iowa town remarked, on the same day that Mahana completed his company, that the men who filled the new regiments would be "no mercenary hirelings," but the editor who made that prediction had no opportunity to examine the finances of the Iowa City volunteers. Excluding the officers and sergeants, 77 percent of the men whom the newspapers described as clamoring to join Mahana's company had not owned enough property the previous year to meet the median wealth in their states, which came to only $295 in Iowa. At least one-fifth of Mahana's recruits had not lived in the state as long as ten months, having migrated there in search of greener pastures. Furthermore, many who had had work when the census marshals took their names in the summer of 1860 were unemployed by the spring of 1861.[5]

The harsh winter continued into April across Iowa, northern Illinois, and southern Wisconsin, with late frosts, high winds, and drenching rains that prevented plowing or planting. Iowa and Wisconsin farmers who brought livestock into Chicago could only obtain payment in wildcat Illinois currency that few banks, or none, would accept for deposit; one man was able to exchange a portion of his Illinois money for gold only by accepting twelve cents on the dollar. Next came hog cholera. Then, when the wheat finally headed up, cutworms promptly descended on it. William Bullard, of Macon County, Illinois, was suffering all those agricultural blights that spring, as well as a lack of cash, when his oldest son and namesake enlisted on the first day of recruiting for the president's ninety-day call. Grieving over their penury and the loss of his father's wheat and hogs, the younger Bullard sent money home once his pay finally started; as problems worsened there, he reenlisted. When he was killed in his first battle, his next-youngest brother followed him into uniform.[6]

Under the pretense of helping the poor exercise their patriotism, communities preyed on those in similar straits to satisfy their military obligations. "There are many poor but patriotic men of small families in this city and vicinity," wrote the editor of a newspaper in Ottawa, Illinois, "who are anxious to volunteer for the defence of their country's honor, but are not in a condition to leave their families safe and comfortable. We have noticed in other places provision has been made for such. Would it not be well to get up a movement on behalf of such in Ottawa?" Town meetings and city councils across the nation made the support of volunteers' families an early order of business in the rallies inspired by Lincoln's call, perhaps recognizing that the poor and unemployed would enlist the most readily, and those offers only increased the appeal to men in that condition. Young fathers of precarious means and the sons of struggling farmers responded enthusiastically to monetary relief couched in such flattering style.[7]

It was the same across the North: a plurality if not the actual preponderance of the men who rallied around the flag had recently experienced acute economic need. Of those who enlisted in the first two companies from Iowa under the president's April 15 proclamation who could be found on the 1860 census, 66 percent owned less than the state's median wealth in real and personal property, officers included. In the first company from New Jersey, 89 percent of identified recruits fell into that category; in the first from Minnesota, 83 percent; and 81 percent in the first company raised in New Hampshire. In New York precisely 80 percent of the first volunteers could not claim the $325 in property owned by those at the median. At least 62 percent of the earliest ninety-day militia companies in every state represented the poorer half of the population, and for most states the proportion rose much higher. The cumulative average of below-median wealth of the earliest volunteers from Maine to Minnesota came to 71 percent.[8]

The 3rd Massachusetts Volunteer Infantry claimed the distinction of having raised the first new company for the war from the Bay State. Company A of that regiment consisted of forty-nine men who called themselves the Halifax Light Infantry, most of whom hailed from the neighboring towns of Halifax and Hanson in Plymouth County. Just over half of them reported that they were shoemakers by occupation—the most hard-pressed Massachusetts workers. Others of them had abandoned that trade only recently, when the secession crisis crippled it, and would return to it once the industry recovered. Jacob P. Hill, a thirty-eight-year-old father of three from Hanson, said he was a stonecutter when he signed the roll on April 16, but eight months previously he had told a census marshal that he was a shoemaker—just as he had said in 1850 and as he would claim again when he next enlisted seventeen months later; it was his habitual occupation, and he had left it only temporarily when the shoe market dried up in the secession winter. Both Halifax and Hanson were shoemaking towns, with 41 percent of the male residents identifying themselves as makers or fitters of boots or shoes, but 61 percent of the volunteers from those two towns were engaged in that industry. At least 57 percent of the volunteers in Company H of the same regiment were involved in some facet of manufacturing footwear, including all fifteen men from the town of Abington and 54 percent of those from Plympton, where shoemaking occupied only 38 percent of working males.

TABLE 1. Sampled Volunteers from Families with Below-median Household Wealth, for Each Recruiting Period

	3-month, 1861	*3-year, 1861*	*3-year, 1862*	*9-month, 1862*	*3-year, 1863–64*	*100-days, 1864*	*1-year, 1864–65*
Connecticut	73%	59%	79%	72%	n/a	n/a	n/a
Illinois	68%	63%	63%	n/a	n/a	44%	55%
Indiana	63%	71%	63%	n/a	61%	31%	50%
Iowa	66%	61%	51%	n/a	n/a	39%	n/a
Kansas	64%	87%	68%	n/a	69%	46%	n/a
Maine	68%	70%	50%	41%	66%	n/a	n/a
Massachusetts	71%	80%	78%	38%	81%	33%	68%
Michigan	66%	72%	65%	n/a	n/a	n/a	62%
Minnesota	83%	68%	74%	n/a	n/a	n/a	73%
New Hampshire	81%	65%	75%	66%	68%	n/a	70%
New Jersey	89%	73%	73%	54%	87%	55%	72%
New York*	80%	61%	62%	69%	n/a	33%	65%
Ohio	76%	60%	60%	n/a	n/a	51%	64%
Pennsylvania	68%	62%	76%	73%	75%	76%	51%
Rhode Island**	64%	74%	56%	44%	n/a	n/a	n/a
Vermont	69%	80%	75%	67%	75%	n/a	n/a
Wisconsin	62%	76%	64%	45%	51%	42%	56%
cumulative average	71%	70%	67%	57%	70%	45%	62%

*New York's first long-term regiments for 1861 were enlisted for two years instead of three.

**Rhode Island median wealth was $0; percentages in that state reflect individuals or families at $0 wealth.

The methodology behind these calculations is discussed in the Introduction; data found at https://dataverse.org/.

Another Abington contingent in Company B was composed of shoemakers to a man. Well over one-fifth of the entire regiment consisted of men who plied that trade, although it was recruited from six different counties that encompassed only a few shoemaking communities.[9]

TABLE 2. Median Wealth by State, 1860

Connecticut	$500.00
Illinois	$815.00
Indiana	$300.00
Iowa	$295.00
Kansas	$550.00
Maine	$900.00
Massachusetts	$300.00
Michigan	$900.00
Minnesota	$675.00
New Hampshire	$1,100.00
New Jersey	$500.00
New York	$325.00
Ohio	$750.00
Pennsylvania	$500.00
Rhode Island	$0.00
Vermont	$1,300.00
Wisconsin	$700.00

When the president appealed for soldiers, a disproportionate number of men who had earned their livings at shoemakers' lasts found the promise of regular rations and monthly pay inviting, especially when a frenzied public offered a host of additional economic incentives. As early as April 16, public meetings started collecting subscriptions of cash for the use of Massachusetts troops, beginning with $1,200 for the volunteers from Lynn, the cradle of the shoemakers' strike: by the end of the day, five hundred men had been enlisted from that town. Within days other towns raised even greater sums, earmarking that money specifically for the use of their volunteers' families.[10]

Even at the seemingly paltry pay of eleven dollars a month, military service might have appealed to young men who were barely earning that much already—or were earning nothing—and still had to provide themselves with food, clothing, and lodging. Early Massachusetts recruits were promised supplemental pay from the state, and the government also paid a monthly clothing allowance of $2.50 that soldiers expected to pocket. The war was still in its infancy when men from industrial communities began to comment on how much money they were able to save in the army and to talk about the debts they were paying off. One impetuous lad from Lawrence, who followed the 6th Massachusetts at the first call, remarked with apparent surprise that he had needed barely four dollars to provide himself with personal comforts for the journey to Washington. He expected to come home with the princely sum of $49 if he were required to serve all his three-month term, so he urged his mother not to labor with her customary concern about having enough money. His calculation did not even include her share of the funds raised for the families of hometown soldiers by private charities.[11]

With such ciphering, it was no wonder that underpaid, underemployed, and patently dissatisfied Massachusetts shoemakers enlisted in droves. The 2nd Massachusetts, the first regiment from that state raised for three years entirely from scratch without a foundation of existing militia companies, filled more than 30 percent of its roster with shoemakers. The second such regiment, the 9th Massachusetts, marched off with 1,029 enlisted men, of whom 373—over 36 percent—worked in the shoe trade. Both regiments were recruited over broad areas of the state, and the concentration of shoemakers volunteering in those first three-year organizations greatly surpassed the proportion of that occupation in the working population statewide.[12]

Regiments raised later that spring and summer still attracted inordinate numbers of shoemakers. The 15th Massachusetts originally recruited 232 of them, added 91 later, and gained another 38 with an attached company of sharpshooters, while 351 shoemakers eventually enlisted in the 19th Massachusetts, 236 in the 20th, and 189 in the 22nd—the regiment nominally raised by Senator Henry Wilson, an ex-shoemaker. Shoemakers composed 62 percent of Company C of the 14th Massachusetts, while Company D was nearly as thickly strewn with them, including what one labor historian characterized as the core of the "old strike network."[13]

As enticing as it might be today to interpret such statistics as evidence of support for a war against slavery by active proponents of free labor, there was no credible war against slavery in 1861: President Lincoln took pains to assure that he harbored no hostile official designs against the institution. Furthermore, the strike of the shoemakers had illustrated their unhappiness with both the industrialization of their trade and their financial straits, which the walkout had aggravated and the secession winter had made worse still. They were the poorest of the state's working class as the conflict erupted. Their presence among the earliest volunteers in far greater proportions than any other tradesmen is more indicative of their desperation than of their dedication to any ideological principal.[14]

Large numbers of those shoemakers, along with textile workers and other factory operatives, fell into Confederate hands in an early debacle on the upper Potomac during the first autumn of the war. The 15th, 19th, and 20th Massachusetts Volunteers were all engaged in the lopsided battle of Ball's Bluff, and more than half of the hundreds of Union soldiers who were taken prisoner there came from two of those regiments. Guards marched them to the main Confederate army near Manassas, where they chatted freely with rebel soldiers. "A great many of them gave it as their excuse for fighting that they were out of employment and had nothing else to do," reported a North Carolinian.[15]

Certainly many men enlisted with no thought of money. The 20th Massachusetts, which attracted so many of those shoemakers, went to war with a nucleus of college-educated officers who had never missed a meal for lack of resources. Some of those officers expressed or implied a sense of obligation to enlist, although it can be difficult to ascertain whether their decisions were driven by their perceived duty as citizens or by peer pressure and a desire to distinguish themselves. "I should be ashamed of myself forever if I didn't do something now," wrote Henry Livermore Abbott, who ended up doing a great deal. He was, however, obviously influenced by so many of his friends and relatives obtaining commissions, and his correspondence gave the distinct impression that, for serious field service, he was only interested in going as an officer. The acerbically ironic letters of his aristocratic comrade Oliver Wendell Holmes Jr. left more uncertainty about the reasons he went to war, although both he and Abbott made exemplary soldiers. Among such young men raised in idealistic surroundings, the duty to defend the Union against enemies foreign and domestic may have been too well understood to require comment.[16]

Massachusetts governor John Andrew and his counterparts throughout the Northern states regarded the initial outpouring of so many volunteers as a reflection of the patriotism of the people. Most historians of the period have come to the same interpretation without looking into the economic conditions that coincided with the frenzied recruiting and actually propelled much of it. Contemporary observers in populated areas remarked on the nationalistic adulation and anger flooding different parts of the country. No doubt that ferment existed, although those who reported it were frequently young men of prime military age who were not moved sufficiently by such feelings to exchange their own comfortable circumstances for the hardships of soldiering.[17]

Correspondence from Union soldiers is also replete with patriotic exclamations, especially early in the war. It was therefore natural that, during the late-twentieth-century research renaissance, patriotic sentiment or the more general category of "ideology" should be at least tacitly identified as the most likely reason those men chose to serve. Patriotism had, after all, been presumed to be the primary motive since 1861, and historians uncovered abundant apparent corroboration when they finally started sifting the endless troves of manuscript sources.

In 1988 Earl Hess noted the prominence given to the Union in volunteers' correspondence, concluding that it "was not mere rhetoric" in a population for which "self-government was a living ideal." He also alluded to the connection people felt between the political health of the country and their own self-interest, as did Phillip Paludan that same year. Paludan portrayed the national rising of 1861 as a resurrection of the flagging patriotism of the late 1850s; other scholars saw the phenomenon as the conscious, society-wide cultivation of a completely new national spirit that began with the basic strategy of indoctrinating schoolchildren.[18]

Nearly a decade later, Hess noticed that soldiers whose patriotism survived a brush with battlefield death became "the solid foundation of the war effort." In the early 1990s James McPherson found that two-thirds of the Union soldiers whose diaries and letters he read had "expressed patriotism," while two in five cited more specific ideals such as liberty, self-rule, or constitutional law. "Most of these volunteers professed patriotic motives for enlisting," he wrote in 1997, apparently in reference to Union recruits during the first year of the war.[19]

Calculating the frequency of such comments was not the same as contending that soldiers had enlisted solely or primarily from love of country or support of the government, but subsequent literature sometimes took that view. "Neither pay nor privilege were enough for men to risk life and limb," wrote Joseph Allan Frank, who mistakenly assumed that any man could have made more money staying at home than in the Union army. Frank also discounted the thirst for adventure and all other "traditional incentives." Volunteers throughout the war were drawn by "inchoate patriotic symbols," he insisted.[20]

Refining the question further, Reid Mitchell identified affection for the Union as the specific form of patriotism that provided volunteers with their "principal incentive." Gary Gallagher drew the same conclusion, writing an entire book on the subject. Each acknowledged other motivations, and each judiciously avoided impossible claims that any specific proportion of men had enlisted from devotion to the Union, arguing instead that it was the most common cause. Incidental digressions on motivation now tend to follow this lead, listing ideological concepts and sociological inducements in that order. Economic considerations, meanwhile, are generally discounted or ignored. Gallagher is one of the few modern students of Union motivation to point out that financial attractions tempted the poor.[21]

While the evidence for ideological devotion is undeniable, it may be as misleading to give full credit to all patriotic remarks as it would be to assume a lack of patriotism among those who were silent on the subject. Many of those assertions were no doubt spontaneous and heartfelt, but collectively such statements warrant more interpretive caution than admissions of less altruistic motives. Someone who concedes his own mercenary intent, for example, is probably not disguising some still-less-admirable purpose, but one who ascribes his actions to pure patriotism may be. Then, too, even the most genuine patriots might well enlist for more than one reason, and in 1861 a great many of them were in financial straits. In both correspondence and contemplative reflection, it would have been perfectly natural for such men to emphasize the more noble motives that brought them into uniform than the practical needs or personal desires.[22]

Thomas Taylor, a young father and struggling lawyer, had married into a family in a community along the Ohio River where the economy had been hit hard by currency destabilization and the interruption of river traffic. He helped raise a company at the very first call. To justify leaving his wife, who vehemently opposed his course, he relied heavily (if fruitlessly) on the argument that he had a duty to help "save" the country. Whether or not he amplified that plea in the effort to soften her opposition, he may also have anticipated some of the economic and social benefits that might accrue from his service—which in the end greatly improved both his fortunes and his status. He went to war as a lieutenant in a three-month regiment, immediately returned to the army as a captain in a three-year regiment, and came home after the war as a field officer with a brevet as brigadier general. His worldly estate fell below Ohio's median ten months before he donned his first uniform, but it had increased exactly tenfold by the first census after his return. Walter Gresham, another lawyer with a modest practice a couple of hundred river miles downstream, prepared his own reluctant wife with similar arguments, and his service availed him even more spectacular pecuniary and political benefits.[23]

Determining the proportionate influence of patriotism in making their decisions would doubtless have been difficult for the soldiers themselves at the time, let alone for analysts generations later. Many soldiers who expressed some hint of patriotic purpose—often through the repetition of editorial-page clichés—explicitly or inadvertently revealed more personal incentives elsewhere in their correspondence.

Those incentives usually included some form of compensation, although not always. Alvah Trueblood, a young printer and the son of a physician, responded with boyish excitement to the ceaseless sound of the fife and drum outside his newspaper office. George Andrews, an unmarried carriage maker nearing thirty who owned a little property, left the impression that he was off on a lark when he joined a company bound for ninety days of war; he frittered away a state bounty equal to two months' pay within a couple of days, equipping himself with a revolver and other useless items in the sheer giddiness of the moment. The thrill of new scenery and potentially epic adventures likewise gripped many of those who enlisted for lack of occupation or income. Such emotions lingered decades longer in the memory than did the anxiety their poverty produced.[24]

For the generation within military age in 1861, armed conflict offered an opportunity to assume the mantle of unquestioned manhood through deliberate exposure to at least theoretical danger. Establishing one's courage against either bullies or bullets remained central to the concept of manhood. Those who considered themselves gentlemen felt particularly protective of their reputations, especially for bravery, but most men of all classes felt some measure of that connection. Editors and recruiters often challenged the courage of those who declined to enlist, and it worked: many a soldier admitted that he had signed up lest he be thought a coward.[25]

Recruits revealed the value they placed on such imagery by congratulating themselves on their own manliness soon after enlisting; decades later, as veterans, they still offered evidence of their own disregard for physical danger. Many of those same volunteers also labored under financial disadvantages of some severity, and if they anticipated the esteem of their friends and neighbors for going to war, that expectation could have posed a supplementary appeal rather than a central motive. Pennsylvania recruit Samuel Alexander consoled his teenaged wife with the reflection that she was at least married to someone who was "man enough to fight for his Country," but it was more clearly financial desperation that drove him into uniform. In a family memoir, New Yorker Thomas Southwick adopted an air of gentility in recounting his confrontation with an Irish bully in his company, but Southwick was the son of a poor shoemaker and was an alumnus of the Randall's Island orphanage. His obvious ambition for a better station in life could well have had more to do with his enlistment than any desire to show his mettle.[26]

That yearning may have been stronger among younger recruits who saw the chance to march directly from adolescence into recognized maturity. This may have been a more compelling reason for nineteen-year-old John McClure, from a moderately prosperous Indiana farm family, who went to war with all the impetuosity of callow youth. He felt no antipathy for slavery (in fact he harbored an unusual degree of racial animosity) and gave little indication of soaring patriotism. Instead, his boasting insinuations about the timidity of friends who remained at home suggested that he had enlisted in large measure to establish his own courage and maturity. That motive failed to sustain his enthusiasm, and he soon turned so critical of the war that he discouraged friends and relatives from joining the army. His family seemed not to need any money from him, despite living on a farm within the region suffering heavy crop damage and currency dislocation, but their relative economic stability made the McClures an exception.[27]

Altruistic ideals were not among the notable impulses that an Iowa newspaperman remembered in the soldiers whose campaign he followed during the spring and summer of 1861. Franc Wilkie, a correspondent for the *Dubuque Herald,* attached himself to the 1st Iowa, which ultimately included Captain Mahana's company of preponderantly poor volunteers from Iowa City. The journalist thought the soldiers in that regiment were probably attracted most by "an ardent wish for a change which would relieve the monotony and humdrum of every-day life."[28] Patriotism did not figure among the obvious impulses he remembered the Iowans evincing when he recorded the following description a quarter of a century later.

> I knew the young men who responded to the call—knew them by hundreds. They were clerks on small salaries; they were lawyers with insufficient business; they were young men with no occupation and anxious for employment; they were farmers' boys disgusted with the drudgery of the soil, and anxious to visit the wonderful world beyond them. To these were added husbands

> tired of the bickering of domestic life, lovers disappointed in their affections, and ambitious elements who saw in the organization of men opportunities for command. Others, differing but little from the last named, scented political preferment, and joined the popular movement.
>
> Physicians with limited practice were early and numerous in their applications for permission to enter the service; clergymen with unappreciative parishes, small incomes, and unsympathetic social environments, came to the front and proffered their assistance. Young men well to do, with virile physiques, anxious for adventure, with their hot blood thrilling in response to the sudden clamors of the drum and the shrill invocations of the fife, thronged with eagerness the recruiting stations and wrote their names in bold characters on the list.
>
> There was not one man in a hundred that believed there would be any war or fighting. All were unanimous in the conviction that the South would not fight, and that if the North put armies in the field, the terrified secessionists would hasten to seek shelter from the storm they had invoked. It was a picnic, a pleasure-trip, a triumphal jaunt through Dixie, with flying banners and beating drums, with all the pleasure of a free excursion, sight-seeing, new faces and places, and pay, food, and clothing during their absence. Some there were who saw loot as they contemplated the wealth of Southern plantations; there were romantic dreamers who caught glimpses in the distance of dark-eyed women with raven hair; and others, idlers by nature, who enjoyed in anticipation the languid delights of the orange groves, the flowering hedges, the beauty of the magnolia blossoms, and the genial air of the "sunny South."[29]

A lack of sufficient income constituted the most repetitive theme in Wilkie's description of Iowa's promptest patriots. "Clerks on small salaries," "lawyers with insufficient business," "young men with no occupation," "physicians with limited practice," and clergymen with "small incomes" all relished the prospect of "pay, food, and clothing" on their little adventure. An audit of the personal finances behind the volunteers in Mahana's company fully confirmed that characterization. A chance for at least temporary economic security drew men from every community across the North, even in that first rush of volunteers who were thereafter regarded as the most fervent in their nationalistic spirit. The Massachusetts shoemakers also fit snugly within that description, as did hosts of entrepreneurs and wage earners left unemployed by the many business failures of the spring, most of which had been ignored by the Republican press.[30]

On the day of the first Union rally at Iowa City, a young German immigrant who had been teaching school near Cedar Rapids found, at the end of the term, that the school board could pay him only a fraction of his promised salary. That left him without money and needing to borrow, which he suspected would be impossible in that economic climate: he did not explicitly ascribe it to his sudden poverty, but he enlisted two days later. Another erstwhile schoolteacher who joined a Minnesota company at the same time inadvertently acknowledged his lack of work when he asked his future wife, "who can go better than young men like myself, without business?"[31]

Poor economic conditions often helped persuade men to answer the president's call who were not without a sense of duty. Fledgling lawyer Charles B. Haydon was just trying to establish a practice in Kalamazoo, Michigan, but business was slow when he enlisted on April 22 for three months. When his company was first presented with the choice of reenlisting for three years, which took him aback, he noted that he would have gone home if it were not for business conditions. "After all," Haydon confessed in his diary, "we can do little while the war continues." A few days later he pondered it again, still uncertain whether he would reenlist, although he conceded that he would not hesitate if he had been awarded a higher rank than sergeant. In the end he did reenlist, convincing himself that he could not "honorably do otherwise." Haydon's subsequent service confirmed the sincerity behind that remark, but economic pressure had still helped bring him to the decision.[32]

Most Union army veterans who were unemployed or underemployed when they enlisted forgot that circumstance when recounting their experiences later, and in many cases they probably did not fully recognize the significance of its influence at the time. Memoirs in particular ring with recollections of the authors' patriotic ardor. It was a rare reminiscing veteran who even mentioned the low wages, lack of work, or outright destitution that would have made military service more appealing to him than it would have been to a well-paid, fully employed citizen.

One of those who made no effort to hide his financial need was Captain William J. Bolton, an engineer in the iron industry from Norristown, Pennsylvania. In the preamble to the transcribed diary that served as his memoir, he admitted that when he led a ninety-day company to Harrisburg on April 20, he had only worked four weeks in the previous six months and was, as he put it, "bankrupt." Donning the uniform instantly eased his financial worries. Several people spontaneously handed him small amounts of cash as his company left Norristown, and he sent it all home with his brother for the support of their aged parents. His uneventful three-month campaign ended with his regiment marching for home on the very eve of its first chance at battle, and his monthly pay stopped that day, but he immediately recruited another company and continued wearing shoulder straps for the next four years. Bolton certainly kept up his end of the bargain, suffering two gruesome wounds before coming home in command of his regiment, but the increasing salary and prominence of his position must have rivaled patriotism as his reason for staying on. He might have resigned at any time or accepted a discharge when his term ended, but he had never before earned so much money.[33]

John T. Buegel, a thirty-year-old Prussian immigrant during the secession crisis, showed similar candor in jotting down his own recollections after the war. He was working as a stonecutter in St. Louis when the currency contraction and general instability began to strangle that city's economy. "All work, indeed all trade, came to a sudden cessation," he wrote. Buegel lost his job, and with construction at a standstill he could find no other work of any kind. One week after Lincoln's call, he and a friend who was in the same circumstances walked into an impromptu armory two blocks from the Mississippi River and started drilling with the first company of what would become Franz Sigel's all-German regiment. Buegel would reenlist at the end of his three-month term and serve until the final autumn of the war, going home before the inevitable hordes of discharged soldiers flooded the labor market. "Trade and commerce flourished," he wrote of the St. Louis he found six months before the Confederacy collapsed. "Work could be had in any branch, and workers were sought but could not be found. So I had ample time and opportunity to consider what I wanted to do in the future." Buegel finished the description of his homecoming with a nationalistic flourish, but that was his only indication of patriotic feeling toward his new homeland. He concluded his memoir with a detailed accounting of how much money he had saved while he was in the army, which suggests the primary purpose for which he enlisted.[34]

Another St. Louis Prussian in his mid-forties, Gustav Hammerstein, had eleven children to worry about when the depression of the secession winter ruined his wholesale-grocery business. Like Buegel, he resorted to immediate enlistment in one of the three-month regiments, taking his seventeen-year-old son with him. When that term ended he reenlisted with two more of his sons, obtaining a commission that supported his family until the regiment was disbanded. That, he admitted, threw him out of work again, and it was more than a year before he could find any other employment.[35]

In other cases, circumstantial evidence alone suggested that a man joined the army to take advantage of an economic opportunity that he never acknowledged, directly or otherwise. Alfred Lacey Hough, a Philadelphian in his mid-thirties, had seen his papermaking business wiped out in the wake of the Panic of 1857, and he was still struggling to recover on the eve of war. He owned no real estate, and the personal property he estimated as worth two thousand dollars in 1860 would have consisted mostly of the inventory in a store he had opened. At the first call for militia, he abandoned all that, leaving his wife and children behind and going off as a sergeant with another of the ninety-day Pennsylvania regiments. For so unfortunate a businessman, enlistment reflected more opportunism than patriotic impulse, and Hough almost immediately solicited assistance from political friends in obtaining a commission as captain in the Regular Army. He secured that generous appointment and remained in the service until he retired as a full colonel nearly thirty years later.[36]

Oscar Derostus Ladley, a young man raised in a utopian community in Greene County, Ohio, faced an even more challenging financial situation at the outset of war, escaping from it the same way Hough had. Ladley had been working as a clerk the year before, but by the spring of 1861 he was out of a job and had left home to look for some means of supporting himself, his mother, and his two younger sisters. The first opportunity that presented itself was the three-month service, and on April 23 he joined the 16th Ohio, with which he saw the war's first collision between Union and Confederate forces on June 3 at Philippi, in western Virginia. A few weeks after his discharge, having found no better employment, Ladley reenlisted in the 75th Ohio for three years, rising steadily through the ranks and returning to Ohio as captain of his company. Peace brought no improvement in his occupational fortunes. He failed in business at least once, and a relative put him to work as a clerk while he sought recommendations for a commission in the Regular Army, which he finally obtained in the fall of 1867. Soldiering was the only dependable livelihood Ladley ever found, and he kept at it until he died of pneumonia on the frontier a dozen years later, as a forty-two-year-old lieutenant.[37]

Ohio governor William Dennison actively appealed to the economic need of citizens like Ladley. He announced liberal provisions for the support of soldiers' families and a hundred-dollar bonus recently authorized by the War Department, which would be payable upon discharge. With adroit use of the passive voice, he implied a perfectly unreliable assurance that each soldier would be granted bounty land once he was discharged—which, Dennison repeatedly suggested, might happen much earlier than three years hence, if victory came quickly. Immediately after listing all those primarily economic inducements, he concluded that "Honor and Glory go hand in hand with Duty and Patriotic Devotion."[38]

Editors of agricultural newspapers from New England to the Northwest tried to persuade subscribers that their patriotic duty to the country lay behind the plow. Those agrarian journalists argued that economic stagnation had created teeming ranks of idle merchants, mechanics, and factory operatives; they advocated letting those multitudes of unemployed fill the armies. Many of those unoccupied laborers and tradesmen did enlist, and they did so in especially heavy numbers in the short-term regiments raised in the first few weeks of the war.[39]

Little Rhode Island filled its entire three-month quota within three days, mainly from the masses of textile workers idled by the cotton embargo. So extensively had the state industrialized, packing tens of thousands of factory operatives into crowded tenements, that a solid majority of families in that little state owned no property whatever—not even the furniture in their homes. The median wealth in Rhode Island therefore stood at zero. State legislators knew what would make such men volunteer in so depressed an industrial climate, and they voted a pay supplement of twelve dollars a month to everyone who enlisted under the call. That did the trick, and nearly two-thirds of the first recruits came from the most destitute men in the laboring class, who could not claim a dollar's worth of personal property.[40]

Some Rhode Island towns and cities showed even more generosity, offering municipal pay supplements for volunteers as high as ten dollars a month. Richer citizens occasionally threw in an additional gift of their own, making public offers of a few dollars to each of the next five, ten, or twenty volunteers, and in short order the state filled a second regiment. That put 1 percent of the state's total 1860 population under arms.[41]

Industrial malaise helped fill much of New Hampshire's lone three-month regiment. Governor Ichabod Goodwin appointed Mason Weare Tappan, a former Republican congressman, to lead the 1st New Hampshire, and the new commander effectively turned the regiment into an employment agency for his acquaintances. Colonel Tappan had already drawn criticism for arranging government offices for his father, brother, and brother-in-law, and now he named his law partner to the unauthorized office of regimental paymaster, giving his local minister the post of chaplain, which paid a hundred dollars a month plus allowances. In the first company to fill up, three-fifths of the enlisted men who listed any occupation called themselves shoemakers, and more than four-fifths of those volunteers had accumulated less property than the state median. The overwhelming majority of them owned little or nothing.[42]

Vermont was farm country. It was poor enough in the rural way, but there were no masses of unemployed industrial operatives anxious to fill the new regiments. Perhaps for that very reason, the state legislature created a special incentive for volunteers in the second week of the conflict, when recruiting seemed to be progressing slower than some had hoped. The solons at Montpelier agreed on April 26 to pay an additional seven dollars per month from the state coffers to any resident who went into military service: he could assign it to his family as supplemental support, or if he chose he could collect it when he came home. That alone amounted to another month's pay for a farmhand or laboring man who enlisted for ninety days. Recruiting stations came to life as soon as the bill passed, and within four days all ten companies of Vermont's three-month regiment were ready to report at Rutland, their ranks full.[43]

A couple of weeks after his initial proclamation, President Lincoln began to regret squandering the national outrage over Fort Sumter on such short-term recruiting. Even without congressional authority, he decided to expand the Regular Army and issued a new call for volunteers to serve for three years. In accordance with administration wishes to avoid more short-term regiments, the secretary of war tried to convince state governors to reorganize their unfinished three-month regiments for three years. Goodwin passed that proposal along to Tappan a week after appointing him to command the 1st New Hampshire, but the colonel blanched at the prospect. "To attempt to disturb it now," he pleaded, "would Break the regiment to pieces, but at the end of the term, if the war continues, I have little doubt it could be persuaded to remain in the field." Aside from illustrating the common delusion that the Confederacy might be suppressed within the three-month service of the militia regiments, Tappan's letter hinted at his own disinclination to sacrifice any more of his own time. Still, he assured the governor that "patriotism and self-respect" would compel his men "to see the thing through" once their brief enlistment ended.[44]

For all the patriotism that had ostensibly driven ninety-day volunteers to arms, a great many of them balked at the request to reenlist. The man who expected to command the 5th New Jersey saw his hopes dashed when the prospective three-month companies all disintegrated under pressure to reorganize for three years. The willing men proved too few to form more than four companies, and he lost that chance to wear a colonel's eagles. "I done all I could," he wrote his wife on May 14, "but they would not go into it for three years."[45]

The emoluments would have to improve before more of them made so long a commitment.

As a group, the three-month men seemed terrified of being held beyond the limits of their contracts. They also showed far more interest in when and how much they were to be paid than in performing the more dangerous aspects of the duty for which they had ostensibly volunteered.

In Maryland, Virginia, and Missouri, three Union armies moved against the enemy just as the ninety-day regiments neared the end of their terms, and the commanders of all three armies had to maneuver under the pressure of completing their campaigns before the militiamen went home. In Missouri a new brigadier general by the name of Nathaniel Lyon, recently elevated from captain in the Regular Army, strove to demolish insurgent forces with a small army that included a heavy proportion of ninety-day volunteers. One thing he noticed about them was how disgruntled they were over not being paid: until its discharge the 1st Iowa received only eight dollars per private from the state for the partial month of duty before the regiment was mustered into national service. The Iowans' uniforms and shoes were already falling apart, but that was not a deficiency they could solve with money, for only the Quartermaster Department could produce a sufficient supply. The men did like to supplement their bland rations with pies, cakes, cornbread, and biscuits bought from greedy farmers, but despite rumors of half-rations they appear to have found enough to eat, if mainly by foraging. At least in part, the anxiety for pay may have reflected demands at home, where community generosity toward soldiers' families was proving inadequate. A petition circulated through the Iowa regiment calling on the officers to inform General Lyon that they did not intend to reenlist when their three-month term ended, mainly to discourage him from asking them to stay on.[46]

The Missouri State Guard had mobilized to confront Lyon's transgressions against state sovereignty, and a number of Northern men of a states'-rights persuasion had joined them in the field. Lyon responded by chasing the state legislature and the State Guard out of Jefferson City and into southwestern Missouri. One of his subordinates fought a little battle near Carthage early in July, leaving behind some prisoners from a regiment raised in St. Louis. A Pennsylvanian serving with the State Guard asked those captives why they were fighting a war of aggression, and to a man they said that they had joined the army because they were out of work—as their comrade John Buegel would confirm in his memoir.[47]

Hoping to complete his mission before losing his summer soldiers, Lyon assailed a rebel army twice the size of his own along Wilson's Creek, below Springfield. He attacked on August 10, four days before the three-month enlistment of the 1st Iowa was due to expire. The Iowans still feared Lyon would not let them go, and their eagerness for soldiering waned in the presence of an armed enemy. The best-paid man in the regiment, Colonel John F. Bates, reported himself sick just as his command moved forward to its only battle: he went back to Dubuque to sit out the rest of the war. When the fight ended, Lyon lay dead and his army fled back toward Springfield. The Iowans kept going, headed for home.[48]

In the Shenandoah Valley, Robert Patterson—a major general of Pennsylvania militia—commanded another Union army filled with short-term militia, including the 1st New Hampshire. He was supposed to prevent the enemy from combining against the third and last national army, under Brigadier General Irvin McDowell, who was maneuvering against Confederates near Manassas Junction, outside Washington. Patterson should have begun offensive operations in the third week of July, but that was precisely when he expected his army to evaporate. More than a week before they were to go home, the officers of the 6th Pennsylvania petitioned the general against holding them over their time, and the officers of several regiments warned that they would not remain an hour beyond their enlistments. On the morning of July 18, some of the Pennsylvania companies that had first responded to Lincoln's call started back to Washington—men who later formed a self-congratulatory society called First Defenders of the National Capital. Their departure began a flood of discharges that drained Patterson's force from more than two dozen regiments to six in less than a week.[49]

Correspondent Wilkie had correctly observed that most of the ninety-day militiamen had not expected any real fighting. A boy who followed the 6th Massachusetts through the Baltimore riot doubted that he would ever see another shot fired once all the troops reached Washington. Another Massachusetts wanderer with the 1st Iowa supposed, before Wilson's Creek, that there might be one serious scrape with the rebels—or perhaps not—and within his three months he expected to march through a defeated Confederacy. A third Bay State youth soothed his sister with the assurance that there would be no killing, anticipating that the government's show of military force would sufficiently preempt Confederate aggression.[50]

Wilkie had also detected, with equal accuracy, that plunder played a part in the visions of the ninety-day men. A few weeks before their discharge, the 1st Iowa and the 2nd Kansas seem to have spearheaded the looting of Forsyth, Missouri, during Lyon's campaign. An Iowan admitted that his comrades "ransacted" the town; a Kansas lieutenant described the soldiers invading private homes. Even the chaplain of the Iowa regiment was said to have stolen items from a store, and the soldier who made that accusation expressed dismay that everything of value had been taken before he arrived. The pillage drew such attention that Lyon issued an order denouncing it.[51]

Union armies in the East showed similar rapacity. The 1st New Hampshire spent late June and early July guarding the upper Potomac, but the men wandered from camp frequently to prowl the countryside for food and plunder, making little distinction between loyal and disloyal citizens. The regimental historian claimed that they paid for what they took—at least when the residents greeted them "respectfully"—but regimental court-martial records indicate otherwise. A sergeant, corporal, and three other men from one detached company swam the Potomac on July 14 to see what they could steal on the Virginia side, but rebel cavalry caught them in the act and took them prisoner. In an altercation with an unarmed Maryland teenager who objected to his thievery, Private Samuel Webster of the 1st New Hampshire produced a revolver and killed the youth on the spot.[52]

McDowell left the environs of Washington on Tuesday, July 16, headed for a Confederate army ensconced behind a creek called Bull Run, twenty-five miles away. With him marched thousands of troops who expected to be home by the following Sunday. His campaign quickly degenerated into an orgy of vandalism and looting. Three-month and three-year men participated indiscriminately in the theft and destruction of private property all along the route of their march. Their marauding reached particularly obnoxious heights at Vienna, Fairfax Court House, and Germantown, where Union soldiers burned the entire unoffending village on the evening of July 17 out of pure malice.[53]

McDowell's three-month men showed even less enthusiasm for facing armed Confederates than Lyon's had. His vanguard had a sharp brush with a Virginia brigade on the afternoon of July 18, and the entire 12th New York fell apart under relatively light punishment, fleeing the field in abject panic before three companies of the enemy. Officers took to their heels, abandoning their men, and the fugitives only slowed down and rallied after they had put a mile between themselves and the firing line. So striking a demonstration of battlefield inferiority alarmed their comrades generally. The next morning, after burial details recovered some of the mangled corpses from the skirmish, the rest of the ninety-day men in that division started demanding their discharges. No one wanted to be killed so close to going home, and short-term militiamen throughout the army turned suddenly punctilious about the precise dates their service was supposed to end. Nervous officers in Joshua Varian's New York artillery battery and in the 4th Pennsylvania (which included Captain Bolton and his Norristown company) pointed out that their time would be up on July 20, although their muster-in date left them a few more days of federal service. The most earnest plea of the commanding general on the eve of a great battle could not persuade them to remain through the hour of peril.[54]

Before dawn on Sunday, July 21, McDowell's army was already moving out to attack the Confederates. The 4th Pennsylvania and the New York artillerymen still refused to participate in the assault. Of the thousand men who composed those two units, only the colonel of the Pennsylvania regiment agreed to stay and fight.[55]

Twelve of the three-month regiments did stay on. Eight of them took part in the actual fighting at Bull Run, but they contributed some of the most embarrassing performances during a day that left Union forces unusually mortified. A brigade that included all three of Connecticut's militia regiments undertook an inexpert assault on Henry Hill that resulted in the first repulse of Union soldiers during the battle, though much of the fault lay in the failure to provide them with enough support. The 8th New York Militia bolted away at the first volley, and only a fragment ever returned to the fight. Toward the end of the battle, as the tide swayed one way and then the other, the 5th Massachusetts Militia demonstrated even less nerve: a conspicuous number of the Bay Staters dropped their muskets and ran as soon as they caught sight of the Confederate battle front, with most of the rest following suit as the first shots came their way. One of their own officers commented contemptuously on his colleagues and comrades, even in his own company.[56]

Some of the longer-term volunteers who had enlisted right after Fort Sumter also showed the white feather at Bull Run. The 11th New York, famous as Elmer Ellsworth's Fire Zouaves and infamous for its core of debauched hooligans, made a poor showing in support of the Union batteries on Henry Hill; hundreds of them utterly disgraced their regiment on the retreat by leading the flight and then deserting for home after they reached Washington. The 2nd New York State Militia never crossed Bull Run to the battlefield, yet Colonel George W. B.

Tompkins reported 140 men missing; several of his officers absconded from the army altogether, fleeing all the way back to Washington and boarding trains for New York. Colonel Tompkins was himself accused of misbehavior before the enemy.[57]

Fresh from its fruitless campaign in the Shenandoah Valley, the 1st New Hampshire arrived at the Concord railroad station before breakfast on August 5, barely ten weeks after it had left. Colonel Tappan had assured Governor Goodwin that his men would reenlist at the end of their ninety days, citing their "patriotism and self-respect," but no such emotions motivated him: like the Iowa colonel, he went home for the duration. Abundant opportunity for reenlisting surrounded his men, but with their pockets full of mustering-out pay only a minority of them immediately joined other units. A great many of those who went right back into service sought commissions on the strength of their brief experience.[58]

By the end of 1861, only a third of the veterans of the 1st New Hampshire had rejoined some branch of military service. Another third of Tappan's troops eventually saw additional service in some form, especially after it became compulsory, but the rest stayed home. The 260 men who never reenlisted could hardly have considered such brief service sufficient to satisfy patriotic obligation, assuming they had enlisted from any sense of national devotion in the first place. Likely their motives had varied, but a summer of soldiering may have quenched most of their thirst for adventure, and distaste for military discipline or camp life doubtless depressed the reenlistment rate. Political disaffection later exerted significant influence as the war shifted from defense of the loyal states to invasion of the Confederacy, and especially as the administration goal of restoring the Union expanded to include emancipation. The same variety of factors inevitably delayed some from rejoining the army until after conscription loomed, encouraging them to choose the security or ease of rear-echelon units or to enlist for tempting bounties. Others only reenlisted when they saw another opportunity for short enlistment terms—demonstrating either a reluctance to neglect their personal affairs or an insider's understanding of how to reduce the odds of going into battle.[59]

One of those who did quickly reenlist was Oscar Frink, who admitted to finding the army a haven for a man otherwise unable to support himself. In his new regiment Frink gravitated to the hospital on the plea of a lame leg, then resisted a discharge because he could not work. When the surgeons forced him out of the army, he reenlisted once more, quickly going on the disabled list yet again.[60]

Charles Rogers of Dover did reenlist soon after his discharge from the 1st New Hampshire, apparently succumbing to an impulse other than patriotic sentiment. Abby Rogers had written to her husband three days after he mustered in with Tappan's regiment, imploring him to come home and care for her and their children. There was nothing in the house to eat, she told him, but when he failed to respond she appealed to the selectmen of her town. The chairman of that board, who happened to be a physician, conveyed her request to Tappan, explaining that Mrs. Rogers suffered not so much from a lack of food as from chronic psychological disorders and acute anxiety. The doctor nevertheless supposed that Rogers "may have mistaken his motive for volunteering to serve his country." Neither the colonel nor Rogers relented, and the beleaguered husband served with the regiment until it came home that summer. Barely seven weeks after his return, he reenlisted.[61]

Rogers apparently fell within Wilkie's category of husbands tired of bickering, for he choose death before domesticity. He also suffered from the financial limitations that Wilkie recalled being so prevalent among the early volunteers, laboring under an economic disadvantage that was typical of men who answered Lincoln's first call to arms. Rogers was a shoemaker by trade and among the poorest 15 percent of residents in his state.[62] By the time he reenlisted, the compensation for military service had been augmented sufficiently to provide an unquestionable improvement over what he might have earned at a cobbler's bench. Towns and cities had initially established local funds for subsidies to soldiers' wives and children, or to their dependent parents if they were not married. Some states had formalized such payments, granting two, three, or four dollars a week to most wives, depending on how many children they had. In addition, the War Department raised the monthly clothing allowance from $2.50 to $3.50 late in May of 1861, at the same time establishing the bonus of $100 that would be granted to long-term volunteers when they earned an honorable discharge. Then, just as the last of the three-month regiments were mustering out, Congress authorized an increase in the pay of enlisted men, adding two dollars to the monthly pay of a private. Going back into uniform as a sergeant, Rogers could expect to realize well over thirty dollars a month from his pay, clothing allowance, and family subsidy, besides his own daily keep. That was probably half again the money he had earned in a good month of making shoes, even without considering the freedom soldiering gave him from an unhappy home life.[63]

It seems unlikely that men of so little means harbored greater interest than the wealthy in preserving the Union, which was the stated and presumed purpose of the war at that time. Far more likely, a lack of satisfactory employment gave them the freedom to indulge an itch for adventure and join the army, while financial need provided the practical incentive to do so. Generations of historians have debated whether the burden of the Civil War was borne primarily by those at the lower end of the economic scale, but the argument has always hung so dependently on anecdotal information that no reliable conclusion could ever be drawn. Now, finally, an ambitious compilation of census data allows the calculation of median wealth for each state, which was not previously feasible. Comparing the wealth of the ninety-day volunteers to those medians leaves little doubt that the war did, indeed, begin as a poor man's fight. It would remain one to the bitter end.

3

ARM'D YEAR

THREE-YEAR VOLUNTEERS, 1861

Six weeks into the war, the country had exceeded Lincoln's initial appeal for 75,000 militia, primarily by mining the ranks of those citizens in chronic or acute pecuniary distress. From the Atlantic to the Missouri came 101 regiments and a few miscellaneous battalions in answer to the call for three-month militia—nearly 100,000 men. The vast majority of those who first responded had already been counted among the poorer half of their state's populations by the 1860 census marshals, and many of the rest had been financially undone by the political and economic events of the succeeding winter.[1]

Lincoln's first proclamation for three-year volunteers had gone out on May 3, accompanied by the new provision for a hundred-dollar discharge bonus, which turned soldiering into a more inviting alternative occupation for unemployed, restless, or desperate men. The savings potential of army pay and allowances on top of food and nominal shelter most readily attracted those in the lower working classes, to whom the promise of a hundred dollars represented an inviting windfall. That looming reward appealed particularly when recruits expected a short war, and it took a while for wartime inflation to diminish the allure. One youth from rural Vermont spurned the idea of a discharge six months into his enlistment, despite all the discomforts of soldier life, because he would have lost his bonus. An overage Wisconsin cavalryman with a big family felt the same after a year. Then there came widespread offers of community support for the families left behind by volunteers and all the speculation about 160 acres of bounty land. Those accumulated incentives, or at least the promise of them, opened the floodgates. Volunteers came forward by the thousands daily. The nature of the inducements virtually assured that they would be most attractive to the poorest elements of society and the momentarily unemployed. Predictably, those populations again figured disproportionately among the applicants.[2]

Recruiting proceeded with the greatest dispatch where pay subsidies were most generous and where industrialization made more of the population vulnerable to the recession. Young men who were still earning good wages showed greater resistance to the patriotic fervor. Of the four New England states that paid no general subsidy to their soldiers, New Hampshire, Massachusetts, and Connecticut failed to meet their census-based 1861 enlistment quotas, while Maine barely did. Vermont, with its seven-dollar monthly contribution, covered its 8,950-man requirement with a 6-percent margin, while Rhode Island, where the state initially paid a monthly supplement and towns offered as much as ten dollars more a month, exceeded its quota by 27 percent.[3]

Political dissatisfaction with Lincoln's war left Maryland, Delaware, and New Jersey far short of their anticipated contributions—despite New Jersey's four-dollar monthly stipend—but Pennsylvania exceeded its quota slightly. New York, where a man who had recently bought a mercantile enterprise complained in late September that the war was still "playing hell" with business, provided 120,231 men instead of the requested 109,056. Farther west, every state suffered from both the currency contraction and the decline in river traffic and trade, and all except divided Missouri sent more troops than expected, often by tens of thousands of men. Indiana provided nearly 60 percent more soldiers than required, and almost a quarter of those troops were raised along the Ohio River, where businesses had been ruined and men thrown out of work by the thousands. Illinois, laboring under agricultural blight and undependable currency, exceeded its quota by more than 70 percent. Sparsely settled Kansas, where drought and famine had wrought disaster and made the state an object of nationwide charity the previous winter, sent more than twice as many men as the president had requested.[4]

Faced with the War Department's rejection of any more ninety-day militia, many states simply reorganized their unfinished regiments for the three-year service, despite grumbling or refusal from men who had hoped for only a season's occupation. Other states lobbied their recruits to sign for an additional three years, beginning at the end of their initial three months. The 2nd Maine had already left for the front in dark-gray uniforms when officers confronted the entire regiment with the choice of remustering for two years, which the overwhelming majority accepted. Nearly three dozen New York regiments also enlisted under state auspices for two years, and scores of other regiments extended their terms from three months to three years. The mayhem and defeat at Bull Run caused troublesome dissension among some veterans of that fight who had consented to the extension, and in some units many of them tried to repudiate the agreement.[5]

The three-year requirement nearly frustrated William O. Sides, who craved a lucrative army commission. Sides considered himself New Hampshire's first volunteer of the Civil War. He owned no real estate, and most of his personal resources were tied up in his livery-stable venture, so a captain's pay would have improved his income substantially. At word of Lincoln's appeal for three-month militia, Sides secured authority to raise a company of ninety-day men, enlisting his younger brothers and casting about for others who might serve under him.[6] The president required only 780 militia from the Granite State, but about 2,000 volunteered, and the governor started another regiment with the surplus recruits. When asked to reenlist for three years, three-fifths of the would-be soldiers refused, and even many of those who agreed supposed that they would never have to remain so long from home. Sides, whose main interest seemed to lie in the commission, did not hesitate. Eventually his company filled up with three-year men, and in June he led it to Washington as part of the 2nd New Hampshire.[7]

The sergeant major of Sides's regiment, George W. Gordon, had spent the four years since the Panic of 1857 trying to find a sufficiently remunerative job to support his wife and daughters and buy a farm, yet something always intervened to confound him. The panic had interrupted his employment as a machinist, but by the opening of autumn in 1860 he had finally begun putting a few dollars away with a job in Boston. Then the economic effects of secession left him hard up for money again, and at a bad time, for he had just installed his family in a mortgaged house in New Hampshire. People to whom he had lent his savings at interest were dodging those debts, and a married couple boarding with Gordon's wife—workers in one of those hard-hit Merrimack River mill towns—had fallen behind in their rent. Gordon could claim some militia experience, so at the first news of the president's call he, too, started gathering childhood friends and relatives to form a company. Most of his prospective recruits also begged off when faced with the three-year commitment, and that left him too few men to claim a commission, so he accepted the highest enlisted rank in the regiment with the hope of rising to the first vacancy among the lieutenants. A few weeks later that vacancy appeared, allowing him to wear shoulder straps and collect a salary and allowances equivalent to four times the pay of a common laborer.[8]

Like their counterparts in the West, many of the early volunteers in the East seemed reluctant to keep up their half of the bargain when they learned how dangerous it might be. Captain Sides, his brothers, and Sergeant Major Gordon all participated in the battle of Bull Run with their regiment, which behaved badly during much of that engagement. As other raw troops did that day, the poorly trained New Hampshiremen scattered to the winds as soon as the bullets began buzzing about them; one lieutenant felt such shame in his comrades that he abandoned the regiment a few days later for a commission in the Regular Army. The worst of the day's performance came during the retreat, when the largest remaining agglomeration of New Hampshire soldiers approached the Cub Run bridge. Two or three company officers tried to rally the regiment there to help cover the retreat, but a Confederate battery dropped a few shells on the bridge, overturning vehicles and blocking the main road back to Washington. The disorganized retreat turned into a panicked rout from that moment, and what remained of the 2nd New Hampshire dissolved in terrified flight. The fugitives swept across the waist-deep creek, blending into the promiscuous throng swarming back to the Potomac River.[9]

Captain Sides vaulted into Cub Run and up the far bank with such undignified velocity that he complained of an abdominal strain. He resigned from the service only ten weeks into his new career, citing the injury he had allegedly suffered in crossing the creek, and he immediately secured a pension for it. Two years later Sides obtained a commission among the light-duty troops of the then-new Veteran Reserve Corps, again on the excuse of his disability. Until the shooting stopped he commanded units guarding prisoners or manning coastal forts, sleeping under cover every night and still drawing $1,400 a year. After the war he exploited his status as a veteran to secure a succession of political appointments, beginning with the post of customs inspector in his home town. By 1870 his wealth had tripled, and he had invested most of it in real estate. Financially the war had made him.[10]

Sergeant Major Gordon evinced a decided predilection for saving money and accumulating property, but he seemed much more willing than Captain Sides to actually earn the benefits he derived from his service. The flurry of resignations after Bull Run quickly brought him a commission, and he stuck with the regiment in every battle thereafter. For the next three years he sent his wife more money than he had ever been able to earn, advising her on improving their house and buying land, all with the plan of returning to a mortgage-free home with some acreage for farming or speculation. Eventually he commanded a company, suffered three relatively minor wounds in the Peach Orchard at Gettysburg, and was killed at Cold Harbor the week before his enlistment expired, leaving his widow to mourn him for fifty-five years. Yet even so conscientious an officer showed unmistakable signs of having been drawn into uniform by the income, prestige, and opportunity it offered.[11]

In his initial search for an advantageous military post, Gordon may also have been attracted by the hundred-dollar discharge benefit attached to the president's three-year proclamation. Recruits would not receive that money until they had completed their term, but it amounted to an inviting sum in the spring of 1861, with so many people unemployed. The regular monthly pay and clothing allowance—both of which Congress raised as soon as the three-month militia started going home—posed fair competition even for the wages of those unskilled laborers who could still find regular work.[12]

The unusually sluggish commerce of the secession winter quickly reverberated from the mills and factories to their supporting industries, affecting the farmers who produced the wool, the machinists who fabricated the tools, the foundries that forged the equipment, and those who transported both the raw materials and the finished products. By the outbreak of hostilities, the Southern cotton embargo had already begun to force cutbacks of hours, days, and entire shifts in those cotton mills that had managed to keep running through the winter. Stockpiles of material served to supply government needs for some time, delaying the stimulating effects of war production. In many regions and industries, the recession persisted well into the summer of 1861 and beyond, keeping workers idle and creating personal financial crises that inspired reflection on the monetary advantages of joining the army. Dismal demand for timber and mineral products prompted a roving speculator in Michigan's Upper Peninsula to report in July that "times here now are as hard as in other Countries," with money scarce, nothing selling, and everyone discouraged; more than ten months later that same man reiterated that "times are so very hard here now." An Illinois merchant who had taken an army commission amid the stagnant commerce of 1861 learned early in 1862 that his town was "still dull, and very little business is transacted." A New York lieutenant who was the sole support of his sisters, mother, and unemployed father wrote, as late as May of 1862, that they were lucky to have at least one family member working amid such "hard times."[13]

Credit-reporting firms recognized "Bankrupts of Sixty One" as a class, and eventually Congress would entertain a bill for uniform bankruptcy laws to relieve them. The sponsor of that bill contended that many of those ruined by the recession had gone into the army. An editor in Dubuque, Iowa, observed as early as mid-September of 1861 that the poor and propertyless had, "to a great extent," filled the ranks of the army, and a survey of early recruits corroborates his impression. Two-thirds of the men in a sample company of the 1st Iowa fell below the rather low median wealth in that state, as did three-fifths of those in the 2nd Iowa. In the adjoining states of Illinois and Minnesota, those figures were even more striking, while 76 percent of the first three-year volunteers from Wisconsin represented of the poorer half of that state's people.[14]

Recruiting advertisements and journalistic encouragement for volunteers reflected the dismal economic conditions of the summer of 1861. Recruiters perceived glaring opportunity in the hordes of men cast out of work by weather and politics. A man who wanted to raise a company in Beardstown, Illinois, on the Illinois River, targeted the very men who spent their time waiting for a boat at the river landing, and the local newspaperman promoted that strategy. "There is a great many men out of employment who might as well take a little trip as not," the Beardstown editor reasoned. "The pay of volunteers has been increased, and there is now more clear money in that business than any other we know of." The same opinion prevailed a month later in Vermont, where a Rutland paper reminded readers that the state would add seven dollars to the monthly pay of each of its soldiers. "Aside from all considerations of duty and patriotism," the editor lectured, "no business pays so well as soldiering now days. Twenty dollars per month from the date of enlistment and all expenses paid, is not to be despised in these hard times."[15]

Letters from men who enlisted that summer also revealed, overtly or by implication, that some financial imperative or the absence of gainful employment had led them to take up arms. Schuyler Coe, a former clerk from central New York, tried his entrepreneurial luck in Council Bluffs, Iowa, but during the summer of 1861 he found "everything was dull and promised to remain so untill after the war is over and I concluded to enlist." Thanks probably to the scarcity of money, all across Iowa the only advertising that seemed necessary to draw recruits was a newspaper list of the army's monthly pay scale. One young teacher in Wisconsin had lost much of the term because the schoolhouse was not weathertight, and the school board withheld his pay, so he crossed into Iowa looking for a position: finding none, he enlisted. Another teacher in Michigan accepted discounted local money for part of his contract, and for the balance he received only promises that had not been met in late August; he had long since enlisted by then, counting on army pay and a state-mandated subsidy to support his parents and their brood.[16]

By the late summer of 1861, numerous difficulties had beset Joseph Lester, a cabinetmaker in Sauk County, Wisconsin. He had four young daughters to raise alone after the death of his wife, and the paralyzed economy of the West left tradesmen like him begging for work. With hundreds of dollars in mortgage and other debts, he arranged boarding for his girls and enlisted in the 6th Wisconsin Battery, in which he soon started a business to supplement his pay and the state subsidy. With a promotion to artificer, he gained access to dry, secure storage in the battery wagon and started buying quantities of stationery and newspapers for resale to his comrades, who composed a captive market. With the proceeds he promptly paid off his debts and started supporting his daughters in style.[17]

Luther Cowen, a surveyor in northwestern Illinois who owned nothing and owed much in 1861, assured his wife and children that he was determined not to "play around" as much as he had and to try making money in the army. Raising a company among his acquaintances around Galena, he took command of the unit and rose to the rank of major after a year. He often mentioned his fear of being thought a coward, but he never made any allusion to national pride or devotion to the government, instead returning repeatedly to the concept of finally paying off his debts. He was killed leading his regiment in a charge at Vicksburg, but in the end he left his family comfortably fixed through the money he was able to save, the insurance he left, and the pension his wife drew for half a century.[18]

Samuel Thoman, a miller in Dauphin County, Pennsylvania, was several years over the age limit for military service, but he enlisted as a solution to indebtedness. In letters to his illiterate wife that had to be read to her by their son, he assured her that he wanted "to get you all I can draw on my service," and he assumed that she would be eligible for about seven dollars a month from the county. Adjuring her to ignore his debts and buy nothing if she could help it, he promised to send money whenever he could and specifically reminded her to apply for his pay and his hundred-dollar bonus if he were killed, which he soon was.[19]

Depending on the local relief committee's promise of liberal distributions to soldier's families, one near-penniless Pennsylvania shoemaker did not even wait for the government pay raise. Samuel Alexander was boarding in a private home with his teenaged bride and their baby daughter in a village across the river from Pittsburgh when he signed the roll of a new company on July 22. The financial incentives had meant much to him, and he flew into a rage when the money came up short. Two months passed before he saw a paymaster, who gave him only a fraction of what he was due, and then the relief committee decided it had been too generous, reducing the amount his wife could receive.[20]

At the opening of hostilities, Maine's legislature established an immediate bounty of two months' pay, or twenty-two dollars, for each recruit. That bounty helped the state meet its quota, but it may not have been necessary because the army posed such an obvious solution to extensive unemployment. "The number thrown out of work by the almost total suspension of commerce, trade, and the various branches of mechanical industry is very large," complained a Portland newspaper, urging its readers to find something for idle laborers to do. "The wages of their labor is their chief if not their sole reliance. It is all that stands between their family and want on the one hand, or the work-house on the other." The same paper later scolded employers who did find work for some of those men and then failed to pay them on time.[21]

Joseph Manchester, the oldest son still living on his father's heavily mortgaged farm in Cumberland County, Maine, enlisted toward the end of the summer. That left all the work to his father, who was in his mid-fifties, but the family's need for cash was clearly paramount, and the state bounty dangled alluringly, along with the promise of regular pay and voluntary community assistance. Joseph sent nearly all his money home against threatening foreclosure, complaining that his married older brother failed to help, but it was all for naught. Joseph died of wounds less than two years after he enlisted, and the farm had been lost by the time his mother obtained a pension.[22]

Similar luck befell Simon B. Carlton of Penobscot County, who was the oldest of his father's six surviving children. Theirs was a poor family on a tiny farm, and all Simon's wages went to his father, who was disabled by a hernia. These earnings totaled barely $100 in 1860, but he and his father bought more farmland together on the prospect of drawing army pay, and he enlisted in the 4th Maine in June, probably hoping to pay off the last of the mortgage with his discharge bonus. He religiously sent the bulk of his pay home every month, but most of it probably went for the support of the family. When Simon was killed at Chancellorsville in May, 1863, his father was forced to let the land go.[23]

John O. Stevens, a farmer in his early thirties from Wentworth, New Hampshire, had struggled hard to provide a home for his parents and sisters. His mother had turned mentally unstable, and the county court had appointed a guardian for her. His aged and rheumatic father showed signs of inattention to business, so John, as the only son, became head of the family. His labor had maintained the family home and bought the land he worked, but accumulated debts were catching up with him when he enlisted in May of 1861. He entered the army as a corporal and soon rose to sergeant, which gave him more extra cash than he had ever had, and he sent almost all of it home, expecting his father to pay the debts with them. After more than a year he began to wonder if the money was being spent as he directed and if his sacrifice was being wasted. In frustration he spoke of selling out and using the proceeds to pay off what obligations he could.[24]

A preoccupation with money also flavored the correspondence of most soldiers from factory towns. When recruits started broadcasting their sudden relative affluence, other poorly paid, underemployed, and unemployed workmen began to think of the army as a form of economic salvation. In July, 1861, Congress authorized President Lincoln to call on the states for up to five hundred thousand men, abetting that request early in August with the increase in a private's pay to thirteen dollars per month. Originally the bill had proposed a four-dollar raise, to fifteen dollars, but congressmen cut that in half at the final hour when one of them pointed out that the war was already costing $1.25 million a day with no revenue to cover the expense.[25] The extra two dollars nevertheless proved sufficient—for a time. Edward Plummer, a sixteen-year-old farmhand who had been earning nine dollars a month plus board, enlisted with the news of the increase, and he may have cited the better pay as an argument to win his parents' consent for an alluring adventure. That kind of money even caught the attention of men who earned a dollar or more a day in civilian life, where they spent most of their income on shelter and sustenance. The expectation of three meals a day and a place to sleep promised to transform the monthly military salary into a surplus.[26]

Thomas and William Jones, Irish immigrants working as farm laborers together in New Jersey, enlisted with the news of that pay raise. "My pay came from the time I first penned down my name," one of them informed their sister. He urged her to make their friends aware of it and tell them that any fare they paid for travel would be reimbursed, no matter how far they came.[27] Such stories of relatively acceptable compensation spread rapidly among the poorer elements of society by the end of the war's first summer, when higher prices were already driving living costs up and real wages down for the working class. After the first bimonthly visit from the paymaster, in September, a captain in the 10th Massachusetts went home on furlough with over $1,000 for his friends' relatives. That same payday the 2nd New Hampshire deposited in excess of $12,000 in one bank for the accounts of soldiers' families, representing more than $15 for each man on duty with the regiment.[28]

Private and public accounts of surprising accumulations of savings attracted men who might otherwise never have thought of enlisting. David Day, who worked in a boot factory in Milford, Massachusetts, had passed his fortieth birthday and sired four children by September of 1861, when he enlisted in the 25th Massachusetts. He reported owning no property whatsoever in 1860: he, his wife, and their children lived in a rented (and presumably crowded) house with another working family, indicating strained financial circumstances even before the economic troubles of 1861. As he began preparing his diary for publication in the 1880s, Day conceded that patriotism alone had not moved him. A couple of decades after the fact he was able to remark scornfully on the low monthly pay of thirteen dollars, citing instead a thirst for excitement, but he neglected to point out that he served as a noncommissioned officer from the outset at more than thirteen dollars per month. Neither did he allude to the relatively generous public assistance from Massachusetts, for which his wife and children were eligible, or the recession that had blighted the industry in which he made his living. All those factors surely bore on his decision at least as much as any wish to escape the boredom of his personal situation. His failure to mention such obvious incentives may suggest their importance: like many veterans, he seemed to be publishing his diary in part to support his pension application, and he may not have wished to reveal how much he had benefited from his wartime service.[29]

A young widower named Amos Stearns joined the same regiment less than a week after Day did. Stearns was an unassuming, matter-of-fact man in his late twenties who described himself as a "machinist," and like Day he lived in Worcester County, where mechanized shoe factories dominated the manufacturing districts. In a preamble to the published version of his own wartime diary, he attributed his decision to join the army to a long bout of "the war fever," but he also admitted that he had been "out of work most of the time that summer" and that he was about $100 in debt, besides. He illustrated how important money was to him by recounting virtually every penny he spent or saved during three and a half years of service, including more than nine months as a prisoner of war. With ill-disguised resentment he recorded the high price of shipping a box of comfort items through Confederate lines and the cost of buying unnecessary uniforms that the quartermaster forced on him when he returned from prison, months after his enlistment had expired. A quarter of a century after completing an unspectacular but highly creditable enlistment, Stearns—like the St. Louis soldier John Buegel—seemed proudest of having saved about $342 "on a private's pay." His little memoir lacked the common ingredient of a lavish patriotic prologue. In fact, he made no reference at all to such sentiments. The only recurring theme was his concentration on money.[30]

Up in Auburn, Maine, Marshall Phillips enjoyed somewhat better circumstances than either Day or Stearns. He was a year younger than Day and owned his own home, but he, too, was a shoemaker, and the combination of Southern embargo and Northern recession had crippled the Maine shops as much as it had those in Massachusetts. Phillips was not among the few who enjoyed a flurry of hectic, short-term employment when a local harness maker won the contract to make the leather equipment for Maine's first regiments. With a pregnant wife and three children, and the town of Auburn promising aid to soldiers' families, Phillips waited only until news of the federal government's additional monetary incentives began circulating, late in July, before he agreed to a three-year commitment.[31]

Leander Harris, another shoemaker living a hand-to-mouth existence in southern New Hampshire, enlisted that summer to fight in a war that his wife never really supported. Emily Harris received town aid, but she wore her fingers raw sewing hoods and shoes to feed their daughters when her husband's pay came late or fell short. The hardship only aggravated her political resentment. In their correspondence the couple would wrangle over it repeatedly, and Leander tried to convince her that love of country had dictated his course, although eventually another incentive surfaced. The federal discharge bonus offered in 1861 equaled the value of his entire earthly estate when he first enlisted, and after thirty months of bickering with Emily over his absence Leander revealed how much the money motivated him: ignoring her heartrending pleas, he reenlisted for a bounty that had been sharply devalued by inflation, arguing that it "would be a nice little sum for us to start with after the war is over." More to the point, he admitted, "I am determined that I will never set down again to try to get a living by shoemaking."[32]

George Upton, also a shoemaker, lived in the next town to Harris, where he had gone heavily into debt to buy a house. He had three small children at the beginning of the war, the last of whom had been born a couple of weeks into the conflict. His trade could not have been producing any more income than that of others in the shoe industry at that time, and his mortgage posed a significant liability. Later he wrote of his desire to preserve "our glorious Country" and to leave his descendants the legacy of "the government in all its greatness," but he was probably also thinking of his vulnerable investment when he enlisted that autumn. The state bounty, his pay, and the monthly stipend for his wife and children would have exceeded anything he had earned over the previous year, and the federal discharge bonus promised to at least reduce his mortgage. He worked hard for promotion so he could send more money to his wife, whom he often asked how much she had been able to reduce their debts. Few more devoted patriots ever served the Union cause, but had it not been for the money so conscientious a man might well have felt duty bound to stay home and support his family somehow.[33]

The depression among shoemakers and textile workers persisted through the summer of 1861. The sprawling riverside cotton mills of Lowell, Massachusetts, and Dover, New Hampshire, first reduced their production because of the economic downturn itself, later cut back still more because of the cotton shortage, and finally fell completely silent by the end of August. So dismal did the future appear to the wife of an unemployed mill mechanic in Fall River, Massachusetts, that she threw herself into the river. Woolen mills had remained somewhat active during the winter and spring, having no shortage of raw material, but even they had not had much call for whole cloth: clothing manufacturers ordered little because retail sales were so slow, and wholesalers of readymade clothing in the West were suffering from collapsed local currencies. It therefore created a small boom in some regions when the burgeoning armies began consuming mountains of woolen uniforms. By the first of May, 1861, one small Hartford clothier had all his tailors working seven days a week and well into each night to fill an order for a thousand overcoats. The recession had nevertheless left a vast surplus of finished flannel that satisfied the government's needs for months, delaying any demand for increased mill production.[34]

Rhode Island's big mills also lay silent or ran on shortened hours most of the summer. "Three-fourths of our laboring classes are out of steady work," noted a Providence paper early in August. "Every day we meet sober, industrious men, with large families, who say that for three months past they have not been able to earn more than two or three dollars. Most of them have earned but little for the last eight months."[35]

Those destitute masses threatened the prosperity of men who still had work. The Navy Department had ordered a fleet of new steam frigates for blockade duty, and the contracts for those vessels promised to put some life back in the shipyards of the Atlantic Coast after many idle months. In Boston, where the business climate was still "strongly marked by inactivity," ship carpenters who would work on those corvettes chose that moment to demand higher wages from the contractors who would undertake the construction. They agreed to demand $2.50 per day for first-class carpenters and $2.00 for second-class, in line with the Boston Navy Yard, and to seek concurrence from carpenters who might come from afar for those jobs. It was widely understood around the shipyards that the contractors had bid lower than the likely cost of building the ships and that they intended to offer no more than $2.00 and $1.75. Newspapers reported that those contractors had already collected applications from more men than they could employ who were willing to work for $1.50 per day. Predictions ran against the success of the carpenters' action. "Very many of them have been out of work for a long time," admitted the editor of the *New York Times,* "and they and their families need all they can earn," but he tempered his implied sympathy with market-based practicality, adding that "men are flocking in here from all quarters to get employment. With the great number of men out of work here and in other places, it is hardly probable that Boston shipwrights can obtain their prices." The editor of the *Journal* warned that if the Boston workmen insisted on the government rates, the contractors might simply import more desperate competitors, of whom there were plenty.[36]

A lethargic business climate did not immediately jeopardize the job of an intermediate-level bank officer, but army paymasters earned about twice the salary at the rank of major. Lyman Hapgood, the treasurer of a Boston bank, had made powerful friends as a promoter of abolitionism and the infant Republican Party, and that first summer of the war he called on those friends for assistance. They obtained for him the appointment of additional paymaster in the volunteer service. His precise penmanship and accurate figures provided him with three and a half very comfortable years in Washington, and the army sent him back to Boston toward the end of the war, as paymaster at the draft rendezvous on Galloup's Island. Hapgood left no journal or private letters to reveal his personal reasons for seeking an army appointment in 1861, but the pay of a field-grade officer must have had something to do with it. As much as he clearly wanted to return to Boston, Hapgood strove mightily to secure a permanent appointment as paymaster with the Regulars when the army mustered him out of the volunteer service. That effort failed, so he returned to banking, this time as a mere clerk rather than a treasurer; five years after the war, his net worth had increased only to the extent of the money he had been able to save while in the army.[37]

The more meager compensation of a private soldier struck thousands of less fortunate New Englanders as attractive enough. Still, even with such economic doldrums stimulating recruiting, those responsible for providing men to the army took the precaution of offering additional cash early in the war. Massachusetts recruiters making nominal appeals to patriotism also touted the practical advantage of the state's provision for family subsidies, which ran as high as twelve dollars a month. When the governor of New Hampshire called on his constituents for a third regiment of infantry late in July of 1861, he accompanied it with a state enlistment bounty of ten dollars, to be paid as soon as a man was mustered in. Recruits from mill towns along the Merrimack, Sowhegan, Cocheco, and Exeter Rivers filled the 3rd New Hampshire within nineteen days after the first tent was pitched on the heights overlooking the Merrimack. Late that month the governor appealed for a fourth regiment, extending the bounty, and in barely another fortnight the same towns supplied recruits for those ten companies. Manchester accounted for three of the companies in the 3rd New Hampshire and for five companies in the 4th Regiment. Despite all that competition for those unemployed mill hands, two prospective officers seeking men for an artillery battery opened their books in Manchester on August 16 and signed up more than three dozen men on the first day; within a week nearly a hundred mechanics, weavers, spinners, dyers, and belters had offered their services for the battery.[38]

Alfred Wheeler, an unskilled factory worker, was scouring Connecticut for a new job in the spring of 1861. He heard that the silk and woolen mills east of Hartford were still in operation, but he lacked either the funds to establish himself there or the expertise to compete with all the applicants who already had experience in the textile industry. A few days before the guns opened on Fort Sumter, he wrote to his brother, back in the southwestern corner of the state, asking if there were a job for him in the local box shop; if the shop was not hiring, he would take anything that was available. His brother could do nothing for him, so Wheeler looked in New York City, but the streets there teemed with men in the same predicament as him. After a few weeks he continued on to Philadelphia, where the situation may have been worse still. Nearly every manufacturer there had laid off workers or cut operating hours; 40 percent of that city's factory employees had already been jobless or were not working enough to support themselves in late February, and Wheeler saw no improvement by summer. There he remained until August, when he finally fell flat broke and enlisted.[39]

Ambrose Hayward hailed from Massachusetts, but he, too, had migrated to Philadelphia in search of work during the secession winter. All he could find was a job in a needle factory, and that ran out as the war got under way. His employer could not pay him the wages he had coming for the previous month and tried to compensate him with needles that Hayward found difficult to sell. He owed money as well, and finally, after he had been without work four weeks, Hayward concluded that he had "loafed long enough" and enlisted in a company that formed part of the 28th Pennsylvania. In April he had recorded his outrage at the Confederate attack on Fort Sumter and joined a drill company, but he had been working then. Only after spending the last of his money did Hayward actually go to war.[40]

Alfred M. White, who had married in necessary haste at the age of nineteen, already had two toddlers when the shooting began. Over the previous year he had found and lost at least three positions, which forced him to leave his child-bride and children with relatives as he traveled New Hampshire and Massachusetts looking for work. His last job had been as a weaver in a central Massachusetts textile mill, where a new hand like him would have been among the first discharged during the economic doldrums of that winter and spring. White left no hint of what inspired him to enlist that spoke more clearly than his work history, his financial status, and his obvious family obligations.[41]

Newlywed Herbert Willand was employed in a cotton-starved Massachusetts textile mill when he first heard about Fort Sumter. He claimed decades later that he yearned to enlist from the start, and entertained the vain hope of replacing some militia member "who found it quite inconvenient to leave home." In a memoir that did not echo with persuasive logic, Willand blamed his wife's opposition for his hesitation through the summer and early autumn of 1861, during which he was unemployed—ostensibly after leaving his job voluntarily. He blamed his bride's "health" for holding him back, using that euphemism to explain the birth of their first child that summer. Her "improvement" allowed him to exercise his patriotic impulse, according to his late-life recollection, and he finally enlisted in October. The burden of a new family after months without work in a depressed community may have contributed substantially to that martial impulse: with no other evident means of earning an income, his pay and his wife's benefits under state law would yield her a minimum of five dollars a week.[42]

Fred Clark, who worked in one of the Connecticut River paper mills in western Massachusetts, had certainly not joined the army for the excitement it might offer, for he proved to be an especially timid spirit. The only surviving evidence for his motive suggests that he enlisted from financial embarrassment, finding the combination of community relief and army pay more adequate than his mill wages for the support of his pregnant bride. She moved into smaller lodgings with a roommate from the mills where they had all worked, and he sent her twenty-five dollars at the end of his first two-month pay period. Writing from his camp near Washington, Clark told her that his comrades saved more of their money at thirteen dollars a month than they could at home on wages of as much as two dollars a day. "I know that I do," he wrote, "and it will do me one good thing, my coming down here."[43]

It was the same, or worse, in all the industrial regions. The army had already taken up thousands of idle ironworkers from Troy, New York, but the big works there still considered shutting down for a season or two as summer waned, which would have put the providers of another five thousand people out of work. One New York City newspaper of a Democratic stamp estimated that the sectional troubles had displaced twenty-five thousand factory workers in that city within three weeks of Lincoln's election, and those men figured prominently in the recruiting that had followed the massive rally of April 20 in Union Square.[44]

Timothy O'Meara, a very capable young fellow from the Fourth Ward of New York City with a widowed mother and disabled brother to support, rectified his lack of employment by going out to Long Island with some friends and enlisting. He may have signed up with an eye to the pay increase and the hundred-dollar discharge bounty, but his superiors instantly recognized his potential and selected him for the adjutant of the regiment, at more than a hundred dollars a month. Thomas McDermott, an out-of-work day laborer and recovering alcoholic, responded to the two-dollar raise and the bounty as soon as he heard of it and ended up in the same regiment as O'Meara.[45] Late into June a minister could still remark that "immense numbers of men are unemployed" in New York City, and he found that they were "now ready to enlist in the war because they cannot earn their bread." Even many skilled, veteran tradesmen could find no work. One well-educated young man in the city decided that he himself need not enlist, observing that there were so many unemployed men ahead of him who were anxious to do so "because they had no other means of support."[46]

The chance for some kind of income provided William Willoughby with a greater incentive than he was willing to admit. At forty-four he had not earned enough to accumulate any property or savings, but by the summer of 1861 the recession had evidently put him out of his job, at least temporarily. With a wife and child and the wolf at the door, he enlisted as a private soldier. A year later, when generous local bounties sparked conversation at home about the motivation of Union soldiers, someone remarked to Nancy Willoughby about her husband's lack of employment leading him into the army. In a vehement retort Private Willoughby insisted that he had gone to war to support the government—although he did not deny having been without any income when he enlisted.[47]

Charles Thomas Bowen, a young New York farmhand of no property and few prospects, married a teenaged girl in 1861 and promptly enlisted in the 12th U.S. Infantry, leaving his bride about three months pregnant. Bowen showed extremely equivocal devotion to the cause and the service. He expressed support for the war much of the time, but once he also conspired with some of his comrades to surrender themselves to the first rebel they met in their next fight. He signed one letter to his mother "your boy for liberty & union" and insisted that if he were sent home he would only reenlist—yet less than four weeks previously he had asked her to see a lawyer about trying to get him out of the army. Bowen worried how he would support his family after his discharge since he had no trade, and at one point he explained to his wife that he had no desire "to plod along from hand to mouth through life." Like many men with no house, no land, and no savings in August of 1861, he coveted the hundred-dollar discharge bonus, and he still counted on it nearly halfway through his term. He had enlisted just as New York newspapers were reporting the army pay increase, and most communities were then raising funds for the benefit of soldiers' dependents. Some of the more loyal correspondence coming home from the army may have reflected soldiers' knowledge that their letters might be read by officers, and Bowen himself was aware of one man who was arrested for "writing Treason home." He may well have been sporadically stirred by the patriotic sentiments his letters sometimes implied, but his obsession with personal economy and his horror of indebtedness bespeak a strong pecuniary influence behind his enlistment.[48]

Vermont's seven-dollar subsidy to volunteers continued after the three-month quota had been met, and it exerted a tremendous effect on farm boys—

and their fathers—in the Green Mountain State. In northern Orleans County one semiliterate farmer, a man well past military age and with a large family, was evidently behind on his mortgage deadline when he enlisted with his oldest son at the end of the harvest season. He showed particular concern about his wife's ability to collect the seven-dollar supplement; his next son enlisted as soon as he could pass for eighteen.[49]

Darius Priest, a laborer from Mount Holly, Vermont, had acquired no land and hardly any personal property by his mid-thirties, but he did have a wife and three young children. He enlisted as soon as newspapers announced the three-year call and the bounty, leaving his family little for support except a promissory note from Francis Gould, a neighbor who owed them money. Like many of the soldiers who gathered around Washington in July, he took his first pay in gold, but sending coin through the mail invited theft. Until he could send the money home safely, he advised his wife to have his father try getting something out of Gould.[50]

Proctor Swallow faced a problem typical of young men in Vermont who were not working on a family farm they could expect to inherit: he had no trouble finding employment, but he spent the summer and autumn of 1861 trying to get his pay from various employers. Working as a hired hand just across the state line in New York, he explained to relatives back in Vermont that "money is awfull tight." A horse breeder who owed him wages complained that he had "not had twenty dollars at one time this summer." During the harvest Swallow tried to improve his lot by renting a threshing machine, but he lost money on the enterprise and went back to boarding with a farmer for monthly pay until he decided to enlist. Thereafter he pitied farmers in Vermont who "have to mow and sweat for $15 a month" when he could relax on "$20 and found" (meaning food and housing, in addition to pay), and he tried to persuade his brother-in-law to abandon his own farm for the army.[51]

New Jersey also paid a monthly subsidy for its volunteers, perhaps feeling particular need because so many in the state opposed fighting a war to keep the seceded states in the Union. The stipend amounted to only four dollars at first (it was later raised to six), but that much was often enough to tip the scales for many whose desperation overcame or complimented their political scruples. It may have helped Oscar Westlake choose soldiering over insolvency, for he had come from a respectable family and must have been mortified when the Somerset County sheriff seized his horse, wagon, and jewelry inventory on behalf of his creditors. That had been his second disappointing business venture inside a year, leaving him penniless, but the president's call for militia had saved him. He enlisted immediately, was appointed one of the original sergeants in his company, and performed so well that he rose to captain within two years. At that rank he earned what he considered a "pretty good salary" of $1,500, and hoped his savings would provide him with a stake in some more successful peacetime endeavor.[52]

Despite his relatively wealthy upbringing, Westlake's entrepreneurial misadventures had transformed him into one of those men for whom the war inspired visions of improved financial and social position. The same was true of Charles Harvey Brewster, the only son of an aging widow whom he had tried to support—along with his two spinster sisters—on a clerk's salary. Brewster showed a pretentious side, representing himself as a "merchant" when the census marshal came calling, but his income was such that he, too, found the rank and pay of a sergeant an improvement over his civilian calling. Like Westlake, he attended conscientiously to his duties, but he still considered it a manifestation of perennially bad luck when he failed to win promotion quickly. The pay of a second lieutenant astounded him, at about six times that of a sergeant, and he lusted after it until the commission finally came to him six months into his enlistment. He sent fifty dollars a month home via an allotment—certainly more than he had ever earned as a clerk—and reminded his mother that as his dependent she would be eligible for a pension of fifteen dollars a month if he were killed, rather than the eight dollars paid to enlisted men's survivors.[53]

It was often only after they had joined the army that soldiers discovered how much better officers were paid, and occasionally they regretted having enlisted so impulsively in the ranks. Seven months into his commitment, an ambitious private in one of New York's first two-year regiments let his sister and brother-in-law know that he would accept a three-year enlistment in a new regiment in return for a lieutenant's commission, and all for the money. "I would rather have $100 per month than $13.00," he explained.[54]

Lavant Jones, a twenty-year-old law student in Lawrence, Kansas, may have volunteered with similar visions of improving his lot. He had already been married for a year and a half to a teenaged girl when he helped raise a company for the 1st Kansas Volunteers, going with it as first lieutenant. For a young man with no property or savings and little income, his commission provided a distinct financial boost, but he reminded his bride that his love for her was "all the legacy, unfortunately, I can leave you in case I should fall." He must have known better than that, for he had enlisted amid all those promises of bounties and pensions for the survivors of those who died in uniform. As it happened, by the time his wife received his letter, she was already a widow: she collected his back pay, the hundred-dollar discharge benefit, and a pension of seventeen dollars a month.[55]

The career of Newton T. Colby of Corning, New York, supplies one of the more undeniable examples of economic opportunism to be found among the early volunteers. In private, at least, Colby freely admitted his lack of patriotism and his mercenary motivation, although in official correspondence he played up his devotion to cause and country. During the presidential campaign of 1860, he was twenty-eight years old and clerking in his father's hardware store to support a young wife and their five children, but the store was not doing very well. Like thousands of others unhappy with their occupations, Colby traveled to Washington after Lincoln's inauguration, seeking a government post. On March 29, 1861, he noted the difficulty of competing for a position with "a decent salary" against such a flood of applicants, and he returned to Corning in April, having failed in that effort. At Lincoln's call for troops only a few days later, he saw another opportunity and immediately took his place with the local militia company, in which he held a commission. Early in May he mustered in as a first lieutenant for two years of service in the 23rd New York, which provided the same "decent salary" he would have preferred as a government clerk. As he would make abundantly clear, he was in it for the money, and incidentally perhaps for the social position. His actions and his own letters would also eventually illustrate that he did not consider risking his own hide to be any part of the bargain.[56]

Of course, the considerations of finances and status that had motivated Colby occupied even those who considered enlisting without the economic necessity of doing so. Frederic Speed, the youngest and most indulged son of an inventor, college president, and prominent merchant from Gorham, Maine, regarded the war as a chance for him to realize some of the success his father and brothers had achieved. His father's connections availed him the position of sergeant major in a regiment raised early in the summer of 1861, but that struck the nineteen-year-old as beneath his capacity, and he hoped his father could arrange for something better. After a few months his family's acquaintance with temperance icon Neal Dow afforded young Frederic a promotion to adjutant in Dow's regiment, but then he wanted something more permanent. He suggested that his father owned enough influence to secure him a commission in the Regular Army, extracting a paternal promise to try, but he felt it necessary to urge his mother to nag about it lest the promise should be forgotten. "I believe it would be *the making of me,*" Frederic pleaded, hinting more than once that bribery might be expected and expressing his willingness to pay it. No permanent commission in the Regular Army ever came his way, but he did finally wangle a volunteer staff appointment as a captain. Rather than being the "making" of him, that appointment nearly led to his undoing in a court-martial for negligence that entailed distinct implications of bribery.[57]

At the beginning of hostilities, Alvin Voris of Akron, Ohio, asked his wife what she thought of him trying to obtain "a post in the army." Ohio, including their county, labored under a critical shortage of currency as an indirect result of the sectional crisis; long lists of delinquent land and lot taxes dominated each week's newspaper, but Voris may have been somewhat insulated from the financial aftershocks as an established attorney and state representative. He speculated that he might find a civil appointment that could "yield me some $2,500 for you," but government positions that remunerative were not particularly numerous and were the subject of intense competition. In the end he nominally enlisted as a private, but his political connections brought him a prompt appointment from Governor William Dennison as a lieutenant; that unsatisfactory offer must have precipitated further lobbying, because Dennison granted him a second commission as lieutenant colonel a few days later, backdating it to the same day as the first one. That gave Voris very nearly the generous income he had mentioned to his wife: with his allowances for rations, forage, and a servant, he exceeded it.[58]

Ohio had already been suffering as much as any of the western states in April, before the fighting began. The currency question disrupted trade even in that part of Ohio opposite Kentucky, where the money was almost literally deemed as good as gold, because of fears that buyers there would refuse to pay if Kentucky seceded. Cincinnati reported all business "depressed," daily newspapers in Ohio carried as many as fifty notices of sheriff's sales, and courts upriver at Marietta ordered a proportionate number of liquidations. Frustrated retailers, some of them on the verge of closing their doors, placed ads fairly begging their delinquent customers to "settle up" and shutting off all credit, but customers with no cash to pay on their accounts had none to buy with either. These notices often occupied the same page as news of the completion of another company or regiment, which sometimes included the bankrupt merchant as well as his indigent patron. As in Iowa, satisfying the president's appeal for troops required little more publicity than prominently publishing the pay and allowances for every grade in the army, from private to major general, and the editors supplied no corrections when those notices erred on the side of generosity. Thus did Ohio exceed its recruitment quota by a quarter in response to the president's calls of April, May, and July.[59]

Hugh Carlisle was one of the unemployed young Ohioans who finally answered the call after wandering the state for six months in search of work. He apprenticed as a printer at the *Fremont Daily Journal,* living with the editor's family, but early in 1861 he took a new job with the *Springfield Evening News.* The publishers of that paper were in financial trouble by May, and the whole printing staff started grumbling when they found themselves cheated on their composition count, with their pay curtailed commensurately. Then the owners welshed on the printers' basic rate, paying only twelve and a half cents per thousand words instead of the promised seventeen cents. That dropped Carlisle's weekly pay from $3.98 to $2.79. With that he quit, first seeking employment at a Columbus newspaper but getting only an offer to sleep in the office before he moved on. He found a few weeks' work at the *Mount Vernon Republican,* but when that concluded he made his way back to the northern part of the state—on foot. Shops in Oberlin, Elyria, Cleveland, Painesville, and Ashtabula had nothing for him, but in August the *Conneaut Reporter* hired him for a five-week stint. That was his last job as a printer, and he returned to his home in Sandusky County to enlist in a company commanded by his uncle.

Like most veterans, in later years Carlisle attributed his enlistment to less pragmatic motives than an inability to fend for himself. He claimed in a memoir that he had wanted to enlist earlier but had feared that his father would not give him permission, yet his father had not objected to him tramping all over Ohio at the age of eighteen. Young Carlisle may well have felt vague patriotic impulses or an understandable hunger for travel and excitement, but the travails he recorded in his journal suggest it was primarily his difficulty in supporting himself that finally drove him into the ranks.[60]

Ohio farmers, like those in Illinois, began to detect cutworms ravaging their corn by the end of spring, and weevils were working on the wheat. Six weeks later corn and wheat also became targets of the army worm, which appeared in different parts of the state, feasting on oats and potatoes as well. With the encouragement of neighbors and editors, farmers still on fragile financial ground had planted vast quantities of grain for the insatiable new military market, but much of their potential profits succumbed to these parasites. Yet another economic disaster on the tail of the last one threw farmers with mortgages or marginal resources on the threshold of bankruptcy, but an act of the Ohio legislature offered them a chance to avoid foreclosure by enlisting. In May Governor Dennison had signed a bill into law exempting the property of Ohioans from the execution of civil judgments if they were mustered into military service. With the announcement of public support for soldiers' families that soon followed, the owners of heavily encumbered homesteads heard the beating of the drum with particular acuity.[61]

Similar economic need carried across the West, passing for patriotism among those who answered it by scrawling their names on a muster roll. In Indiana, Illinois, Wisconsin, and Iowa, newspapers reported an ongoing depression in all types of business through the summer, and their retail advertisers corroborated the news with sympathetic allusion to the scarcity of money and the "hard times." Lumber could be had in Iowa as cheaply as eight dollars per thousand board feet. The prices of all crops in Indiana had plummeted since the previous year, yet nothing was selling even at those rates through the summer and into the autumn. As might have been expected, the newspaper columns devoted to official notices of sheriff's sales were growing, and other states passed their own "stay" laws to exempt volunteers from attachments or foreclosure. That was an important point for debtors considering the army as an option.[62]

As newspapers did everywhere, Hoosier sheets hinted for the poor and dissatisfied to step forward and fill the new regiments. Opportunity beckoned in the published orders of the state's adjutant general, who appealed to the working class by announcing that a third of the company officers in each regiment would be chosen from among the sergeants. Informational notices about army pay and allowances reappeared, demonstrating for those at the lowest levels of income how attractive the remuneration might be. Predictions of a short war persisted, while visions of free land entranced would-be recruits, who were bombarded with the repeated assurance that it was "quite certain" Congress would pass a bounty-land bill to provide every soldier with "a home." Again came the appeals for relief committees to which indigent dependents of volunteers could apply for aid. The editor of the *Daily Evansville Journal* promised that "we, who, on account of business ties, are unable to follow," would support the families of those who—presumably having no business ties or gainful employment—went to war. Newspapermen of a more cynical tinge confirmed that the promises of relief did persuade poor family men to enlist, adding that those promises were not always fulfilled.[63]

Economics, aggravated by terrible weather and insect infestations, may have been more responsible than national loyalty for Indiana exceeding its recruiting quota by over 22,000 men. The same factors helped explain why Illinois was able to field more than 34,000 men beyond its own obligation. By late June the army worm had devastated crops in Indiana and essentially destroyed the corn crop in Illinois, where it had to be replanted, and the same pest was stripping the timothy, too. In the southern part of the state, where hay was most heavily cultivated, one farmer alone estimated his loss in timothy at four thousand dollars. Grasshoppers descended in some parts of the state, with locusts and chinch bugs elsewhere. "Everything green is being destroyed," one agricultural journal reported. The locusts swept deep into Iowa, where cankerworm had also begun to defoliate orchards. Terrific hail had devastated grain crops in the middle of Illinois, hundred-degree heat left everyone from Louisville to Milwaukee sweltering, and at least one tornado tore through the seat of Bureau County—splintering homes, peeling off rooftops, and ripping the cupola from the courthouse.[64]

Meanwhile, unreliable Western money still hampered commerce all the way from Lake Erie to the upper Mississippi. Gold and Eastern currency had begun to infiltrate the prairie, but not in sufficient quantity to loosen pocketbooks or stir trade; some of the Eastern money turned out to be bogus bills that Westerners could not easily recognize. The Illinois Central Railroad allowed farmers who had bought land from the company's corridor to make their payments in corn, if they had any. As cash disappeared, one business failure precipitated another: a city might see several in a week, or in a single day. Many a merchant developed military ambitions during that ruinous summer and autumn, selling or abandoning flagging business enterprises to join the army, especially if they could secure a commission.[65]

In Milwaukee, still-solvent banks suddenly started refusing the "stumptail" notes of their discredited competitors except as special deposits subject to future rejection. They did so right after major employers there had disposed of massive quantities of such bills as wages to poor laborers. Those mostly German laborers suspected collusion between the bankers and their bosses, and they mobbed the banks late in June, breaking windows and tossing books and furniture onto bonfires in the streets. Troops had to be called from nearby camps before the riot was quelled.[66]

Unlike Illinois or Iowa, Wisconsin at least looked forward to a bountiful wheat crop through the summer, but once it had been harvested it proved to be altogether too abundant. As growers in Minnesota had feared, Eastern wholesalers still had so much left over from the bumper crop of 1860 that they refused to pay enough for it to even cover the cost of transportation.[67]

In such an atmosphere, it was not necessary to dwell extensively on the benefits of joining the army to persuade men to do so. Subtle suggestions brought more than enough men to the colors. When Governor Richard Yates returned to Illinois from a visit to Washington, a Springfield newspaper emphasized that his excellency had been accompanied by a paymaster carrying "*two hundred thousand dollars* to pay the volunteers." Nearby on the same page ran an article proclaiming the trustworthiness of the Treasury notes created by the new federal war loan, which would be distributed for pay. Thanks to the suggestion of John McClernand—a friend, neighbor, and political rival of President Lincoln—army quartermasters had also started tendering that currency for grain and other supplies that growers were prevented from sending to their traditional markets down the Mississippi. Before summer ended, some of those notes were filtering up into the Great Lakes in denominations small enough for daily use, much to the satisfaction of Republicans who reflected nostalgically on the days when U.S. Bank notes were current everywhere. The Democrat McClernand's economic ingenuity appealed to Iowa Republicans, who dared to hope that the war would also help them sell their crops as well as introduce a reliable currency to the region.[68]

Across the vast region that another generation would call the Midwest, the more optimistic journals adopted the mantra that the business disruption could only be temporary. Interpreting the contraction of the currency as a sign of prudence rather than poverty, they applauded the thrift people showed, praising those who "find it agreeable to make last year's dress last another summer." For all too many, circumstances had grown too precarious to correct with spartan fashion. One Wisconsin paper admitted that army pay, especially for men with families, was "very good, much better than prospects now indicate for some time to come, in common avocations." As soon as Wisconsin authorized a five-dollar monthly pay subsidy for married volunteers, family men started swarming to the various regimental rendezvous. When the 2nd Wisconsin passed through Chicago on its way to Washington, a correspondent of the *Chicago Tribune* expressed surprise at how many married men he discovered in it. In addition to the subsidy, Wisconsin papers still held out the false hope of bounty land. Less than a month after recruiting began for the half-million-man volunteer army, the Badger State had already put more than its share of citizens into uniform.[69]

Michigan, Ohio, and Indiana saw similar throngs of volunteers early in August, with new companies filling up every week in some cities. A Republican editor in Flint, Michigan, portrayed the surge as a patriotic reaction to the disaster at Bull Run, despite the lists of mortgage sales filling a quarter of his front page and the exaggerated financial incentives he accentuated. His counterpart in Greencastle, Indiana, granted that "almost everybody is complaining of hard times," reprinting reports of "honest, toiling men thrown out of employment and reduced with their wives and children to beggary and starvation." Yet he denied that such conditions were driving men into the army, instead offering his own opinion that the local volunteers were "actuated by the right motives."[70]

Sixteen-year-old George Young, from southern Indiana, revealed that he had been looking for work when he enlisted. He informed his father that he had had an offer of as much as thirty dollars a month to work as a teamster for the army, but he turned it down because he supposed the job would be more than he could bear.[71]

Men who were still employed that summer nevertheless declined to enlist until the recession finally caught up with them. "As long as I have work to do I shall not go," replied an Indiana brickmason to an inquiring friend, adding that he might enlist if his business petered out and more men were still needed; by autumn he did run out of work, and enlisted in a cavalry regiment. An Illinois schoolteacher who had to resort to farm labor for wages in the spring of 1861 also enlisted when his season's contract expired. Throughout the martial excitement of 1861, an orphaned sixteen-year-old from Ohio who was out on his own stuck with the Illinois farmer who gave him his keep and a dollar per month more as a farmhand than the army would have paid. The boy envisioned staking a claim on a spread of his own in Minnesota, and the idea of entering the army occurred to him only later, when generous enlistment bounties gave the illusion of substance to his agrarian reverie. Young men cutting timber in the forests of upstate New York showed no inclination to go to war so long as the logging lasted. A Wisconsin observer inadvertently acknowledged the economic impetus behind volunteering when he predicted another wave of recruits once the harvest ended and the lake shore froze. With jobs aplenty and good pay they would not enlist, he suspected, but once they were out of work many of them would do so at once. The excess number of regiments mustered over the fall and winter proved him right.[72]

The contraction of credit coupled with political uncertainty had hit the commercial centers of Cincinnati and Chicago hard, but St. Louis fared even worse, bearing the brunt of a trade embargo that was finally being enforced on the lower Mississippi. Long-range naval guns at Cairo, Illinois, overlooking the confluence of the Ohio and Mississippi, prohibited any river traffic below that point by the end of May, but the economic consequences of sectional alienation had already sharply curtailed river travel. Down in New Orleans, on May 8 Samuel Clemens abandoned the last steamboat he ever piloted because his captain had decided to confine himself to plying the river between there and Memphis, throwing his fortunes with the Confederacy. Clemens returned upriver as a passenger on the *Nebraska,* passing out of the South without molestation and arriving at an eerily quiet St. Louis levee on May 21. His was apparently the last boat to get through. The once-bustling city sat dull and dismal, with business at a standstill and boatmen perfectly idle. Commercial houses there were going under, and their owners were losing their homes. The only jobs lay with the government, and most of those required wearing a uniform for an extended period. One St. Louis citizen could hardly believe his good fortune when, instead, he found work at the post office, where he could finally earn some money again.[73]

"St. Louis has never been so dull since it was a place of business," reported a passenger bound farther upriver, "and in every town along the river business is prostrated. Alton looks deserted. Hannibal was as still as a grave-yard, and Quincy is grown over with grass." In Iowa, steamboats had become a rare sight by June, for they had nothing to carry downriver and no one was coming upriver. A Dubuque editor who was unsympathetic to coercion of the seceding states blamed the Union blockade at Cairo for stopping the river traffic and throwing twenty thousand steamboatmen out of work by the first week of July. Some of those men may have been among the hundreds who stormed the St. Louis City Council in its chambers on the evening of July 9, seeking an appropriation on behalf of themselves and their families. The council had recently raised twenty thousand dollars in emergency relief for the city's poor, but the fund had already been exhausted.[74]

A majority of those unemployed steamboatmen may have shared the Dubuque editor's reservations about holding the Union together by force.

Many of them had migrated directly from downriver, or from the Missouri River watershed that had been settled mainly by slave-owning families from cotton-growing country. The Southern-leaning Missouri State Guard, which Sam Clemens made an attempt to join, recruited heavily from the loungers congregating along Missouri levees from Kansas City to Kentucky, otherwise Missouri, too, might have exceeded its quota of Federal troops. Eighty percent of the expected number enlisted as it was, with at least half the state's territory populated by citizens who were largely hostile to the policy of the national government. Those loyal regiments depended heavily on men like those in St. Louis who had besieged the city council, and those who still loitered along the waterfront. The first prisoners from Franz Sigel's command had revealed as much when they unanimously admitted that they had resorted to the army because there was "nothing to do in St. Louis."[75]

James B. Eads, a St. Louis inventor who had made a fortune in the salvage business and enjoyed the friendship of President Lincoln's attorney general, hoped to augment his wealth with a government contract that summer. His cabinet connection had availed him an opportunity to build a fleet of ironclad gunboats for use on the big rivers, and Eads was considering taking the job if he could make enough out of it. He planned to secure the best-possible profit by sharing as little as he could of the proceeds with the men who would do the work. With so many men begging for a chance to earn some money, Eads supposed that he could pay as little as $1.25 a day for mechanics, and he was indiscreet enough to say so within earshot of voluble rivermen.[76]

St. Louis was the hub for fortune-seeking wanderers in the West, and one of them found inspiration for a new enterprise among all those unemployed workmen milling about the city. Josiah W. Bissell, a onetime banker and self-taught engineer from Rochester, New York, obtained permission to organize an engineer regiment composed entirely of "mechanics, artisans, or persons accustomed to work as laborers under mechanics." In that region the principal sources of such men were the river towns, and his regiment gleaned most of its recruits from those acutely depressed communities along the Missouri and on both sides of the Mississippi between Dubuque and Cape Girardeau. The laborers in Bissell's regiment drew twenty-five cents a day over the usual army pay, and his mechanics forty cents. That nearly doubled the pay of a private, giving most of them almost what they had earned before secession. With any supplement from their communities, they would be able to feed their families.[77]

Clemens visited St. Louis for a week or two before turning upriver to Hannibal, his boyhood home, where he and a few acquaintances from his youth struck off looking for some detachment of the Missouri State Guard. In June a couple of greenhorn Iowa regiments that included Bradley Mahana's company landed at Hannibal in chase of such aspiring rebels, and after a fortnight's flirtation with service in the cause of the cavaliers Clemens dropped out. He was lucky: he had saved some cash, and after his brother snared a government appointment in Nevada Territory the two headed west, away from bad money, stifled trade, and civil strife. For many of the acquaintances the former riverboat pilot left behind, the only immediate prospect for supporting themselves consisted of shouldering a musket or strapping on a sword.[78]

4

FAMILIES FIGHTING A HARD WAR

Poor People have to go to War or starve," complained a New Hampshire woman in the first days of 1862.[1] Since the previous spring, the prospect of regular pay with "keep" had lured vast legions of Northern volunteers who were suffering varying degrees of financial embarrassment. Promises of supplemental salaries and support for their families had augmented that response with innumerable men who were the sole or primary support of wives and children, aging parents, or orphaned siblings. In several states the legislatures had passed responsibility for additional pay or family relief on to the county commissioners, city councils, or town selectmen—sometimes with authority to levy local taxes for the purpose, or with the assurance of state reimbursement.

Wisconsin's five-dollar state supplement for married men constituted the only direct state-level support in the West. Additionally, Wisconsin allowed municipal governments the latitude to determine local family subsidies as well as the means to extract those resources from their taxpayers. Ohio gave the responsibility to the counties but added a special state tax to fund those county expenses. Michigan foisted both the administration and the cost of supporting soldiers' families on the counties, eventually capping such aid at fifteen dollars per family but mandating that it be raised and distributed independently of ordinary support for the poor. Indiana passed similar legislation, without the limit, but Illinois refrained from either assisting or interfering with local charity.[2]

In the East most of the relief for the wives, children, and dependent parents of volunteers was left to local communities through funds appropriated by town governments or raised privately by volunteer committees; in most cases the municipal expenditures were eventually covered by state funds. The exception, at least initially, was Vermont, where the state's seven-dollar contribution satisfied the demand during the first fifteen months of the conflict. In New Hampshire the state required each town to provide support, at four dollars a month for the first dependent and two dollars for each additional family member, with an apparent limit of fourteen dollars for a woman left with five or more children.[3]

The maximums set by Michigan and New Hampshire were clearly intended only to supplement a soldier's pay, the combined income reflecting what a laborer would have earned working the traditional six-day week at a dollar a day. Even at such levels the money provided crucial relief, particularly for those families that had already gone for months with no income at all. It also helped rejuvenate stagnant local economies, especially after the army started issuing pay in new federal notes that began to supplant unreliable local currency. Newspapers tended to praise men who sent their pay home, nominally because it provided for their families but also because it gave them more money to spend in their communities. The army calculated pay in two-month intervals but often did not distribute it until well after the end of that time, leaving soldiers' dependents in perpetual need of funds. Commissioned officers were usually paid with their men, so the delays sometimes left them equally short of money, and occasionally they encouraged their wives to apply for the subsidy too. States and towns eventually barred the families of better-paid officers from receiving those funds.[4]

The opportunity to obtain even small amounts of cash at a juncture when it was so scarce inevitably widened the disproportion of poor who joined the army that first year. A New Hampshire man revealed that his community had contributed its most impoverished wage earners to the war when he told a neighbor woman whose shoemaker-husband was in the army that "there has no one gone out of this town as yet that is missed any. They are only shoemakers." Offers of family support had often convinced wavering recruits like that woman's husband, but before winter some of them began to see that they had made one-sided commitments with both the federal government and their home communities.[5]

Public generosity toward soldiers, so boundless in April, had waned in some quarters by the first day of summer. New York recruits on Staten Island saw four of their comrades drummed out of camp to the tune of the "Rogue's March" because, having discovered that their families would not be receiving community aid after all, they refused to be mustered in. In a rare move the Rhode Island legislature retroactively rescinded its twelve-dollar monthly pay supplement in August, granting only a one-time bounty of fifteen dollars to those who enlisted after June 16. At all levels of government, regret over the unbridled generosity of spring grew more general when the summer's campaign failed to quell the rebellion and the army started bulging with hundreds of thousands of men. In May Cincinnati announced that it would distribute anywhere from one to three dollars per week to the families of its soldiers, depending on the number of children, but in October the city cut the maximum allowance back to two dollars. The wife of Samuel Alexander, the impecunious Pennsylvania shoemaker, learned in October that the relief committee of Temperanceville had arbitrarily reduced the allowance to soldiers' families—to the outrage of her husband, who had served barely three of his thirty-six months.[6]

About the same time, soldiers from Dubuque, Iowa, found that their community was no more true to its promises. In the frenzied patriotism of April, that city had formally organized a relief committee, the Volunteer Fund Board, for the purpose of assuring that the families of those who went to war "are fully supported" while the breadwinners were absent. The board had collected several thousand dollars in voluntary contributions, beginning with a host of pledges at Dubuque's first Union rally, but autumn had not passed before all those funds had been exhausted, forcing the board to appeal to the county for a thousand dollars. That money had also run out by the end of the year, and the committee disbanded altogether, depriving many a soldier of a benefit without which he might never have enlisted. With the prolixity common to Victorian indignation, the editor of Dubuque's most critical Democratic newspaper lambasted the federal government for leaving the care of soldiers' families to the uncertainty of voluntary charity. "The life of a poor man is surely as valuable to the State as the wealth of a rich man," he reasoned. "While, therefore, the Government is appealing to the patriotism of the poor to give their lives, let it not neglect to secure from the rich the means to preserve the poor wives and children, the old fathers and mothers of Volunteers from the necessity of soliciting the crumbs and scraps which are thrown into the slop buckets of the rich man's table."[7]

Private committees that relied on donations for the care of soldiers' families started falling short of funds all over the country that summer. Soon after Congress granted the army a two-dollar raise in August, Horace Greeley blamed the failure of family support for what he considered relative lethargy at New York City recruiting stations. Prospective recruits regarded the Union Defense Committee's pledge to support their loved ones as "played out," Greeley claimed, arguing (as he would again later in the war) that volunteers would come flooding in if they were only offered sufficiently generous pay. Wealthy New Yorkers raised small fortunes for patriotic propaganda or vague missions to "uphold the government," but the care of soldiers' families in the Empire State was left to the chance benevolence of local governments, civic associations, or individuals.[8]

With neither state-level nor state-mandated relief, Indiana let down many of its soldiers, despite all the promises of patriotic citizens trying to encourage volunteers. Recounting the story of one local group that failed to live up to its commitments from the start, a Democratic paper in Plymouth suggested that any soldier who depended on the town relief committee to take care of his loved ones might as well dig their graves before he went away. Those groups that did try to accomplish their mission had only limited means, and rather than making regular distributions they instructed needy families to come asking for assistance. Even those benevolent organizations usually ran out of funds after a few months. One aspiring officer who knew that he had nothing better than regular pay to offer recruits for a new Indiana regiment targeted hungry Germans who were "completely without income," describing in detail camp food that he implied would be abundant.[9]

Legislation requiring states or towns to support the families of volunteers was often poorly written, sometimes leaving one municipality liable for the dependents of a soldier who had enlisted under the jurisdiction of another. The more generous a community might be toward such people, the more it made itself a target for those who migrated to maximize their benefits or were shuttled about by different towns in order to get rid of them. A Maine woman and her five children were consigned to the poorhouse by the city of Portland after her husband enlisted, but they left it to stay with her father-in-law, who had moved to New Hampshire. The selectmen there naturally complained when that man billed them for the support of his grandchildren and daughter-in-law on behalf of a soldier who had enrolled under the quota of another community, but they were forced to pay it.[10]

Often—because of poor recordkeeping, complicated requirements for proving eligibility, or suspicions of fraud—those who had a statutory right to supplementary support from their state encountered difficulty when they tried to collect. Paperwork problems seemed most common in the states that shifted responsibility to local government, where provincial officials were often confused by army records and tended to require duplicative confirmation that the applicant was entitled to support. Two men who enlisted in Massachusetts heavy-artillery regiments later in the war spent the better part of a year coaching their wives through a daunting bureaucratic maze for twelve-dollar stipends the legislature had authorized in the spring of 1861. One of them feared that his wife was not receiving the money because she had moved just across the Canadian border from their old home in northern New York. The other, a shoemaker who had lived in the same town all his life, simply suspected that officials were cheating his wife to save money, which infuriated him all the more because he had enlisted specifically so she could receive the supplemental income along with his pay. To the consternation of men whose sons enlisted with them, their states would usually only pay one subsidy no matter how many breadwinners a family contributed to the army.[11]

From May of 1861, the selectmen of Keene, New Hampshire, paid out monthly sums in the exact amount legislated for each family according to the number of dependents, calculating to the penny for partial months. Henry Thompson, a poor tanner with five children, drew the maximum allowance for nearly four years of service, which yielded him more money than the army paid him during that same period, even after another congressionally mandated raise in 1864. At the outset of the war, Keene gave the full amount even to the captains of companies, but that ended with the close of 1861. Thereafter, anyone who entered the service with a commission received nothing from the town, and any enlisted man who won promotion to lieutenant lost his family subsidy the month he was mustered at his new rank.[12]

By January of 1862 larger New Hampshire towns were expending $1,400 a month for soldiers' families, with as much as $2,500 applied to that purpose in the city of Manchester. Local officials in smaller communities might exercise a niggardly control over the distribution of relief to poor and often uneducated women during their husbands' absence. The selectmen of Cornish, New Hampshire, operated under the same law as those in Keene, but they responded with particular parsimony to at least some appeals, including that of Private John Gilbert's wife. Ellen Gilbert had known poverty before the war, and she continued to feel the stigma of it after her husband enlisted. She and her children had lodged for quite some time at the county poor farm in Windsor, Vermont, while he looked for work, but he enrolled in the 3rd New Hampshire Volunteers in the summer of 1861 under the quota of Cornish, just across the Connecticut River from Windsor. He expected the town to allow Ellen twelve dollars a month in accordance with the new state law, but instead of giving her money the selectmen doled out portions of flour and firewood to her, deducting those goods from their obligation at their own prices. Five months after he enlisted, Gilbert missed a visit from the paymaster, and it was not until April of 1862 that he was finally able to send twenty dollars home. Men hoping to alleviate their loved ones' poverty by enlisting sometimes left them poorer than ever.[13]

One student of class tensions between Union soldiers made an incidental and invalid distinction between volunteer soldiers and their officers, on the one hand, and the substitutes and draftees who entered the army after 1863. He described the latter as "economically marginal," as though the volunteers from the first two years of the war represented less impoverished strata of society. John Geary, a division commander given to exaggerated self-congratulation, similarly disparaged his first contingent of substitutes, comparing them unfavorably to the early war soldiers who volunteered "without money and without price." In fact, the earliest volunteers were as "economically marginal" as any in the war: they did come at a price, but because their situation was more desperate, their price had been much lower.[14]

The influence of economic circumstances on men's decisions to join the Union army has yet to be thoroughly examined, and it has seldom been considered except in microcosm. In her study of soldiers from Deerfield, Massachusetts, Emily Harris attributed the enlistment of multiple members of individual families to pure patriotism. She characterized the enlistment of four brothers in one regiment over the course of seven months as an illustration of "the fervoured and self-sacrificing response of Deerfield's citizens." The financial situation of that family sharply suggests instead that their motive lay in money. The patriarch of the Pervere clan, who was in his mid-sixties, owned a very modest farm worth only $500, and he had at least five living sons of working age. Two of them, Dwight and Horace, were married, and Dwight lived on the family farm with his wife and children, although he worked as a farmhand for someone else. The entire family—father and sons—owned a total of only $1,100 in personal property beyond the farm. With three families technically eligible for community support, the four who enlisted represented a regular monthly income of over $80, or one-third more than they could have expected as farm laborers with similar board. They also looked forward to a total of $400 in federal bonuses when they returned. The youngest son remained at home, providing all the additional labor his father might have needed on a farm of that size.[15]

Harris credited other sets of impoverished Deerfield brothers with similar patriotism for their decisions to enlist. None of the three Todd brothers, for example, owned a dollar's worth of property, and their father had only $200 in personal possessions. The situation for the Saxton brothers was even worse: their parents were still feeding eleven children at their table, but everything they owned in the world was only worth $100. Military service made all those men eligible for pay, bounties, bonuses, and regular public aid of enormous consequence to such destitute families—and without incurring the opprobrium that was usually attached to charity.[16]

Clark Carr, a New Hampshire man in his mid-thirties whose soap business had failed, went to his mayor before he enlisted to inquire what town support his wife and children could receive. Once he learned how much they would get he committed himself, allotted his wife ten of the thirteen dollars a month he would earn from the army, and began advising her on the payment—or the avoidance—of their creditors. Months later he counseled her to be frugal "while our financial affairs continue in their present embarrassed condition." In conjunction with his silence about any other motive, that remark revealed his likeliest reason for going to war.[17]

Whether their families were receiving local subsidies or not, few married or single soldiers failed to send at least part of their pay home. The overwhelming majority of diaries and letter collections contain explicit references to the mailing, expressing, or hand delivery of funds to wives, parents, or siblings who often needed it desperately. Most sent as much as they could, sometimes because they had more cash than it was safe to keep in camp, but more often because it was so badly needed by their kin. Sometimes the letters accompanying the soldiers' earliest shipments of money documented that it was meant to remove a burdensome obligation, including mortgages that were nearing default. The men fretted for the home folks when their pay was late, as it often was, and worried whether money had been delivered safely after they sent it.

In the 1860s army paymasters visited regiments or companies wherever they happened to be, often at great distances from reliable post offices or express agencies. In April of 1862 a score of nervous paymasters made their way through the marshy, vine-covered forests of the Virginia Peninsula with five million dollars for the Army of the Potomac.[18] If a soldier was in the hospital, in enemy hands, on furlough, or detailed away from his unit, he missed out and had to wait until the next payday. Most enlisted men preferred not to spend a portion of their pay for Adams Express to guarantee delivery of the rest, so they would test the mail by sending a small bill, following up with larger denominations if the first installment arrived safely.[19]

Because of the demand for military goods, as well as the stimulation to civilian purchases through local relief and the money soldiers sent home, the shoemaking and textile industries of New England began to see a slow recovery in the autumn of 1861. Mills that had shut down entirely resumed partial operations, and those that had eliminated whole shifts and reduced their remaining crews to partial weeks began adding workdays or shifts. That still left a multitude of operatives looking for work, or for more work, even after the volunteer army had absorbed hundreds of thousands of men, and cash remained a scarce commodity in some regions into the new year. During the fall and winter, newcomers filled each state military rendezvous as soon as the most recently organized regiment marched away. As in the early days of the war, devotion to the Union as a bastion of democracy, as an antidote to disorder, and as a symbol for the homeland played a major role in bringing those men to the camps—certainly a greater role than any sympathy with abolition—but even the rhetoric of contemporary correspondence shows less influence from patriotic sentiment than those men recalled in old age.[20]

Seth Bumps, a Vermont farmer with five children still at home, left no record of his personal feelings about the war, but his financial situation projected an atmosphere of desperation when he enlisted at the age of fifty-five. His worldly property in 1860 amounted to less than half the median of his state, and the advice in his letters revealed that much of that property was encumbered with debt. The farm itself may already have been foreclosed on before he enlisted because he instructed the home folks to buy another with the proceeds of the Vermont family subsidy and the money received from him, his seventeen-year-old son, and his brother-in-law. In great detail he explained how each creditor should be handled, adding that the debts for which there was no collateral or written contract could simply be left unpaid until he returned home. If he entertained any political opinions or Union sentiments, they remained unrecorded, and his scribbled letters—written jointly with his brother-in-law—harp only on money and debt. It seems obvious that all three of them enlisted for the purpose of earning as much collective cash as they could, but it would come at tremendous cost, for Bumps did not survive a full season in camp, and his son died a little later. Poor health among recruits in the Vermont Brigade led to heavy initial mortality, moving the brigade commander, William Brooks, to comment that many of those men "should never have been enlisted."[21]

Even those who explicitly characterized their intention to enlist as going to the aid of their country, as James Madison Bowler did, might pluck for themselves what plums they could reach when they finally transformed the impulse into action. Bowler, a schoolteacher who had migrated to Minnesota from Maine, joined a militia company when the president's first call reached the prairie, repairing with it to Fort Snelling. A young lady of his neighborhood, whom he wished to impress, had given him license to "go if you think it your duty," and he assured her that he deplored "the condition of our country that calls upon us to fight for it." He had first enlisted under the three-month mobilization, but he did not agree to the longer term when the 1st Minnesota had to reenlist for three years. Instead he spent the summer pledging his troth, and not until the end of September did he return to Fort Snelling with another company, part of which he had raised with the hope of a commission. After acting as first sergeant until the regiment had been organized, he was disappointed with a warrant as a mere corporal and spoke to his fiancée about soliciting help from her next-door neighbor, Lieutenant Governor Ignatius Donnelly. That seemed to bring the desired appointment. Within a year Bowler commanded his company, rose eventually to major, and clung to the position as long after the war as he could, admitting that he did so only because it paid so well.[22]

William Miller, a freshly married man and new father from Indiana, waited even longer to enlist. When he finally did, it was with the expectation that he would go in with a commission, and he reacted bitterly when the men he had recruited failed to elect him. Miller honored his commitment, although he never rose above the rank of first sergeant, and remained faithful to the Union despite the disaffection of old acquaintances. He had, however, enlisted with the hope of enhancing his social status, and in the end his army service did avail him a desirable profession.[23]

An Illinois sergeant crowed that he was earning "more than I could make at home besides the pleasure of serving my country," but for some volunteers the Union meant as little as it did to the rebels. Joseph Knowlton, a thirty-nine-year-old mechanic in one of the mills along New Hampshire's length of the Merrimack River, obviously belonged in that category. He would have been one of those left unemployed in the wake of secession and may merely have sought to improve his condition when he wrote to the Confederate War Department asking for a commission. The attack on Fort Sumter lay less than a week in the future when he mailed the request, promising to raise five hundred conservative Northern men for Southern service. He assured the Confederate secretary of war (whose name he did not even know) that the offer consisted of no "idle talk." Knowlton's letter passed into rebeldom before hostilities commenced, arriving safely in Montgomery, Alabama, where clerks boxed it up for transfer to Richmond when the capital shifted there. He never received a reply, nor does he appear to have found satisfactory work at home, for in the fall he put his wife and children in the care of local officials and enlisted as a private in the 4th New Hampshire Volunteers. Once discharged from that regiment, he joined the Regular Army.[24]

Henry Baker, a bachelor who owned a chair factory farther up the Merrimack, also felt the pinch of the recession that was throttling the river valley when he started to consider joining the army. He wrote to his sister of feeling a duty to go to war, but his debts had grown too cumbersome for him to afford to enlist in the ranks. He tried for a commission in the 4th New Hampshire during the summer but failed to interest enough potential recruits to strike a deal with the man who was organizing a local company, and the regiment marched off without him. Not until November did he collect enough men and muster in as a second lieutenant in the 7th New Hampshire, moving another married sibling into his home to care for their widowed mother and run what little was left of his business. Baker reasoned that if he should not come home (which he did not), at least he would leave enough money to satisfy his creditors, besides the pension their mother could draw.[25]

Unlike state officials in Rhode Island, which harbored much heavier proportions of unemployed operatives, the governor of New Hampshire dared not retract the bounty offer he had made for recruits in the state's third and fourth regiments. He continued to pay ten dollars a head for every man who enlisted thereafter, and it had an effect. Late in September Ferdinand Davis, a Maine native living in Lebanon, New Hampshire, informed his family of his enlistment in the 7th New Hampshire. He noted that as a single man he considered it his duty to go, but he also revealed how much the financial benefits impressed him. In archaic parlance he jubilantly announced that he would receive "$13 per month and found in every thing," indicating that he expected free food, clothing, and housing as well as pay. In addition to that, he was eligible for the governor's ten-dollar bounty, and the town of Lebanon was offering ten dollars more, on top of the hundred-dollar federal discharge bonus. "So you see," concluded Davis, who might have enjoyed the wages of a carpenter in better times, "the pay is inducement enough for some without any other."[26]

The pay indeed proved a sufficient inducement for Luther Scott, a young man then living in the New Hampshire state capital. He was apparently not finding much work as a house painter and was facing a winter with no income at all. "Do you think I ought to enlist?" he inquired of his father, enumerating the financial benefits. "It would amount to $24 a month for me: $13 pay, $8 for my family, $100 bounty, $10 from the state," and he saw no better prospects. "I should not go if I did not think it was best," he added, "but business will not be good for much, as I can see, untill the war is over." In the end, with a wife and a new baby boarding among strangers, Scott decided to gamble his life against his livelihood—and it was a bet he would lose.[27]

Spencer Bonsall was not exactly poor, but he had been without an income for over a year, having lost his post as surveyor for a district of Philadelphia. While he may have hungered as much for social position as for money, he did need a job, and the army appeared to offer an opening. In 1861 Bonsall was in his mid-forties and was living with his wife and son in his wealthy father-in-law's Seventh Ward home. He probably did not relish service in the ranks and may have sought a commission, but if so he had no luck at it and finally entered a Pennsylvania regiment as a hospital steward in January of 1862. That rank paid no more than thirty dollars a month, and only that much if he were rated as a first-class steward, besides whatever family subsidy the city or local committees offered. That paled in comparison to his salary as a city official, but the flavor of his war stories suggest that Bonsall hungered for promotion and saw the position as a springboard to greater prestige and pay. When he won no promotion, Bonsall complained of illness and reported to the hospital, finally going home on a convalescent furlough. There he stayed, searching in vain for something better, until he was dropped from the rolls of his regiment as a deserter.[28]

If Pennsylvanian James Mitchell enlisted in a patriotic rush, with visions of glory and adventure, he quickly subordinated those sentiments to the cause of personal advancement. Instead of joining a volunteer company, he went straight into the Regular Army in February of 1862 as a private soldier in the infantry—traditionally a dead-end situation, but he immediately started cultivating friends among the officers. Within six months he rose to the rank of sergeant, and had already won the notice of an influential superior who promised to recommend him for a commission. Mitchell apprised his mother that he had been assured of "a fair prospect of a good position for life," and he was wearing shoulder straps before his second summer in the army.[29]

The war's first winter drove a good many men into military service who had resisted that alternative while the weather held, hoping to find more pleasant and remunerative occupation. From Christmas of 1861 through February of

1862, Illinois mustered a dozen new regiments of infantry, two regiments and several battalions of cavalry, and eleven artillery batteries. Across the five primarily agricultural states of the Old Northwest, well over 75,000 men entered newly formed organizations over the course of the winter. New England provided regiments and batteries totaling about 10,000 men of all arms during the same period, with another 25,000 coming from New York and Pennsylvania, exclusive of recruits who entered old regiments. The organization of new military units in New England and the Mid-Atlantic states absorbed something over 3 percent of the population in those regions; in the West the comparison came closer to 11 percent, perhaps reflecting the degree to which the seasons determined employment—or unemployment—in those states.[30]

John C. Ellis had been working in Paducah, Kentucky, when the war began, but the disruption of traffic on the Ohio and Tennessee Rivers had put him out of a job. He started up the Ohio, looking for something to do in Illinois, Indiana, or Ohio, and as his savings ran out he headed for the Great Lakes, where he secured a few weeks' work in Erie, Pennsylvania. Ice on the lakes ended navigation there, leaving Ellis unemployed again. He had a sister living in Pittsburgh whose husband owned a hotel, but he looked for no help there. In the spring he wrote to her to describe his peregrinations since the outbreak of the war, informing her that he had enlisted in February, having seen no other way to support himself. A year later he told his nephew that he had enlisted "to put down the Rebellion," but by that he meant he had *not* enlisted to free slaves, which he felt he had been tricked into doing; his primary reason for enlisting had been economic desperation.[31]

Maine recruiting faltered at the end of summer, after the state bounty had been allowed to lapse. Newspapers and recruiting posters in that state highlighted the federal bounty, payable only on discharge, and characterized it as the "very best chance to enlist," as though the army were a rare opportunity. Recruiters could think of nothing more enticing to add except that pay and subsistence would begin on the day of enlistment, or that the men would join a "crack regiment." Such paltry lures were offset by nearby advertisements for lawyers who offered to act as agents for the widows and heirs of soldiers. Tired-out farms and cutbacks in lumbering nevertheless provided occasional recruits as Maine's northwoods logging industry suffered its second bad year in a row. Less timber was coming down from the forests of the upper Penobscot River that winter than at any time in the previous sixteen years, and despite deep-enough snow for good sledding, only two-thirds the usual number of teams were being sent out. The army provided a handy answer to unemployment for such rugged woodsmen.[32]

Seeking the last few recruits to round out a Maine artillery battery through December and January, Lieutenant John Franklin Godfrey hung a tattered flag outside a recruiting office that he located near the waterfront where he knew the "loafers" of Bangor lounged. "Recruiting was dull work," he confessed a few weeks later, explaining that "those who had any interest in the war went when it first broke out, or a short time after." The men who were enlisting as private soldiers by winter, he revealed, were "not all such as we would wish to look upon as patriots, or care to think about as heroes." For the ears of potential volunteers, he regurgitated a memorized repertoire of passages he thought eloquent and persuasive, "appealing to men's patriotism and oftener to their pockets," but those soliloquies seldom produced the desired result. Adverting to the lapsed state bounty, Godfrey cast sarcastic allusions to the "great pecuniary assistance" his recruiting posters promised. The lieutenant's blandishments wrought no effect on any but the seediest looking in his audiences. After weeks of such monotony, he started for the battery at the head of five "valiant recruits," including at least one lumberjack, all of whom he characterized as "rather out at the elbows to be sure."[33]

Early in January, 1862, three French staff officers on leave from the Army of the Potomac visited a bar in Auburn, New York, that was virtually wallpapered in recruiting posters. The trio interpreted assertive promises of safe and easy duty with good food and regular pay as an indication of how difficult it had become to entice anyone into uniform, and no one seemed interested even then.[34]

Those who resorted to military service because they had fallen on hard times did not always join the army. The navy offered no bounty, but service with the blockading fleet did entail a chance for occasional prize money, a fraction of which would be dispersed among the gobs. More to the point, the most inexperienced deck hands earned twelve dollars a month and able seamen as much as eighteen dollars (as seaport newspapers prominently reported), with more for those in the engineers' departments. As an added incentive, naval service did not usually require sleeping on the ground in the rain and snow, although it did involve other, less well-known discomforts.[35]

William Wainwright, the oldest of seven children, worked as a spinner in the cotton mill where his father served as overseer. His father had spent his life amid cotton looms, as did all his sons, and since coming from England they had followed the textile factories through Rhode Island, Massachusetts, and into New Hampshire. There they had settled when secession cut off the cotton supply and crippled their industry. Their rented house in Exeter lay barely twenty miles from the Portsmouth Navy Yard, where carpenters were working on the hull of a couple of new navy gunboats, and on November 21 Wainwright made his way to the yard. Posters tacked to the walls of buildings there promised that naval recruits would be paid from the day they enlisted, and could assign pay allotments for their families right from the start. Wainwright promptly signed on as a coal heaver aboard the USS *Kearsarge* for three years.[36]

The same recruiting posters caught the eye of Charles Poole, the son of a day laborer and himself a house painter who, with the painting season at an end, was attracted by the offer of immediate pay. He, too, put his name down as a coal heaver. Poole enlisted without the permission of his parents, who would be distressed to hear of it, and perhaps in anticipation of that he did not return to his home, instead staying in Portsmouth that night. The next morning he, Wainwright, and other recruits rowed out to the mastless ship to clear enough lumber out of the way that they might sleep belowdecks, but it was a hopeless job at that stage of construction. They all returned to Portsmouth in the evening and found their own lodgings. Poole made a deal with the owner of the City Hotel to board at $3.50 a week until the *Kearsarge* sailed, but he would pay that out of his own pocket. The promises of pay from the date of enlistment evaporated once the men signed the articles because the recruiting posters had not been officially authorized and old navy traditions prevailed: enlisted men's pay did not begin until they were assigned to a commissioned ship.[37]

Later they were joined by a onetime accountant in his mid-fifties named Carsten DeWit, a native of the Dutch colony of Demerara, in South America, who had come to Portsmouth in the 1840s. Judging by the anguish he expressed at leaving his wife and children, the youngest of whom was barely of school age, only extraordinary need could have moved him to ship for a three-year cruise. At the same time, his shocked reaction to the profanity of the crew left little doubt of his inexperience among seagoing men. DeWit signed on as the ship's yeoman, in charge of reckoning the crewmen's purchases against their pay. As he went aboard he grieved that it was the first time he had left his family for more than three weeks at a time, and only once had they been separated even that long.[38]

The work on the *Kearsarge* went more slowly than officers or men liked, perhaps partly because the enlisted men were not the only ones being cheated of their pay. The previous July, when the Boston shipwrights had struck, they had expected to earn the usual navy-yard rate of $2.00 and $2.50 per day, but in December the Navy Department instructed the commandant at Portsmouth to pay nothing more than what he considered "average" wages. With that he arbitrarily decreased common laborers' wages by twenty-five cents per day, thereby reducing some to as little as $1.00 a day. Adding insult to injury, he insisted that they be at work by sunrise to compensate for the lack of light in a December day. The laborers met to discuss these affronts, but then the commandant cut the carpenters' wages, and they called a strike. Of some 650 men employed by the yard, barely a score turned out for work on the day the strike was to begin. The commandant responded by firing the known leaders and threatening to do the same to the rest, trusting that the significant pool of men who still remained without work that winter could serve as potential replacements if necessary. Within a couple of days all the adzes, axes, and hammers were echoing once again.[39]

Navy recruiters habitually told inquiring prospects outright lies about the emoluments of the service to persuade them to sign on, as George Geer discovered when he took the ferry over to the Brooklyn Navy Yard in February of 1862. Geer, whose father manufactured cast-iron stoves in Troy, had been selling some of them from a rented storefront in New York City, where he had been living since his marriage in 1858. The recession had crippled his father's mortgage-laden business and put an end to his own, leaving him chasing down deadbeat customers; he had fallen far enough into debt that he hoped for a bankruptcy law that would allow him to cancel those obligations. In the meantime he considered the navy as a temporary refuge. Geer had acquired some experience with machinery and steam engines at his father's foundry, and the officer at the yard agreed to accept him at the advanced rate of first-class fireman, which was the highest enlisted grade in the engine room. That same officer informed him that he would receive a month's wages in advance—thirty dollars at that rank—and promised that he could assign half his pay to his wife in an allotment that would start immediately, while the advance would be taken out of his half of the pay over several months. As Geer revealed later, that was the deciding factor: he jotted his name down and went aboard the hulk of the old *North Carolina,* which served as a receiving ship for recruits.[40]

Soon afterward, a navy lieutenant visited the *North Carolina* in a quest for volunteers willing to serve on the navy's first fully armored warship, then in the final stages of construction. The USS *Monitor,* as that ironclad was called, required only forty-two crewmen, and far more men volunteered than were needed, but that did not necessarily illustrate their adventurous spirit or their enthusiasm for the experiment. Fireman Geer stood among the volunteers, and he was no hero or daredevil: he betrayed his views on valor or patriotism by asking his wife, Martha, "what is the Cuntry worth to a man when his wife is a Widdow[?]" His decision took him off the rotting receiving ship and into an active assignment that would start his pay, and similar practical considerations inspired his fellow crewmen. He told Martha that one of those who boarded the *Monitor* with him had been an engineer aboard the Fulton Ferry for seventeen years, but had recently lost that job and had gone into the navy "from necessity."[41]

Within a month Geer learned that he had been duped about the allotment. He had to work off the advance and then earn two more months' pay before Martha could get another penny. He assured her that had he known as much when he enlisted he would never have done so, and her plight drove him to tears of sadness and frustration more than once. He had left her and their two little boys living in an apartment with a crude and demanding landlady, but Martha's sister moved in to share the cost and help care for the children. For living expenses Geer's wife borrowed from her sister and from his parents, who by then were also supporting his two adult brothers, both of whom had lost their positions. Within a few weeks Martha, her sister, and the children all moved into cheaper lodgings, still owing rent on their old place, and Geer had her send him thread and jackknives that he started peddling among his shipmates for an additional couple of dollars a month. Then Martha started taking in washing. She developed a habit of visiting with friends and relatives overnight, prompting her husband to suspect that she did so to save money on the evening and morning meals; she claimed to have no appetite, and he thought she was stinting herself for the sake of the children.[42]

Geer's immediate goal had been to secure funds for her as promptly as possible, but he hoped his service would ultimately provide him with a more remunerative career. He used his Masonic connections to cultivate friends among the engineer officers, who loaned him books on engineering and promoted him to storekeeper of their division, which gave him extra time to study. His older brother had an acquaintance who was friendly with the secretary of the navy, and that begat correspondence that would eventually yield further promotion. "As I never had any trade," he wrote, nearly ten months into his enlistment, "of coarse I could do only what chance threw in my way[,] but now I have a good trade or profession which will give me imployment most any whare."[43]

The chance to learn a trade or hone their skills had attracted many men to the armed services since the previous April, and not all of them had to wear uniforms. Both the army and the navy hired civilians in different capacities, from the building trades and railroad work to clerical and medical services, and among such employees the mercenary motive flourished at least as prominently as it did in the ranks. Teamsters, for instance, were paid better than a sergeant major, if not as much as an officer.[44]

John Vance Lauderdale entertained no sympathy for either secession or the war against it. When he applied for service with the U.S. Army, it was not with any notion of serving his country: his ambitions were solely professional and financial. Having just graduated from medical school in New York City, he responded to his brother's advice, gleaned from army surgeons, that he would learn more of medicine after a year in the army than over a lifetime in hospitals or private practice. "Besides," his brother concluded, "you receive a good salary." Lauderdale needed no more urging than that, and he was soon on his way to St. Louis as a contract surgeon with the forces that were plying western waters.[45]

Recruiting for the army abated slightly over the winter, but enough new units to fill two or three divisions were still being organized each month. Twenty regiments or more of infantry mustered in just during March, 1862, exclusive of cavalry and artillery, and other regiments were yet gathering in the camps. Daniel Sawtelle, a young man who described himself as the son of "poor but honest" folk, enlisted on February 11. He admitted in his memoirs that his father had endured numerous financial reverses in western Maine and had moved his family to the wilds of Aroostook County to live as cheaply as possible. Two years before the war, when Daniel had reached his majority, he bought his parents a hundred acres of land for $450, planning to pay it off by working summers as a farm laborer and winters as a lumberjack for $13 a month. When the war came he had not yet earned enough to make the final payment on the land, and amid a recession he was only able to collect a portion of the previous winter's wages. During the summer and fall of 1861, he had helped his father build a house on the mortgaged property, finishing it during the winter rather than returning to his unremunerative timbering job, and he enlisted once the house was habitable. Despite having earned no money for nearly a year, and facing the threat of foreclosure on a farm in which he had invested heavily, Sawtelle insisted half a century later that he had gone to war from patriotism alone.[46]

"I have heard it said," he wrote in 1912, "that we young fellows did not know what we were doing, that it was the excitement of the times and a love for adventure," but he maintained that he and his comrades had succumbed to none of that. "We felt it our duty to our country," he asserted, "and whatever the cost, we were determined to fulfil our duty." He may have believed as much by then, after decades in the Grand Army of the Republic, which promoted that very image of the veterans who composed it. Patriotism may well have fluttered in his breast that winter of 1862, too—perhaps alongside the excitement and the longing for adventure that he later denied—but economic pressure also exerted some effect. As the only surviving son of a father he described as "feeble," Sawtelle was the principal support of the family. Besides feeding and clothing him, the army offered the same wages he would have earned the previous winter had his employer paid up. In the week before he enlisted, Maine newspapers reported conspicuously on three new regiments in camp at Augusta that drew upward of $200,000 in pay, much of which the men sent home. Those same papers also noted that the legislature was debating bills for a new state bounty and for the support of soldiers' dependents. In his position Sawtelle could not have been oblivious to those prospective benefits, or immune to their attraction.[47]

An atmosphere of imminent victory dissuaded some from enlisting who might otherwise have felt duty bound to quell the rebellion. Beginning on January 19, 1862, with the rout of a Confederate force at Mill Spring, Kentucky, several Union armies small enough to be commanded by brigadier generals achieved a string of victories that continued without interruption for the next two months. In February Ambrose Burnside captured Roanoke Island, in the middle of the North Carolina sounds, and Ulysses Grant took Forts Henry and Donelson, which collapsed the Confederate defense line across southern Kentucky and opened the river route to Nashville. On Washington's Birthday a New Jersey newspaper remarked that "the recent Union victories, following in such quick succession upon each other, have astounded and overwhelmed the rebels, and have electrified the whole country."[48]

Three weeks after Fort Donelson, Confederates lost a two-day battle for control of northern Arkansas, and they evacuated their stronghold at Manassas,

Virginia, outside Washington, as well as their toehold at New Madrid, Missouri. Later in the month Burnside captured Newbern, North Carolina, and established a base there. Other Union forces drove Thomas J. Jackson—the Confederate general renowned as "Stonewall"—out of Winchester, Virginia, giving him the only battlefield defeat of his career. The landing of Union troops at the mouths of the St. Mary's and St. John's Rivers led Northern newspapers to prematurely report that "the whole State of Florida is restored to the Union." The flurry of little triumphs prompted a widespread conclusion, appearing with but little variation on hundreds of editorial pages, that "the backbone of the rebellion is broken." That jubilant phrase would offer cynics an endless source of ironic commentary over the next three years.[49]

The cavalcade of victory had begun just as a new secretary of war entered upon his duties. Edwin Stanton—a sly, scheming lawyer who had ingratiated himself to key members of the previous and present administrations—replaced the negligent Simon Cameron in January, and the sequential successes lulled him into disastrous overconfidence. On April 3 Stanton issued an order halting all volunteer recruiting in every state of the Union. Later, when the order proved to have been a colossal blunder, he tried to pass it off as a temporary suspension, but that was obviously not true. His own handwritten draft of the decree indicated that no more volunteers would be received. All recruiters were ordered to close their offices, sell any furniture, and return to their regiments. A week earlier Stanton had alluded to "this hour of apparent victory" in a private note, expressing his belief that the war had been all but won and no more troops would be needed: one of President Lincoln's private secretaries explained the order in precisely that way in a newspaper column.[50]

On the third morning after Stanton's order reached the Adjutant General's Office, the complexion of the war changed completely when a Confederate army nearly drove Grant's unprepared soldiers into the Tennessee River. The next day Grant recovered his lost ground and Northern newspapers hailed the battle as another victory, but the force of the blow demonstrated intense determination among the supposedly defeated rebels. A couple of days later Confederate defenders abandoned Island Number 10, their northernmost bastion on the Mississippi, leaving it to Union forces that were closing in under the command of John Pope. From a distance, that seemed to confirm the impression of inevitable conquest. Editorial opinion suggested that success in Virginia was all that would be necessary to quell the rebellion completely.[51]

It took some time to absorb the real lesson of Grant's desperate fight, which came to be called Shiloh after a country church on the battlefield. At least twenty thousand men had been killed or wounded in the two days of fighting, and the wounded illustrated the horrors of the war in both their physical injuries and their psychological trauma. A Missouri captain with a relatively minor wound fell into a deep depression over the slaughter and killed himself a few days later. Boatloads of horribly injured men arriving at river ports on the Ohio and upper Mississippi excited no martial aspirations among onlookers who had hesitated to enlist. A nurse who tended Union and Confederate wounded after the battle described men "mutilated in every imaginable way." Dr. Lauderdale admitted that he "did not think it possible that a man could be so riddled and survive," and he incidentally documented the economic demographics of recruiting, observing that the wounded represented "generally the humbler walks" of society. Long newspaper lists of Shiloh casualties spread grief and anxiety from Iowa to Pennsylvania. Even in the East, from which only the occasional westering adventurer had been involved in the fight, accounts of the epic battle tended to cure the malady known as "war fever," especially when they included descriptions of amputations and gruesome wounds of the head and body.[52]

The Confederates had fought like "tigers" at Shiloh, thought an Indiana corporal. If their ferocious assault had not vanquished the invading Federals, it had demonstrated that Southern determination remained vibrant and deadly, indicating that the rebellion might not be so easily crushed. Nearly unanimous support for a broad conscription law arose in the Confederate Congress a few days later, corroborating that impression, and Secretary Stanton evidently realized as much when he read about it in the Washington newspapers of May 1. That same day he sent an unsolicited explanation of his order ending recruiting to Henry W. Halleck, the overall commander of forces in the West: for the first time, Stanton used the excuse that he had issued the edict merely to compel complete enlistment returns from the state governors. In the same telegram, he gave General Halleck the unusual authority to call directly on state governors for reinforcements—thereby avoiding the embarrassment of having to ask for them himself.[53]

A few stray regiments that had been substantially completed when Stanton closed down recruiting were allowed to muster in over April and early May, but incomplete companies and fragments of regiments were simply disbanded. After the bloodbath at Shiloh, those released volunteers were not necessarily anxious for another opportunity to enlist, and some of them had been cured forever of that impulse. Men who had other options for making a living no longer found the attractions of glory and adventure quite so seductive as they had been.[54]

In the wake of Stanton's injudicious decree, the Regular Army posed the only alternative for those few who were still bound to enlist, and twenty-one-year-old Ira Pettit felt that impetus. He had never ventured far from the family farm in western New York, as he noted in a diary that suggested he thirsted after new scenes and activities. Money had no appeal: he intended to send his pay home to cover the wages of a hired hand to take his place. He boarded his first train at Lockport, where no bands or cheering crowds bid his little covey of recruits farewell, and none greeted them at Canadaigua. They saw no other soldiers on the way.[55]

Halleck did ask some governors to mobilize more volunteers, but the well-publicized conclusion of recruiting made that task a lot harder. If any other field commanders took time from their campaigns to exercise Stanton's delegated authority to demand troops, they met with little success. George McClellan, the youngest and most senior of the country's major generals, had arrayed the largest army in American history—the Army of the Potomac, which he was leading toward Richmond up the peninsula between the York and the James Rivers. He felt he lacked the overwhelming force that conventional military wisdom recommended for an offensive against a fortified enemy and begged for reinforcements, but with the source of new troops closed off he could only be accommodated by stripping other departments. Stanton had helped cultivate such fear for the safety of Washington that the president refused most of those requests. The largest corps of the army McClellan had hoped to amass lay at Fredericksburg, fifty miles north of Richmond, under the command of Irvin McDowell. From there the president intended to send General McDowell south toward Richmond by land, keeping him between Washington and the Confederate army, while McClellan's hundred thousand approached Richmond from the east. Their combined columns nearly met the two-to-one superiority McClellan thought he needed. Unless the enemy beat them in detail, the plan promised an excellent opportunity to at least capture the rebel capital, if not destroy its principal army. Barely a year into the conflict, so crushing a blow might have discouraged much further resistance.[56]

With such vast operations about to begin, Stanton finally realized that more troops would be needed, but he still avoided asking for a formal proclamation that would emphasize his misstep in ending recruiting. He inquired of all the governors on May 19 how soon each of them could raise new regiments, but he met with disappointing responses, ranging from an optimistic forty days to three months or more. One governor offered implied criticism of Stanton's April 3 order, predicting great difficulty because, "having discouraged all idea of further volunteering among the people, they have engaged in other pursuits for the season." The governor of Minnesota was trying to fill Halleck's requisition, but found it extremely difficult. New Hampshire's governor reported slow progress raising a couple of hundred men for an existing regiment. Israel Washburn of Maine hinted how desperately people in his state still needed cash when he suggested paying a quarter of the hundred-dollar federal discharge bonus in advance. "It will help amazingly," the governor predicted.[57]

Through the adjutant general of the army, Stanton instructed the governors to begin recruiting, but the last of those telegrams had just gone over the wire when Stonewall Jackson transformed the secretary's concern into panic. Jackson brought what by then was considered a small army down the Shenandoah Valley, slamming into Union forces commanded by Nathaniel Banks, first at Front Royal on May 23 and two days later at Winchester. Banks put his division into full retreat, and his men did not stop short of the swollen Potomac River, thirty-five miles away. In Washington Stanton quaked with fear that Jackson would assail Harper's Ferry, or even the capital itself. He telegraphed frantically for men, asking the governors for militia and acceding instantly to their proposals for three-month regiments. With so few other troops available, the president canceled McDowell's march on Richmond, ordering a quarter of his men to the valley to prevent Jackson's escape and another quarter of them up the Potomac to bolster Banks, protect Harper's Ferry, and lend force to the pursuit. That stymied the pincer movement on Richmond, ending what more than one Union general considered the best possible chance to capture the Confederate capital.[58]

Had Stanton allowed recruiting to continue even at the more relaxed levels of February and March, something like fifty thousand more men would have been in uniform by then, and enough of them would have been in Washington to allay any panic over Jackson. An adequate force could have been sent to confront the incursion without jeopardizing McDowell's advance, which had such a fair chance of delivering Confederate hopes a fatal blow. Stanton's frenzied call for more than twenty thousand new ninety-day militia reflected his recognition of how much his mistake had cost. A Massachusetts congressman who thought the threat from Jackson overdrawn even with the force then available around Washington sneered at Stanton's wild appeals for troops as "the flurry of a girl who meets a cow in the street."[59]

After learning that three-month troops were no longer legal, Stanton rescinded his impulsive order, using deceitful ambiguity to explain his erratic behavior. Five governors had instantly begun appointing officers and raising men for three-month regiments, however, and Stanton let them complete those for which recruiting had started. Advertisements boldly promising "Good Clothes, Good Rations and Good Pay, and only For the Summer Months" worked wonderfully, and five regiments had left New York, with three more ready to follow, when Stanton countermanded his request. Late May was a bad time for farm boys to leave home, as three more months would cover the heart of the harvest season, but the spring had been so wet in Illinois that many a farmer there may have despaired of a crop anyway. Enough men for three ninety-day regiments were soon camped outside Springfield and in Chicago by the first week of June, and two more were filling up. Ohio raised four regiments, and Indiana one. There were still enough men and boys out of work in Rhode Island to fill two regiments of infantry and a company of cavalry, all for three months. Eighty-five students from Dartmouth College and Norwich University formed another company of cavalry, taking advantage of a chance to taste field service without inconvenience to their academic calendar; for most of them that would be the only service they ever saw.[60]

The cavalry excepted, none of the ninety-day men saw more than garrison or guard duty, the probability of which fueled the enthusiasm for that summer service. Three-year recruiting proved more difficult. Men coveting commissions advertised for volunteers, or canvassed their friends and neighbors, but the pool of interested men had almost entirely evaporated. "I have not heard of anyone enlisting or even talking about it," a young man at an Iowa college told his fiancée. "The war fever has pretty generally subsided. The students are not quite so anxious now as former[1]y War has lost its idial beauty and become a hideous real[ity]."[61]

The demand for military materials had initiated sufficient industrial recovery by the summer of 1862 to compete with the army's economic appeal, aggravating the discouraging effect on recruiting wrought by the war's sudden brutality. Many men who had not enlisted had gone back to work in the textile, clothing, and shoe industries. That in turn had diminished the surplus of idled workmen whose desperation had allowed employers to pay poorly without fear of losing their help, and wages had risen accordingly. "Shoe makers are getting better pay than they have had for years," a Massachusetts tanner would soon inform his soldier-son, and the shoe boom carried into the winter; nor would it end soon. A Philadelphia correspondent to a Kansas newspaper reported late in June that the "avenues of trade, commerce, and fashion seem to be as much crowded as ever."[62]

Recruiters for long-term regiments met with little success even in the hinterlands, where industry was scarce. Ohio, which had so quickly mustered four of those three-month regiments, struggled from the first of June through August to fill its first three-year regiment under the late-May call. Recruiting for New Hampshire's one-regiment quota dragged—despite ads heralding pay of thirteen to twenty-two dollars a month, the hundred-dollar federal bonus, and a state bounty that the governor had recently doubled to twenty dollars. In Carroll County a man raising a company for that regiment spent all of June scouring his rural domain for willing recruits, turning up only one seventeen-year-old boy who barely met the height requirement and an impoverished widower in his forties. Connecticut, also called upon for one regiment, could not scrape together more than a few officers and a handful of enlisted men under the incentives of May and June, despite the alleged emergency.[63]

Newton Colby, antebellum office seeker and former lieutenant of volunteers from Corning, New York, had the same trouble. He had resigned his commission in May, as his regiment was preparing to embark on McDowell's campaign to Richmond, giving the excuses that his father had had to close his hardware store and that his family needed him, but all that appears to have been pure pretense: Colby showed a talent for avoiding combat and finagling promotions, and the resignation served both purposes. He had been back in Corning barely two weeks when he started drumming up volunteers for a company to be commanded by him in a new regiment, but after eight weeks of recruiting he still had not found enough men.[64]

The first three-year regiment completed anywhere in the nation that summer was the 9th Vermont. Governor Frederick Holbrook telegraphed Washington on May 26 that he had initiated recruiting for it across the state, with a company to be raised in each county, and he hoped to have it organized in thirty to forty days. The regiment was full within thirty-eight days, mustered in within forty-four days, and left the state for Washington exactly fifty days after Holbrook's telegram. It was probably no coincidence that this first unit to respond to Stanton's frenetic appeal of May came from the state with the most generous supplementary pay for all its volunteers—and with too little industry to have gleaned much early benefit from the production of war matériel. On June 19 a Vermont newspaper announced that recruits would be allowed a month's pay in advance as soon as they were mustered and that they would also receive a two-dollar recruiting premium that the army traditionally paid to the person who brought in a volunteer. Within a week captains began reporting that their companies were full.[65]

The 9th Vermont was still incomplete when the Confederacy's most prominent general complicated the Union recruiting process even further. Robert E. Lee had taken command of the rebel army defending Richmond early in June, renaming it the Army of Northern Virginia. With McDowell's approach forestalled by Jackson's Valley Campaign, Lee orchestrated a stunning attack on McClellan. Leaving a skeleton force in the trenches around Richmond, he fell on his adversary's isolated right wing on June 26, driving it across the Chickahominy River after two days of unrelenting attacks. McClellan abandoned his base of supplies and began withdrawing his whole army to the James River. Lee harried this retreat for four days, striking the Federals every day and trying to drive them into the James with furious, deadly assaults at Malvern Hill on July 1. After seven straight days of fighting, McClellan settled in behind a defensive perimeter around Harrison's Landing.

Confederates had cut the telegraph lines early in the counteroffensive, leaving Washington atremble with uncertainly. Lincoln felt a desperate need for more men, but he wanted to avoid asking for any directly, especially after Stanton's injudicious dismantling of the recruiting system and his frenzied plea of late May. In a plan that bore the fingerprints of Stanton and Secretary of State William Seward, Seward headed north on a mission to persuade all the governors to "offer" the president troops as though by spontaneous concurrence. Asking publicly for more men to rescue McClellan and avoid disaster again would only create "a general panic and stampede," Lincoln maintained. In direct meetings and by telegraph, Seward managed to convince most of the governors to go along with the ruse, but it included a touch of bait and switch. In a letter Lincoln had sent with his secretary of state, he had specified that the governors should "give us 100,000 new troops," but that number started growing before the recipients of that letter even acceded to it. On June 30 Seward reported that he was "getting a foundation for an increase of 150,000," but on the morning of July 1 Lincoln suggested raising that to 200,000, and later in the day he decided it should be 300,000. When the governors signed their backdated memorial on the subject, they did not know how many men they had supposedly agreed to provide until Lincoln specified 300,000 in his formal decree. Governor Edward Morgan of New York expressed surprise when the morning papers of July 2 reported the number.[66]

As a New Hampshire editor observed ten days afterward, the epidemic ardor for volunteering had withered wonderfully since the real fighting began. To attract such numbers of men while the newspapers carried page-long casualty lists, with tens of thousands of the unemployed already absorbed by the army and so many others now back at work, the governors insisted that recruits had to be offered more money. The War Department had already started advancing a month's pay and the two-dollar premium, but Seward indicated that state officials also wanted to see a quarter of the federal bonus paid upon enlistment, like a bounty. That would mean a minimum of forty dollars cash to any man who signed up, which was still a fair amount of money in the summer of 1862 for most young men—as well as for some who were not so young.[67]

The call for 300,000 troops fell felicitously on the eve of Independence Day, which assured that recruiting appeals would be broadcast amid the routine rhetoric at thousands of picnics and town greens. Newspapers supportive of the administration made much of the cash advance on the federal bounty, and some went further, speculating on the progress of the conflict and predicting a relative absence of danger. "The inducements are much greater than at any previous time," proclaimed the *Cleveland Plain Dealer.* "The big battles will have been fought, and much of the duty will no doubt consist in holding places already captured, or ferreting out Guerilla parties to let them swing."[68]

Soldiers at the front expected another rush to the colors at least in the East, where they envisioned multitudes still out of work, but that impression was based on stale information. Three days after its predictions of safe service and imminent peace, the *Plain Dealer* mourned an extremely feeble response, observing that popular support for the war in Cleveland had all but disappeared.

The *Chicago Tribune* correctly diagnosed the economic impetus behind the enlistment fever of 1861 as it interpreted the recruiting lethargy of 1862: hundreds of thousands of men had lacked any income in the first months of the war, the *Tribune* noted, but the army had absorbed many of them and the production of war materials had employed many of the rest, often at the highest wages they had ever seen. Now volunteers would not come forward very enthusiastically in any state until the governors, legislatures, and the people themselves began competing with those wages by adding to the federal government's financial incentives.[69]

A record crowd gathered at Allyn Hall in Hartford, Connecticut, to hear patriotic speeches by the state's governor and senior senator, but few of the listeners enlisted until they saw more money in it. In the middle of July the city of Hartford established a six-dollar monthly stipend for married men's wives, with another thirty dollars a year from the state, which would also contribute fifty dollars in advance to all recruits. Tallying up all the pay, bounties, and subsidies, the *Hartford Courant* reported on its front page, in bold headlines, that a married man who enlisted for a three-year term would realize $458 "if the war ends within a year," and a bachelor would make $338, besides his clothing and rations. "Very few laborers, clerks, or mechanics earn such wages as these," the *Hartford Weekly Times* pointed out. Both those totals were reported too high, and perhaps strategically so. The tantalizing rumor also surfaced that the president would later reduce the three-year enlistments to a single year, but still the response remained disappointing. Near the end of July the *Courant* suggested another patriotic rally, lecturing the citizens of Hartford that they were "not as yet sufficiently aroused to the importance of the crisis" and complaining that nearby towns were posting bounties as high as $150 for men who would enlist before a deadline of August 20. It surely reflected a widespread interpretation of public sentiment that recruiting appeals consistently emphasized economic incentives over love of country or the need to defend the Union as a bastion of liberty.[70]

Most of the more economically desperate had already gone to war, and local bounties caught on quickly as towns and cities began to vie with one another to persuade the remaining potential volunteers to fill their new quotas. For many the quota had become a goal in itself, because no one knew for certain what the government might do if a community failed to supply the men demanded of it. Lewistown, Pennsylvania, added ten dollars to the federal bounties, conspicuously announcing that a recruit could have "$48 pay in advance" by assigning himself to that town. By the end of July Boston and the biggest Massachusetts towns voted to pay a hundred dollars to each man who enlisted against their municipal credit, while others offered seventy-five dollars. Rockingham, Vermont, decided on twenty-five dollars per man, as did the states of New York and Pennsylvania and some of their major cities. Cleveland may have been the first city in the West to settle on a bounty as high as fifty dollars, after which a meeting at Brainard's Hall drew so many people that it had to adjourn to the open air.[71]

With incentives as inviting as those, some men started responding who had been hanging back—or who might never have considered going to war for the monthly pay alone. One such recruit was a young Massachusetts man just out on his own named Charles Reed. Despite his wizardry with pen and ink, Reed admitted that he was discouraged about finding a position as a commercial artist. As a last resort he followed the advice of a friend, who then introduced him to the aspiring captain of an artillery battery in the process of organization near Boston. Reed's fields of talent included music as well as art, and the captain offered him a position as chief bugler, with higher pay than a sergeant and elevated status as part of the battery staff. He would also collect nearly $150 with the combination of local and federal bounties and his first month's pay of $21. He consulted with his brother-in-law, who thought the risk worth the financial benefits—having perhaps been influenced by all the newspaper jabber about the flood of new troops ending the war quickly.[72]

Despite concern about waning enthusiasm for the war, and after its initial endorsement of such monetary incentives, the *Cleveland Plain Dealer* published one of the earliest and most prescient of reservations about paying bounties. On July 26 the editor cautioned against allowing the bounties to turn into an auction, with each community trying to outbid all the others: he suggested that it might be better to raise money for the benefit of soldiers' dependents, thus satisfying a moral obligation at the same time. A man could serve either by enlisting or supporting the families of those who did, the editor remarked. Those who stayed home and risked no danger, increasing their wealth daily, owed that much to those in the army. The soldier might have no legal claim for that kind of assistance from such a man, but he had a moral claim. Citing the detrimental effects of bounties paid during the Revolution, a conservative New Hampshire editor later echoed similar concerns about an "auction of men." Those payments had not only led to extravagant expense, he argued, but had demoralized the troops and destroyed their discipline and effectiveness, encouraging short-term enlistments that left the army with no veteran core: anticipating the bounties would go higher still, men had hesitated to enlist, and the bounties had therefore increased until they became "insupportable."[73]

Few people then or later seemed willing to admit it, but money had posed a significant lure from the moment the first man enlisted. By the end of summer in 1862, that phenomenon became more obvious as the size of the bounties began to determine who, and how many, would go to war. The auction had begun.

The governor of New Hampshire started the bidding at ten dollars per man in 1861. Library of Congress.

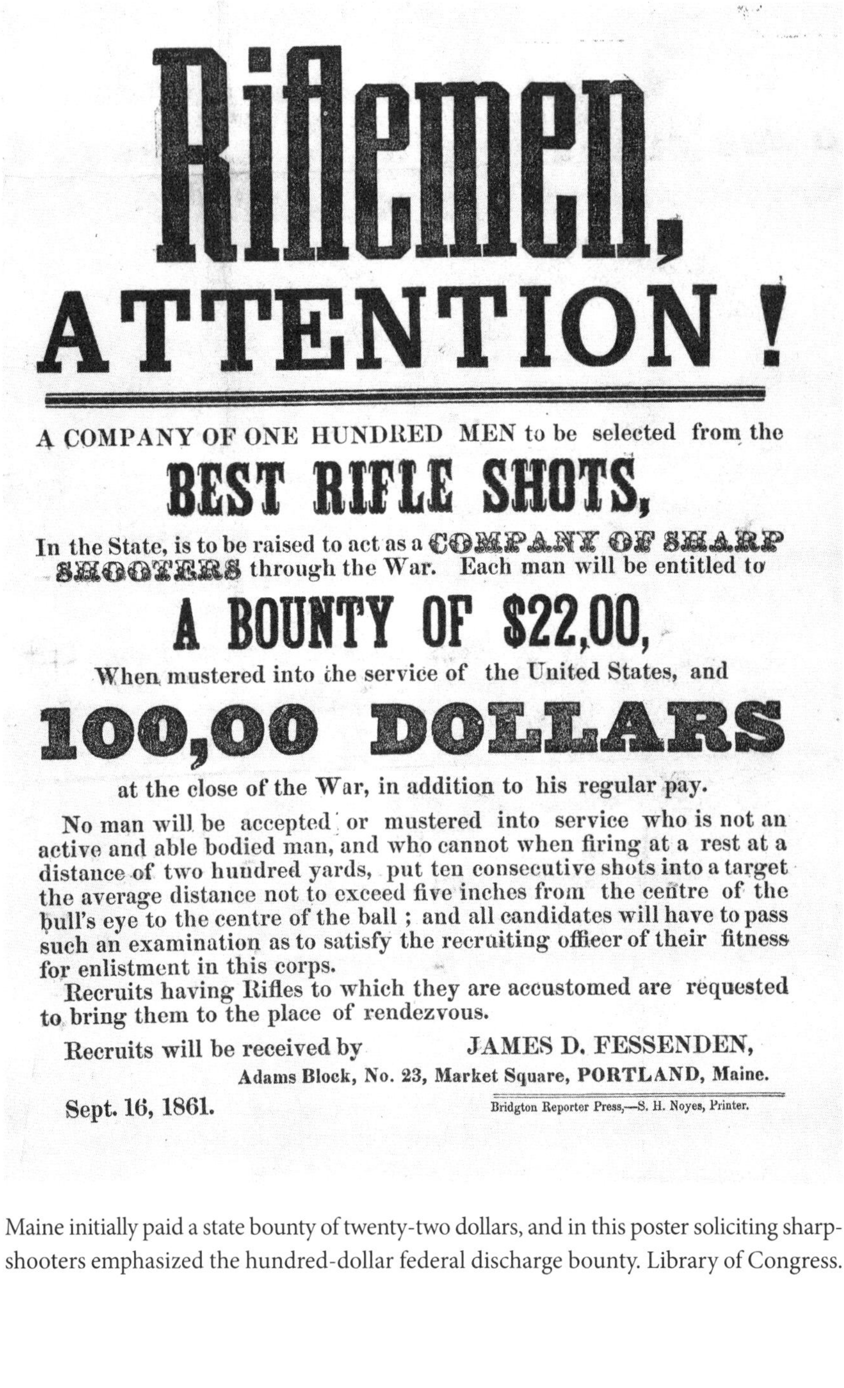

Riflemen,

ATTENTION!

A COMPANY OF ONE HUNDRED MEN to be selected from the

BEST RIFLE SHOTS,

In the State, is to be raised to act as a **COMPANY OF SHARP SHOOTERS** through the War. Each man will be entitled to

A BOUNTY OF $22,00,

When mustered into the service of the United States, and

100,00 DOLLARS

at the close of the War, in addition to his regular pay.

No man will be accepted or mustered into service who is not an active and able bodied man, and who cannot when firing at a rest at a distance of two hundred yards, put ten consecutive shots into a target the average distance not to exceed five inches from the centre of the bull's eye to the centre of the ball; and all candidates will have to pass such an examination as to satisfy the recruiting officer of their fitness for enlistment in this corps.

Recruits having Rifles to which they are accustomed are requested to bring them to the place of rendezvous.

Recruits will be received by JAMES D. FESSENDEN,

Adams Block, No. 23, Market Square, PORTLAND, Maine.

Sept. 16, 1861.

Bridgton Reporter Press,—S. H. Noyes, Printer.

Maine initially paid a state bounty of twenty-two dollars, and in this poster soliciting sharp-shooters emphasized the hundred-dollar federal discharge bounty. Library of Congress.

After the call for 300,000 more three-year troops in July of 1862, the New York legislature authorized a fifty-dollar state bounty to meet its quota, while congressional districts and municipal entities sometimes added their own. Recruiting posters, like this one asking recruits for New York units to "look at the bounties," usually strove to maximize the economic appeal. Library of Congress.

ATTENTION!

THE UNION FOREVER!

ONE HUNDRED DOLLARS BOUNTY!

FOR

NINE MONTHS' VOLUNTEERS!

The above bounty will be paid twenty able-bodied men to fill the quota from Houlton, for nine months; making the pay from 25 to 32 dollars a month, with clothing and rations. A Bounty of $100 dollars for nine months, is equal to $400 for three years.

Persons wishing to enlist as above will apply to ADRIAN VANDINE or J. H. BRADFORD of Houlton, Enlisting Officers.

A TOWN MEETING

WIL BE HELD AT

HOULTON VILLAGE, MONDAY, SEPTEMBER 8, 1862,

At 9 o'clock A. M., for the purpose of enrolling all who wish to volunteer; and voting the above Bounty. All who enlist to fill the above quota, will be paid the above bounty as soon as mustered into the service.

A draft will be made for the above quota of men on Wednesday, Sept. 10th, unless filled by volunteers before that time. All persons interested in raising the above volunteers are requested to be present at the Town Meeting on Monday, the 8th inst., at 9 o'clock, A. M.

Houlton, Sept. 3, 1862.

PER ORDER.

The nine-month-militia call was the first that could be enforced by draft, which prompted even small communities like Houlton, Maine, to raise generous bounties for volunteers. Aroostook County Historical and Art Museum.

An artist for *Leslie's Illustrated* depicts the threadbare, the inebriated, and the reluctant being persuaded to enlist at a New York City recruiting station in March of 1864. Library of Congress.

The best inducement these brokers and recruiters at the Brooklyn Navy Yard could offer was the potential for five hundred dollars in prize money, little of which was shared by many sailors. Library of Congress.

5

RAISING A BOUNTY ARMY

VOLUNTEERS AND DRAFTED MILITIA, 1862

Only the fear of conscription initiated widespread demand for state, county, city, and town bounties. Since the beginning of hostilities the president had periodically called on the states to mobilize troops for federal use, but several governors had refused and others had fallen short of his requisitions without consequence. No practical process to force compliance had ever been established, so idle talk of holding a draft had not previously provoked much anxiety. That changed abruptly with the passage of a new law facilitating compulsory service.

No sooner had Lincoln announced the 300,000-man levy of three-year volunteers on July 2, 1862, than Senator Henry Wilson of Massachusetts proposed legislation making it easier for the federal government to compel the states to supply troops. On July 8 Wilson introduced a bill to amend the Militia Act of 1795, which had authorized Lincoln's first ninety-day call. As it came out of Congress a week later, it gave the federal government, rather than the states, ultimate control over enrolling citizens in state militias. That avoided one major impediment to compulsory service because some states no longer kept up with militia enrollment—that is, compiling lists of citizens whose age made them subject to military service. The bill also extended the term for which the president could call militia into federal service from three months to nine months. The measure contained other ingredients that states' rights conservatives found obnoxious, including a section about the military use of "persons of African descent," but it was the enrollment provision that troubled most citizens. It deprived reluctant states of any excuse for delaying or averting conscription if the requisite number of men failed to come forward voluntarily: the federal government would simply force a draft to fill the militia, then call it into federal service. On July 17 Lincoln signed the bill into law.[1]

Thereafter, if the ranks of the militia were not filled by the willing, they would be composed of the unwilling, who naturally supported incentives to inspire others to volunteer, including negative inducements. An atmosphere of opprobrium soon surrounded those touched by conscription, and those who most feared being forced into the conflict had an interest in artificially cultivating that atmosphere. Having to be drafted was quickly stigmatized, as though it indicated a shortage of patriotism, and that stigma became a favorite tool for stimulating voluntary enlistment. Newspapers supportive of recruiting also cited a litany of practical disadvantages faced by the drafted man, most of which were either false or exaggerated.[2]

Positive inducements brought better results and therefore attracted more support. Where bounties had already been offered, mass meetings passed resolutions calling for them to be increased; where they had never been offered, similar citizen gatherings asked their representatives to establish them. Two days after Wilson's bill became law, Vigo County, Indiana, announced a ten-dollar bounty for those who enlisted there; as stingy as that seemed, times were still hard enough in the West to lend it an air of substance. John Lauderdale, the contract surgeon whose hospital boat docked at different towns on the Mississippi, found the river towns dingy and depressed, predicting that a place like Keokuk, Iowa, would never recover its economic health until the war ended. Some activity had resumed at Ohio River boatyards, where government gunboats were under construction, but they were the glaring exception. Bad weather, uncertain currency, and the curtailment of river traffic continued to keep enough people between Ohio and Iowa in such precarious circumstances that the forty dollars a recruit would instantly realize remained reasonably attractive in the sixth season of the war. The wheat harvest provided some short-term work farther west, where farmers were forced to pay their hands $1.50 to $1.75 a day "cash down and no grumbling" for a couple of weeks, but that was over by early August. As one Iowa paper noted, wheat was about the region's only source of income.[3]

Instead of raising their own bounties to entice volunteers, most communities in the West relied at first on emphasizing the potential benefits a drafted man might lose. Innumerable newspapers, including some in the East, presumed that the advance pay, the premium, the federal bounty, and any family support would not be available to the conscript. They often asserted, falsely, that the drafted man would also be held to monthly pay of eleven dollars. Sometimes they invoked the old rumor of 160 acres in bounty land, insisting just as inaccurately that this as-yet-unfulfilled pledge would also be reserved solely for the volunteer.[4]

On July 14 Congress provided one rather somber attraction for potential recruits who worried about the welfare of their families if they came home crippled, or failed to come home at all. The Pension Act of 1862 updated antebellum allowances for disability or death suffered in the nation's service, extending benefits not only to the widow and children but also to the dependent parent or even dependent orphaned siblings of any soldier or sailor who should die on duty. In accordance with the traditional aristocracy of military rank, the survivors of anyone above the rank of lieutenant colonel would receive thirty dollars a month as before, those of majors would draw twenty-five dollars, captains twenty dollars, first lieutenants seventeen dollars, and second lieutenants fifteen dollars. Enlisted men's heirs were still eligible for only eight dollars per month.[5]

The new militia bill only helped facilitate a draft in the case of a shortfall in the call for militia, with its nine-month service limit. The July 2 levy of three-year volunteers carried no threat of compulsory service. That was an important point, but some confusion existed over it, which injected a measure of anxiety into the discussion of raising bounties.[6]

As though resisting the idea of paying cash for volunteers, the governor of Michigan confidently surmised that men did not serve their country for money, but from a sense of duty. He praised his state's provision for community support of soldiers' families and doubted that increasing bounties would accelerate the flow of volunteers. Ohio, Indiana, and the states along the Mississippi also hesitated to establish a statewide bounty, frustrating poorer towns and cities that had to compete with their richer counterparts. Men who had promised themselves to a local company in Quincy, Illinois, decamped for Chicago when Cook County offered a sixty-dollar bounty. Citizens in Ottawa, Illinois, lambasted the commissioners of LaSalle County for their reluctance to authorize a similar payment, citing the Chicago offer as a probable drain on their own available manpower. The occasional editor railed that a state bounty was the only antidote to such cutthroat local competition.[7]

Inaction at the state level left individual communities to engage in what sometimes turned into rancorous debate over whether they should make their own offers, and if so how much. Vanderburgh County, Indiana, instituted what, for the Ohio basin, amounted to an extremely generous fifty-dollar bounty late in July. Before the month ended, the town of Viola, Minnesota, raised fifteen dollars for each man, while Stearns County and St. Paul, Minnesota, agreed to pay twenty dollars, although in most of that region official liberality lagged for the present.[8]

Private funds for bounties, similar to those subscribed for the care of soldiers' families, arose as alternatives where government officials balked. For many, that may have seemed the fairer and more politically palatable method since those funds depended on the largesse of those who could afford it and supported the war, but they seldom accumulated enough to match government offers. Donors in Grand Haven, Michigan, managed to give $12 to each of that town's recruits, suggesting how tight money still was that so small a bounty would exert any effect. A massive rally on Detroit's Campus Martius passed resolutions begging Wayne County's commissioners to offer $15 per month to each volunteer and to appropriate $75,000 for additional distribution. Organizers there and elsewhere created a "Citizens' Bounty" fund when their commissioners failed to do so.[9]

Lee County, Iowa, appointed a War Committee that optimistically sought $12,500 in donations for a bounty of $50 per man, but in ten days Linn County's Union Defence Committee obtained less than a tenth of that in subscriptions, and even then few of the subscribers paid up. Lancaster, Ohio, only collected enough to allow $10 for each man required from that town. Citizens of Ann Arbor, Michigan, pledged $750 immediately, and added $1,650 a few nights later, all for raising the first new company, which would have yielded about $20 per man if not diluted by further volunteers. In Dubois County, Indiana, residents agreed to raise a variable amount that they called a bounty, ranging from $10 to $20, "for any volunteer who needed it," although that sounded like a one-time offer of aid for which the recruit would have to actively apply.[10]

Such modest efforts seemed satisfactory out on what was then known as the Middle Border, but the combination of an executive demand for troops and the implied threat of conscription had initiated something like hysteria in the East. Conservatives regarded Massachusetts as a hotbed of abolitionists whose activism had precipitated the war, yet men there betrayed intense fear of being forced to fight, and a mania for municipal bounties infected most of the state. The town of Clinton established a $75 bounty as soon as the new draft law was signed, much to the aggravation of at least one local soldier who resented that such liberality was not accorded disabled veterans when they came home. On Nantucket Island the people acceded to a $100 bounty in mid-July, and even then the local editor carped about the "loafers and idlers" of the town, who scattered and took to the sea at news of the military levy. New Bedford, another whaling town, matched Nantucket's offer; so did Westfield, Sutton, and South Scituate. Northampton raised its $70 bounty to $100 as though in self-defense. Cambridge jumped from $75 to $100, and offered twice as much support for soldiers' families as the state would reimburse. Brighton ratified the highest bounty in the state at the time, offering $125. A good many small towns determined to pay at least $50, all just as the widely misunderstood draft law was announced.[11]

Towns in southern New Hampshire felt bound to follow suit before their eligible residents migrated across the state line to enlist. Nashua posted a bounty of $100 for all who enlisted before August 15; a little farther north, Dover started with $75. The same border panic set in south of Massachusetts. In July Providence, Rhode Island, adopted a $100 bounty to be paid in installments over the course of a year, and the legislature of Connecticut passed a $50 state bounty for those who enlisted before the deadline for the quota. The New York State Assembly also enacted a bounty of $50. Maine inaugurated one for $45 if a man enlisted in a new regiment—or $55 if he enlisted in an old one—and reports soon spread that Maine men were enlisting in droves. That surge must have abated quickly, because by early August most of the state's towns had added their own bounties, generally settling on $100. The Buffalo Board of Trade alone contributed $8,500 for volunteers from that city. In Pennsylvania Governor Andrew Curtin refrained from calling the legislature into special session, at least just yet, trusting instead that the people would contribute to bounty funds either privately or through local taxation, as some did; by the end of July the bounty fund in Philadelphia had reached $272,000, exclusive of contributions from the railroad companies. New Jersey, which had been supplementing the wages of each of its soldiers to the tune of $4 a month, raised that to $6. Delaware saw a few war meetings even in conservative Sussex County, and one in Wilmington succeeded in prompting a $50 city bounty.[12]

Vermont, which had exceeded its quota under previous calls in part through its $7 monthly supplement, felt no need to change anything for the moment: that stipend was already siphoning volunteers out of New Hampshire. Some Vermonters argued presciently that bounties would actually impede recruiting by encouraging wavering volunteers to wait for a better offer, and would only attract an undesirable element when they did bring men in. Those critics seemed vindicated when a Colchester photographer was arrested at his home by the Chittenden County sheriff for enlisting in the newest Massachusetts regiment for an $80 bounty and then absconding with the money. Numerous newspapers repeated that the $7 supplemental pay amounted to a $252 bounty over three years, questioning the need of complicating the process and raising the expense with local bounties. Still, a few towns started to vote their own bounties: $25 in Rockingham and Waitsfield, and $50 in Hancock. A big crowd filled the Burlington Town Hall on a rainy Sunday at the end of July, adjourning until the following Tuesday, when citizens contributed $2,840 to encourage local men to enlist.[13]

Funds solicited privately sometimes surpassed official appropriations, especially when those appropriations required voter ratification, perhaps because they were raised without fear of being voted down as extravagant. The town of Windsor, Connecticut, needed thirty men to cover the July 2 call, and a single war meeting raised $4,500—enough to give each man $150; two other donors then promptly contributed enough to raise that to $180. Such liberality prompted the *Hartford Courant* to prod the capital city into another war meeting of its own, as though Windsor's generosity might cut into Hartford's potential recruits.[14]

The frenzy over bounties escalated wildly in the first week of August, when Secretary of War Stanton exercised the president's authority under the revised Militia Act. Henry Halleck, newly appointed general in chief of the nation's armies, suggested mobilizing 200,000 militia, but Stanton boosted that to 300,000 and on August 4 ordered them out for the maximum term of nine months. He imposed an impossible deadline of August 15 that seemed designed to force a draft: it had taken well over a month, after all, for the country to supply the 75,000 militia Lincoln had requested in 1861.[15]

When that order appeared in the newspapers, all hell broke loose, particularly in the East. People lapsed into momentary shock at this "astonishing" news, and war rallies sprang up everywhere, with far greater fervor and urgency than ever before. Organizers began calling them Union meetings, lending a patriotic flavor to the efforts of more affluent citizens to entice a poorer class into an unpleasant civic task by appealing to their mercenary spirit. Those rallies followed a familiar pattern wherever they were held, with solemn expressions of patriotism, solicitations of money—presumably for the support of soldiers' loved ones—and appeals for volunteers. A woman who attended a couple of those meetings in Beverly, Massachusetts, found them deceptive and unpersuasive, except insofar as the money spoke. A number of grandiloquent orators promised wavering recruits that they would "have a pretty easy time of it," with good food and the best medical care; their wives and children would be well taken care of by those whose duty it was to stay home and see to such things. "Nobody spoke who meant to go to war," the woman noted dryly, adding that conscription had infected many previously healthy men with strange diseases. In Beverly as on Nantucket, some of the wealthier residents suddenly took to the sea for a season.[16]

Edward Hall, who had enlisted in 1861 as an indigent shoemaker with a wife and son, had profited only to the extent of his monthly pay, family aid, and the ten-dollar bounty from the state of New Hampshire. The readiness of men at home to spend so lavishly on volunteers only when they themselves were threatened with compulsory service roused him to deep anger. Hinting that he had not gone to war for any moral or political principle, Hall raged that those who had wanted the war thought they could wage and win it vicariously, with no cost to themselves in either blood or money. Those bellicose "stayathomes" had gotten more than they bargained for, wrote Hall (who would eventually give an arm for a cause in which he had no heart), and they raised bounties reluctantly, merely "to save their precious selves from the chances of a draft."[17]

A Maine soldier serving with the Army of the Potomac evinced similar contempt for the profligate spirit of the patriotic meetings at home—the reported proceedings of which he interpreted with cynical asperity, scorning the organizers and pitying their prey. "They call a town meeting," wrote Marshall Phillips, "make patriotic speeches[,] get those poor fellows who are of no account in the world and who might as well be killed as not excited up to the highest pitch possible, and then with the greatest self complacency and noble generosity vote a big bounty to those who enlist." Then, he added bitterly, the meetings expected soldiers like himself, who had received no local bounty, to help cover the cost of such generous gratuities for those new recruits through taxes on their homes.[18]

His pique was shared by many a man who had joined the army in 1861, who resented the munificent rewards lavished on late-coming volunteers. John Ames, who had obtained a Regular Army commission a month after Fort Sumter, despised the mercenary appeal of what he called "the miserable bounty business." Why should men answer their country's first call, he wondered, "when by waiting a comfortable year at home, they can enlist and get the glory & the bounty?" As Phillips implied, forcing early war recruits to help pay the cost of those enticements merely added insult to the injury. "I have to to [sic] go home and pay my taxes," echoed Private Roland Bowen, who had enlisted from recession-crippled Worcester County, Massachusetts, "to pay a Soldiers bounty money, because he would not enlist until a year after I did."[19]

Ignoring such inequity, little towns that had previously floated no bounties now voted unanimously to approve them, and the prices skyrocketed where the precedent had already been set. In states such as Connecticut, which had passed a general bounty to provide uniformity and allay the complaints about unfair competition between towns, communities with deeper pockets renewed the auction by adding their own inducements to the rest. For a three-year enlistment, Hartford paid $175, and the state gave $50 down plus $30 a year, while a man with a family could collect an extra $16 a month if he had enough children. With the federal bounty, premium, and monthly pay, that represented half again the best income a common laborer could expect.[20]

Wethersfield, Connecticut, combined a $125 bounty with a $25 bonus to be paid if, and only if, the town filled its quota. When Stanton postponed his initial draft date of August 15, the people of Windsor renewed the $150 bounty for which they had originally specified that day as the deadline. By stopping the bounties at the draft deadline or the quota limit, almost all towns demonstrated that the prevailing purpose of the bounties was not to provide soldiers for the cause but to save the citizens from conscription. Branford voted a $200 bounty but refused to pay two men who had enlisted from Clinton, while that town declined to award those two residents anything because it had already met its quota by the time they signed up. The pair thus went to war with no local bounty at all.[21]

The possibility of being shortchanged by such technicalities helped less prosperous towns attract recruits from among their own residents with half as much money. Canaan, Connecticut, still managed to gather a score of men for the war with a $100 bounty, and by way of encouraging others to follow their example the editor of the local newspaper published what he called a "Roll of Honor," listing them by name. All but two of them had appeared on the Canaan census two years earlier, and they ranged in age from seventeen to fifty-one. Had they been moved by some motive other than the financial windfall, all but the youngest one could have enlisted anytime since the beginning of the war. Of the eighteen whose family wealth was recorded, fifteen—83 percent—fell beneath the state median. A dozen of them did not own a dollar's worth of property, while one of the three wealthier volunteers never mustered into service, either because he was rejected or because he changed his mind. The gradual increase in the bounties, which paused at each level until that amount failed to attract additional men, always drew the greatest proportion of recruits from the most financially distressed stratum of the remaining civilian population.[22]

Now the confusion over application of the draft came into play. Two recruiting drives were under way simultaneously, both of which aimed to mobilize 300,000 men, so each of those levies required precisely the same number of men from each state. The first, authorized by the president's proclamation of July 2 for three-year volunteers, came with no danger of compulsion. Failing to meet that quota might weigh against local or state pride, but without congressional legislation there was nothing the government could do to enforce it. The second call, issued on August 4 for nine-month militia, did have the power of conscription behind it by virtue of the revised Militia Act.

On August 14, in the same order that announced his initial postponement of the militia-draft deadline, Secretary Stanton added that "if the old regiments should not be filled up by volunteers before the 1st day of September, a special draft will be ordered for the deficiency." This was pure bluff, because there was still no statutory provision for such a draft, but a public growing accustomed to autocratic behavior from Stanton's department had to wonder. Newspaper editors who never mentioned Stanton's threat, and surely recognized how hollow it was, still seemed intent on conflating the mandatory nine-month levy with the unenforceable demand for three-year men. From the very first news of the militia draft, before it had the excuse of Stanton's mid-August bluster, the *Providence Daily Journal* overtly and inaccurately warned that conscription would be applied to deficiencies in the three-year call of July 2; in Minnesota the *St. Cloud Democrat* published an alleged order to that effect. In their zeal to encourage volunteers and higher bounties, many editors aggravated the confusion by deleting the term "militia"—which only applied to the nine-month regiments—in discussing the impending draft. A more common tactic consisted of harping on the approach of the nine-month-draft deadline in the same paragraph, or sentence, that reported the progress on recruiting for the three-year quota. Most citizens had no ready access to statutes that would clarify the discrepancy for them, although the editors should have been aware of the difference because most of them had published the law in their own pages.[23]

One New Haven newspaper carried recruiting advertisements for nine different companies during August, mostly for nine-month regiments. Several of them relied primarily on pitching the financial benefits, contending that with state bounties, family support, and army pay, a married volunteer with two children would pocket $279.50 by the time he came home, "and without doubt the town will vote you a liberal bounty." Combining the canard of lower pay for draftees with the mathematical manipulation of presumed victory inside a year (which was "almost certain"), Republican editors in particular gauged the overall benefits to a three-year volunteer at $510 and those to a draftee at $156. As the militia draft loomed closer, an editorial ploy went the journalistic rounds, beginning with the *New York Herald,* to the effect that the nine-month service was going to be the lightest and safest duty of all. According to this short-lived fable, the militia would not be sent to the front but would instead be kept in camps of instruction as a reserve, training within reach of home while collecting the same pay, allowances, and bounties as the three-year volunteers. There was not a fiber of truth in it, but the report accelerated nine-month enlistments for the week or two before it faded away.[24]

Recruiting posters presented equally tempting (and equally deceptive) enticements. Advertisements pasted to buildings and fences in Portland, Maine, listed emoluments only slightly lower than those offered by Connecticut, topped by prominent headings carrying the dollar amount of the largest bounty or the total of all of them. The posters had been designed by men endeavoring to lure enough recruits to earn a commission, and the recruiters obviously understood that money would have the greatest effect. In Augusta one recruiter published an ad spicing the total bounty payments with the old promise of 160 acres of public land, as though the benefits of the new Homestead Act were available only to veterans. The town of Saco evidently regarded filling its nine-month quota as a priority, paying one hundred dollars apiece for militia recruits and only forty-five dollars more for each three-year volunteer. Meanwhile, nearby Dayton gave the three-year men two hundred dollars—the best bounty in Maine at that time—and only twenty dollars to the militia recruits. Numerous Maine towns approved a cash-down bounty of twenty dollars for the militia but added another eighty dollars to be paid to a soldier's family, or to a friend, in installments. Enough men signed the roll on that offer in one day to retire Oxford's quota.[25]

Having just increased its bounty, Cambridge, Massachusetts, also offered to insure the lives of its volunteers, raising a significant subscription for either the payment of individual premiums or direct distribution to any of the soldiers' wives who should become widows. The common council also adopted a fifty-dollar bounty for nine-month militia, ignoring the objections of critics who feared that paying half as much for only one-quarter of the service would slow recruiting for the three-year quota. The council finally rectified that flaw by doubling the three-year bounty. Competing for the same pool of willing volunteers, neighboring towns in northeastern Massachusetts rapidly boosted their offers from one hundred to three hundred dollars in increments of fifty.[26]

Secretary Stanton provided hesitant Massachusetts recruits with another inducement. Governor Andrew had asked if he might enlist men for old state regiments on the condition that they would be mustered out with the original members of those units, which would shave a year or more off a recruit's commitment. Professional soldiers recognized that a new man serving with veterans was worth much more than any in a regiment of novices, and generals had long been clamoring to fill up the old regiments instead of raising new ones. Stanton replied ambiguously, leaving himself the option of reneging, but the governor took it as his authorization. Andrew had the secretary's telegram by the morning of July 22, and it had no sooner appeared in Massachusetts newspapers than young men and boys began taking advantage of it in a new wave of enlistments rippling across the Bay State. Eighteen-year-old George Hitchcock may have used it as an argument to gain permission from his parents, who had refused all his earlier requests to join the army.[27]

The ominous prospect of a draft had the unintended consequence of filling up the navy's receiving ships, too. That did not relieve the various towns or cities of their recruiting obligations—naval enlistments were not counted against army quotas until July of 1864—and navy recruiting depleted the number of available men. Frederic James, a ship joiner of draft age who owned his own home in East Boston, enlisted for a year as a landsman during the recruiting frenzy of August. His navy pay would have amounted to less than he would have earned at his trade, he would receive no bounty, and the city would not provide support for his wife and young daughters, so money was an unlikely motive. Like others who entered the navy just then, James may have simply regarded it as a safer alternative to being drafted, besides presenting the attractive possibility of being promoted to ship's carpenter.[28]

As the August 15 militia-draft deadline approached, meetings turned frantic in towns that had not filled their quotas, and most towns fell into that category. A Democratic paper in Cheshire County, New Hampshire, reported that bounties were "all the rage" there. Isolated, hardscrabble communities where the war was not popular in the first place started their bounties at $100 but raised each other like poker players until they reached $200. That seemed to have become the minimum amount that would pry men out of civilian life, at least in that region and at that stage of wartime inflation: when Epping approved the leap to $200, it satisfied its entire quota of fifty-two men in a single day. More desperate towns elsewhere in the state raised the ante even higher. Hempstead and Deerfield tried to make certain of avoiding the draft with a bid of $300, but Durham voters passed a phenomenal offer of $440, outstripping every town in the state until the next day, when Stratham countered with $500—and, almost incredibly, $400 for each nine-month man. The farther north one went in the Granite State, the more conservative and tightfisted voters became, but frugal Democrats would spend as freely as Republicans to avoid fighting in a war they increasingly opposed. The stream of recruits from the customarily impoverished hill farms of the northern counties, meanwhile, had been constricted by the sudden economic benefits of military consumption. The scarcity of cotton and the demand for uniforms and blankets had driven the price of wool higher than at any time since the War of 1812. Farmers in the foothills of the White Mountains had gone heavily into sheep, and sternly Democratic Ossipee, way up in hardscrabble Copperhead country, had had to offer $300 per man to bring in enough volunteers.[29]

Rhode Island showed similar panic, with early volunteers reaping anywhere from $200 to $350 in most municipalities. Middletown voters had settled confidently on $125, but only three of the eighteen men they needed would submit for so little; a couple of days before the deadline, the town went to $500. A few other prosperous little communities matched that figure.[30]

The financial incentives were climbing by late August even in Vermont, which congratulated itself on having enacted the first and most liberal of the state subsidies. Organization of a tenth regiment of infantry had been under way since publication of the July 2 levy, but it had not proceeded with the same celerity that had characterized recruiting the previous summer. Several companies had compiled partial rosters that included the names of men who had enlisted tardily under Stanton's frantic requisition of late May, but most of them had not signed up until after the enactment of the new draft law. The remainder of those companies and most of the men in the other companies only enlisted in the aftermath of the militia draft. That 300,000-man levy forced nervous townspeople to recognize that the state subsidy would no longer lure enough men without the additional incentive of immediate cash, and the resulting bounties filled the rest of that new regiment.[31]

Most Vermont towns started holding meetings within a few days after seeing the nine-month draft reported in the newspapers. Many of those assemblies passed resolutions for the selectmen to pay a fifty-dollar bounty for three-year men, and one in Berlin, adjoining the state capital, filled the town hall with what was described as "one living mass of patriotism." In addition to their fifty-dollar demand on the selectmen, Berlin voters contributed voluntarily to a purse to be divided among those who enlisted. Seventeen men raised their hands that day, and (with the same evident aim as his Connecticut counterpart) the editor of the Montpelier paper listed their names under the heading "Soldiers of the Republic." Two of the seventeen appear to have been transients who never reported for duty, either disappearing with what cash they received or thinking twice about the bargain they had made. Three others were later rejected by surgeons. Fifteen of the original seventeen appeared on the 1860 census, all but one of them in Berlin, and thirteen of them or their families—87 percent—had accumulated less than Vermont's median wealth. Most reported owning no property at all, while one was the son of a well-to-do farmer and the other was himself a somewhat less prosperous farmer who was promptly discharged for disability. Only twelve ever saw active duty, going into the same company of the 2nd Vermont. Five of those, all from among the poor, eventually died on the battlefield.[32]

Calais, Vermont, raised more than its quota of volunteers on a $50 bounty. Moretown offered only $25 for the nine-month service, but individuals added another purse of $500 to be divided among recruits. Every town in Lamoille County approved a bounty of $50 per volunteer for the militia draft, but they did so by coincidence rather than by consensus. Once they learned that the other towns had matched their bounties, some communities decided to offer more. There was some question whether Vermont would pay the $7 monthly subsidy for the nine-month men, but recruits for those regiments expected it, so the town of Eden promised to give that amount to its militia volunteers if the state did not. Citizens in little Cambridge, which was called upon to produce ten men for the three-year call of July 2, raised $565 on vocal pledges at a rally, and ten men instantly accepted a $50 bounty. Patience paid off for prospective recruits, however, and a week later Cambridge had to raise the bounty offer to $90 apiece for ten more men to satisfy its obligation of nine-month militia. Residents in Westminster, along the Connecticut River in southern Vermont, pledged funds sufficient for a $100 bounty to each volunteer if the town failed to vote one in that amount, and enough men to complete the town's quota enlisted on the spot. Voters in Charlotte, on the shore of Lake Champlain, raised their bounty to the same level a few days before the draft deadline, impelled by the anxiety of knowing that they still owed twenty-eight men.[33]

The militia draft heightened anticipation in the West too, but more optimism prevailed and many welcomed the twin 300,000-man calls as evidence of executive impatience with the rebellion. One editor in Kansas speculated that with so many men in uniform, it would be easy to hold captured territory "while an army of 800,000 will be free to sweep over the Southern states," and nine months was plenty of time in which to do it. "If 1,200,000 men cannot do it," opined another Kansan, "the thing will begin to look dubious." So many still struggled to earn a marginal livelihood in the Western states that communities did not have to provide bounties quite so high as those that burdened New England and the Mid-Atlantic. Anxious volunteers no longer flocked to the colors at the first emotional appeal, as a frustrated editor in Appleton, Wisconsin, hinted by pleading that young men come forward, but moderate inducements did eventually draw them. Most states in the West attracted enough three-year volunteers to meet their quotas under both the July 2 call and the nine-month militia levy after the War Department credited them with four militiamen for every surplus three-year volunteer.[34]

Public rallies in various Wisconsin counties petitioned their commissioners for formal bounties, but with only occasional success, and in most cases they had to rely on private donations to lure recruits. The legislature did finally fix a state bounty of fifty dollars in the face of the mandatory militia levy, although the state treasurer had only recently announced that the fund for the five-dollar supplement to married men was temporarily exhausted. As many towns in the East had done under pressure of a looming draft, some deficient Wisconsin communities undermined the stability offered by the state bounty by adding still more of their own money. That may have begun to irritate citizens who thought the mercenary spirit was being carried much too far, and it certainly aggravated those who had become disillusioned with the progress and the evolving goals of the conflict. At a war meeting in Portage, Wisconsin, in the third week of August, one dissident snapped at a collector who asked how much he would contribute to the bounty fund. "Nothing," the man replied, to the astonishment of that patriotically animated body. "Not a damned cent."[35]

After a few weeks of newspaper lobbying about the enormous bounties in New England and the Mid-Atlantic states, Goodhue County, Minnesota, eased into the bidding with a $20 offer, while Mankato appropriated enough to pay $25 to each of the forty men demanded from that town. Just as critics had predicted, a couple of small towns in Michigan began bidding against each other for a handful of required men, causing bounty offers to rise to $50, $75, and finally $100.[36]

By a vote of 13 to 4, the commissioners of Benton County, Iowa, passed a $15 bounty about the same time, but payment was predicated on enough volunteers coming forward to relieve the county from a draft. Private donations to the bounty fund of Lee County met only half its goal, despite the local newspaper publishing the names of those who contributed and those who refused: the balance was raised the day before the draft deadline by county voters, who approved municipal promissory notes at 8-percent interest for a $75 bounty to married men and $50 to bachelors. Under similar pressure, Waterloo citizens gave up on the prospect of official compensation and held a rally on the first Saturday after the announcement of the militia draft. The Waterloo Brass Band came out to entertain, and speakers regaled an enthusiastic crowd that contributed $1,500 within half an hour. That yielded $20 for each soldier the town was expected to send, and a few pledged themselves to enlist, sometime soon; none actually did so at the moment. Iowa's governor urged a state bounty on the Des Moines legislators, but Stanton's April order to end recruiting had persuaded them to appropriate no money for that purpose, and the summer levies had already cost the state a great deal of unanticipated expense. Privately raised bounty funds, therefore, still served as the principal alternative, and few Iowa communities could afford much, although Keokuk collected over $5,600 and some smaller towns raised $1,000 or so.[37]

Citizens in East Saginaw, Michigan, contributed (or promised to contribute) $7,500 for the 250 men they had to raise. The governor of Ohio hoped to provide a $50 state bounty, but that burden was ultimately left to subordinate levels of government and private subscriptions. Cincinnati's city council came up with one of the more appealing proposals, including a $20 bounty and a supplemental monthly payment of $5, similar to Wisconsin's state subsidy, while a committee in Columbus raised enough for a flat fee of $20 per man. Wyandot County officials considered selling bonds to finance a $50 bounty, but the proposal did not survive a popular referendum.[38]

Most of the bounties prominently mentioned in newspapers across the West referred to the $25 down payment on the federal bounty. The advance of a month's pay constituted no bonus, but it was almost always lumped with the bounty. So was the $2 enlistment premium—an offer so small that it illustrated the anticipated appeal of any amount of cash. The premium may have been added to round off the total amount a volunteer could receive on the spot: that obviously mattered a great deal, since the most prominent portion of most recruiting ads promised $40 in "bounty," with any local contribution added to the total dollar amount. Besides those ominous, disingenuous references conflating the draft of nine-month men with the three-year service, that was the best direct inducement for enlistment the majority of those communities could provide. Council Bluffs, Iowa, proposed the innovative idea of canceling the city tax for residents who enlisted once they showed certificates proving they had been mustered in. Far more Western communities offered support for the families of the soldiers than tried to appeal to the avarice of the volunteers themselves, and at least through 1862 those efforts produced better results.[39]

One Ohio editor observed that a good many men showed sufficient patriotism to enlist with no local bounty at all, but that impression reflected the continued scarcity of either cash or employment. The economic climate remained so bleak there that the government's $40 advance payment still satisfied many. Where greater bounties were offered, men came pouring in.[40]

The Chicago Board of Trade passed the hat among its members, raising $17,000 to pay $100 bounties to recruits for a field battery, and within two days all 170 men had been signed up. Cook County offered the $60 bounty that had caused jealousy and resentment among other Illinois counties, and the *Chicago Tribune* reported that it initiated "a perfect mania for enlisting." DuPage County paid $35 dollars, and in fear of losing men to Chicago the LaSalle County commissioners asked residents to match that city's $60 bounty. LaSalle County's newspaper reported that the proposal elicited greater recruiting excitement than anything since the outbreak of the war, but the editor admitted that many of those men predicated their enlistment on the voters approving the payment. More than enough men for an entire regiment agreed to enlist in LaSalle, on the condition of getting the money, and the regiment was formally organized the day after the last dollar of the bounty was distributed. The county appropriation had specified that the offer would be withdrawn when the quota was met, and several hundred surplus volunteers went home disappointed, declining to commit themselves without the cash.[41]

Sixty-three percent of the earliest of that summer's Western volunteers came from the poorer half of the populations in their respective states. In Minnesota 74 percent of those who first answered the July 2 call for 300,000 men belonged to families that did not own property valued as high as the state median. The comparable figure for the first Michigan volunteers under that call was 65 percent; in Wisconsin it came to 64 percent; and in Indiana and Illinois, 63 percent. The surveyed recruits from Iowa were almost evenly split at 51 percent—a rare result among long-term units, which usually filled up with an overwhelming majority of poorer volunteers. Except for Rhode Island, where a majority of families owned nothing, Iowa tallied the lowest median wealth of any Northern state, which may account for so small a majority from the poorer half of Iowa's families: even those at or a little above the median were still fairly poor by the standards of older states. The apparent near-equity of "rich" and "poor" among the Iowa recruits is further exaggerated by those figures being based on property claimed in the summer of 1860, while the wealth of many in the West had dramatically diminished since then.[42]

The armies were still filled almost exclusively with the volunteers of 1861 and 1862 in the summer of 1863, when a well-educated Illinois sergeant observed how large a proportion of the nation's poorer citizens the Union forces had absorbed. "The army is not made up of clerks and the worlds favorites," he explained to his mother, "it is composed of the lower classes. Not that I wish to speak disparagingly of our soldiers, but two thirds of the rank and file are totally incapable of anything but the most ordinary pursuits of life."[43]

A graduate of Jefferson Medical College serving as a surgeon in Louisiana found Union soldiers of equally common stock, especially among those who had enlisted before the autumn of 1862. Describing them for his mother a week before Christmas that year, he showed none of the charity the season usually imparted. "That class of men that enlisted up till recently are made up of the roughest material," he wrote, "men that if they never returned to their homes, with few exceptions would be but little missed."[44]

Such unflattering assessments of the men in the ranks corroborated the occupational limitations that had left millions of unskilled wage earners vulnerable to the economic tribulations of the early war years. That vulnerability had driven multitudes of them into the army, seeking relief from acute financial distress.

By the summer of 1862, a lot of breath and ink was being expended on the question of who was really doing the fighting. Much of that dispute took on a partisan flavor, but the political aspect of the argument also bore economic implications. War Democrats, who insisted on the integrity of the Union but did not support the war as a vehicle for emancipation, maintained that more of their adherents had filled the armies than had Republicans—whom they blamed for having precipitated the crisis. Democrats went to the front, they contended, while Republicans devised plans, such as the draft, to remove even more of them from the political scene while Republicans stayed home to vote. In York County, Pennsylvania, which had voted Democrat by only a 2-percent margin in 1860, a newspaper reported less than six months into the war that the vast majority of the county's soldiers were Democrats, including one regiment he considered "almost unanimously" of that persuasion. The question even divided families. One Pennsylvania Democrat who commanded a company in the Army of the Potomac chastised his Radical Republican brother for sitting back and lobbying for abolition policies while Democrats battled the rebels. Since the first summer of the war, Democratic editors had illuminated cases of prominent Republicans of military age who pleaded for others to volunteer (and especially Democrats) while they remained at home. A dissident editor in Iowa characterized the bounties as bribes toward that very end.[45]

Their complaints had some substance, for some of the more compelling recruiting appeals did emanate from men who could easily have gone into uniform themselves. George Ithamar Parsons, the editor of the *State Republican* in Lansing, Michigan, was one of those who tried to encourage enlistments by publishing misleading reports about the disadvantages endured by draftees. Two days before volunteering was supposed to end and conscription was to begin, he ran an anguished appeal for men to come to their country's aid. Asserting that it was every citizen's duty to offer his services, he feared that one man seemed to hold back only because another did, and he doubted that even bounties would fetch them. At the age of forty-four, Parsons was younger than many a man who enlisted that summer, and his plea might have had better effect had he proposed raising a company himself, or had he joined someone else's. Instead he kept to his newspaper office, from which he also worked as an attorney, regularly representing the claims of clients against the same government he was begging others to protect.[46]

Wallace Hanford, editor of a Republican paper in Vinton, Iowa, promoted a bounty fund to satisfy the local quota, offering fifty dollars from his own "limited funds," but at twenty-nine he had less excuse than Parsons for not going into the army. The obvious political motivation behind such inconsistency translated into class tension when Democrats represented the poorer classes of any region. While Hanford claimed no property at all on the 1860 census and thus fell below Iowa's deceptively low median, Parsons owned property worth nearly seventeen times the much higher median wealth of Michigan.[47]

A Douglas Democrat who addressed the August 9 war meeting in Cambridge, Massachusetts, ridiculed the faint recruiting response from the largely Republican elite of that community, whose antislavery agitation had helped convince Southerners to secede. He had collected a platoon of recruits by holding Republican challengers to their pledge of hiring a bass drum and brass band to march through the streets with him, and he was going with that platoon as a mere corporal. Alluding to an election-eve Republican rally on the same spot in 1860, with paramilitary "Wide-Awake" Lincoln clubs marching by the light of their whale-oil lanterns, he remembered one phalanx of them bellowing for the crowd to "make way for six hundred Wide Awakes from Ward One."

"Where are these six hundred Wide Awakes tonight?" he asked. "Has their patriotism gone out with their oil, and are they asleep in the shades of old Harvard?" Indeed, Boston Brahmins had not flocked to the colors with nearly the same alacrity as Massachusetts shoemakers. Governor Andrew had appointed the sons of some prominent Bay State families as officers in many regiments, hoping to give those units the political tinge he preferred, but most of that intellectual elite had not volunteered. Faced with conscription, some of Boston's more gallant young blades formed private "insurance" cooperatives, pledging a portion of the cost of hiring a substitute or two for any of them who might be drafted. The alumni and undergraduates of Harvard who wished to wear a uniform could always obtain a commission from the governor, but those who entertained no such desire had no need to worry about compulsion. As Henry Adams discovered while serving as private secretary to his father at the American legation in London, the slightest impediments could divert someone of his privileged station from any transient warlike impulse. Parental indulgence could also serve as a prophylactic against any caprice of that nature. In September of 1862 young Adams probably encountered Willie Matson, a recent Yale graduate whose father had sent him on a foreign tour of unlimited duration as the draft deadline approached. Squire Matson had provided his son with an introduction to Ambassador Adams for the first leg of his journey away from the seductive allure of bands and banners.[48]

Bluebloods who did take up the sword drew conspicuous journalistic attention at the time, and their eloquent memoirs ensured them historiographical prominence, but theirs was not the society that bore the brunt of the conflict.

A comparison of military service and mortality among alumni at one of the nation's most prestigious educational institutions with that of a more pedestrian population illustrates the extent to which the mandarin class exercised its privilege. Graduates of Dartmouth College showed significantly more reluctance to serve in uniform than the public at large did, and their service much less often concluded fatally. The graduating classes best represented in the Union army were those of 1860, 1861, and 1862, which respectively contributed 26 percent, 19.5 percent, and 18 percent of their numbers, while 13 percent of those youths died in uniform. Those classes carried the college's honor during the conflict, according to a collective alumni biography compiled in 1867. Only three members of the class of 1863 served, and all survived; the graduation list for the class of 1864 did not include any veterans. The alumni biography recorded 1,381 living graduates of the college who fell somewhere within military age at least at one point during the war, representing the classes of 1837 through 1864. Only 142 of them—barely 10 percent of the living, eligible alumni—participated in the war, including the 35 who enlisted only for a summer of cavalry service that offered them more excitement than danger. Of the 142 soldiers, most joined short-term regiments or obtained staff positions, and 21 died in Union service, for mortality rates of 14.8 percent among those who served and 1.5 percent among the age-eligible graduates.[49]

Plebian populations fared much worse. The majority-antiwar town of Conway, on the other side of New Hampshire from Dartmouth College, sent 23.6 percent of its eligible men to war and lost 25 percent of those who enlisted, amounting to 3.9 percent of male residents born between 1816 and 1849. Even in relatively inactive Cape Elizabeth, Maine, 18.6 percent of those who were of age served, and 2.5 percent of that part of its population died in the war. A conservative calculation of service among white men of military age across the North yields an overall participation rate of roughly 30 percent, with a death toll equivalent to 4.6 percent of the service-age white males.[50]

The educated gentry did not take up arms in nearly the same proportion as the common folk. Most of the young men who could afford the time and expense to attend Dartmouth during the Civil War came from well-to-do families, and they could dream of dabbling in military glory without the pressure of economic or governmental compulsion. Early in September, 1862, recent Yale graduate Cornelius Kitchel wrote to his classmate Richard Cary Morse Jr. to say that he had thought about enlisting in the nine-month service but had not done so. At the time of his letter, recruiting for both three-year and nine-month regiments proceeded at full tilt, especially in New England, and there was still plenty of time left for Kitchel to have chosen one. Demonstrating how quickly such rash whimsy evaporated, Morse himself had asked his father's permission to enlist immediately after the July 2 call, stressing the "*urgency*" of the president's appeal. His fabulously wealthy father had insisted that he wait until his twenty-first birthday, which lay barely ten weeks away, but in the interim young Morse's bellicose vagary subsided. Both he and Kitchel continued their studies at Princeton and Yale during the Maryland and Pennsylvania invasions, and neither ever went into the army.

"Are we not weak, Dick?" Kitchel concluded.[51]

Governor Andrew had promised in May that if the administration showed more sympathy with abolition the roads would "swarm" with soldiers. Instead, the more closely Lincoln's policy resembled the Radical agenda, the slower those troops came, especially from the cradle of American abolitionism. In the Bay State money appeared to be a more powerful incentive for military service than any progressive ideology. Of the three-year New England volunteers surveyed for this study, the Massachusetts samples showed by far the highest average proportion of below-median wealth at 80 percent—four "poor" men to every "rich" man. The poorer men of Massachusetts doubtless did not harbor four times the patriotism of the state's wealthier citizens; more likely they simply found the financial incentives four times as appealing. A lieutenant forwarding volunteers from the Cambridge depot saw some evidence of that when a file of Irish recruits refused to board the train before they had received the last portion of their promised bounty. A young man from West Dedham who enlisted in July quickly suspected that some of his comrades had enlisted "more from motives founded in dollars and cents than from those drawn from true patriotism." With army service as deadly as it was by the summer of 1862 and the local economy steadily improving, those who were volunteering primarily for the money required considerably more of it to enlist than their unemployed counterparts had in 1861. Recruiting remained slack in Massachusetts, as in most parts of the country, until the financial inducements began to rise sharply, suggesting that many of the subsequent volunteers were either specifically looking for money or were beguiled by it.[52]

President Lincoln personally acknowledged that economic considerations exerted a noteworthy influence on recruiting. In a defense of compulsory service that he left unpublished he admitted that, since the beginning of the war, men had enlisted from "a variety of motives," naming them in the order he probably hoped reflected their prominence. As might have been expected, he listed patriotism first, followed by "political bias, ambition, personal courage," and "love of adventure." He concluded with a "want of employment, and convenience." Most of the first five motives have been liberally examined, including the desire to demonstrate one's manhood, which Lincoln characterized as "personal courage." His last two categories—including "convenience," which euphemistically suggested a wide range of economic inducements—have evaded extensive examination by students of motivation.[53]

In contrast to his affluent political opposite in Lansing, Michigan, the publisher and editor of a Democratic weekly in Prairie Du Chien, Wisconsin, represented the poorer part of that community. William D. Merrell owned barely a quarter of his state's median wealth, and his editorials reflected as much. Like many Democrats he supported a draft, although he was apparently eligible for it himself, hoping that it would either scoop up the wealthy or at least force them to contribute monetarily by hiring substitutes or paying taxes on bounties. In an editorial that appeared before Stanton ordered the militia draft, Merrell pointed out that Wisconsin had thus far sent more than twenty thousand men into the army, most of whom were poor men with wives, children, or parents depending on them for support. He calculated that the state treasurer was paying over a thousand dollars a day in supplemental support for those families—and in so doing he underestimated the cost by nearly half. It was time for someone besides those of limited means to start bearing the battle, he concluded:

> Of this class of material the state has been nearly drained. Is it not time that those should be called on to enlist, who can afford to go without leaving their families in want? We have able-bodied men enough among us—men whose families would not suffer for bread even if their natural protectors should accidentally happen to get shot, or die of fever in camp. It would save the state a vast amount of money if this class would go. Not half the suffering would occur among families if men of property would cheerfully set themselves up as marks for the enemy.[54]

Merrell expressed an opinion with which editors of his political persuasion usually agreed. Alluding to the Chicago Board of Trade's bounty contributions for a pet artillery battery, the Democrat who edited the *Chicago Times* sneered that the enlistments of the wealthy would be more acceptable than the donations of the wealthy. Reporting a feeble response to the July 2 call in Portland, Maine, the editor of that city's principal Democratic paper estimated that there were at least a hundred "young men of wealth if not leisure" residing there who could help fill the quota.[55]

Michigan betrayed the same willingness to leave the fighting to the poor and idle. "As long as it is left to volunteering to fill the army," wrote a Vermonter living in Detroit, "a busy man will want to do a little more business. A rich man wants the poor man to risk his life first, and *he* will stay at home. Clerks and accountants and salesmen and idle young men want the laborers and farmer boys to go. It will soil *their* white hands to be soldiers. They want to stay at home and make money."[56]

An Ohio newspaper of Democratic proclivity tore into Governor David Tod over a statement he had made regarding the traditional right of drafted men to hire substitutes to serve in their places. The changes in the Militia Act had left many wondering whether that old privilege enjoyed by militia raised under state authority would survive in a draft administered by the federal government. In addressing that doubt, Tod had indicated that he would apply his executive prerogative to try to protect anyone from conscription who either hired a substitute or contributed to a fund for that purpose. Taking that as outright gubernatorial deference to the wealthy, the *McArthur Democrat* suggested that it might be better if the rich went to war in place of the poor. "It is much easier for a rich man to leave home than a poor one," maintained the newspaper editor, echoing his counterpart in Prairie Du Chien. "The rich can provide for their families in their absence while the poor man's family requires his daily labor and watching." To accentuate his point, the editor engaged in some venomous sarcasm about a theoretical contractor who contributed a thousand dollars toward a relief fund for soldiers' families after making hundreds of thousands of dollars from lucrative army contracts.[57]

The *Boston Journal,* as Republican a sheet as Massachusetts produced, rebutted such thinking with a condescendingly didactic editorial entitled "Why Should the Poor Enlist?" They should do so to protect the country that gave them so great an opportunity for advancing their own economic interests, claimed the editor, who seemed oblivious to the contradiction inherent in that argument. In trying to justify the imbalance of poor men in the army, he offered implicit corroboration that it existed. Moreover, his effort to encourage still greater participation by the poor suggested that the imbalance was the product of deliberate design.[58]

Dennis Mahony, the impecunious and heavily mortgaged editor of the *Dubuque Herald* and the principal spokesman for the Irish of that city, had been ranting for a year over the unequal burden borne by the poor in the war for the Union. He amplified his rhetoric on that point when, in response to the July 2 requisition for three-year men, Iowa Republicans tried to excite interest in a regiment gleaned from the state's largely Democratic Irish population. The suggestion illustrated all the political and economic manipulation Mahony and other Democrats had complained about, since it would relieve relatively wealthier Republicans of having to fight while enhancing their electoral majority at home. One Republican in Dubuque recommended appointing Mahony colonel of that regiment, believing that he was poor enough to accept the commission and influential enough to attract recruits by the hundreds. Irishmen were already enlisting in other regiments with at least as fair a representation as other factions, Mahony noted, so why did they need their own regiment? "Why not form a Regiment of Republicans, and of Abolitionists," he asked. Those groups seemed perfectly warlike "on the streets, and on the stump, and at war meetings," he observed.[59]

The revisions to the Militia Act had included legislation making it a criminal act to "discourage enlistments." The vagueness of the new law made it an easy tool for arbitrary application, and Republican enemies annoyed by Mahony's incisive journalism made haste to put it to partisan use, reporting him for that very offense. Mahony probably did not know that Secretary Stanton had personally ordered his arrest as soon as he received the complaint, but the mere knowledge that he had been reported provoked the irascible editor to further acrimony. In a front-page editorial he denounced his rivals again for trying to enlist poor men and save themselves from the dirty work. "Is it discouraging enlistments," he asked, "to make personal appeals to leading Republicans of this city to follow the example of their poorer Democratic neighbors and give their services to the country? So it appears they consider it, by the petition they sent not long since to Washington to have the *Herald* suppressed and ourselves imprisoned. Now, if they think this discouraging to enlistments let them say so, and we shall cease urging them to go and fight the rebels."[60]

By then the militia levy had been announced, with the draft scheduled to commence on August 15. Implementation of the selection process was postponed at the last moment—as were most initial draft dates during the war, because the main purpose of conscription was to coerce men into volunteering. Great anxiety nevertheless prevailed. On the eve of the deadline, the unabashedly partisan Republican who held the post of U.S. marshal for Iowa, Herbert M. Hoxie, made the trip from Des Moines to collect affidavits against Mahony. Then, acting on those accusative affidavits while ignoring contradictory testimony, he arrested the *Herald* editor and another Democratic Iowa newspaperman, sending them finally to Old Capitol Prison in Washington. The bitter Republican opponents who asked for Mahony's arrest—both of them military-age lawyers of considerable property who never served in the army—filed affidavits specifically accusing him of dissuading Irishmen from enlisting. Although they obviously crafted their claims to fit the only charge that might lead to an arrest, the specifications also suggested how badly the two complainants and the rest of Dubuque's Republican establishment wanted poor Democrats to enlist.[61]

Higher government officials may also have prioritized luring the poor into the army. Denunciation of the administration's hesitant emancipation policy by Radical editors theoretically discouraged wealthier Republicans from going to war, but such diatribes drew no punitive action or even objections from the secretary of war.

Whether the mobilization of Dubuque's humbler citizens amounted to a tacit Republican aim or simply an incidental benefit of disposing of their foremost political opponent, it proceeded with vigor thereafter. Of one company raised that August, only 43 percent of those who enlisted before Mahony's arrest fell below median wealth, but that figure rose to 69 percent for those who enlisted after his arrest.[62]

That differential may have resulted more from increased economic incentives. With Mahony out of the way, the county made its best appeal to his former readers and constituents with the offer of a fifty-dollar bounty to anyone who enlisted by the new draft deadline of September 1. Still publishing during its editor's incarceration and showing no inclination to help with recruiting, the *Herald* made no mention of the bounty but reported within four days after it was approved that the quota under the three-year call had been exceeded; the only question was whether the surplus men would be counted against the nine-month quota. An exclusively Irish regiment never materialized, but two other regiments and most of a third were organized by the middle of September at a rendezvous outside Dubuque.[63]

Differences grounded as much in class as in party kindled similar conflict nationwide. The rising issue of freed slaves drove a wedge between the working and the propertied classes, as farmhands and other workmen of lesser skills heard exaggerated tales of "contrabands" coming north to replace white laborers at pennies a day. Mahony and other Democratic editors had exploited undocumented squibs of that nature as they tried to foster animosity for the emerging war aim of emancipation. They also emphasized that the new Militia Act carried a provision that essentially authorized the recruiting of black soldiers. Those issues struck deeper in the poorer echelons of society, where indifference to the enslaved or outright racial prejudice stiffened adherence to states' rights principles.[64]

The Lincoln administration's gradual shift toward a general emancipation policy did not go unnoticed in conservative communities, where it exerted its own discouraging effect on enlistments. When one town in southern Indiana failed to supply a single man for the county company, the local editor deduced that those residents had come to believe that "freeing the nigger is the principal object of the war." That opinion tended to alienate those who might otherwise have joined a struggle to save the Union "as it was."[65] At a war meeting held in St. Paul to recruit a new regiment of Minnesota infantry, an assembly of workmen presented a resolution declaring that "when those who had nothing to do but blather about the Negro filled the Sixth Regiment, we will go into the Seventh without a bounty." That ambiguous comment could have indicated annoyance with those of either Radical or conservative opinion, but there were plenty on either side of the question who refrained from enlisting for fear they would satisfy the principal war aim of the other faction without achieving their own. Facing hesitation among such focused idealists, recruiters were left to direct more of their attention than ever before on men dissatisfied with their employment, men without enough employment, and men of sufficiently mercenary inclination who could be persuaded to enlist for the right price.[66]

Serving one's country for profit evoked a decidedly unflattering image in that era, as indicated by the intense vilification heaped on government contractors. A soldier who went to war for money could also be made an object of contempt, and the extreme government action deployed to counteract any imputation of that nature hinted at how effective it might have been in dampening recruiting.

The War Department threatened arrest for anyone "discouraging enlistments" just as hefty enlistment bounties began to proliferate, and accusations of mercenary motivation sat high among the most feared of all potential discouragements. Exactly how high was demonstrated by the imprisonment of Dr. Nathaniel Batchelder, one of the earliest and most prominent victims of arbitrary federal arrests. His crime consisted principally of interrupting a New Hampshire recruiting rally to allege that the men who were volunteering cared less about their country than about the generous town bounties. Popular scorn for mercenaries gave that comment the power to shed a disgraceful light on volunteering, and federal officials reacted with the swift severity repressive governments often reserve for dissidents whose criticism lands too near the truth. Batchelder soon found himself confined in a coastal fort, where he remained until he promised to refrain from further statements that might exert so devastating an effect on recruiting. The War Department's new judge advocate general, Joseph Holt, deemed the doctor's offence particularly odious. "If any case of disloyalty Short of taking up arms against the government justified the arrest and imprisonment of the offender," Holt scribbled on the back of one document in the file, "this is one."[67]

The draconian response to Batchelder's outburst backhandedly revealed government recognition of how deeply the public disdained soldiers who fought for pay. That contempt helped explain the reluctance of individual soldiers to mention the attraction of monetary incentives in their correspondence, except perhaps to win the assent of resistant parents or wives. Soaring bounties later attracted a class of opportunists who permanently blackened the reputation of all bounty recipients, and after the war most reminiscing veterans grew especially sensitive about admitting any appeal money might have exerted on their decisions to enlist.

6

BOUNTY MEN GO TO WAR

John Henry Pardington worked unhappily as a store clerk in Trenton, Michigan, just south of Detroit, and he felt a bit trapped. He had been married just a year and a half, and his wife, Sarah, had given birth to a little girl three weeks before the president's July appeal for troops. John had been raised on his father's farm, and he missed the rugged outdoor work. Clerking did not "agree" with him, he confessed to his older sister, complaining that it gave him no appetite. He later admitted to a drinking habit that may have betrayed his discontent. "If I could get any thing to do out-doors to Pay me as well I would quit," he told her. In August he found something else that paid as well. Massive July war meetings in nearby Detroit had already initiated bounty donations that yielded a hundred dollars for each married man, with monthly supplements of five or ten dollars. The donors were often people hoping to relieve themselves or their family members of any military obligation, and news of an impending draft increased the contributions to the fund. Furthermore, Detroit's bounties were enhanced by the state provision for family support of fifteen dollars a month.[1]

Pardington, like many another dissatisfied or underpaid employee, anticipated receiving enough money between the local, state, and federal offers to take the leap. On August 6—the day news of the militia draft appeared in local newspapers alongside an article about the bounty—he impulsively enrolled as a musician in a new regiment recruited entirely within Wayne County. Pardington departed with his new unit at the end of the month, leaving behind enough money that both his father and father-in-law asked him for loans. He refused his own father, telling him that he would not lend to his wife's father, either, but his father-in-law waited and asked Sarah directly after John was gone, knowing she would be unable to refuse. In correspondence John occasionally adverted to his affection for the country and the cause, but it was evident that neither patriotism nor politics alone moved him powerfully enough to have pried him from his family. Money matters, descriptions of his own activities, and inquiries about his family's situation dominated his correspondence. He sent most of his pay home, and with her municipal support Sarah was able to accumulate enough savings that in his last letters he authorized her to make a substantial down payment on a house they had decided to buy.[2]

Pardington belonged to the 24th Michigan. Of the men from that regiment surveyed for their economic condition, 65 percent did not own the state median wealth of nine hundred dollars in 1860, either personally or within their families. Pardington eluded the census marshals that year, but his letters imply that he fell well below that figure if he owned anything at all.[3]

The primary reason for a Union soldier's enlistment cannot be inferred with any confidence without digging beneath the surface of his correspondence. Those who wrote anything about what led them into uniform usually cited some level of duty, but such explanations often accompanied revealing remarks about finances. A more practical reason frequently underlay the patriotic rhetoric that helped young men persuade their parents and allowed husbands to justify leaving their wives. Letters and other evidence sometimes prove, and often suggest, that money served as a (or the) major attraction for a volunteer, or that daunting odds of being conscripted had convinced him to enlist for the largest bounty he could get.

Professional opportunities also posed an occasional consideration. Each of the hundreds of new regiments coming into existence that summer and fall provided regular employment and steady pay for two or more doctors. Dr. John Bennitt of Centerville, Michigan, met the median wealth of his state four times over, but he had spent the fall of 1861 and the subsequent winter complaining about his "pecuniary embarrassment." He recognized that he could rectify his financial distress by entering the army as a surgeon, but in one letter he remarked that he did not want to enlist "unless it was necessary." By the following August he found it necessary, taking a commission as second assistant surgeon in the 19th Michigan, and the prospect of a regular salary of $123.81 a month moved him to propose that his wife go out and buy a new silk dress. "Do not deprive yourself of any comfort so long as you have money to buy it," he wrote. Pay came slowly, however, and that fall he modified his profligate advice, telling her to sell their buggy and harness for enough cash to pay a pressing bill. By the time he received his first pay, after New Year's Day of 1863, Congress had cut the salary of a surgeon to $110, but that was still more than most country doctors could have cleared in private practice.[4]

During the draft fright of early August, William Child, a young doctor with a relatively new practice in Bath, New Hampshire, took advantage of the highest local bounties yet to accept an appointment as assistant surgeon. In his first wartime letter to his wife, he urged her to see that someone collected his town bounty. A little farther north, across the Connecticut River on the Canadian border, Dr. Joseph Rutherford took the same position with a new Vermont regiment. Rutherford owed money that he could not be sued for while he was in the army. The pay meant a great deal to him, too, despite (or perhaps because of) the extensive property he owned, so he bitterly resented the congressional cut in salary. He endured a long spell without a visit from the paymaster but assured his wife that he would soon send her enough to retire their debts, promising that she would feel much better once she had three or four hundred dollars in hand. For all the inconveniences, he reminded her that there was no other way for him to earn so much money "so easily." He supposed it would be "an utter impossibility" to make anything from a practice at home at that juncture, and he soon expected a promotion that would add another fifty dollars a month to his income.[5]

Under the pressure of mounting debts and stubbornly delinquent patients and tenants, fifty-one-year-old Dr. Asa Ames Bean of Ashtabula, Ohio, had taken a position as a contract physician with the army. The pay of civilian doctors working for the army fluctuated from as little as $80 a month to a maximum of $125, with no benefits beyond free transportation between the contractor's home and the assigned post. Dr. Bean's salary fell toward the lower end of that range, and the five dollars a week he had to pay for board bit so deeply into his income that he hoped to find something cheaper. His comments on the war revealed no overwhelming support for the conflict, but when he saw an opportunity for a commission as assistant surgeon with the 114th Ohio, he jumped at it. His pay increased, and he received free housing and sustenance, or at least a cash allowance to pay for them. He failed only to consider the risk: his regiment occupied a miasmic camp along the Mississippi River, where he soon came down with a fatal fever.[6]

Seneca B. Thrall, who was twenty years younger than Bean but equally burdened by debt, also began as a contract surgeon in the army hospital at Keokuk, Iowa. He, too, gave that up for a place as an assistant surgeon with the 13th

Iowa, landing on the lower Mississippi near Dr. Bean. Despite the separation from his family and the misery of the location, Thrall felt that he had made the right choice. He told his wife he would have been dissatisfied had he remained working in Keokuk, where civilian physicians were paid only the minimum of eighty dollars a month. Still, a few months later he showed some dissatisfaction with the speed and regularity of his pay, only a fraction of which he received after he had served six months. "If I only had the full amount," he groused, "we could nearly pay off our old debts."[7]

Younger still was Myron Underwood, a newlywed doctor practicing in central Iowa, who thoroughly resented the families who never paid for his services. "I was a good fellow," he complained, "as long as I would work for them for nothing." In August he accepted an appointment as assistant surgeon of the 12th Iowa, with which he served for three full years, coming home only once in an attempt to collect overdue fees from his former patients at home. The experience he gained during the war and the money he saved would help lift him from antebellum penury to postwar prosperity.[8]

Service as an assistant surgeon with a Maine regiment and as surgeon of the 96th U.S. Colored Troops vastly enhanced the worldly estate of John B. Wilson. In 1860 he had been a struggling young doctor living in a Maine boarding house, owning personal property amounting to barely half that state's median wealth. Two and a half years later he was married, living comfortably in Gulf Coast assignments, supporting his bride in ease at home, and all the while building substantial savings. In the spring of 1864 alone, he ordered federal bonds equal to twice what he had been worth on the eve of the war.[9]

Benjamin N. Bond, who was doctoring in Randolph County, Illinois, claimed to have a large but unproductive practice when he wrote to Senator Lyman Trumbull for help in finding a government job of some kind. The imminent passage of an internal-revenue law stirred the ambition of perennial office seekers for the trove of new positions as federal tax assessors or collectors, and Dr. Bond wanted one of those jobs. "I cannot get money enough to live on & support my family," he confessed, asking Trumbull if he could arrange a situation for him. Barring such a local appointment, Bond said he would accept the administration of one of the Indian agencies under the Interior Department—or a consulship, if one could be had. Almost anything would do, although he listed the army or navy as his last choices. In the end all Trumbull could manage for him was a commission as surgeon in a Missouri regiment—but a full surgeon, with the rank and pay of a major—which fed Bond's family until the end of the war.[10]

As newspaperman Franc Wilkie had noticed, professional men of limited practice and insufficient business tended to think of the army as an environment in which they would inevitably thrive. Yet even as they sought such opportunities, many of them declared in apparent sincerity that saving the country meant more to them than living, or earning a living. Altruism seemed more common among Massachusetts officers, whom Governor Andrew tried to select for that very quality. A captain in the 32nd Massachusetts explained to his wife that he hoped he would be spared for her sake and their children's, but he asked her how he could "meet death more nobly than in defence of the old flag and freedom."[11] Another captain in the same regiment assured his wife that he would prefer to come home but insisted that first he wanted to "crush out this Rebellion." Yet another Massachusetts youth, after taking a commission in the U.S. Colored Troops, assured his mother that he was willing to die "in pursuance of the great work I have undertaken."[12]

Those sentiments were not entertained solely by commissioned officers or by Massachusetts men. A Pennsylvania cavalryman who enlisted that summer vowed that he was ready to endure any hardship, and while he did not comment on the risk that lay before him, he did consider himself "on the path of duty."[13] A New Hampshire boy who sent his money home to the foster parents who had raised him told them plainly that "money is not what I came out here for."[14] After two years of misery and mayhem, an Ohio youth had enough spirit left to tell a correspondent that he did not want to "lose sight of the vast interest the nation has at stake."[15]

Others exhibited a sense of genuine obligation leavened with motives of personal interest. Samuel Nichols, a sophomore at Amherst College, spent half of July, 1862, working himself up to enlist, melodramatically urging his brother that it was "our imperative duty to take the place of our fallen soldiers" and rebuking himself for not going sooner. At first he imagined that he would enjoy the privileges of elevated rank from the outset, but when that reverie evaporated he still found enough determination to match his rhetoric, shouldering a rifle as a private. Eventually he satisfied his ambition for advancement, earning a commission.[16]

Whatever feelings of national devotion volunteers may have harbored, their own admissions or close inspection of their circumstances indicate that many Union recruits of 1862 were drawn into the army by the need or desire for the money it would bring. Except for the bounty jumpers who deserted with their advances, the proportion who enlisted primarily for the cash in 1862 appears to have been about the same as at the height of the bounty mania in 1864. Not so many of them were as desperate as the volunteers of 1861, but men who contemplated enlisting usually thought about the pay and the bounties and considered the economic consequences. Some enlisted even though they expected their service to cost them a financial loss, some joined when the compensation at least promised to equal the income they would sacrifice, and some were thinking mainly of the money. The rest combined profit with patriotic impulse or other motives.

Economic analysts Claudia Goldin and Frank Lewis examined the direct and indirect costs of the war, finding only a slight difference in the pay received by soldiers and their civilian counterparts and concluding that those who enlisted enjoyed little "risk premium." Based on those findings, they deduced that either "patriotic duty was a sufficient incentive" or that "soldiers underestimated the probabilities of death and injury." Their study did not calculate the extensive unemployment at the beginning of the war, which would have disguised some of the disparity in pay that Goldin and Lewis assumed, and rising wages for wartime production further explained the relative parity. The need for escalating bounties, meanwhile, fully demonstrated the limitations of unadulterated patriotism. Most recruits did misjudge the dangers they would face, however, especially in the first year of the war and to a lesser degree through the summer of 1862. In other words, the more opportunistic volunteers miscalculated their gamble.[17]

Philip Arsino, the son of a Vermont shoemaker, left no question of his opportunism. He had served briefly in a Massachusetts regiment during the first year of the war, while his father enlisted in Vermont despite having reached the limits of military age. Both had been discharged for disability when the army was shedding such men like feathers from a molting chicken. Philip returned to Vermont in the summer of 1862 to take advantage of his home state's seven-dollar subsidy, and he adorned his motives with no pretense of patriotism, promising his mother that he would never be caught in a battle. "I didn't come ought here again to fight for old Blake or old Sowles," he told her, alluding to two of Swanton's richest men, whom he apparently regarded as representative beneficiaries of the war effort. "I come ought for twenty dollars per month."[18]

Few recruits would have admitted at the time, and even fewer later, that they enlisted primarily for the money it would bring, but they often left clues. George Caverly, a farmer in Barrington, New Hampshire, kept a diary in which he recorded only his daily activity, and nothing to indicate his thoughts, but the details he chose to enter suggested what was important to him. Through late July and early August of 1862, he worked with a few neighbors to cut and gather their hay, his own, and his father's. August 9 looked a little lowery, so they decided to let that day pass and it was well they did, for showers came in the afternoon. Caverly chopped some firewood and "chored around" until his wife had dinner ready, and after eating he went to a special town meeting called to decide how much Barrington would pay its volunteers. They needed ten soldiers and determined on paying them $200 apiece, besides raising $1,000 to cover the required family support. That quite obviously started Caverly thinking. The next day he went directly to the home of a married cousin, a shoemaker of modest means, and discussed the possibility of enlisting. Together they visited a third neighbor, and all three gave notice to town officials that they would accept the bounty offer. A couple of hours after midnight, they piled into a wagon for the trip to Dover, where they caught a 6:30 A.M. train to Concord. They came home the next day in their soldier suits. After the selectmen gave the recruits promissory notes for most of their bounty and $50 in cash apiece, Caverly and his wife set out to pay off their debts before he left home.[19]

What might have possessed Caverly, with a wife and three children and still living on his father's farm a few days short of his thirty-ninth birthday, to throw himself into a war that had turned so bloody? A descendant might reflexively credit patriotism, yet Caverly had not taken up arms during the frenzy of 1861, when he could have done so for a much shorter commitment. Army pay and state-mandated support levels had not changed in a year, and he would have been no less able to afford leaving his family in August of 1861 than in August of 1862: at either time his wife and children would have been eligible for about $192 a year, in addition to his pay of $157. That should have equaled or exceeded Caverly's annual income, but the timing of his decision implied that the bounty money decided the question for him. The combined value of the town bounty and the advance on his federal bounty represented more than one-third his share of the family farm.

John Henry Jenks, a Massachusetts shoemaker, had moved to New Hampshire in 1859 to try selling his wares, first by peddling them to general stores and later by selling them from a storefront he rented on Main Street in Keene. His ambitious two-column advertisements in Keene's Republican and Democratic newspapers failed to overcome competition from the shoe shelves in established clothing stores, while mass production in his native state dropped prices lower than he could offer on such a limited scale. By the summer solstice of 1862, in his fortieth year, he had a wife and children to support (including an infant son) and he had run out of money, besides having accumulated burdensome debts. At the first news of the president's July 2 call, he let the weekly newspaper advertisements lapse, closed the store, sold his inventory for what he could get, and began to think about the only way he could earn a lot of money fast. Eight weeks later—just after the town bounty in Keene reached its peak—he enlisted. During the interim he must have convinced a few neighbors to go with him because he was mustered in as a sergeant, despite a lack of military experience. From camp he wrote his wife instructions for the disposition of his federal, state, and town bounties and his advance pay, hoping she could survive on what little he withheld from his debts and the twelve dollars a month Keene allowed for her and the children.[20]

Jenks enlisted for three years, but he comforted his wife with the expectation that he would be home by spring; even in the autumn of 1862, he credited rumors that the war would soon end. He had still not seen an armed Confederate by the height of the following summer and considered seeking a commission in the Regular Army, but he burned with no war spirit. His letters home offered no word to suggest that he had enlisted for any purpose beyond resolving his financial difficulties.[21]

The Combs clan of Winchester, New Hampshire, enlisted en masse in the same company as Jenks as soon as their town approved a $200 bounty. Brothers William and Reuben were both in their mid-thirties, painfully poor, and each had a houseful of children to feed. William had bought a steam-operated sawmill on a mortgage that he was having trouble paying, and his creditors were not patient. Reuben, the older of the two, had a son on the verge of turning sixteen who enlisted with them, as did the son of their oldest brother, who lived in the same neighborhood. A fourth brother who had some military experience joined them, and took command of their company. Reuben and William both more than doubled their net worth with the town bounties alone—aside from the federal bounty, their regular pay, or the town support for their families—and both were eligible for the maximum monthly aid. William's matter-of-fact letters home offered little to suggest that he had enlisted for anything beyond the financial advantage: he made only one early, sidelong allusion to wanting the war over before he came home, but he harped almost exclusively on money. He advised his wife on the handling of creditors and in the purchase of a farm from a miserly neighbor, instructing her to offer a price equal to his town bounty and the pay he had been able to send home. The proceeds of his enlistment and service provided William with property for the first time in his life, and forever transformed him from a debtor tenant into an independent farmer.[22]

Eighteen-year-old John McMahon, a pious lad from west of New York's Finger Lakes, succumbed to the confusion over drafting, supposing that the three-year regiments would be filled by force if not by volunteers. He also fell for a modified version of the propaganda about pay: not only did he think he would earn only $11 a month if he were drafted, instead of the standard $13, he further believed that if he enlisted for three years he would earn $16. While he alluded to "the disgrace of being drafted," he coveted the $200 local bounty for volunteers, not to mention the federal bounty, because his parents were deep in debt for their farm. The previous autumn he had remarked on that debt in his diary, noting that they needed his help, which prompted him to add that he did not consider it his duty "at present" to go to war. "I think until I see more clearly I shall not go," he had concluded in November of 1861, but he began to see his duty more clearly with the bounties offered in August of 1862. So, apparently, did his parents, who had previously forbidden him to enlist and might still have interceded during the several weeks his company was camped near their home. They did not object. He never mentioned receiving his bounty money, and it may have gone directly to them. He also allotted them more than three-quarters of his pay.[23]

Sarah Wakeman, a short, sturdy young woman of nineteen who preferred to dress as a man, left her family in New York's Susquehanna River valley in August of 1862 after an apparent tiff. Taking a job on a canal boat at Binghamton, over the course of two weeks she made her way up the Chenango Canal to the Erie Canal, where the boat turned east for its destination at Canajoharie. There Sarah's job ended, and she walked into town with the few dollars that stood between her and hunger. A group of recruits spotted her, taking her for a man because of her blocky build and powerful hands, and invited her to join their company. Between her gratification at their acceptance and her need for more permanent employment, she complied, signing herself as Lyons Wakeman. The examining surgeon gave her a cursory glance, evidently making no examination for hernias, and the mustering officer accepted her although she stood three inches below the minimum height. Had she gone on to Albany and shopped around, she might have found a better financial offer, but as it was she received $152 in bounty and advance pay. Most of this she sent home to her mother, evidently as a peace offering, and continued to send part of her pay—along with a wish to see her family again that was destined to go unfulfilled.[24]

Cyrus Stockwell, a tinsmith who had migrated with his wife and children from the mill town of Lowell, Massachusetts, to the Illinois prairie, assured his parents that he had enlisted out of a sense of duty. He reiterated that in a diary entry on the day he mustered in and confirmed it by faithful service to the bitter end. Yet he had not prospered in Illinois and stood well below the median of that state in terms of accumulated property, while an infant daughter no doubt reminded him of the limitations of his trade in an economy that was still struggling. Enlistment yielded him enough money that his wife sent some of it to his parents, but regular pay and the inevitable stipend for his growing family would have improved their situation even without the moderate bounties of that region.[25]

Money meant something to Fred Kappelman, a teenager who had come to America as a child with his parents. He enlisted at Chicago in a regiment thick with German immigrants like himself. He turned down an offer to serve as company fifer because the duties would interfere with his plans to earn money at barbering. He served briefly as a private, meanwhile shaving everyone "from the colonel down to the corporal," and then secured a spot in the ambulance corps that won him a pay raise and exemption from duty. His father tried to wangle a discharge for him, supposing he had enlisted only in apprehension of being drafted and would want to come home, but Kappelman declined, finding his new employment perfectly agreeable.[26]

Charles Caley, a young farmhand in Ohio's Western Reserve, used the bounty money raised by the townships there as a stake, marrying his sweetheart and enlisting five days later. He allotted most of his pay to his bride, and when he sent his advance bounty and first month's pay home his first instruction to her was to cover his bills with it. Nor was Caley's an uncommon course for those who took advantage of the enlistment benefits. Ransom Merritt Neal, a dainty and diminutive young man from Unity, New Hampshire, declared that he joined the army from "a sense of duty," but he enlisted immediately after Claremont established a town bounty, which he accepted. He also arranged to serve as the substitute for a local lawyer against the militia draft, and with that double windfall he married a local girl the day before he left home. Lewis Caswell, a Massachusetts fisherman who would later enlist for one of the war's biggest bounties, observed that Marblehead's hundred-dollar offer of 1862 had impelled a good many men toward the altar: writing to an absent brother, Caswell remarked that everyone was "geting married and going to the war."[27]

The monetary incentives would have seemed especially inviting to Gilbert Gulbrandson, a Norwegian immigrant who had just reached his majority. In the summer of 1862 he lived with his parents and six younger siblings on a prairie homestead in southern Minnesota, where extreme weather had blighted crops and business all year. "Times are wors than ever this summer here," reported another resident of that region in late July. Gulbrandson went down into Iowa—where, as the deadline for the militia draft neared, bounties were more frequent and a bit more generous than north of the state line. The day of that nominal deadline, August 15, he enrolled in a new company. His parents owned less property than the median Minnesota family and had accumulated hundreds of dollars in debts, at least some of which Gilbert offered to pay with the proceeds of his enlistment, to ease their grief at him going to war. He soon found that the money would not come all at once, or very quickly, but it eventually helped bring his family out of debt.[28]

A hundred miles farther south in Iowa, Amasa Orlando Allen would have been equally anxious to get out of debt and accumulate some property of his own. What little he earned from his work in a sawmill came in the form of dubious Western currency, but there was not much call for his services with lumber selling at only eight dollars per thousand board feet. He owned nothing after seven years of marriage. He and his wife, Agnes, a slight woman unsuited to farm labor, had a five-year-old son and one-year-old daughter when he enlisted on August 11, hoping to leave a little cash in the form of bounty money and a small but steady income through community support. Amasa bought some hogs and cattle to tide Agnes over the winter, penning them and their provisions on land far enough from her boarding place that she had to appeal to friends to drive her there. Her situation soon began to deteriorate: the cattle broke into their grain and ate themselves sick, the hogs had to be sold to pay for more feed, and inflation ate up what money she received. Agnes shrank to 115 pounds on too spare a diet; Amasa initially fattened up on army rations, but he sickened from fever when his regiment descended to the lower Mississippi. His economic plan for going into the army finally achieved a limited version of his apparent goal only the next year, when Agnes secured a pension as his widow.[29]

Jacob Hunter, a forty-year-old cabinetmaker in central Iowa, identified with the Union cause and the government sufficiently to incur the wrath of local

Democrats, who were growing hostile to the conflict. Still, he took up arms with distinct expectations of economic benefits, much of which did not materialize. Five of his and Mary Hunter's six children were still alive when he enlisted on August 11 under local promises of support to supplement his federal bounty and pay. He had hardly arrived at the regimental rendezvous in Iowa City before he learned that Mary's anticipated benefactors were not following through with their pledges and that she was expected to pay for some of the supplies she did receive. Like most of those who had been beguiled under false pretenses to commit themselves to the harsh rule of military law, he raged for a time at the injustice of it but finally concluded that he would have to "make the best of a bad bargain." The worst of his bargain lay only a couple of months away.[30]

An Indiana volunteer whose wife and children were also suffering from broken municipal promises realized that he, too, had to accept such treachery. "They have got us fast," he scrawled, in recognition of the military code that could see him executed for violating his own vow of service, no matter how badly the government or society failed in their parts of the contract. For all those soldiers who lacked sufficiently sustaining political support for the war to remain on duty, the bayonets of the provost guard and the image of the firing squad supplied effective substitutes.[31]

The relative weight of patriotic purpose to monthly pay in the decision to enlist is no easier to determine after a century and a half than it was at the time. In Wisconsin a nearly penniless tenant farmer and would-be schoolteacher named Thomas Sterns enlisted on August 14, 1862. When he left home his wife, Lavinia, was only twenty-one and had a child who would soon be walking. Sterns had harvested his wheat, but it had to be threshed by a roving crew after he was gone; by the time they were finished with it, Lavinia had spent all the money she had and had to borrow until she saw the first of her husband's bounty money. He had allotted her ten dollars a month, besides the five-dollar state supplement, but it was clear that they had not been prospering, even as next-door neighbors to her parents. By the end of the war, Lavinia would lose her husband and her youngest brother, both of whom might have remained at home had the bounties not lured them away.[32]

One sergeant who enlisted from a Wisconsin farm that summer revealed the relative value of that kind of money when he wrote that he thought his regiment's acting hospital steward had "a pretty good place with $20.50 per month."[33] Sterns, who hinted at patriotic sentiments, may not have enlisted entirely for money, but like so many others he had failed to enlist until he saw an opportunity to earn what was, for him, a fair sum of money. More than one man who had clearly been beguiled into the army by a chance to improve his financial situation began leaning heavily on political arguments to respond to the baffled, worried, or angry reactions of family members.

The tendency to cast a more glorified light on a practical decision is well illustrated in the letters of Peter Welsh, who completely revised his reasons for enlisting during the ninety weeks of life that remained to him after he entered the army. Welsh, an Irishman from the Maritime Provinces, had migrated first to Massachusetts and then to New York City, where he struggled to support a sickly wife through irregular work as a carpenter. During a bout of unemployment, he traveled back to Massachusetts for a family visit that turned sour, and the sadness of that episode drove him into a drinking binge that left him penniless and depressed. Lacking the means for even a meal, let alone train fare home, and feeling so deeply ashamed of himself that he could not face the relatives he might have borrowed from, he impetuously enlisted. The recruiting officers sent him to the front immediately, with no opportunity to see or communicate with his wife; when he arrived there he informed her that there were "hundreds of men here who got into it the same way i did." Initially he tried to mollify her with her eligibility for a community stipend as the wife of a soldier, supposing that he could at least support her between his army pay and public relief, but after a few months he tried to offer her consolation on a higher plane. With a leavening of religious analogy to strengthen his political argument, he quoted from both Saint Paul and the archbishop of New York to demonize the rebellion and sanctify the cause of union—and, almost incidentally, liberty.

"[T]he amediate cause of my coming here is no more than one grain of sand to all on the sea shore compared to the cause in which we are engaged," he contended. He went on for pages in an effort to persuade his wife (or himself) that he had done the right thing, however inadvertently, and that his adopted land represented the best opportunity on the planet for religious freedom and economic equality. Less than five months after his enlistment, he seemed to have forgotten that economic inequality, more than any other factor, had driven him to a decision that would soon enough cost him his life. For her part, his wife remained adamant in her opposition to the course he had taken. So bitterly did she resent all reminders of military service and national devotion that she appears to have objected when he wrote to her on stationery bearing lithographed patriotic totems.[34]

Welsh's epiphany may have been genuine; at least he may have convinced himself with those borrowed arguments. He did, after all, serve honorably and well even in the face of mortal danger. His early letters nevertheless demonstrate that political idealism and nationalism played no part in bringing him into the army. As he admitted was the case with many of his comrades, he had enlisted out of personal shame at his acute destitution, regarding his situation with remorse and a touch of horror when his hangover subsided. That regret may have helped prompt his conscious interpretation of the war as a sacred cause, and certainly such noble imagery consoled hundreds of thousands of other soldiers for the sacrifices they and their families endured in the name of union and freedom. In later years those grandiose ideals would dominate most veterans' recollections of going to war, whatever the reality may have been.

Even those who tried to infect others with the doctrine of liberty and union betrayed a more pragmatic attention to their own interests. John H. Coggeswell, a roving printer and boisterous Republican from Bridgeport, Connecticut, had long been preaching party rhetoric, but he leaned closer to the mercenary end of the motivational spectrum when he finally translated his words into actions. He had passed several months at the financially faltering *Housatonic Republican* in little Falls Village, in the northwest corner of the state, where he complained of having to act as editor, compositor, pressman, and printer's devil. "Our record is that of a toiler," he wrote, in the confused first-and-third-person parlance of newspapermen and monarchs,

> and we think the balance-sheet of labor and reward intimates a decided lacking on the part of reward. We therefore content ourself to wait for a more convenient season to go on with our publication. Meantime there is plenty of work to do, by every man who has the soul to do it. We propose to lend our assistance to Uncle Sam for a little while, and if it be in the providence of things sublunary, we intend to re-commence the *Republican* when the din of war is changed to that of the usual industrial pursuits of life.

While Coggeswell obviously congratulated himself on having "the soul to do it," in fact he had found a better-paying job as quartermaster sergeant for a nine-month Connecticut regiment. He had encouraged local men to enlist in the three-year regiments with exaggerated calculation of the profits they would see, assuring them all the while that the war would surely end within a year. He had published their names under his "Roll of Honor," praising them for their courage and patriotism, and cast a Parthian shot at "Bombastes Furiosos,"as he called the "army of exempts" who clamored for preservation of the Union while ducking service on the excuse of physical frailties. Despite his implied intention of serving through the war, once Quartermaster Sergeant Coggeswell had been released from his safe and well-paid assignment he remained at home, although the contest did not end within the year he had so confidently predicted.[35]

Itinerant printers often hovered on the brink of insolvency, and Edwin O. Wentworth had known as much of that anxiety as any man in the trade. Having lost his job in Maine, he boarded his wife, Caroline, and their infant daughter with relatives and returned to seek employment in Massachusetts, where he had worked previously. After much hunting, he turned up nothing. By then the third week of July had come, and Massachusetts towns began offering bounties for volunteers at news of the new draft law. Wentworth inquired about municipal support for his family and learned that if he enlisted his wife and child would be paid two dollars a week, besides the local and federal bounties and his pay. From his room in Springfield he wrote to his wife that he had decided to enlist. When she failed to object, he outlined how much money she would receive, detailing the debts he could pay, the belongings he could recover, and the furniture she could buy with the proceeds, but the next day he wrote again to say he had abandoned the plan. One of the foremen and three journeymen of the *Springfield Republican* had enlisted, vacating their press positions and opening one for him, which he accepted only two hours before he had planned to sign the muster roll. "Now," he wrote, "there is no occasion for me to enlist, I can have work without." It was a night shift, and he was to begin immediately. Wentworth admitted that he had been apprehensive about going into the army because of the risk of leaving his wife and their daughter without support if he should be killed. Clearly he felt that he had been delivered from a desperate predicament.[36]

That relief did not last long, for something happened at the *Republican*. Wentworth attributed it to the night work ruining his eyes and his health, but he always had some ready excuse for his inability to find work—or keep it. Whether he quit or was fired, he enlisted within a fortnight after he started the job, on the day after word of the militia draft appeared in the paper. Springfield had raised its bounty again, and Wentworth was completely taken in by all the recruiting propaganda: he consoled Caroline with the belief that the new regiments, including the one he would join, would likely go to garrison duty; the war would be over in a year because so many troops were being mobilized.

Upon his discharge he would get 160 acres of land, he fully believed, and with the rest of his bounty they could finally have a home of their own. He allotted her fifteen dollars a month from his future pay, and proclaimed that with this income and the family subsidy she would essentially be independent. "Enlisting seems the best thing I could do," he confidently assured Caroline, but to others he admitted that he had really had no choice in the matter. A couple of weeks afterward he defended his course to his father, insisting that "necessity compelled me to enlist" because he could find no satisfactory employment.[37]

Samuel Cormany waited a few weeks longer. Over the next half century he recorded conflicting reasons for enlisting, and may have overlooked one important factor all the while. He had grown up in southern Pennsylvania, near Chambersburg, but for the better part of two years he and his bride had lived in Canada, where she was born and her family lived. Early in August of 1862 Cormany, his wife, and their infant daughter returned to the United States, traveling by train to his boyhood home, where they lived with friends and relatives for a few weeks. Lee's invasion of Maryland early in September set the population around Chambersburg ajitter, especially when some of his troops started toward Hagerstown. As the enemy neared, Cormany decided to enlist. "I really inwardly feel that I want to go and do my part," he recorded in his diary, "as a Man—as a Volunteer—leaving others to wait and be drafted." Both he and his wife were devout United Brethren, and he described the two of them spending "a great deal of time" on their knees that night before concluding that he, "as a loyal, patriotic Man," should enlist.[38]

Cormany transcribed his diary from its original notebooks into a more durable ledger during the First World War. The originals were discarded before a professional editor prepared the transcripts for publication, and no one will ever know how much of the content he added during the transcription. The portion quoted above probably came straight from the original, with the commentary about manhood and patriotism dating from September 9, 1862, but below that paragraph lies a rare appended sentence that echoes with much later reflection. "The fear of being drafted, if I did not volunteer—had possibly some weight in inducing [the] decission." The opprobrium of conscription did influence some men, but Cormany may have worried that it would lead to service as a private soldier in a unit of someone else's choice. To avert that fate, he joined his future captain in recruiting men for a cavalry company, expecting a commission that did eventually come to him, but until then he enjoyed a privileged position as company clerk.[39]

What Cormany failed to note, either in 1862 or in 1916, was that when he enlisted he had been without employment since leaving Canada, more than five weeks previously, and he had cultivated no prospects for earning a living. Instead, he had planned to migrate eventually to Missouri, where he owned land, but that move had been forestalled by the war. Just before leaving Canada he had tallied his entire cash resources at $112.17, and it had cost him $5 just for his family's train fare on the first leg of the journey across the border. His purse would have been considerably depleted on the way to Chambersburg via New York City, and in the intervening weeks he did not mention replenishing it or doing anything to warrant compensation. They had been visiting and dining as guests in various houses, and it was only after he was under military pay that Cormany started looking for a home where he could board his wife and child regularly. A little later he received a small bounty, and while he remained an enlisted man he complained enough about the extent of his clerical duties that his captain paid him an extra $10 a month out of his own pocket. Cormany's enlistment solved a pecuniary problem that he never alluded to, but it could not have failed to worry him at the time he made the decision.[40]

A few weeks later still, another Pennsylvanian who was having difficulty finding work considered rejoining the army if he could find a position with adequate remuneration. Henry V. Christy, who worked as a clerk in Philadelphia before the war, had been discharged for disability from an early regiment but had never afterward found a position. He wrote the adjutant general of Maryland, a former neighbor, for help in finding something to do in Baltimore, pleading, "I cant get nothing to do here, and am almost dead for want of Work." He could depend on his surgeon's certificate to save him if the militia draft should sweep Philadelphia, and he hoped it soon would, thereby emptying out some clerkships and reducing the competition, but conscription failed to open any vacancies for him. Writing back to the adjutant general in Baltimore, who was fielding similar requests from other friends pleading "hard times," Christy asked for a cash loan and the prospects of getting a commission in one of the Maryland regiments. Much later he found a place as first lieutenant in a Pennsylvania regiment.[41]

The unemployed, the commercially unsuccessful, and the financially straitened were not the only men whose patriotism was being prodded that summer by enlistment bounties and officers' salaries. William Wirt Henry operated a shop selling drugs, patent medicines, perfumes, hair restoratives, and other allegedly beneficial liquids, and while that business did not seem to be failing he nevertheless considered reenlisting when the bounties began rising. He had served as a lieutenant in the 2nd Vermont but had resigned in the first autumn of the war, promising his wife that he would not rejoin the army. Henry's letters reveal him as a man who kept a close eye on how much money he made, and the siren song of position and profit—perhaps amplified by the fear of conscription—overcame him when he read about the militia draft: within hours after the order for that draft was published, he convinced his wife to let him try raising his own company. Officers lost out on the federal bounty, but they counted against the town quotas and usually drew local bounties, besides which Henry anticipated even higher pay than he had earned as a lieutenant, hoping for a captain's commission. His previous experience instead won him the office of major, and when a spate of resignations quickly led to further promotion he asked his wife if she was not glad she had allowed him to "serve my country." Thereafter his old concern about earning enough money evaporated: he told his wife not to fret over how much she spent, and he lent his surplus funds to the regimental sutler, who gouged the men for edible treats and camp gadgets.[42]

In Corning, New York, the shadow of conscription and the bounties it inspired helped Newton Colby finally complete the company he had begun recruiting right after resigning from the 23rd New York. The new company became part of the 107th New York, and Colby secured a fresh commission as captain, which yielded him 25 percent more than he had drawn as a lieutenant—which, in turn, had been quite an improvement over his income as a clerk. Colby, as pure an example of a mercenary as the Union army supplied, defied that categorization only by his reluctance to bear the dangers of the battlefield. As he would soon divulge unequivocally, his own personal safety was the only factor more important to him than how much the paymaster doled out to him.[43]

Colby and his new regiment reached Washington in August, 1862, just before McClellan brought the Army of the Potomac back to the capital under orders to abandon his stalled campaign before Richmond. The new Army of Virginia—commanded by John Pope, who had been promoted to major general for the capture of Island Number 10—soon came streaming back into the Washington defenses from another disaster at Bull Run. Lee led his Confederates into Maryland in the first days of September, and McClellan took most of both Union armies in chase of the rebels. The 107th New York went along on the pursuit, and within days Colby found himself in his first battle.

The Union army confronted the Confederates at Sharpsburg, along Antietam Creek, on September 17. The 107th New York went in with the Twelfth Corps during the early morning, in reserve behind its brigade. The New Yorkers did not spend much time under fire before the enemy receded, and when the brigade rolled out of the East Woods to renew the attack the 107th remained behind in support of a battery. The brigade commander reported casualties in the 13th New Jersey and 107th New York "unusually light," with the big new 107th suffering least of all. Any action at Antietam was daunting, however, and the experience unnerved Captain Colby. Ten days later he confessed to his father that he was frantic to escape further combat, asking for help in getting away from the front.[44]

Dozens of new regiments had marched with McClellan into Maryland, and each included plenty of men who, like Colby, had begun to rethink the prospect of facing the cannon's mouth. Officers had the option of resignation, and plenty of them took advantage of it after coming under fire for the first time; some even reported to their surgeons at the initial sound of gunfire and remained under medical care until they could resign. One New Hampshire regiment that was thrown into the thick of the Maryland fighting less than three weeks after it left home lost five company officers, the quartermaster, and its colonel within the next few weeks, all by resignation. Nor was that sort of anxiety-driven attrition unusual.[45]

The option of resignation must have occurred to Captain Colby, who had already exercised it when the 23rd New York marched toward the enemy, but he did not avail himself of it again just yet because the salary meant so much to him. Unlike many other officers who felt that same natural aversion to danger, Colby suffered no qualms about leaving the men he commanded; he worried only about losing the emoluments of his rank. He wanted a "more quiet place," he told his father, "where I might get the *pay*." A few weeks later he was even more blunt, "I care little for the war," Colby admitted, "and profess no enthusiasm and patriotism—only aiming to make the utmost I can out of it—with the least risk of life and health—I believe that most men in the army now think as I do." He pleaded with his father to wield what influence he could to procure him an assignment drilling recruits at the Elmira rendezvous. In particular, he suggested that his father might ask for assistance from the former colonel of his regiment, whom the captain hypocritically accused of having resigned after Antietam because he had been afraid.[46]

Lieutenant James H. Nichols of the 20th Maine knew plenty of officers like Colby. The next winter he remarked to a friend at home that "a large proportion never lived so well, or received such pay (I mean the officers) as they do now. The longer this war continues and the less fighting there is, the better they like it."[47]

Officers of that stripe inhabited even the best of regiments, including the renowned 5th New Hampshire, commanded by Edward E. Cross. Colonel Cross harbored a low opinion of two cousins from Newport who held commissions in one company of his regiment. The first of them to resign, Captain Ira Barton, left early in September of 1862. Lieutenant Sumner Hurd hung on with the regiment, but he did so for the money. During the last battle of 1862 he left his place in the front line on the excuse of illness, later claiming that he had not followed into the thick of the fight because he had been knocked down by a piece of shell—although he was back on duty the next day. Cross marked him for a coward over that, which gave Hurd dual reasons to get out of the army. So many officers were trying to resign that the War Department had started to either deny their requests or summarily dismiss the applicants dishonorably, but Hurd intended to resign, honorably or not, if he could only find some way to support himself at home. "But for the life of me I do not know what I am to do," he informed his cousin. "I am not strong enough to be a Farmer[;] you must find something for me to do if it is only to light the street lights in the village of Newport." Barton was busy trying for a sinecure of his own in the heavy artillery, and with or without his help Hurd resigned in the spring.[48]

William H. Cotton, a first lieutenant in the 5th Iowa, had spent the first months of 1862 slogging the marshy banks of the Mississippi in Pope's campaign against Island Number 10. In March his captain resigned, opening the way for promotion, but sometime in April Cotton informed his wife that he, too, was thinking of sending in his resignation. A few weeks later, however, he wrote that he had changed his mind because he needed the money. Between those letters he had received long-overdue pay, and his regiment had shifted inland to firmer ground, both of which doubtless improved his morale, but he focused on the rebels' recent capture of his uncle, whose wife and children needed support. In his antebellum life as a newspaper editor, Cotton had owned nothing he could call his own and had barely been able to support his wife and children, but a lieutenant's pay now allowed him to support two families: his sense of duty to the nation had therefore not borne heavily enough on his conscience to keep him in uniform, but obligation to his extended family had. Like many of those whose service was somehow predicated on economic need, however, Cotton gave good measure in return for his pay—and a little over a year later he gave the last full measure.[49]

Lieutenant Edward A. Acton had just returned to the Army of the Potomac from convalescent leave in the middle of June, 1862. He was still essentially disabled from wounds suffered during his first battle, six weeks previously, when he considered submitting his own resignation. Having just come from home, he felt the separation all the more acutely, and the danger hung conspicuously before him because his regiment had been handled even more roughly only two weeks earlier. In the wake of those bloody encounters, numerous company officers had already resigned or were about to. Acton remained enough of a Quaker to use plain speech: he had saddened his entire family by going to war, which testified to a powerful sense of purpose, and he had succumbed to deep comradeship with his men. Still, it was money that dissuaded him from the resignation. He admitted to his wife that he would "certainly" have resigned if there were any opportunity to go into a paying business at home. His only chance for a decent living would have been to buy out a going concern, he explained, and even if such an opportunity could be found he could not raise the money. "I have no choice but to remain here," he wrote. It would pain him to leave the brave men he led, he confessed, but he would have done it but for his inability to make a better living. Acton also mentioned that he was being promoted to captain in place of one who had elected to go home, which would bring him a substantial increase in monthly pay.[50]

Regiments usually saw fewer resignations when they were located in quiet theaters of the war, where the officers did not have to endure perpetual danger to earn their salaries. Lieutenant Richard Goldwaite and his comrades of the 99th New York encountered very little excitement during two years of service, spending most of that time in the vicinity of Hampton Roads. The middle-aged Goldwaite had not enjoyed financial success before the war, but he had married just prior to the opening guns and quickly fathered a daughter. A new child tended to make the presumed breadwinner of that era think about money. Goldwaite did that most of the time, and his in-laws had applauded his good fortune when he landed his commission. On paydays he always sent most of his money home, noting that it was the first time in his life that he had been able to save for "a rainy day." After more than a year of monotony his wife started applying pressure for him to come home, and he seemed amenable to doing so if it had not been for the money he was earning. Reminding her that "without money we are without friends," he suggested that she look into the potential for some business he might follow to keep them comfortable, but he had heard that there was little in the way of inviting opportunities back in Albany. When she was unable to come up with anything, he reasoned that it would be foolish of him to give up his commission "when I am doing so well." The presence of the enemy often initiated a reassessment of such financial benefits, however. Soon after fighting finally erupted near his post, Goldwaite went out of the service, going home to open a tobacco store with his rainy-day fund.[51]

From the moment Edwin Stanton announced the demand for militia on August 4, the nine-month service proved very popular—especially since it might be mandatory anyway. So brief a term in a new regiment reduced the likelihood of immediate immersion in battle and diminished the potential for fighting over the course of the entire enlistment. Rumors of the militia regiments going into training camps as a reserve also posed a significant attraction for recruits of all grades. For enlisted men, local bounty offers for nine-month volunteers often rose proportionately higher per month of service, especially as the nominal conscription date drew closer. Towns and states frequently betrayed the basic goal of bounties—avoiding the forcible induction of unwilling citizens—by stipulating that payment would cease the day drafting began. Volunteers, in turn, sometimes revealed their economic motive by waiting until the last possible day, and anxious voters encouraged such gambling by passing additional bonuses at the eleventh hour. Three days before the first deadline, Stratham, New Hampshire, offered nine-month men a bounty equal to $44.44 for each of those nine months, while the town bounty to three-year recruits only broke down to $13.89 a month. As the first draft postponement ran out, Cambridge, Massachusetts, established a $50 bounty for nine-month militia, having paid only $100 to those who had just committed to thirty-six months of service.[52]

Under such circumstances, there seemed no good reason to enlist for three years except for those with an urgent need for a slightly larger amount of immediate cash. Many who did sign for three years supposed that the war would end within nine months anyway: one Maine volunteer expressed perfect confidence "that the war *must* end before that time." Continued confusion over conscription added further impetus to three-year volunteering. Newspaper editors who surely knew better mixed their commentary about the draft with discussions of volunteering in general, as though still trying to convince their readers that the three-year call would also be completed by draft if necessary. Men who believed they might have to serve three years under compulsion would have felt more pressure to enlist, and thus secure the state and local bounties before the cutoff dates for those offers. Better-informed citizens knew that the new draft law applied only to the nine-month militia regiments, and the politically savvy might have guessed that the serial postponements of the draft would continue until volunteering abated. Understanding of the law and the process implied a level of education—and therefore class—that may have accounted for some of the economic superiority so visible in most nine-month regiments.[53]

Except in Pennsylvania, which actively tried to recruit more nine-month troops than called for, restricted opportunities for nine-month enlistments also helped reduce the disadvantage to three-year recruiting. To encourage three-year volunteers, most states delayed organizing nine-month regiments until most of their three-year regiments were complete. Massachusetts men who joined for the longer term during that cycle tended to be significantly poorer than those who waited long enough to choose the militia: 78 percent of Company A of the three-year 34th Massachusetts, for example, fell below median family wealth, while Company A of the nine-month 45th Massachusetts included only 38 percent with so little property.[54]

That contrast was even more pronounced among the officers. The 41st Massachusetts, the last of nine Bay State regiments raised for three years that summer, was still languishing incomplete as recruits began flocking into companies for the first of a dozen nine-month militia regiments. The 45th Massachusetts Militia was under organization at the same time and across the same territory as the 41st, lending much equivalence to any comparison between the two units. Officers were usually much better situated financially than their men, and in the 41st the original company officers reflected an average family wealth of $7,148, with 38 percent of them coming from families below the Bay State's median wealth. The captains and lieutenants of the 45th, meanwhile, were nearly five times as wealthy, with an average family fortune of $33,354, and only 9 percent of them did not rise above the state median. The roster of the 44th Massachusetts, another nine-month militia regiment, revealed a downright aristocratic flavor. One-sixth of Company F in that command was composed of undergraduates or alumni of Harvard, including four clergymen, eight lawyers, two doctors, four "litterateurs," and a couple of engineers. A well-employed young man from Boston supplied himself with a tailor-made uniform so he could look his best for the photographer before going off for nine months as a private in the 43rd Massachusetts Militia.[55]

The tendency of richer men to gravitate to the nine-month service was nearly universal. In every state that provided nine-month troops except New York (which raised very few for that term), sample companies chosen for economic examination showed higher proportions of soldiers with above-median family wealth. In Massachusetts the disparity was particularly striking; it was substantial in New Jersey and Wisconsin as well, and noticeable almost everywhere.[56]

A close study of enlistment patterns in one Maine community yielded a similar result. The 17th Maine Volunteers, a three-year regiment raised during the summer of 1862, attracted only twenty-four recruits from Cape Elizabeth, and 41 percent of them owned less than $200 worth of property. Recruiting for the nine-month 25th Maine began after the 17th was full, and thirty-seven Cape Elizabeth men responded, but only 14 percent of them claimed so little property even though nearly half the contingent consisted of teenagers; barely one-fifth of the volunteers in the 17th Maine were still in their teens. Odds alone suggested to potential recruits that the short-term units would be the safer bet, and sure enough the 25th Maine came home in July of 1863 without losing a man to combat. By then dozens had been killed in the 17th Maine, and that regiment left more than two hundred of its number dead on different battlefields by the end of the war.[57]

While officers of lesser means equivocated over the balance of risk to reward of remaining on duty with front-line three-year regiments, young men of better fortunes or families strove vigorously for commissions in the nine-month militia. Their efforts brought a distinct economic stratification to recruiting and to the army in the latter months of 1862. In their anxiety for commissions in those exclusive short-term units, hopeful officers were not averse to "buying" coffles of men from other recruiters to fill out their muster rolls—an unseemly practice not uncommon in Union recruiting.

Oliver Peabody, an enterprising merchant and soon-to-be affluent banker from Boston, purchased recruits to form the core of his prospective company in the 45th Massachusetts Militia. He went fishing for them on Nantucket Island, where the local editor had described all those young men rusticating on street corners. Peabody did not put much direct effort into persuading them to enlist, instead taking a room at the Ocean House while a local man rounded up some prospects for him at ten dollars a head. Within a few days he had collected fifty-four of them, along with a few more from Martha's Vineyard. That was enough to earn Peabody the signature of Governor Andrew on his commission as captain; in the election of field officers he lobbied for higher office, leaving the state as lieutenant colonel of the regiment. The commanding officer of the 45th later said of Peabody, "no man ever made a better use of his opportunities."[58]

Governor Andrew commissioned all the officers among Massachusetts volunteers, and in the dispensation of that patronage he showed conspicuous deference to the upper class. He appeared to be saving the nine-month regiments as a refuge for some of the state's more privileged sons, and on their behalf he asked an accommodating Secretary Stanton to assign his favorites to a relatively quiet theater of operations. Not one of the fifteen militia regiments from Massachusetts was subjected to the bloodbaths between the armies in either of the major theaters; instead they all went to North Carolina or Louisiana, where they lost an average of only eleven men apiece to hostile fire.[59]

Pennsylvania's drafted militia made up for the absence of Massachusetts regiments in the Army of the Potomac. The Keystone State ultimately supplied the government with thirty-four infantry regiments for nine months of service because, for political reasons, Governor Curtin unilaterally chose to recruit more short-term men than three-year troops. Curtin dispensed no obvious favoritism in organizing the militia regiments, which may explain why his surplus nine-month troops contained only 3 percent fewer men of less-than-median wealth than the three-year sample; in the Massachusetts samples, the nine-month militia had nearly three times as many wealthier soldiers as the three-year volunteers. The Lincoln administration ultimately accepted Curtin's additional nine-month regiments, but the War Department sent twenty-five of them to the Army of the Potomac, where on average they suffered two and a half times the battlefield casualties of Governor Andrew's pets. Two of the Pennsylvania militia regiments fought in three major engagements in less than eight months.[60]

Many of the nine-month men nevertheless went off feeling they had struck good bargains in terms of both money and service. One Pennsylvania lad who was counting his bounty money congratulated himself that he had enlisted late in September, which he mistakenly believed meant that he would serve a month less as a result.[61] Another Pennsylvanian, whose debts were bringing the sheriff's attention to his farm, departed with his father-in-law's injunction to find a lucrative office and "make all the money you can."[62] A dissatisfied Maine shoemaker let his mother know that he was "fairly engaged in 'Uncle Sam's famous Excursion,' where the excursionists receive one hundred & fifty dollars in advance & are clothed & fed during the whole show."[63] A printer working in Massachusetts informed his parents in New Hampshire that he was going to join a nine-month company himself, citing reasons that were entirely personal. "It is the most favorable season of the year," he wrote, "the term is short, the bounty is ample, the draft is almost certain & may come at such a time that the conscripts will be in service during the hot weather & above all we are getting the very *best men* in town. Not a paddy or a nigger is received."[64]

The local bounties paid in the summer and autumn of 1862 paled in comparison to those offered after the middle of 1863, but the soldiers who took them encountered derision and contempt from the veterans, especially in the Army of the Potomac. John Pardington's 24th Michigan was among the reinforcements regarded as "bounty men" because of the private funds raised in Wayne County to entice them into uniform. A sergeant in the 2nd U.S. Sharpshooters sneered at the "big bounty men" as "no men at all," concluding after a few months' observation that "most of them came out just to get the bounty."[65] Those sentiments circulated a year and a half before the bounties reached their height, and the sting of such opprobrium lingered long after the war, prompting disingenuous denials in reminiscences published for popular consumption.[66]

Nor was that scorn confined to the eastern armies. Writing from Louisiana, an early Connecticut volunteer described great discouragement among his comrades because of the money and plaudits lavished on the later volunteers. Men who had not responded to the patriotic appeals of the previous year had to be smoked out of their holes like woodchucks by the threat of a draft, that soldier complained, after which they were "petted, praised, and paid a year's salary before they even start." It was "ridiculous to think of," concluded that disgusted veteran.[67]

One Illinois private recoiled at the very notion of paying any special reward for what he considered a citizen's duty, and a doomed Massachusetts cavalryman complained bitterly of the recruits who replenished his regiment—some of whom were so unfit they were discharged after a couple of months but still kept two or three hundred dollars in bounty. Even if they had been "good men," he wrote, "they have only 1/2 the time to serve and get twice the amount we do who have probably seen more hardships and done more than they will ever be called on to do." The bounties caused hard feelings between the men, he added, laying into the nine-month militia with particular venom.[68]

Envy of their abbreviated enlistments only amplified resentment toward the nine-month militia. A Massachusetts man who had been through the Peninsula Campaign lashed out at his community for such generosity to soldiers who would have been drafted if they had not volunteered; his townsmen pinched pennies when he enlisted, he fumed, and now they insulted him and his comrades by calling the nine-month militia "the best men in the state."[69] Joseph Spafford, a lieutenant in the last nine-month regiment from Vermont, felt the reproach keenly. Seven months into his service he complained to his sister that "all the three years men, & in fact many who are neither 3 years or 9 mos. men, but have staid at home, seem to have a kind of spite against the 9 mos. men. When have you or anyone else ever heard a good word spoken for them? The 3 years men say they have no patriotism, were *bought;* call them the *Pick Nic* party, etc."[70]

Associating army service with ready cash became reflexive by August. One Connecticut youth who was living and working with his brother-in-law returned from attending a recruiting rally in the nearby town when the brother-in-law accosted him to ask whether he had enlisted. "Did you get that money?" he wanted to know, in all eagerness.[71] When a Maine boy went off to the state capital to enlist, his father worried that he might not negotiate as good a deal as he could at home, but the son did well for himself. "I did not lose anything by enlisting here," he assured his father, reporting nearly a year's income from town, state, and federal bounties.[72]

Military service seemed so profitable by the second summer of the war, at least for those still without steady work, that some who answered the July and August calls felt compelled to assert that they had not done so for lack of employment. "Be assured I have not enlisted because I could not get work," insisted Myron Wood, a young Massachusetts man who had hired on with a Worcester County farmer for the hay harvest. Describing his employer's understandable agitation over his only hand abandoning him at so critical a period, Wood claimed that he might have gone to Connecticut and earned sixty dollars a month for the same work. Even if that assertion was not exaggerated, he joined the army as the haying season began winding down, when seasonal wage premiums were about to disappear.[73]

Another farm boy from Steuben County, New York, harbored a measure of national pride, especially when he heard rumblings of foreign intervention, but it was embarrassment and economics that started him thinking about donning a uniform. John D. Hill, then nineteen, had left home for a job a couple of towns away in an effort to earn some money for the family. He admitted to his sister that he began to feel ashamed as other young men started enlisting again in the Tioga River valley, but he harped most on the economic opportunity enlistment offered. He pointed out that if he and his older brother Alonzo both enlisted, they would immediately pocket more in bounty alone than he could "lay up" in an entire year, and he grew even more exuberant when he learned of the advance pay. Hill supposed they would be able to leave enough for their family to live on until they were paid—naïvely assuming that they would be compensated in timely fashion. "I am not making anything here to speak of," he confessed, "and Lon is not much better off."[74]

The chance to improve his lot, and perhaps escape an importuning wife and growing family, drove Daniel Hopper to join the army and make the most of it. Hopper owned little but his carpentry tools, and the market for such tradesmen had not improved markedly in Youngstown, Ohio, by the autumn of 1862. Much to the distress of his wife, Delina, he enlisted for $220 to serve as a substitute for a man liable to the militia draft, and he made further arrangements with the prospective captain of a cavalry company to bring in a few more recruits in return for a warrant. Hopper rode away as a sergeant, leaving Delina pregnant with their third child. Her pleading letters reveal his tendency to neglect her as he strove for advancement, withholding money while he banked his salary. Within a few months he earned a commission, ending the war as a first lieutenant with considerable savings, and by 1870 he enjoyed economic stability and a measure of comfort. Delina and most of the children were dead by then, but he lodged their surviving boy with her sister and began a second family with a child bride. For him, the army served as a bridge to prosperity, as he had apparently intended.[75]

One man who sought a commission to better himself regretted the decision immediately and unexpectedly because of the separation from his family. Ellsworth Phelps, a middle-aged Connecticut farmer who was poorer than a great many who enlisted as privates, had raised a company for the nine-month service and had become its captain. The other officers elected him lieutenant colonel. For all the unaccustomed compensation and personal connections of that office, after a couple of weeks away from his wife Phelps vowed that no inducement could persuade him to do it again. His promise implied that one of his significant reasons for joining the army had been "inducements," which usually served as a euphemism for financial and social advantages—and the financial and social gains that followed his service were significant.[76]

In distant corners of the Old Northwest, fortune had also escaped Louis Morrison. He had fared well enough as a bookkeeper in the mining country along Lake Superior, but like much of his generation he thirsted after commercial success, and—again like so many in his generation—therein lay his downfall. He must have been sufficiently familiar with accounting practices, but his judgment about investments may not have stood him in good stead, for one venture after another failed. The secession winter scuttled a mercantile enterprise he had undertaken in Minnesota, and he sent his wife and children to live with his in-laws in the East before forging back into his old haunts on Michigan's Upper Peninsula. There he bought an interest in some land, but a year of one disappointment after another ended with his resources dwindling and commerce still flat. What business opportunities he entertained required more capital than he had left. No one would buy his portion of the jointly owned land, even at substantial loss, and a partner declined to advance him a loan against his share. In desperation Morrison mortgaged some land he owned outright, producing enough cash to last through the summer of 1862. The remains of that money carried him across the Great Lakes early in the autumn, when he decided to rejoin his family, but the last of it ran out in Buffalo. Broke, overweight, and nearly forty-four years old, he joined a company of sharpshooters on the spot, sending his wife a portion of his federal advance and promising her the city bounty from Buffalo.[77]

The bounties for which such men enlisted signaled no insidious transformation in recruiting, as many then and later supposed. A lack of conspicuous cash incentives had simply disguised the economic motivation among the volunteers of 1861: their desperation had required little additional inducement beyond regular pay and rations, with some assistance for their families. The bounties that proliferated in the late summer of 1862 merely attracted those at the next level of economic need, after the army had exhausted its appeal to the poorest stratum of society.

Bruce Catton, the poet laureate of the Civil War centennial, excused the Army of the Potomac's disdain for the bounty men of 1862. He believed that the earliest volunteers of the war had come out with no mercenary intent, while the draft-era bounties infested the army with men whose principal aim had been "the acquisition of sudden wealth." Exactly one of those 1861 recruits was still alive when Catton described them as "volunteers in the purest sense of the word, men who had enlisted for no earthly reason except that they wanted to go to war, moved by that strange and deceiving light which can lie upon the world very briefly when one is young and innocent."[78] Innocence had indeed afflicted most of those 1861 volunteers. Huge numbers of them had also suffered from acute financial distress, and many of them had enlisted for reasons not so different from those that brought the first bounty men of 1862, whom some of them now jeered.

7

SOLDIERS OF MISFORTUNE, 1862–1863

Paying off debt remained a common theme in soldiers' correspondence throughout the war. When the new quartermaster of an Indiana regiment sent home six months' accumulated pay his wife retired their account at the local store, but other obligations remained for her to juggle while she instantly incurred new ones. A young tenant farmer just east of Indianapolis used his enlistment bounty to pay some of his debts, then sold his livestock to pay more, and depended on an older brother to manage the pay he sent home for the benefit of his teenaged wife. A Vermont man in his mid-forties tried to save his farm with an infusion of bounty money, leaving his youngest son in charge of the family finances, but within a few months he had to coax the boy into selling their cattle to reduce their debt further. Another Vermonter of the same generation, in similar financial straits, also pared his farm debt by enlisting, and as soon as his oldest son turned eighteen he enlisted, too, collecting an even bigger bounty than his father had. With that, their monthly wages, and Vermont's seven-dollar stipend, the father presumed they could "pay the dept right alonge." Two brothers from Sudbury, Massachusetts, enlisted together when their father was declared an insolvent debtor and his property was seized for auction, after which they sent their pay home to keep the rest of the family fed.[1]

From the first beat of the drum in 1861, droves of men had entered the army saddled with debt that they hoped they could retire on their monthly pay. That phenomenon had abated somewhat as military mobilization and war-induced industrial recovery shrank the ranks of the unemployed, but inflation-driven depletion of real wages again augmented the number of insolvent recruits by the end of 1862. Some of them offered endless, solemn promises of eventual payment to those they owed money, in the perennial way of reflexive deadbeats; others begged for patience as they chipped away at their obligations, especially when they involved mortgages on a house or farm; still others ignored anyone they owed money, relying defiantly on the stay laws that protected soldiers in several states from debt collection and foreclosure. Those laws appear to have been the primary reason a good many deeply indebted men enlisted in the first place, and they would simply bid their wives not to pay either taxes or bills. That practice only discouraged potential lenders from advancing money to soldiers' families—or even to men who might thereafter be drafted—and one doctor in Indiana refused medicine to the wife of a soldier unless she paid in advance. In their letters home, men in such circumstances burdened their kin with little or no patriotic discourse, usually opting instead to offer guidance in balancing family expenses and encumbrances.[2]

Many of those who had resorted to military service as a solution to financial distress met with prompt disappointment. Through the autumn of 1862 and the succeeding winter, the newest Union soldiers learned that the U.S. government did not attend to its obligations with the same prompt compliance that it now demanded of its citizens. Army pay came due only at the end of even-numbered months, and the actual payment of the accrued wages had almost always been slow; many of the three-month soldiers of 1861 had been forced to wait until they were mustered out for any compensation at all because paymasters often lagged at least a month behind. By the second year of the war, that backlog had grown much longer. Some of those who enlisted in August of 1862 drew two months' pay late in November, but at the end of January, 1863, most were still waiting, wondering if they were ever going to be paid. Six months of accumulated arrearages became fairly common, and a wait of eight or even ten months was not unknown. One New York regiment raised during the summer of 1862 indignantly refused payment of less than a quarter of the nearly seven months' pay it was due late in March, and a Connecticut regiment organized in the fall saw no pay until the first week of May. Such administrative negligence inconvenienced even officers, and prevented recruits from giving their wives the cash they needed for winter supplies. Soldiers with needy families were forced to borrow at interest, take on additional duties for comrades, seek special details that brought extra pay, or try their luck in speculation.[3]

If a soldier went to the hospital for sickness or wounds or fell into enemy hands, or if there were the slightest discrepancy in the descriptive list that served as individual identification, his pay would be held up until the next time he saw a paymaster. If he was sent to another unit and his records failed to follow, as often happened, he might be left penniless for months at a time. An older Connecticut soldier whose pay fell months behind by the spring of 1863 was transferred to the Veteran Reserve Corps not long afterward and had to spend most of 1864 trying to convince the pay bureau that he still existed. Only after writing directly to President Lincoln did he finally collect, just before the end of his enlistment.[4]

The problem persisted throughout the war. Men who had calculated that their families could survive on their monthly pay and the support their communities promised discovered early how bad a bargain they had made. Morale plummeted as husbands and fathers learned of the privations their loved ones were suffering at home, with food short and eviction imminent. At one critical juncture, when a sizable force of Confederates threatened the suburbs of Washington, long-unpaid troops striding through the city to confront the threat bellowed angrily for "greenbacks" as they passed the Treasury Department.[5]

Much of the problem lay with the unanticipated expense inherent in the duration of the war, for contractors might refuse further matériel if they were not paid, but soldiers could only withhold their services on pain of death, for desertion or mutiny. When the House of Representatives responded to furious demands for soldiers' pay at the beginning of 1863, Treasury Secretary Salmon P. Chase reported that the arrearages amounted to $60 million, while he had only one-fifth of that amount available unless he dumped government bonds for cash at heavy discounts. The Treasury collected about half a million dollars a day that the War Department allocated to paying the men, but at that rate it would take another four months to pay off what was then due. Congress finally passed a joint resolution insisting that the army and navy be paid up to date immediately, authorizing the issuance of more federal bonds and the printing of another $100 million in currency for the purpose. By late April of 1863 the last of the overdue pay had been issued, and early in May Chase reported that all the government's outstanding debts had been met, although that was no longer true: on April 30 another two months' pay had come due, and soldiers did not fail to notice that sly timing. At the end of August Chase was already begging for another $25 million to meet the army's payroll.[6]

Soldiers also wondered whether they would receive the $100 federal discharge bonus after newspapers reported that it would only be paid to those who completed at least two years of their enlistments. One wounded Maine man, the father of a large family, expected to be discharged before that time limit, and he had seen so many of the army's promises broken that he assumed this one would be, too. A Pennsylvania widow had not received any of her husband's bonus sixteen months after he was killed, despite all the expense she had incurred submitting affidavits, and it took her congressman's intercession to get it for her. Enlisted men who earned commissions were often denied that discharge benefit, and some were asked to repay the advance portion they had received at enlistment. An Indiana sergeant who won promotion to lieutenant had to wait nearly a quarter of a century after his discharge before his persistent appeals for that money were rewarded by a check issued in badly inflated dollars, minus ten dollars for attorney's fees.[7]

After men had mustered in to the credit of their town and county quotas, and could not back out, municipal governments often held back their promised bounties so long that anxious recipients supposed they had been swindled. Sometimes local officials did cheat men out of town bounties, and in Vermont one soldier had to nag his wife about chasing down their selectmen. After waiting fourteen months for his town bounty, another Vermonter hired a lawyer to shake it out of the town fathers.[8]

With the advent of those local bounties, spontaneous community generosity toward the soldiers' families began to fade too, and voluntary relief funds proved increasingly unreliable in states lacking statutory provisions for family support. An Indiana harness maker who had depended on a county fund to assist his wife and three little daughters indignantly observed more than a year and a half later that not a dollar had been paid from the fund, besides which his pay was again long overdue. Promises of regular pay and family support from the moment of signing the roll routinely went by the boards, and soldiers often had to guide their womenfolk through the bureaucratic details of collecting what they were due, with a letter to the governor as a last resort. The failure and refusal of supplementary income from the state or community aroused something approaching rage among men who, as a Massachusetts soldier frankly acknowledged, would never have enlisted without expecting that additional money.[9]

Even when the paymaster arrived in good season, many a man who had just signed three years of his life away came to the grim realization that his pay might be insufficient for his own purposes, let alone leave enough to send home. Army rations ranged between bland and revolting, and they were not always issued with the regularity everyone had assumed: one Pennsylvanian who may have enlisted hoping to support his widowed mother and younger siblings instead had to write home for money after spending all his pay buying palatable food. A Maine youth warned his brother-in-law, who was contemplating enlisting, how quickly he would tire of a constant diet of beef, coffee, and cold bread without butter. Most men were accustomed to an ascetic diet and stood commissary fare well enough, but the more epicurean soldier's entire pay might not be sufficient to keep him in food he could bear to eat. "I have not had a decent meal of victuals since I left N.Y.," complained a Granite State soldier in Louisiana, "only what I bought."[10]

Clothing and equipment drained off much of the soldier's pay too, despite the highly touted clothing allowance. It came as a great shock, usually on the payday at the end of the first calendar year of service, to learn that the entire initial uniform would be deducted from the forty-two-dollar annual clothing allowance, consuming most of it. Men who had been issued flimsy shoes that they traded off for fifty cents or a dollar before buying sturdier footgear seethed to learn that they had been charged nearly two dollars for such shoddy. Having to pay for that first issue aggravated men particularly when they were forced to abandon perfectly good clothing, as happened in the 4th Michigan. Like many Union regiments organized early in the war, that one had left home in gray uniforms that officers eventually required everyone to discard because they looked "too Secesh," and the men had to pay for that decision.[11]

The two U.S. Sharpshooter regiments in the Army of the Potomac originally wore forest-green uniforms, but regulation blue gradually replaced them until one regiment's colonel required his men to draw costly new green apparel at their own expense. Whole regiments occasionally lost winter clothing when the men were ordered to pack it up for shipment back to Washington by the Quartermaster Department, which often managed to misplace everything. Perhaps most infuriating, and most unfair, was the frequent requirement that men who had lost arms, clothing, or equipment in battle bear the cost of replacing whatever they lacked through the quartermaster. All but the most economical soldiers bridled when they learned how little money remained (or how much they still owed) after deducting their clothing and equipment.[12]

The sutler also extracted his mite each payday from those soldiers impulsive or desperate enough to patronize his varied but overpriced stock. These peddlers were assigned the monopoly of selling goods to a specific regiment when it lay in camp; sometimes they followed it on the march, too, always offering credit but standing beside the paymaster every payday to collect on their accounts. They filled their wagons with an array of merchandise that might include clothing, footgear, canned food, jellies, fresh fruit and vegetables, notions, tobacco, gambling materials, and usually whiskey to sell to the officers. The profits could be enormous, and enterprising former soldiers occasionally took up the trade themselves. When rations fell short or monotonous, the sutler supplied the missing ingredients of the domestic table—asking several times the home-front price for moldy cheese or butter that was nearly rancid, and perhaps skimping on the weight as well. When they gave change for cash, it might be in discounted state currency. Now and then the treats and comforts they offered looked suspiciously like the goods sent by the Sanitary Commission for free distribution to soldiers. A judicious sutler might hire a soldier to drive an extra wagon and watch the store while he made a trip to the rear to replenish his inventory. At least one sutler teamed up with the regimental commissary sergeant, who drove for him, provided added security, and contributed government supplies of ham, tea, beef, coffee, sugar, and bread to his larder.[13]

The profit motive was hardly limited to poor enlisted men. Quartermasters often engaged in shady dealings with government stores or vouchers, sometimes in collusion with senior officers determined to gain from military service. The lieutenant colonel of the 10th Vermont, himself a patent-medicine merchant who had once sold his elixir to soldiers in camp, lent money to his sutler but kept the arrangement secret. Sutlers were the most conspicuous of innumerable profiteers who made it their business to fleece soldiers, and it would not do for the rank and file to know that their executive officer benefited from their exploitation.[14]

Despite earning so much more money, some officers found they could save little. Before the war ended, the price of officers' uniforms had risen enough to spawn complaints in the field grades, and the cost of personal servants ate deeper into their income as the war progressed. Regulations allowed for one civilian servant to maintain an officer's clothing, care for his horse, set up his tent, and prepare his meals. Commissioned officers could not draw food from the commissary if they collected ration-commutation money, and keeping their own mess meant having someone to cook for them. An enlisted man could be assigned if no civilian servants were available, but to discourage that practice the War Department started charging the officer for that man's pay, allowances, and rations, which might come to seventy-five dollars a month. Subalterns of the class one aristocratic lieutenant characterized as "the common farmer sort" did without a servant, letting their crisp blue uniforms turn a "dowdy green" to save money. That snobbish lieutenant, whose family needed nothing, predictably expressed dismay at how much of his own pay he spent.[15]

Lieutenant George Kies does not appear to have kept a servant while his regiment occupied one of the forts in Baltimore Harbor, but he sent his wife only thirty dollars per month and expected her to support herself and their son on that amount. That was more than most enlisted men's wives could expect between their husbands' excess pay and public subsidies, but it was less than a third of a lieutenant's income. Mrs. Kies heard rumors that her husband was spending some of his money on another woman, which he vehemently denied, but her grievances prompted a sudden spasm of generosity from him and the promise of an increased allowance.[16]

George Chittenden, an Indiana surgeon, had expected to earn enough money to finally buy a home for his family, but after two and a half years that hope had fled. When he admitted that he could make no money in the army, his wife let slip the extent of her despair after exercising "the closest economy" for so long. Dismissing his latest scheme of resigning and moving on to more promising surroundings, she wrote that she had given up dreaming after seeing "so many 'palaces' crumble."[17]

Greenbacks, with which soldiers were usually paid, were only worth fifty-three cents on the dollar in gold during the winter of 1863, requiring a premium of nearly 90 percent for conversion to specie. They recovered that summer, after Gettysburg and Vicksburg (a merchant in Union-held New Orleans reported the premium for gold as only 55 percent even before that rise), but with military deadlock a year later paper money dropped to forty cents on the dollar. A navy surgeon who had accumulated sizable savings in two years worried that his family would no longer be able to subsist on his salary because prices were rising so fast. To counteract that vulnerability, he let his savings out at 6 percent, some of it redeemable in gold, in hopes of building up an additional cushion for after the war, when he expected prices to come back down. He supposed the government would stop issuing more currency then, allowing its value to rise, and hoped that would give him something to live on after his inevitable discharge.[18]

The wife of a private soldier might have cast a sardonic sneer at the inability of any couple to thrive on eight or ten times the income her own husband earned. Mothers who tried to feed their children on three dollars a week and took in piecework to buy them winter clothing would have found it difficult to sympathize with someone whose worst complaint consisted of living in a rented house—or having to borrow several hundred dollars from a bank to buy furniture, using government bonds as security until her husband's pay came through. The plight of the women and children left behind by enlisted men more often came down to a choice between buying medicine or food—or selling the family dog. A Vermont housewife asked her pained husband if she might shoot his dog, so she could avoid paying a new town dog tax imposed to help cover the cost of bounties.[19]

Captains of companies and field officers in command of regiments devoted so much of their time to their duties that they usually had to bear the expense of a servant, but lieutenants of an economical bent could put away substantial sums. "Officers are in many respects a privileged class," remarked a Michigan hospital steward who had just been elevated to lieutenant, adding that the promotion had also brought him a very attractive salary. His initial outfit would cost $75, he admitted. In ignorance of the War Department policy of reclaiming the federal discharge bonus from men who won commissions, he expected the remainder of his bonus to cover the cost of the uniform, but even without that he had the chance to accumulate an enviable stake for the future: with his rations commuted to cash, a lieutenant earned $129.83 per month, and an extra $10.00 if he commanded a company. An 1862 Iowa volunteer who rose from second lieutenant to captain during the war came home to $3,100 in government "five-twenty" bonds that his parents had bought with his pay, and a Maine captain nearly tripled his net worth during the war. Less than halfway through his service, a lieutenant in the 6th Vermont was already calculating his first $1,000 in savings; the commander of the 10th Vermont accumulated $8,900 in under two years, and most of it before he was promoted to colonel.[20]

Men in the ranks occasionally cursed themselves for having come into the army at the pay of a private, especially with all the menial labor and misery that fell to their lot. The most they could hope for, short of extensive attrition in their companies, was a warrant as corporal or sergeant, with precious little more money and no additional comfort. Even men who grew to feel that the army was the best they could do lusted after a commission, while the educated and talented saw no sense in accepting anything less.[21] A Dartmouth-educated schoolteacher in Iowa avoided service altogether until late in the third year of the war, but as conscription closed in on his community he secured a commission as commissary for the 11th Missouri Cavalry; in so sheltered a position, he reasoned, "I might thus serve the country better, with more of honor and profit to myself."[22]

The pay and privileges of commissioned officers seemed so enviable to enlisted men that many in the ranks believed the men wearing shoulder straps would be happy to see the war continue indefinitely. Officers absent from their commands on business, on leave, or on parole crowded Washington City, lounging in the hotel bars, visiting their congressmen, and pestering the Paymaster's Bureau. A Regular Army captain opined that many of the young lieutenants recently appointed by the president "didn't come into the service except to draw their pay." Junior officers often felt the same about the field officers and generals, and indeed the generous income remained a significant incentive for some career officers. Less than a fortnight after Fort Sumter, future brigadier general William Brooks considered retiring if he could find a means of supporting himself, and that sentiment was not uncommon among conservative professional soldiers. "If I could see my way clear for making a decent living," wrote Major General William Franklin two years into the war, "I would resign to-morrow."[23] Lewis Fales, the brother of a nine-month man serving in the Gulf Department, told him it was believed throughout their community "that if the Officers were not making so much mony there would be more energy displayed by them in bringing the war to a close." So thought an unlettered New Hampshire private serving along the Potomac, who assured his sister that "if it was knot for the big pay that the ofices have this war wood vary soon come to close."[24] "This is a war of shoulder straps and money to the officers," wrote a middle-aged farmer from New York's Delaware River valley, "and not to put down the rebellion."[25]

Nearly everyone of all ranks in the army, meanwhile, believed fervently in the mercenary motives of the politicians and other civilians who seemed to be profiting from the conflict. An engineer lieutenant with one of the western armies revealed that suspicion to his wife, recognizing the opportunities for speculation and expressing his hope that "the war will soon be conducted by men who want to get through with it and not to make money out of it."[26]

Officers of Wisconsin's only nine-month regiment, which was raised largely by draft, begged to have it ordered south because it was hemorrhaging deserters—lest the regiment should be disbanded and their salaries end. The monthly pay in any commissioned grade appealed tremendously to all former laborers, and to those professionals in law or medicine who had not seen particular success in their civil endeavors. One captain thought the majority of surgeons had joined the army because their civilian practices were flagging, and much surviving correspondence sustains his opinion. A private observed that "monney is all that they care for."[27]

It was chaplains, however, who were most frequently accused of seeking commissions because it was the only way they could earn a living. Perhaps betraying denominational disdain, the son of a Methodist minister concluded, after hearing a brief and unsatisfactory sermon from Unitarian Daniel Foster of the 33rd Massachusetts, that chaplains were "a class of men that could not get employment at home." He supposed that such clergymen secured their appointments by means of "underhanded work."[28]

Occasionally a chaplain would earn the respect of his men, particularly if he joined them in battle. Veterans of the 12th New Hampshire always revered Chaplain Thomas Ambrose, who was captured at Chancellorsville while tending their wounded and was killed in the trenches at Petersburg the next year. Chaplain Joseph Lovering followed the 17th Maine to Appomattox, helping amputate limbs on the battlefield, but men like these were not common to the position. More often chaplains were described loitering about the post hospitals, where the more conscientious might tend the sick or write to the family of a soldier who died, and if a chaplain was mentioned in a letter home it was not usually in a positive light.[29]

A man in the 8th New Hampshire refuted a newspaper assertion that his regimental chaplain was well liked. "I have yet to meet the first man that does like him," that soldier informed his wife.[30] An officer in the 2nd New Hampshire suspected his chaplain and regimental surgeon of conspiring to steal delicacies and comfort items sent by the Sanitary Commission for the benefit of sick soldiers. When the chaplain of the 27th Indiana went home on furlough, a lieutenant remarked that he was not much missed, for he had been of little use and had not preached a dozen times in a year and a half: the officer judged him "the worst 'bore' we have."[31]

A Massachusetts corporal in New Orleans attended a Catholic mass conducted in Latin that made as much sense to him as the sermons preached by his chaplain, George Sanger, whom he described as "a fat, lazy man" prone to cards and alcohol.[32] Other soldiers criticized their chaplains' doctrinal narrowness, their neglect of duty, or their consumption of the tastiest Sanitary Commission delicacies.[33] On the eve of William Sherman's Atlanta Campaign, a Massachusetts captain complained that the division chaplains gathered for a religious meeting near his quarters and "kept up a dismal howling far into the night."[34] A couple of months later a major from Massachusetts who had spent more than three years in the service told a party of Boston Brahmins that he was "entirely down on" chaplains and had never heard of a good one. He, too, insisted that the army received "only poor specimens, who couldn't get settled at home."[35]

Rarely, a chaplain who had displeased his captive flock might win them back. A Connecticut captain recorded a delegation of officers from his regiment reproving their new chaplain, John Morris, for his nosy intercession into the men's choices of recreation, warning him that he had better mend his ways if he wished to remain. Sixteen weeks later the same critic had become Morris's champion, describing his courage in helping bring off the wounded at Antietam, where he was among the last to leave the field and was slightly wounded himself. "All praise to him this time," concluded the captain. All too often, though, the men who wore the black coats and crosses on their epaulettes fit the description offered by the cynical newspaper correspondent Franc Wilkie: "clergymen with unappreciative parishes, small incomes, and unsympathetic social environments."[36]

Occasionally a miscreant chaplain might face court-martial, as did one in the renowned Iron Brigade. James Richmond, a fifty-two-year-old Episcopal priest with a contentious past in the church hierarchy, had left a large family in New York and moved to Milwaukee just before the war. He signed on as chaplain for the 2nd Wisconsin, but early in 1862 he was brought up on charges of neglect of duty, conduct prejudicial to good order (specifically through heavy drinking), and for signing a false certificate. Perhaps he simply gave up and went home without waiting for trial, for his name was dropped from the rolls of the regiment the following May like that of a common deserter. As though his bad example had soured the regiment on the very idea of a spiritual advisor, his place was never filled by anyone else. Back in New York, Richmond obtained another volunteer appointment as a hospital chaplain.[37]

Supply officers had abundant opportunity for personal gain, and often made the most of it, as though handsome profits had been their purpose in obtaining their appointments. Early in 1862 a War Department investigator reported extensive quartermaster fraud along the Ohio River, charging much of it to Major Reuben Hatch, the brother of Abraham Lincoln's old friend Ozias Hatch. The president had commissioned Hatch in July of 1861, and testimony indicated that the major had been bilking the government ever since. General Grant, who commanded in that sector, had Hatch arrested and planned to prosecute him for "great frauds," but—against the explicit advice of the army's judge advocate—Lincoln appointed a friendly commission that authorized all of Hatch's expenditures. The major retained his position and won promotion, but the war did not end without his name coming up in conjunction with the tragic explosion of the steamboat *Sultana,* the overcrowding of which bore a hint of corruption.[38]

Early in 1863 Lewis Fales specifically told his soldier-brother about an army quartermaster of his acquaintance who boasted that he had already made $2,000 from the service, and that his potential profits only increased the longer the war lasted. Quartermasters and commissaries could skim small fortunes from the goods that passed through their hands, and court-martial records demonstrate that for many the temptation shone too brightly to resist. Republican newspapermen were often rewarded with quartermaster appointments, as Francis Hurtt of the *Ohio State Journal* was, but the administration could not save him when Hurtt bought a luxurious house for $12,500 cash on his $1,200 salary. Hostile editors who had long suspected Hurtt's peculations quipped that either the newspaper or the quartermaster business seemed extraordinarily profitable, and a court-martial led to his dismissal from the army. About the same time, evidence of a costly fraud in the sale of mules came to light in the Quartermaster Department at Louisville. A few months later a pair of quartermasters outside Washington were caught participating in a broader conspiracy to defraud the government in grain purchases, in which their share alone came to $31,000 in five-twenty bonds. Such dishonesty permeated the system. When the judge advocate general and secretary of war wanted to squeeze government contractors for Republican campaign funds, army quartermasters advised them on the most undetectable means of extortion; no less a personage than a department commander collected the kickbacks for them.[39]

Profits from the supply departments sometimes trickled down to knowing enlisted men, too. In 1862 William Bradbury, a British immigrant, abandoned a failing business and an untrustworthy business partner to enlist in an Illinois regiment. He assured his wife that he would soon obtain a field commission or an appointment as a staff officer, but promotion never came, and instead he took the post of company clerk. He supported his family with extra money earned through illicit arrangements with successive quartermasters and commissaries, with whom he shared a hefty portion of civilian clerking salaries that he was not supposed to receive. Later he sold letters describing affairs in Tennessee to an assortment of newspapers in the North. He finished the war as an official stenographer, and all the while collected his regular army pay and those additional stipends, legitimate or otherwise, making more money than he had earned at home. That, rather than any service to his adopted country, appears to have been his principal aim.[40]

Soldiers in the Army of the Potomac thought their quartermasters particularly corrupt, which perhaps reflected an ethos percolating from the top. Rufus Ingalls, a native of Denmark, Maine, had been a quartermaster since 1848 and served as chief quartermaster of the Army of the Potomac during most of its existence. The provost marshal general of that army frowned on Ingalls for what he considered questionable practices, especially in connection with sutlers of dubious ethics. Corporal James Brown of Brownfield, Maine, bordering Denmark, informed his brother that Ingalls had gotten at least three of their common neighbors in the Bean family appointed to lucrative positions in the department: Sylvanus and Eli Bean both had commissions as assistant quartermasters, while their youngest brother, Charlie, was serving as a wagon master with the supply trains, with "big pay." Sylvanus also had his teenaged son along "as a sort of orderlie for himself," and Brown said the boy was "drawing his 13 dollars a month with nothing to do." The Beans were bound to get rich out of the war, predicted their knowing townsman, who added wryly that it was a pity their father was too old to come out and "help the Boys to plunder uncle Sam" because "he would be the bigest thief of them all."[41]

A position in the supply departments was not absolutely necessary to milk supplementary income from the system. Officers from the company level to corps command exploited the unsettled conditions in Confederate territory for their own profit, and they enjoyed the collaboration of colleagues all along the lines of communication. Cotton offered the most reliable return, although the trade itself sometimes led participants into trouble with functionaries who were antagonistic to that underground market—or envious of its profit margin. The Southern embargo on cotton sales had steadily increased the price from its antebellum level of between nine and thirteen cents a pound until, two years into the war, it was selling for ninety-five cents in New York. Plunder of cotton was rampant on the lower Mississippi and its tributaries by late 1862, and Andrew Johnson, the military governor of Tennessee, believed that the Army of the Cumberland remained inactive during the summer of 1863 to glean such riches from the countryside. The military governor of Arkansas, John Phelps, suspected the same of Samuel Curtis, commander of Union forces west of the Mississippi, whom he accused of coveting the cotton stockpiled at Helena. Phelps further charged that Alvin Hovey, one of General Curtis's division commanders, was trading men from the contraband camps back into slavery in return for cotton at the rate of two per bale.[42]

Testimony from the ranks corroborates some of those accusations. Soldiers in the Trans-Mississippi took it for granted that their generals were growing rich by sending north the cotton they had either stolen or bought dirt cheap, and Hovey's exchange of cotton for once-and-future slaves was widely credited. A sergeant in the 29th Wisconsin, part of Hovey's division, denounced the generals for profiteering in cotton while men died, and a private in that regiment specifically described a nighttime raid in which the captain of one company stole cotton and destroyed the property of landowners who resisted. When speculating officers did not wrest the cotton by force, they often took it at bargain rates—usually less than twenty-five cents a pound—as payment for salt, fabrics, or other trade goods for which they charged outrageous prices, sending the bartered bales up to Cairo, where they brought at least twice as much per pound.[43] The provost marshal at Keokuk, Iowa, found that soldiers returning from service on the lower Mississippi harbored "an almost universal feeling of bitterness from the conviction that they have been, and are, used principally for the benefit of cotton speculators, officers, and outsiders."[44]

The states east of the Rockies had completed all their new infantry regiments under the levies of July and August by the first day of 1863, and the lucrative local bounty offers expired once those quotas had been satisfied. With the financial inducements reduced to the federal bounties, state bounties, and state or local family aid, recruiting diminished to a trickle of men joining the Regular Army or existing volunteer regiments. Moreover, the unprecedented bloodshed of 1862 had sharply curbed the impulsiveness of patriots and adventurers. From Fort Donelson and Shiloh to Fredericksburg and Stone's River, at least twenty thousand Union soldiers had been killed on the battlefield or died of wounds, and that many or more had survived, visibly or psychologically maimed, to come home and illustrate the brutality of the fighting. Few had not seen the empty sleeves and the missing legs, read letters describing horrible wounds, or heard of the veterans' raving dreams. Too many had watched sons, husbands, brothers, and friends march off, only to die in battle or camp. The picture-book war had lost its luster.[45]

The president's announcement of his Emancipation Proclamation in the wake of Antietam likewise cooled the fervor of conservatives who had approved of a war to preserve the Union. Thousands of such men had enlisted during the summer and autumn, only to feel that they had been tricked into fighting the abolitionists' war for them. A few days after the proclamation appeared in print, declaring all slaves free in rebellious territory on January 1, 1863, a New Hampshire recruit suddenly wondered what he was fighting for—adding that there were few abolitionists in the Army of the Potomac. Fitz John Porter, the commander of the Fifth Corps and General McClellan's most trusted lieutenant, reported that the president's announcement "was ridiculed in the army," provoking "disgust, discontent, and expressions of disloyalty . . . amounting . . . to insubordination."[46] The son of abolitionists commanding a company in a Massachusetts regiment confirmed that he and his colleagues met the proclamation with "universal disgust." Nor were there many abolitionists in other Federal armies, if the bitter commentary coming home from the various fronts reflected the general feeling.[47]

Economics also contributed to the lethargy in volunteering. Business and agriculture had recovered substantially since the recruiting delirium of 1861. Joel Fales, a cabinetmaker in South Dedham, Massachusetts, wrote that business of all kinds was "quite brisk." Over the winter his brother Lewis, an architect in nearby Milford, drew plans for a house he estimated would cost $18,000 because of rising materials prices: he supposed those prices would discourage construction in 1863, but both brothers were surprised to find the economy booming as that year progressed. Joel remarked that the boot business was "never better," but he could not understand why: the army could not make such a difference, he reasoned, because "they would all wear boots at home." He seemed not to consider that soldiers would wear their shoes and boots out faster than civilians.[48]

In the West, where the price of wheat served as a barometer for agricultural health, the pessimism and uncertainty of 1861 had given way to boom times. Wheat had been selling for forty to fifty cents a bushel on the prairie in the winter of 1861, and the best price that year had come along the wharves of the Mississippi River in late April—where, very briefly, the best quality brought about seventy cents. In 1862 the price had dropped back to fifty-five and sixty cents, and Iowa growers found grain prices mixed, but Minneapolis entrepreneur Peter Wolford assured his brother that business was "brightening up" in the region. By late January of 1863, wheat was up to eighty cents in Minnesota, and it would rise to ninety-three cents in Indiana by August, with other grains rising apace, while hay cost $12 to $14 a ton. Land had appreciated tremendously as well, and Wolford sold forty acres of prairie for $1,500, throwing that money and more into another land purchase so vast that he could not estimate how many thousands of acres it entailed. His only complaint involved the widespread availability of money, which prevented him from lending out his growing fortune for any more than a hefty 12-percent interest.[49]

Despite the high price of wheat, many farmers had gone deeply into debt to men like Wolford, both for land and farm equipment, and they were still struggling. Two brothers from Vermont who settled in southeastern Minnesota to farm and operate a tavern and stable faced daunting debts; one of them had to sell off 160 acres to meet some of them, while the other could not afford harvest help. In New England the rate of pay for laborers had jumped 20 percent by the beginning of 1863, and work could be found with ease, but the cost of living had far outstripped compensation. Elsewhere there was more work than within recent memory, and fewer people to do it. In the Ohio and Mississippi River valleys, unoccupied common laborers had grown scarce, especially in farm country, but the cost of essentials was still soaring beyond the reach of wages. If the price of wheat measured the health of agriculture in the West, the price of butter seemed to indicate how much money was worth everywhere: it was selling for eight or ten cents a pound in Minnesota at the start of 1862 but bounded to twenty cents a pound toward the end of the year in Sheffield, Ohio.[50]

Such increases reflected an alarming general inflation, and at about the same time an artilleryman's wife in western New York underscored that "*Prices are ruinous,*" while a man north of Boston offered specifics: coal had risen to eight dollars a ton, wood to eight dollars a cord, and rum to ninety cents a gallon, while tobacco was "god dam dear" at ninety cents a pound.[51] By March of 1863 butter was up to thirty cents a pound in Massachusetts, and early in 1864 it quickly escalated to sixty-five cents a pound in New York before settling back down to thirty-five. Prices for most items rose and fell in parabolic fashion, depending on military fortunes or political news, but an upward trend predominated until well into the fourth year of the war; the congressional decision to print more money for paying the troops only increased that trajectory. The firewood that seemed so expensive at six dollars and eight dollars a cord in the fall of 1862 was selling for twelve dollars early in 1863. The gallon of rum that went for ninety cents in 1862 cost two dollars by the spring of 1864.[52]

Far worse were the prices soldiers had to pay to sutlers, local farmers, or peddlers around the army camps: butter began at thirty-eight cents there, and after several great leaps reached a dollar a pound. The men routinely gauged the value of a dollar in camp as half what it would have been at home, but that resulted less from the predictable result of production costs or an oversupply of currency than from sporadic, opportunistic gouging. Perhaps no soldier paid more for the emblematic commodity of butter than a Vermont colonel did while following Lee's army back from Gettysburg, when Pennsylvania farmers extorted every cent they could get from their protectors. The colonel had to give one greedy householder a dollar for eighteen "miserable" biscuits smaller than a pocket watch, and he paid seventy-five cents for half a pound of poor-quality butter. A New York lad began a letter home with the indignant announcement that he had been forced to give five cents—nearly one-eighth of a day's pay—for the sheet on which he wrote. A few months later a Delaware private suffering from the common nicotine addiction had to pay three dollars for a plug of tobacco as his regiment skirted the heart of Virginia's tobacco region.[53]

While the soldiers suffered from the avarice of vendors who held an unfair advantage, their families at home had become victims of the greenback phenomenon. Less than a year into the war, Congress had established a national currency, commonly called "greenbacks" for the ink on the reverse of the notes, and the enabling legislation had assured that it would depreciate from its very inception. Originally the currency had been intended as legal tender for paying all debts, public and private, but New York bankers had objected to taking it in payment of the interest on government bonds, for which they wanted gold coin. They had prevailed on the Senate to amend the bill to exempt interest on the national debt from the legal-tender clause, and that had precipitated a populist battle in the House of Representatives. Some congressmen objected that the soldiers who were putting their lives on the line would be paid in that depreciating medium, but bankers whose only risk consisted of lending money would collect the gold premium. Thaddeus Stevens of Pennsylvania remarked that the bill created one class of money for bankers and another for the people. The bill and its obnoxious revision nevertheless passed late in February of 1862, and by early August greenbacks had depreciated badly enough to weigh heavily against foreign exchange and crimp international trade.[54]

In reducing real wages on the home front, rampant inflation could theoretically have enhanced recruiting, if only by encouraging enlistment as a means of obtaining the basic necessities. That may have brought a few footloose young men into the army after the frenzied, draft-induced recruiting drives ended at the close of 1862, but army pay and provender alone appealed little thereafter to those with families to support. Without bounties as a supplement, the most tightfisted army private could no longer send home enough money to provide for a wife or parent, even with regular community support at the levels then current. That tended to reduce the pool of willing recruits to two basic types: desperate loners and drifters, or eager patriots whose families could fend for themselves. Nearly two years of bloody warfare had sharply reduced the number of both types in the civilian population.

Those who were looking far enough ahead could see that Union manpower needs were still growing at the beginning of 1863. In May and June nearly three dozen regiments of volunteers would be going home from the eastern armies, having reached the end of the two-year enlistments that the War Department had reluctantly accepted in 1861. By the time the last of the two-year men were gone, scores of nine-month regiments would have begun mustering out, and those men had seen just enough of the army's worst conditions and treatment to deter a majority of them from reenlisting, even if they had not endured combat. Those discharges would severely reduce the strength of both the Army of the Potomac and the Army of the Gulf, operating on the lower Mississippi.

As a solution to that impending reduction, Senator Henry Wilson introduced a bill for outright national conscription, bypassing the state militias and drawing citizens directly into the national "volunteer" force for three years. It passed both houses late in February, 1863, with amendments providing for the hiring of substitutes, a flurry of exemptions, and a clause for commuting personal service to a cash contribution that would become the primary target of the law's opponents. In this context commutation entailed the drafted man paying a fee, set finally at three hundred dollars, which bought him freedom from that particular draft levy. If his name were drawn in a subsequent call, he would either have to pay the fee again, hire a substitute who would exempt him for three years, or take up a musket himself.[55]

Proponents of commutation contended that it would keep the cost of substitutes down by offering an affordable alternative, and the law provided a pool of teenagers as substitutes by setting the minimum draft age at twenty; the War Department decided that even minors would be acceptable, with parental consent. If a draftee could be excused for three hundred dollars, substitutes would have to compete with that price, and some congressmen who did not calculate the added benefit of a three-year exemption assumed that a substitute would have to accept less than the commutation fee. Even if that had been correct, three hundred dollars still represented most of the average laborer's annual wages, notwithstanding wartime increases. From the day it was announced, critics assailed commutation as protection for the wealthy, who could easily afford the fee if no substitutes were available. A Massachusetts lieutenant thought it an "outrageous" provision that left "only the poor to fight," and it became the foundation of the claim that the war was "a poor man's fight."[56]

The law did not clearly explain the extent of exemption allowed by the fee. Section 13 implied that commutation and hiring a substitute both relieved draftees from reporting under "that draft," which suggested that they would be liable again under any later draft. Section 17 released the man who hired a substitute "during the time for which he was drafted," which meant three years, but nothing further addressed those who paid commutation.[57] That led to widespread uncertainty, but after innumerable inquiries the War Department declared that paying the fee freed the conscript only from that particular draft.[58]

The draft law itself diminished the number of men liable for service by incorporating thousands of office seekers into a new bureaucracy. All congressional districts had to have provost marshals, enrolling officers, examining surgeons, and all their assistants, each serving with a sought-after federal appointment. In addition to their level of compensation, those positions became doubly desirable in the face of compulsory service. Congressman Stevens, who had voted for conscription willingly enough, sought a provost-marshal sinecure for his nephew as a personal favor from the secretary of war. Richard Thompson, a former congressman from Indiana, secured for himself the position of provost marshal in that state's Seventh Congressional District; he had also obtained a commission in the Commissary Department for his son—whom he then had to dissuade from resigning, which would have cost him a comfortable assignment as well as making him subject to the draft.[59]

Additionally, the provost marshals were to exercise their arrest authority through the assistance of armed troops, which strict constitutionalists found as obnoxious as the federal draft itself. To supply a goodly portion of what was essentially a new national police force, the War Department created a legion of light-duty soldiers from the ranks of those who had already been discharged from the army for wounds or service-incurred ailments. They would be dressed in light-blue uniforms and serve as guards, clerks, or hospital attendants at the same pay and allowances as regular troops, but they would be kept out of the field. Such safe duty attracted a lot of men who had recovered from their disabilities and, seeking a means of employment, might have reenlisted in field regiments. They received no federal reenlistment bounty, but nothing prevented them from accepting local or state offers—and they were counted against recruiting quotas, which would soon elicit large sums in local bounties. For nearly a year the War Department called this light-duty police force the Invalid Corps before settling on the more glorious-sounding Veteran Reserve Corps.[60]

Preparing for a draft required canvassing every portion of the country under Union control to compile enrollments lists, and in some locales that task was not even begun until June. Most enrolling officers took responsibility for only their own townships and spent a week or two completing their lists, but resistance delayed the results in some districts. On July 1 Provost Marshal General James B. Fry ordered the first draft, requiring one-fifth of all enrolled men rather than calling for a specific number. For the first imposition of this new and unpopular government power, he selected safer districts in eight states from Maine to Delaware, skipping those such as New Hampshire and New Jersey with heavy concentrations of oppositional Democrats. In an effort to establish a precedent of peaceful acceptance for this federal intrusion, Fry flatly ignored the western states, where violent resistance had flared during both the June enrollment and the 1862 militia draft.[61]

The national draft was first imposed in Rhode Island, which harbored such extremes of wealth and poverty, and well over half of all families did not own a dollar's worth of property. Lottery drawings began on July 7 without incident, with the editor of the administration-friendly *Providence Daily Journal* among the first to see his name drawn. Three days later the governor conveyed his premature and unsubstantiated opinion that the citizens were responding enthusiastically, unjustifiably asserting that they regarded commutation or the hiring of substitutes "almost dishonorable." Nothing could have been further from the truth: all but one Rhode Islander in forty selected for service that week avoided answering the call. Of 4,321 men whose names were selected, 249 failed to even report for examination. Sixty-nine percent of the remaining 4,072 were excused on one exemption or another (including several provisions designed to relieve the poor), leaving only 1,259 to be held to service; 1,142 of those either furnished substitutes or paid the commutation fee. In the end, only 117 men were ordered into uniform—less than 3 percent of those called—and fewer may have actually served. The *Journal* editor was not among them.[62]

In Providence the son of a rich widow ignored the impending draft while he examined diamonds as a gift for his intended. When his name was drawn, he did not even bother looking for a substitute. Instead he interrupted his jewelry shopping only long enough to drop off three hundred dollars at the provost marshal's office and pick up his discharge papers.[63]

These local lotteries passed peacefully—but, when Fry added some New York City districts to the draft order, that city exploded. On July 13 demonstrators attacked the provost marshal's station, setting it afire, and by evening a full-scale riot had engulfed the city. The image of the commutation clause as the rich man's shield may have ignited the mayhem, but racial tensions and economic competition seemed to spread the flames. Crowds that residents characterized as primarily Irish battled police, destroyed the Orphan Asylum for Colored Children, and began roving the streets, beating and lynching black victims and searching for loot. For the next three days terror reigned; the mob obtained arms that gave them an edge against club-wielding police, and they were finally only quelled by veteran troops diverted from the pursuit of Lee's army as it retreated from Gettysburg. A smaller disturbance erupted in Boston, as though in sympathy, and other Massachusetts towns braced for an uprising of the poor. Minor violence rattled state authorities in New Hampshire as the draft started there, and Wisconsin officials who had seen a riot in 1862 feared another when their turn came.[64]

The riots marked the high tide of violent draft resistance. Thereafter, those who opposed the draft worked toward evading it—and aiding others to avoid it—rather than disrupting the selection process. The voters of Standish, Maine, took the lead in what soon became a popular solution in that state and in New Hampshire: before the first draft was even ordered, Standish agreed to provide every drafted citizen with three hundred dollars to buy his way out of service, which he could also presumably apply toward hiring a substitute or keep as a bounty if he chose to serve personally. Some communities withheld payment until after a draftee or his substitute was mustered in, preventing the money from being applied to commutation, but most allowed that use, too, or even intended it. Critics called it a "bounty for cowards" since most conscripts might be expected to simply hand the money over to the provost marshal, but other towns quickly copied the example of Standish.[65]

If everyone paid commutation, a draft might yield millions of dollars without raising a single soldier, which would immediately precipitate another draft, but most men seemed inclined to pay the fee if their towns subsidized them.

Soaring bounties and disappointing draft returns showed that the nation had been swept nearly clean of men, or at least white men, who were still inclined to fight without better compensation. The willingness of frugal New Englanders to incur unprecedented municipal debt illustrated how averse those voters were to military service. The numbers hiring substitutes or paying commutation demonstrated that most were unwilling to fight for any price. In Rhode Island 97.3 percent of all the men whose names were drawn that July evaded or avoided service. In Massachusetts 97.5 percent escaped, as did 97.6 percent in New York, 97.7 percent in New Hampshire, 98.1 percent in Maryland, and 98.4 percent in Connecticut. Only Vermont, Maine, Delaware, and the District of Columbia held as many as 5 percent of their drafted men to service, and fewer than that finally reported for duty.[66] If those statistics did not prove that support for the war had vanished, they did confirm that patriotism alone was no longer going to fill the armies—if it ever had.

From the outset of the federal draft, men who would have preferred not to serve at all sought less obnoxious ways of meeting the new obligation than going to the front with a rifle, and the heavy artillery offered one solution. Recruiters had long advertised this branch as a means of avoiding "all the hardships and privations of camp life" (and implicitly the danger of battle as well) by permanent service in the forts around Washington.[67] In the spring of 1863 New Hampshire's new governor, Joseph Gilmore, started raising a company of heavy artillery to garrison Fort Constitution, at the mouth of Portsmouth Harbor. Even for that comfortable service, men were slow to come. Gilmore admitted in June that the state could no longer provide soldiers except by force or by the payment of "most liberal bounties," and similar difficulty would prevail throughout the country during the rest of the conflict. The draft accelerated Gilmore's recruiting, and in July, while draft violence rocked New York City, startled Boston, and even disturbed Portsmouth, the company for the fort quickly filled up with misfits and idlers who made unenthusiastic soldiers. In his anxiety to complete the state's draft quota, the governor started a second company and had it mustered in, complete, inside a month.[68]

Among the officers who snagged a spot in these companies was Ira Barton, a former captain in the 5th New Hampshire who had resigned from that regiment after drawing unfavorable notice from his colonel, Edward E. Cross.

Barton had tried earlier for a commission in the Invalid Corps, but Cross had striven to quash that effort by informing the provost marshal general that Barton had received no recommendation from him or his erstwhile brigade commander, adding "*nor can he receive any.*"[69] Barton nevertheless had the backing of his father, a prominent Republican, against which the disapprobation of the Democratic colonel meant nothing to the Republican governor, who named the captain to command the second company. The duty was soft enough, with dry beds, cooked meals, frequent furloughs, and no enemy presence. Elmer Bent, a private in the 14th New Hampshire whose older, married brother joined Barton's company, waxed sarcastic over how easy the artillerymen had it. His brother did not have to leave the state, was allowed to go home for four days every three months, and had earned three hundred dollars in bounty, all of which provoked Bent to propose writing a letter of sympathy. Benjamin Marshall, the unemployed son of a widowed mother, gladly took that opportunity to sidestep the draft and make some money, admitting that the bounty, board, and clothing amounted to "more than I could get any other way." The raising of the second company also offered a "chance" for his brother, he suggested.[70]

The heavy-artillery option suited those who saw no promise of their neighbors footing the bill for commutation or a substitute, and had no hope of raising that much money themselves. With relatively few such regiments, most of which quickly filled with men looking for safe duty, that relief valve for public anger over the draft closed. As that anger peaked, the seemingly blatant discrimination of the commutation clause became the focal point of animosity.[71]

Newspapers friendly to the administration or the war effort defended commutation as a brake on the escalation of substitute prices. An Ohio editor called it "the poor man's friend," but that relationship would have been more obvious had the fee afforded the same three-year exemption as a substitute. Commutation did tend to curb the cost of substitutes, as developments would show, but restricting the exemption to a single draft levy greatly increased the value of a substitute. Under the militia draft of 1862, with no provision for commutation, potential substitutes had seemed satisfied with a payment of $150 from their principals. By the spring of 1863, soldiers looking for someone to take their places were willing to pay $200, and rarely as much as $300, although one militiaman refused even that much to reenlist in place of a rueful three-year volunteer.[72]

Once Congress established commutation at a maximum of $300, that became the minimum price for substitutes, and it rose from there, partly in response to municipal subsidies. During New Hampshire's first draft levy, the town of Hampstead made the common offer of a $300 stipend for whatever its drafted citizens decided to use it for, and substitutes immediately started charging that town's conscripts $500. Men who were drafted from Granite State towns that contributed lower sums did not pay so much: a farmer from less-generous Claremont made a trip to the draft rendezvous at Lebanon and paid a volunteer there to act as his son's substitute for so little of his own money that he failed to even record the amount. Substitutes and their brokers naturally tried to charge all the market would bear, and the larger the public subsidies rose, the higher the market price went. In the West, where communities voted less generous bounties for volunteers and avoided appropriating commutation funds for conscripts, substitutes could be had a year later for as little as $400 at a time when prices in the East ran to two or three times that figure.[73]

In addressing the fairness of the draft law, supporters often regurgitated a letter of Senator Wilson's in which he emphasized those provisions for exemption that seemed to favor the poor. The only son of a widow or of aged and infirm parents would not have to serve if he swore that he was their primary support; if there were two sons, the parents had the right to select which would be exempt. The only adult brother of orphaned children under the age of twelve could be excused on the same grounds, although there was no provision for exempting one of multiple such brothers. If a family had two sons or a father and son in the service, up to two other brothers might be exempted. A widower with children younger than twelve was not subject to conscription—but he would be if his children were twelve and older, no matter how many he had. All men aged thirty-five and under would theoretically be called first, along with unmarried men as old as forty-five, while married men over thirty-five composed a second class that was to be drafted last.[74]

The class division was applied at the basic municipal level, within towns or by county if there was no town government. If the first class in any community had been exhausted by demographic quirks, heavy recruiting, conscription, and evasive or incidental migration, older married men with large families were sometimes compelled to serve. More often those same patriarchs were forced into uniform by simple economics, while single young professionals routinely resorted to substitutes, although those with fledgling careers might lament the rising prices.[75]

Conscription's more careless defenders occasionally argued that its adverse effect on the poor was counterbalanced by the opportunity to fight in place of wealthier men, which provided them with employment at more appealing wages. Poorer soldiers often saw it that way themselves, as their disproportionate representation in the army had intimated right along, but publishing apparent approbation of those unequal class distinctions seemed to invite unfavorable observations. A Michigan editor probably made few friends for the law by arguing that it would be mutually beneficial for a drafted businessman who had many people working for him to hire "another man, without family or business or employment," to fight in his place.[76]

Travel, either to foreign lands or to the territories, may have afforded the most pleasant means of evading conscription for those with the resources to set themselves up elsewhere. South American sheep raising sparked particular interest among young men in western Maine, including the sons and nephews of former governors, and a number of them took ship for Buenos Aires. Gold fever drew other men toward the mining country of Idaho and California, where distance and desolation made enforcement of the draft more difficult.[77]

The province of Canada offered more convenient refuge. A saddler from northern Vermont found work a few miles over the border, where Americans of his age were congregating in considerable numbers, and he assumed that he could remain there for the duration of the war if necessary. A New Hampshire youth boarded a train for Stanstead, Canada East, accompanied by two dozen other draft evaders; once established there, he counted about thirty others passing through town daily. So many flocked to Stanstead that they filled all the available jobs, driving the price of labor down, and the local newspaper encouraged them homeward by reporting the money offered to soldiers and substitutes in the Union army.[78]

Some potential conscripts did not need the excuse of faraway employment. William Newton Matson, a well-to-do lawyer and insurance investor from Hartford, had sent his boy Willie abroad during the militia draft of 1862 and kept him overseas through 1863. Willie's mother rejoiced that her son lay beyond the reach of the government, yet she still defined the nature of the conflict in glorious terms. "We are fighting for our liberty and freedom," she wrote, presumptuously using the first-person plural. Then she listed the names of five of her son's friends who had been drafted. "None of them will probably go," she concluded, assuming that they would take advantage of their family wealth just as her son had.[79]

By early September administration officials claimed that a thousand conscripts a day were arriving in the national capital, but those men came under increasingly heavy guard. Most of them had enlisted as substitutes, and they brought little cheer to rank or file when the first of them arrived in the camps of their assigned regiments. Captain Andrew Stone of the 9th New Hampshire had to escort one contingent, describing them as "the ugliest sett of Devils that ever went unhung" and congratulating himself on getting rid of them. Thieves thickly seeded every lot, ready to stomp or stab anyone who resisted their pilfering. Edwin Horton, who had neglected to report for induction, ended up confined to a guardhouse with two or three dozen "roughs" from Boston and New York who beat him into submission and robbed him of everything he had. He and they were delivered to the Vermont Brigade in late September, but more than a quarter of the two hundred conscripts bound for the 2nd Vermont deserted on the way. Sergeants were soon tying or locking up many of the rest to prevent them from running off, but still they drained away to the rear—or to the enemy. These men were "simply rascals," judged a colonel of artillery, "who never intended to serve, but merely wanted the bounty or purchase money offered."[80]

Escalating the disdain they had shown bounty men the previous year, the veterans disparaged their latest reinforcements as "four hundred dollar men"—or some costlier variation of that epithet, depending on the prevailing bounties and fees. Yet some of the substitutes and most of the men who had been drafted showed promise. Quite a few discharged veterans of two-year regiments had reenlisted in New York, either as volunteers or as substitutes, but often they, too, were brought to the front between bayonets, along with the conscripts and bounty jumpers. The major of the 4th Vermont deemed the men he received in late September of 1863 superior to any reinforcement of volunteer recruits the regiment had received; the drafted men lived up to his expectations if the substitutes did not. Men like Charles Biddlecom, who was drafted from central New York about the same time, may have typified many of those who came without choice: Biddlecom had not the least shred of patriotism—he did not think the Union worth a single life and had no use at all for Lincoln's emancipation plan—but he did not want to be thought of as a coward or a shirker.[81]

Of the 196 men delivered to the camp of the 4th Vermont late in September, nearly one-quarter deserted, but 60 of them died in service—mostly from wounds or as prisoners—while 88 left the regiment with honorable discharges or legitimate transfers. The 92 drafted men proved to be the most reliable: only 6 of them deserted, and 33 died in uniform, leaving 53 to serve until they were formally released. The lot included 104 substitutes, 42 of whom absconded sooner or later, but 27 of them died in the service, including a number who were killed, wounded, or captured in battle, and 35 of them finished their terms.[82]

A substitute sometimes came from the same town or the same family as the drafted man he replaced, but more often he would be a stranger, just arrived from out of state or from the Old World. The provision for substitutes created an entire new profession among glib entrepreneurs unhampered by an excess of conscience: men who styled themselves "substitute brokers" prowled the rougher edges of society, gathering up prospective recruits as a peddler stocked up on merchandise. Usually they scoured the cities, scanning hotel bars for loungers indifferent to their futures, or they ambled the streets with an eye for the frayed cuffs and battered hats that bespoke strained resources. They preferred the uneducated or the alien unfamiliar with English, who were easier to dupe. Underage boys out on their own or running away from home also made easy marks: one sixteen-year-old who enlisted during a disciplinary dispute with his father was still waiting for his bounty six weeks before his discharge. Substitute brokers were supposed to limit their fees to between $10 and $25, but most of them skimmed all they could from their clients.[83]

Shortly after the draft riots, a substitute broker with a long, black, pointed beard calling himself Carter staked out Carle's Hotel in New York City, where he approached a likely looking fellow going by the name of Oliver Davis. He told Davis that he might be able to pay him $200 if he were willing to enlist in the army. Davis balked at the price, so Carter said he could go as high as $225 but no higher, because he would get so little for himself, and they agreed on that amount. About the same time, Charles E. Sherman had been drafted from Naugatuck, Connecticut, and went to Charles G. Wilson, a New Haven insurance agent who was dabbling in the substitute market. Wilson guaranteed him a substitute at a price of $325, choosing from among men solicited by wholesale providers including Carter, and it happened to be Oliver Davis who took Sherman's place. The $100 difference between what Sherman paid and what Davis received disappeared into the pockets of Carter and Wilson. Davis was operating under an alias, as did most substitutes who thought they might find the work unpleasant enough to desert, but he turned into a good soldier and earned sergeant's stripes before the war ended.[84]

Among the conscripts and substitutes who signed up that summer came the occasional down-on-his-luck volunteer. Having recently fled a pregnant sixteen-year-old in England, James Horrocks informed his parents that he had been unable to find employment in New York City and had therefore enlisted in New Jersey, which offered a $200 state bounty. With that, a $50 city bounty from Hudson, and the advance on the federal pay and bounty, he thought he had done very well for himself—but he, too, enlisted under a false name, just in case.[85]

Thomas Johnson would have been a little pressed for cash about then himself. He was a Cape Breton Islander who had brought his big family to Maine in the early 1850s, working as regularly as he could at manual labor in the town of Westbrook. In 1861 he had reached his early fifties and still owned nothing. Promises of community support for soldiers' families drew many men in his position to neighboring Portland, where he signed the roll of the 10th Maine for a two-year term. At his discharge in the spring of 1863, both his pay and the community support for his family ended, and as an aging, unskilled laborer he would have had some difficulty supporting his brood at the high prices of the war's third summer. By the middle of August he was back in Portland, meandering up and down Congress Street and browsing at recruiting posters.[86]

As a positive counterbalance to the coercion of conscription, in June the War Department offered all able-bodied, honorably discharged veterans a $402 bounty for a three-year reenlistment. The minimum requirement of nine months' service betrayed the order as a special plea for the militia troops who were then preparing to go home, but it also applied to veterans of the two-year regiments discharged that spring. Lieutenant John Gould, formerly of the 10th Maine, went to Portland to raise volunteers for a new regiment of such "veteran volunteers," but even with the $402 bounty recruits remained scarce. Most substitutes realized at least $500 from their principals, aside from the state and federal bounties, and the veterans who were willing to go at all seemed to be choosing that route. From his office at the Preble House, Gould anxiously awaited an administrative decision on whether the new $100 state bounty for drafted men and substitutes would apply to veteran volunteers; when that was resolved satisfactorily, he lobbied Portland's mayor and alderman for a $100 city bounty and got that, too. Yet even with $602 to offer his recruits, Gould brought in only three men during all of August. The first to volunteer was the gray-haired veteran Thomas Johnson, who had been married since February of 1832 but insisted that he was only forty-five years old. Gould described him as "an old man," but for the sake of signing him up wrote him down as forty-five—just within the upper limit of military age.[87]

Conscription vastly worsened the labor shortage and forced an increase in wages, especially in the East and particularly during the critical agricultural seasons. James Nichol, who owned a fair-sized spread in Darien, Connecticut, lost a favorite hired hand right after the haying season ended, just as names were being drawn for the draft; the young man simply went away, as though to enjoy a little vacation with his wages, but then he never came back. Later Nichol learned that he had been scooped up by a substitute broker and sold off at a profit of $330 to himself, which the new recruit gave to his family. "I think it was the best thing he could have done," his ex-employer reasoned, "if he is spared." Commutation and the profusion of exemptions for physical and economic conditions merely forced another call for troops in October, and Nichol observed that the threat of conscription behind that levy chased the last potential farm laborers out of the state.[88]

Combined with the intense demand for substitutes, Nichol's assertion that "you can get no help" because of that draft-driven exodus reflected how thoroughly his region had been denuded of ardent patriots. Increasingly it was the aged or infirm who preached the gospel of arms—or those able-bodied men regarded by one soldier's resentful wife as puny, puling patriots, begging others to bear the burden of a war they only dared wage through proxies.[89]

8

THE RISING PRICE OF PATRIOTISM, 1863–1865

The Civil War turned the United States into an insatiable man-eating machine. To feed that appetite, as early as August 8, 1862, Secretary of State William Seward charged his diplomatic corps with apprising unemployed Europeans of the opportunity the United States offered to immigrant laborers. With the militia draft just then being imposed, one of Seward's correspondents advised that to encourage more immigration he should also publicize that aliens would not be subject to military duty. The secretary coyly replied that he could not imagine anyone thinking that foreign nationals could be drafted, and he refrained from offering the suggested assurance because military recruitment posed one of his foremost motives. Aliens might be exempt from the draft, but they could certainly volunteer.[1]

U.S. diplomats fully understood the hint. Writing to Secretary Seward from Paris just three weeks later, Consul General John Bigelow asked for specifics about the bounty mania in the United States. "If you would send to the Consuls full particulars of the bounty paid by the government to volunteers and when, where and how soon after enlisting it could be touched, I think they might induce a considerable emigration to the U.S., especially from those ports whence the bounty money would defray the expenses of the voyage." Answering Bigelow another three weeks hence, the secretary cautioned him that "nobody is authorized to do anything or pay anything," but that was only the official response. In cryptic approval Seward immediately added that he had asked Secretary Stanton for a schedule of compensation for soldiers, which he would send to Paris. Noting that the war amounted to an effort by each side to "exhaust the other,"

Seward supposed that "immigration of a large mass from Europe would of itself decide it."[2]

After the passage of national conscription, immigrants also became perfect candidates for substitutes because, under the 1863 draft law, substitutes themselves had to be exempt from conscription. American ministers and consuls were also encouraged to advertise that citizens could claim land under the Homestead Act, which might move immigrants to apply for naturalization, and the mere application for citizenship would make them eligible for the draft. The tenant farming that dominated Ireland made cheap land in the United States particularly attractive to those prospective émigrés, and enlistment bounties seemed to bring its purchase price within reach.[3]

On February 8, 1863, Seward divulged his intentions even more obviously when he instructed overseas officials to give priority to male emigrants between the ages of twenty-one and forty. Despite his earlier stricture, he ambiguously suggested that the diplomatic corps might surreptitiously aid such emigrants financially. Those policies contributed to some 117,000 Europeans sailing for America in 1863 and another 114,000 in 1864—mostly to join the Union army, according to a contemporary observer. More than half of them came from Ireland, driven by extensive crop failures. Immigration in 1863 at the port of New York alone more than doubled over the previous year.[4]

Immigrants from England's cotton-starved textile region had flooded the labor market in Canada, which was already inundated with American deserters and draft evaders. The resulting unemployment drove many British subjects south of the border, and the low wages in Canada made the average federal enlistment bounty gleam like a prince's ransom. Eventually the stream of Americans fleeing to Canada was met by floods of Canadians boarding trains for the States, ostensibly (and often truly) looking for work where it was plentiful and wages were high. Substitute brokers who risked arrest by transporting men over state lines to more generous climes thought nothing of casting their lines in the Canadian provinces, where desperate British soldiers would desert for as little as a hundred dollars.[5]

Combining the tactics of such crimping brokers with Seward's oblique diplomacy, the Boston Board of Trade formed a subsidiary organization called the Foreign Emigrant Society, hiring its own agents to sail to Europe and solicit men. With another draft quota coming due, those agents engaged three shiploads of Germans in ostensible labor contracts in which they agreed to work for three years under any employer in return for passage to the United States and a hundred dollars cash: the difference between that payment and the bounties the immigrants signed away mitigated the expenses of the venture. Everyone seemed to understand that these men were being recruited as mercenaries, including Governor Andrew and the men themselves. Once the Germans had been shuttled to Boston by way of England and Portland, Maine, they were mustered into service, mostly in the 20th Massachusetts, and headed for the front. The ships that had brought them returned to Europe for the next of several more loads.[6]

The richest source of volunteers as the summer of 1863 came to a close consisted of the men who had enlisted in 1861, and they became the object of an intense reenlistment campaign. Those veteran troops would start going home the following May, and the War Department gave them an opportunity to reenlist early. As it turned out, that was the only way those men could be kept in the army: an apparently unintended ambiguity in the Enrollment Act led to a ruling that anyone who was in the army on March 3, 1863, the day the law was passed, was permanently exempt from the draft. Those who had been discharged even a day earlier, or who had enlisted a day afterward, could not take advantage of that loophole.[7]

On June 25, 1863, the War Department had appealed to nine-month soldiers on the brink of discharge, offering them a chance to reenlist for a four-hundred-dollar bounty (plus the traditional two-dollar "recruiting premium"). That same order specified that the three-year men could begin reenlisting on September 24, which would keep a steady flow of veterans returning to the field. The reenlisted men would receive their original one-hundred-dollar discharge bonus and enjoy a thirty-day furlough—besides being credited to the quotas of their communities, which would presumably afford them additional state and local bounties. The June order had been as badly composed as the draft law, however, and it would have allowed several hundred thousand of the three-year volunteers from 1862 to reenlist after less than a year. Poor men who had enlisted for meager bounties the previous summer and autumn considered taking advantage of that offer for the sake of their families, reasoning that it only added one year to their commitment.[8]

As fair as it would have been to offer the same benefit to veterans of one year's service as the department gave to nine-month men, the intent of the June

25 order had been to reenlist those soldiers who could soonest claim their liberty. A revised order that circulated on September 11 required soldiers still in the service to have completed two years of their original three-year terms before they could reenlist. That would spread the reenlistments out indefinitely—as well as staggering those thousands of furloughs. Garrison troops who had manned comfortable forts in quiet backwater posts produced a great many veteran volunteers, but a surprising number of men who had seen hard service also accepted the bargain. For most of them, the hardest service was yet to come, but as late as the autumn of 1863 some soldiers still gambled that the war would be over before their original enlistments ended anyway, transforming the bounty into an unencumbered gift.[9]

Officers applied some pressure on the men to reenlist, partly to preserve their regimental organizations, for regiments that fell below minimum strength might be consolidated or disbanded, forcing most or all of the officers to be mustered out. Especially in regiments that enjoyed less deadly service, many officers cherished their commissions because they could never have made as much money at home. A New Hampshire captain made that argument to his mother when he considered reenlisting, adding that he led "a lazy life" in the army, earning money whether he was sick or sound. Considering that, he asked her, "don't you think I had better remain?"[10]

More than one colonel threatened to reduce all noncommissioned officers who declined to reenlist. Others started finding fault with the conduct of those who hesitated, launching a spate of courts-martial until the men started coming around. One regimental commander called his men into formation to leave camp on a brutal winter campaign, announcing that anyone who reenlisted on the spot could instead go home on reenlistment furlough. A lieutenant threatened to arrest some of his men who vocally disparaged the idea of reenlisting. Some of the pressure came from comrades, for if enough men in one regiment reenlisted it would be allowed to go home as a unit to recruit, which would save every man the travel expense and perhaps prolong the furlough. That was important, as travel could cost two or three months' pay and consume a week of the furlough, and men had frequently passed up an opportunity to go home because of the cost alone. Furloughs themselves became bargaining chips as unit commanders refused to approve them under any circumstances unless a man reenlisted.[11]

Most of those who might have reenlisted did not. Many remembered indignities and injustices they had endured in the army, and for some the reenlistment effort itself posed another example of that injustice, with sly tricks and coercion employed to lure men back. A Maine corporal of a cynical mien informed friends and family that he would not consider it. "I would not trust my patriotism to carry me thru another term of service," he protested.[12] As many a soldier had observed, a man might hear a lot of praise and promises when the army wanted him, but no one in or out of the army cared about him once he had been bound to service. Most who had seen the worst of the fighting in the two main theaters managed to resist the temptation of the money, although they often admitted the power of its attraction: "the bounty is almost *fabulous,*" conceded Musician James Holmes, who nevertheless was having none of it. Recuperating in the hospital for paroled prisoners at Annapolis, a Massachusetts lad who had been captured at Gettysburg dismissed claims that he could earn $1,300 in bounties, absolutely refusing to serve again. They could even forego the prospect of a likely promotion, when discharges would remove the commissioned and noncommissioned officers above them.[13] "When I get free," remarked another Massachusetts man, "you never will catch me in Uncle Sam's clutches again."[14]

Soldiers whose enlistments would end in the spring of 1864 could fairly smell the air of home and feel the comfort of peace. John Cuddy, a Pennsylvanian who had enlisted at sixteen, assured his anxious parents that he could not wait to go back to the happy life he had known. As Vermonter William Stow explained to his mother, "three long years have I bin surrounded with the trim sentinels of death & I want to get out of it." Neither of them reenlisted, yet neither of them made it home, either.[15]

The anxious supplication of women at home often dissuaded even those who might otherwise have succumbed to the offer of so much money, which would have seemed even more appealing in the poorer Western states. A veteran of the 8th Iowa, which had been cut to pieces at Shiloh and Vicksburg, implied that he might have considered another term had he not gotten a "small mesage" from someone who meant a great deal to him. He went home in 1864, and in evidence of her appreciation his bride delivered their first child before the year was out. Silas Sadler of the 4th Michigan thought enough about reenlisting that he wrote home about it. The notion drove his mother to tears, and when Silas learned of this he apologized. "I won't reenlist, now," he promised.[16]

Conjugal pleading did not always prevail over the lure of bounty money. "You talk rather saucy about my reenlisting," a Michigan fifer chided his wife, when she informed him of her opposition. He might have shown his independence by reenlisting anyway had he not been ineligible under the two-year minimum-service requirement.[17] Susan Miller had obviously wanted her husband to come home when his time was up, especially after their little boy died, but James Miller was not about to be guided by his wife's wishes either; he reenlisted over the winter, and she seemed to know that it was their last goodbye when he returned to his regiment in April.[18]

James Miller's letters suggest that nationalism impelled him at least as much as the bounty, but some men's patriotic appeals rang a little hollow. Emily Harris had struggled to support her two children in Hampstead, New Hampshire, battling skyrocketing prices as well as her own growing opposition to the war while Leander Harris was away with the army. Lonely after more than two years by herself—and probably depressed by her travails—she begged him not to reenlist, knowing how susceptible he might be to an offer of so much money. "I could bear almost anything better than that," she wrote. She knew her husband well, and he placated her for a time by suggesting that he would reenlist if not for her opposition, mentioning more than once that the bounty would be such "a nice little sum for us to start with after the war." He often declared his support for the government and claimed that the greatest temptation to reenlisting would be the chance to come home on furlough, but the economics that had impelled him into the ranks in 1861 still obsessed him. In alluding once more to the bounty, he informed Emily that he had no intention of ever making his living as a shoemaker again, but until the last moment he allowed her to believe that he would heed her wishes. She may not have known that he had already reenlisted until he came to the front door on his furlough late in February, 1864.[19]

Sometimes the chance of climbing to higher rank in a recruit-swollen regiment added extra incentive. The sergeant major of the 4th Michigan considered it, but his regiment had lost so many enlisted men at Gettysburg that officers survived in disproportionate numbers, reducing the chances of any promotion among them; he refrained from committing himself to a second term, and never regretted it. Corporal Nathaniel Parmeter saw a better chance in the 29th Ohio, letting his reenlistment bounty out at interest and perhaps hoping for a commission, but for him promotion was slow and slight; he came home without shoulder straps. Charles Howe, who had served nearly three years as a volunteer but was not yet nineteen, reenlisted in the Regular Army with the promise of an ordnance position equivalent to the rank of lieutenant: instead he was sent to a fort on the plains for three years as a hospital steward.[20]

For most, money seemed to pose the main argument for reenlisting. Federal, state, and local bounties for reenlistment were the highest yet paid, and many who might have returned to peaceful pursuits found them too enticing to refuse. Indeed, it was cash that attracted John Wilmot. He had gone away from Vermont as a teenager, but a few months later a young woman had surprised him with a letter announcing her pregnancy, and by the end of 1863 her child was a year and a half old. Vermont was offering its reenlisting soldiers $125 if they waived their monthly state supplements: with that, the federal bounty, and his discharge bonus, Wilmot could collect $627, aside from anything the town of Thetford might give him. He had long anticipated his $100 discharge bonus as a stake for starting out on his own, and had already reenlisted for what he considered a small fortune when he went through the motions of asking "Annie" whether he should. Wilmot was not the only soldier who used the bounty and furlough to get married, although he was among the tardiest of the grooms.[21]

Proctor Swallow wavered for a time, obviously preferring to go home, but economics decided the matter for him. He would pocket the same minimum as Wilmot if he commuted his monthly stipend to cash, and that amounted to more money than he had ever owned. He could make a living in the army, which he had been hard pressed to do before he enlisted, and he had plans for being detailed as a tailor that would earn him even more. Not a word about the cause, the country, or any altruistic doctrine cluttered his scribbled consideration of the matter; he was, after all, the young man who had said in September of 1861, "I have no desire to enlist." But for the money, he evidently would have had no desire to reenlist, either.[22]

Yet another Vermonter sensed the motivation of his comrades who went home on reenlistment furlough. Martin Clark, who had just come out in the fall himself and would end his life in a Georgia prison pen, revealed to a correspondent that he doubted the patriotism of the men who were reenlisting. Judging from what he had seen and heard, he guessed that the money was what most of them were after. A boy in the 23rd Massachusetts who had enlisted at the beginning of the war chose not to try another term, and he had harsh words for those who did: most men who had seen hard service would not opt for another three years, he insinuated, and he assessed the reenlisted men of his regiments as the shirks who ducked as much work and danger as possible. He supposed that the citizens who sent those "defenders of their country" back with music and accolades "will laugh and say they have got rid of them for three years more."[23]

Sergeant Charles Maxim also belonged to the 23rd Massachusetts. He calculated that his bounty and pay over the course of three more years would come to about $2,000. That was more than he could make anywhere else in a long time, he reasoned, and his decision may have been influenced by the relative ease of his service. His regiment had seen little serious fighting, and almost none within the previous two years. In the end he did reenlist, although he intensely disliked the army, but he regretted the decision during the butchery at Petersburg the next year, and resented his more cautious comrades when they went home.[24]

Thomas Covert, a young shoemaker who had snared the job of saddler for the 6th Ohio Cavalry, wanted to reenlist despite his wife's fervent prayers that he would accept a discharge. "I am getting more wages here than I could make at hom [sic]," he argued, mentioning a recent pay raise for saddlers, the $402 veteran's bounty, and $100 from their town in Ashtabula County, which he had not expected. He was in the hospital just then and would not have been able to work at home anyway, so he ignored her wishes and took the bounty.[25]

Edwin Wentworth, an equivocating dreamer who had never been able to hold a job for any length of time, repeatedly assured his wife that he would not reenlist. The generous bounty would not match the wages he could earn as a printer at home, he reasoned—forgetting how sporadic his employment record had been. He had not come into the army until the summer of 1862, so he would have been unable to reenlist for the foreseeable future anyway, but the potential profit began to tantalize him as he came within a few months of eligibility. Only two weeks after he had dismissed the idea of reenlisting, he began to argue himself into it. With state and local bounties from Massachusetts, the state subsidy for soldiers' families, the federal bounties, and his regular pay, he, too, ciphered out an income of $2,000 over three years. As he had when he first enlisted, Wentworth augmented that vision of riches with an arbitrary prediction that the war would end soon in any case and he would be sent home early, with all that extra money. He could buy a house and land on installments, he thought, and provide his long-suffering wife "a chance to live comfortably."[26]

Commissary Sergeant Rufus Mead, who had lived very well as the partner of the 5th Connecticut's sutler, long resisted the reenlistment frenzy that gripped his regiment through December of 1863. On January 4, 1864, he wrote that the fever still raged, with over three hundred men signed up already, and reenlistment was the sole subject of conversation. The 5th Connecticut had not had two dozen men killed since Second Bull Run, where it escaped with a few men missing, and it had just watched the Confederate Army of Tennessee driven from its namesake state, so morale was high. The sergeant nevertheless told the folks at home that he felt he had done enough for his country—but he had done a little for himself at the same time, and in the end decided to do a little more for Rufus Mead. Three days later he sent another letter, forewarning everyone that he would be home on furlough after all, with the other reenlisted veterans who were coming to collect their generous town bounties.[27]

Vermonter Wilbur Fisk, who wrote ironic but faintly patriotic letters to a hometown newspaper, showed more candor in his own pocket diary. In describing the progress of reenlistment in the Vermont Brigade, he portrayed his comrades as conscientious, loyal citizens intent on a task they could not neglect, but of himself he privately admitted, "I have never earned money easier all things considered than I have here in the army." Money meant a great deal to him, although he tended to disguise the trait because he considered it unseemly: when a discharged veteran reenlisted in his regiment as a substitute, Fisk disparaged him for having come out for the money and claimed that the man elicited little sympathy when he died. That same week Fisk himself reenlisted for the $402 bounty and the lump-sum state payment of $125. When his town declined to give him an additional bounty because it had already met its quota, he waved the flag, editorializing on paying the local bounty as a matter of fairness to the country's defenders.[28]

More common by far was the soldier who gave the proceeds of his reenlistment to his wife or parent, or invested it for the day he would come home, if he ever did. Yet there were those who, like sailors after a long cruise, squandered their bounty receipts in an orgy of self-indulgence—drinking heavily and buying rounds or renting horses and rigs for long, wild drives. Still others put the money to more direct, immediate use toward a peaceful future, financing their illicit flight to parts unknown. Three original members of the 2nd Vermont lit out during their furlough—as did three others who reenlisted just before the spring campaign, and were still at home on leave when the Vermont Brigade was shot to pieces on the first day of fighting in the Wilderness. Francis Boland, who had enlisted from among the Irish coalminers of Schuylkill County, Pennsylvania, had fended off creditors during the two years and more he had served, but he absconded instead of paying them with his bounty. The War Department realized that lump-sum payments "both encouraged and facilitated desertion" and so paid the $402 federal bounty incrementally, but it had no control over how much money states and towns paid in advance. With his discharge bonus of $100 and the $40 advance on his reenlistment bounty, plus his state and local bounties, a Maine or Vermont veteran could still raise up to $400 in cash as soon as he reenlisted. A volunteer from elsewhere in New England might realize even more, and that would cover the cost of relocating to an undisclosed location, while the furlough offered the opportunity for a head start on any pursuit.[29]

The reenlistment offer stood for the rest of the war, although the bounty was eventually reduced. While the War Department crowed over the success of the effort, it failed to preserve the organization of as many regiments as army headquarters and the officers of those units had hoped. In the spring and summer of 1864, so many troops were going home that everyone noticed the depletion, and a Sixth Corps staff officer worried that his division was "dwindling away," with regiments "going out of service every week."[30]

Historians of the conflict, with Bruce Catton first among them, have assumed or implied that the reenlistment offer applied only to the 1861 volunteers and that a majority of the veterans who might have reenlisted did so. In 1866 the provost marshal general reported that more than 136,000 veterans were reenlisted under the program from first to last—that is, from June of 1863 through April of 1865. By the terms of the War Department offers, the reenlisted soldiers necessarily came from the nine-month, two-year, and three-year volunteers who had entered the service between May of 1861 and April of 1863: that encompassed most of the nearly 1,360,000 men who entered the army during that period. Even if half that number had been killed or permanently and severely disabled—or disqualified by receiving discharges before completing nine months of service—680,000 could still have taken advantage of the reenlistment offer sometime during the remainder of the war. Only in the face of such devastating and unlikely attrition would the 136,000 who did reenlist have represented as much as 20 percent of those who might have done so—let alone more than half.[31]

Money obviously exerted a powerful stimulus on the reenlistments, too, as it had on other enlistments throughout the war. Catton cited a single regimental history to show that the generous bounties "seem to have had little influence" on the reenlistment of veterans, trusting that source over the contradictory remarks of the one soldier whose original letters he used. He concluded that "the dominant motive, finally, seems to have been a simple desire to see the job through," but in fact money appeared to be the main draw for those reenlistments. Directly or otherwise, the men's own correspondence often indicates as much, including most of the examples cited above. The extent of mercenary incentive became most obvious immediately after the War Department rescinded the special veteran bounty, whereupon reenlistments all but stopped.[32] The economic backgrounds of the men who did reenlist also confirms that they would have regarded the amount of money they received as a significant windfall. Of those surveyed for Table 1 as samples of the two- and three-year volunteers from 1861, 70 percent came from families claiming less than the median wealth in their states. Those who reenlisted from those same samples were a little poorer still, with 71 percent of them falling below the median.[33]

The reenlistment program did little to augment the ranks beyond bringing back some of the discharged nine-month and two-year men. The offer served mainly to alleviate by a fraction the homeward hegira that would begin in the middle of spring, 1864. Because of the popularity of commutation, neither had the summer draft levy of 1863 much replenished the armies in the field, which barely kept pace with natural attrition. Besides that, the infusion of substitutes had strained military resources by presenting a new level of resistance to discipline. As a consequence, the last conscripts were just being broken to the harness in their new regiments when the president issued another call for troops on October 17, 1863, this time specifying a goal of three hundred thousand more men.[34]

Soldiers, including short-term troops who could hardly wait for their enlistments to end, supported the draft as a means of ferreting out able-bodied men they and their families sneered at as "stay-at-homes."[35] That epithet was often cast at administration opponents, who declined to serve over political differences, but wealthy loungers earned equal scorn in comments on the payment of commutation as a means of escaping the draft. A Maine captain hinted at such animosity when he expressed his frustration that "one class" was doing all the fighting, and a Michigan soldier probably spoke for a majority of his comrades when he observed that the poor man seemed bound to be drafted. Even when a rich man's son did join the army, he often enjoyed special privileges and protection, to the muffled outrage of men who had to carry the load for them. Mostly, however, that sort of youth avoided the army altogether.[36]

The Hartford lawyer and his wife who had sent their draft-age son abroad at the first hint of compulsory service earned phenomenal profits from insurance investments, luxuriating in high society at home and in New York while they cheered the war on. With abundant leisure to correspond with her peripatetic young patriot, the mother kept him abreast of a struggle that seemed impossibly distant from their circle. She told him it was "an almost unprecedented time to make money," and there were so many men in Hartford that it was as though the war did not exist. For all the reports of the killed, the presence of wounded on the streets, and the large number of names called in the draft, she had never witnessed "so much gaiety and extravagance" or seen the city so prosperous. One of her greater concerns over the previous year had been finding a camel-hair shawl without paying the exorbitant prices brought by the poor exchange rate on greenbacks; finally she bought one "at a great bargain" from a woman dressed in widow's weeds.[37]

For the rich and well-connected, the war consisted of a long series of thrilling events as troops gathered and trained, mustered in, marched through town to the depot, or came home on furlough, escorted by bands and entertained by spellbinding speakers. President, governors, congressmen, and most of their lesser appointees could always keep their sons safely at home, if they and those sons preferred, or have them installed as hangers-on in safer corners of the army. For those who earned their living by the sweat of their brow, the threat of conscription hung like a perennial cloud.[38]

The draft call of October 17, 1863, disguised as an appeal for volunteers, launched another flurry of public meetings in every municipality across the country. It did not escape the notice of many who attended those meetings that the option of commutation had contributed significantly to the need for this call. Communities that had voted to stand that expense for their drafted citizens would have to do so repeatedly if successive levies failed to raise reliable men. The strategy therefore turned toward offering money for actual soldiers, preferably from among the citizens of the community. The deadline for each town providing its quota of volunteers was set for January 5, 1864, which allowed plenty of time for deciding how much of a bounty to offer and advertising it to prospective recruits.[39]

The approach of the January deadline rekindled a modified version of the auction initiated by the militia draft of 1862, with the leading men in every community pleading indecorously for young boys and men desperate for money to save their towns from a draft. Perhaps recognizing that the most vigorous recruiting took place just prior to the deadline, the War Department granted one extension to February 1 and another to March 10—but with another 200,000 men added to the demand. The recruiting drive thus ran from autumn through the winter, and on March 14 the president ordered another draft for 200,000 more. Enthusiasm fluctuated, as did the bounties, with the approach and passage of each announced deadline. As had been the case since the concept of bounties first took root, it required more money to raise men in the East than in the West, but the federal government had begun paying $302 to any first-time volunteer. That winter and spring a $200 local bounty prevailed along the

Wabash, while in Minnesota a veteran considered himself lucky to get $140; in the East the most popular amount offered for that draft by towns and cities was the $300 suggested by commutation, although some paid $500 and occasionally $600 per volunteer.[40]

The federal bounty was to be paid in installments over the course of three years, but New Hampshire enjoyed a special relationship with the administration because it held the first state elections every year. After a close call in the bellwether March election of 1863, the War Department made every effort to keep Granite State voters happy, including helping the state meet its recruiting quotas. Toward that end Governor Gilmore won permission to pay out the entire federal bounty in cash from state coffers on the promise of reimbursement from the U.S. Treasury, and to that he added a state bounty of $100. This made the state a favorite haven for bounty jumpers from Boston and New York, earning New Hampshire's depleted veteran regiments the worst reputation in the army. It also tempted residents of military age who worried that they might be drafted anyway.[41]

As a town that had soured on the war after emancipation came into play, Conway, New Hampshire, needed to make a generous offer. Cash spoke loudest, as Conway citizens had learned from experience. In 1861 the town had had to be primed for any recruits at all by the flash of a rich resident's ten-dollar gold pieces, and 81 percent of its recruits that year had represented below-median wealth. At a special town meeting on December 5, 1863, voters decided to offer a $300 town bounty. That was the maximum of the moment, and it, too, was to be paid on signing. Still, for most of the rest of December, no one in town responded, but on New Year's Eve three residents volunteered and started for the state capital, where they each expected to pick up $700. William Perkins and Daniel Babb would probably have been excused from a draft, with so many men still at home, because they would have been counted in the second class: both were married and had children, and Perkins was forty years old while Babb claimed to be thirty-six. Marquis Heath would probably have been passed over as well, already having been discharged once before for illness, and he was not what one might have called healthy when he reenlisted.[42]

The three, all of whom would be dead before the next winter, were rushed through the draft rendezvous at Concord and led away the next afternoon with 320 other recruits for their brigade, then encamped in Kentucky. A freshly appointed lieutenant traveling with their escort may have counted Babb, Heath, and Perkins among the score or so he thought "likely," but the rest he dismissed as "consummate rascals" and complained of having to guard them more diligently than he would as many rebel prisoners.[43]

Like many who enlisted from winter onward, thereby collecting large amounts of money from multiple sources, the Conway trio did not reach their assigned company without being cheated. When they arrived in Kentucky, Perkins and Babb both complained that the federal paymaster, who had required their signatures on the payroll, had not actually given them their advance. Besides the outright thieves who infested the various draft rendezvous, picking pockets and beating or murdering men for their cash and belongings, confidence men beset conscientious recruits at every hand, lusting after the money they could smell.[44] Brokers and even recruiters bilked the alien and the ignorant; would-be officers borrowed money from their own enlisted men against payday, then slipped away without mustering in when they failed to win their desired rank. The new soldiers no sooner departed for the army than alleged creditors dunned their wives or parents for some of the bounty they presumably left behind.[45]

Daniel Babb went directly to the hospital—also like a great many of those who enlisted as volunteers or substitutes after the autumn of 1863. The standards for health and fitness had plummeted by then, partly in response to the need for troops and partly because of corruption among assistant provost marshals and the examining surgeons. Soldiers had long suspected that some army doctors would certify a man sufficiently disabled to be discharged for a price that one soldier estimated at $100. From the beginning of the bounty era, recruits drew attention when they enlisted for one bounty, played off sick long enough to be sent home, and then recovered in time to enlist for another bounty.[46] Now the process ran in reverse, with mere boys, wizened grandfathers, cripples, and consumptives trying to get into the army to reap beguiling bounties or substitute fees, either by greasing the way themselves or having it done for them by brokers. If one surgeon would not pass a recruit, he would try somewhere else. A boy barely turned fourteen was successively rejected for bad lungs, a faint heartbeat, and suspicion that he was lying about his age in the final months of 1863, but in January, 1864, he passed muster in a New York cavalry regiment, taking $450 in bounty and spending all of it before he left the state. A surgeon in the Hudson Valley accepted volunteers under the winter draft whom he had turned down during the last call because they were too old or weak.[47]

Three-quarters of a platoon of recruits might not be fit for service: one could not hide a rigid knee; another would fall down in the ranks with epileptic convulsions; a third might show unmistakable symptoms of contagious disease. By

March of 1864 the incidence of syphilis and inflammation of the lungs throughout the army had nearly doubled over the previous year, and that month produced more cases of chronic alcoholism than surgeons saw anytime during the war. Wily provost marshals and their examining surgeons seemed responsible for much of the trouble, but even those who were suspended for negligence could often mobilize enough political support to win reinstatement. Several officials in northern New York and Vermont were suspended early in 1864 for passing manifestly disabled recruits, yet only one was actually dismissed. Even those who grew too bold usually came away clean: corruption ran rampant in Ohio provost marshal offices, but the governor suggested that suspiciously wealthy officers there should simply be allowed to resign to avoid prosecution.[48]

The bounties triggered cupidity among adolescents and the aged alike. Soldiers in the field grieved or raged, as they had since the first enticing bounty offers, when they heard that their fifteen- or sixteen-year-old brothers were trying to talk their parents into letting them enlist. Often the father himself, who might be past fifty, described the bounty as the nest egg that had eluded him throughout life, and the frantic soldier-son would beg him to abandon the idea. Almost invariably that dissuasion included a forceful declaration that the bounty was not worth the risk—illustrating that the son who was already in the army recognized money as the driving force behind his relative's warlike impulse.[49]

From the advent of national conscription, money appeared to be the impetus for most enlistments, whether accompanied by patriotic motives or not, although the allure of the money was often amplified by the threat of compulsion. The possibility of being drafted weighed on the consciousness of many a family man—including those who technically belonged to the second class—in areas where struggling economies or lavish bounties had already coaxed most of the younger men into uniform. That description fit many communities in the Old Northwest. As 1864 opened, an editor from western Wisconsin who was himself enrolled in the first class touted recent recruits from his state as "*better men,* socially, mentally, and physically" than previous volunteers: unlike the "needy adventurers" of 1861, he observed, these men had property and responsibilities.[50] Distant as they were from urban centers, the states of the upper Mississippi saw fewer bounty-jumping opportunists and attracted a narrower selection of potential substitutes. Land-rich farmers in their thirties and forties, with or without mortgages, frequently could not afford commutation or the greater expense of substitutes. They often took what bounties they could get, leaving wives or teenaged sons to manage the homestead.[51]

David Coon found himself in that position as he passed his forty-second birthday. He had lived in central Wisconsin for about a decade, accumulating a little more property than the state median by the summer of 1860. In February of 1864, with regional newspapers warning of another draft deadline, extolling the state's $900,000 expenditure for soldiers' families, and joking grimly about precipitous price increases, Coon joined a new infantry regiment. He told his wife that he passed the physical so easily that he would never have escaped had he been drafted. At first he agreed to $165 in local bounty—a little less than the average in the Sixth Congressional District—but when his recruiting officer claimed that he could only pay $150, Coon assigned himself to a different town for $200. He advised his wife to use that money to pay off the outstanding mortgage on their sugar bush as well as some other debts, including a cow for which he was being sued, after which she should buy herself new shoes and finally tombstones for long-unmarked graves. His oldest son was already in the cavalry, so fifteen-year-old Herbert was left to grow their food and some market produce, while Emma, at thirteen, was expected to help him cultivate an acre of beans and tend the vegetable garden. As the payments on the rest of Coon's federal bounty came in, he wanted his wife to "salt" it down, presumably at interest, and hoped that his family would be able to get by on the state supplement of $5 a month plus $5 from him. Along with his single-minded attention to how they should run the farm, his references to the pain of parting made it obvious that he would never have enlisted had he not felt trapped between the dollar and the draft.[52]

Daniel Chisholm left his home in southwestern Pennsylvania on February 26, 1864, his nineteenth birthday, heading for Pittsburgh with his sixteen-year-old brother, Alex; three days later they enlisted together in the 116th Pennsylvania. Daniel hinted at the importance of their bounty payments in the second sentence of his first letter home, in which he told his mother that they had each sent $200 to their father. The boys appear to have been wiser about money than their father, a carpenter whose entire worth in 1860 had amounted to only $200, and they urged him to use their bounties to buy a house so he could stop paying ever-escalating rent. They both made good soldiers and earned noncommissioned warrants, but the money they would or could receive preoccupied them to the end of their service and was evidently part of their purpose: when soldiers' pay was raised the following August, Alex considered it "so much the better." They earned more in the army during the war than they could have anywhere else, and the subsequent fortunes of their family demonstrated that they squandered none of it. Even Daniel Chisholm's great-grandson, who edited the brothers' letters, concluded that they enlisted "because of the bounty money."[53]

The mercenary incentive had become so common by then that men boasted of it. In January of 1864 Meshack Larry, a Maine soldier, encountered a former comrade who had reenlisted. The surprised Larry asked why, and—as Larry relayed it—his friend candidly replied that he had come out again for bounty money and to avoid being drafted. "He thought that New Englanders would fight better for Big bounties than they would for patriotic motives." Larry wrote, registering his agreement with that opinion and adding that his friend admitted not having a "might" of patriotism.[54]

At barely eighteen, the orphaned Frederick Hooker was cajoled by desperate older women into enlisting for the money it would bring. Nancy Sheldon, a household servant of twenty-five, married the unemployed youth at Bristol, Connecticut, on January 7 and moved in with her widowed, indigent mother while Frederick went looking for an opportunity to enlist at an "advantage." He tried the navy first, but that service was too popular with a draft threatening, so not much money could be had there. After a few days he took what seemed like a safe haven in the 2nd Connecticut Heavy Artillery, then garrisoning the big forts across the Potomac from Washington. He told his bride and her mother, whom he also now called "Mother," that he expected $385 in cash before leaving the state and reminded them to apply for his town bounty and the state-aid payment of $6 a month. In May his regiment marched out of the forts to fight Lee's army as infantry, but the new Mrs. Hooker lived comfortably until her husband died, after which she secured a pension and survived without occupation.[55]

John Carvel Arnold hesitated until the enrollment list of Snyder County, Pennsylvania, had been culled enough for conscription to snag a man like him, with a wife and five children. Convinced that he would be drafted, on February 26 he took the best bounty he could get, but it was five months before he could collect any of it. His endless apologies for being unable to feed his family or pay his creditors suggested how badly he had needed the money. At one point his wife asked if she could sell his dog, for which she had been offered five dollars, and he reluctantly gave her permission to do so.[56]

John Jackson had served a bloodless term in a nine-month Maine regiment, looking on it all the while as something of a frolic, but he had been unable to find satisfactory work when he returned home. He moved to Boston in the fall of 1863 for better employment opportunities, but harvest season had just ended and the best shoe-factory jobs had all been taken. He worked for a time in a shop with few windows, so they kept the gas lights burning all day, causing the air to turn bad. He was exempt from conscription by virtue of having been in service when the law was enacted, and he hoped the draft would clean out a lot of operatives and open a better spot for him, but the War Department kept extending the draft date. Finally he gave up and went back to Maine, where the state and the towns had posted seductive bounties to fill two new regiments; late in March he enlisted in the 32nd Maine. With his experience he secured the stripes and lozenge of a first sergeant, and the proceeds of that venture may have underwritten the farm he bought when he left the army for good.[57]

Bounty money was high among the priorities for Wilbur Huntington Proctor when he tried to enlist as a drummer boy. At a few months past his fourteenth birthday, he was already on his own, and like many an unemployed fellow in March of 1864 who had seen nothing of war, he considered the army for a refuge. For three weeks he tried to enlist in Boston, Philadelphia, and several places in New York City, mingling and conspiring with bounty jumpers and substitute brokers who intended to bilk him of most of his bounty. Finally he responded to an ad in the *New York Herald,* giving a false name, and was accepted immediately. Four days later he boarded a steamer for the front, $373 richer.[58]

Henry and Eliza Van Deusen still had one son, eighteen-year-old Edward, on their Wisconsin farm as the fourth spring of the Civil War opened. For months Henry had been too sick to work, and Edward was frail to begin with, leaving the family in want—but if Edward was too weak for farm work, the examining surgeons of that season thought him strong enough for a soldier. At the end of April he left for the Army of the Potomac with the brand-new 37th Wisconsin, leaving behind enough bounty money to carry his parents through a couple of years.[59]

In April of 1864 young John Rowe left his family's home in Michigan to look for a job in the oilfields of northwestern Pennsylvania. When he could not make a living there, he enlisted in a Pennsylvania regiment. His company commander noted that Rowe arrived for duty flush with cash.[60]

The bounties had to compete with rising wages, especially among skilled workers, in addition to compensating for the dangers and privations of a soldier's life. Army teamsters were paid forty dollars a month, as was an express messenger in Cleveland. Civilian blacksmiths and bridge builders with the armies drew two dollars a day, and carpenters around Alexandria, Virginia, reportedly earned three. Teachers in California were paid a hundred dollars a month, although they found it inadequate. Wagon masters in the West earned thirty-five dollars a month or more: John Miner gave up leading migrant trains from Omaha to go east and enlist as a substitute only at the nagging of his wife, who must have been dazzled by the lump sum it would bring. In contrast to the early days of the war, soldiers living in mud, misery, and mayhem often envied friends and relatives who were earning even a dollar a day at home. One young Ohioan who knew where he could work in a lumbering camp for twenty-two dollars a month plus board and lodging disdained a bounty of four hundred or five hundred dollars; another hundred dollars might make the difference, he intimated as he struck off for the piney woods, but without an offer that high he had no opportunity to test his resolve against soldiering.[61]

Captain Thaddeus Stevens Jr., whose congressman uncle had arranged for him to become provost marshal at Lancaster, Pennsylvania, revealed the effectiveness of the higher bounties by describing the sharp reduction in recruiting when the federal offer momentarily expired. To accelerate volunteering, Congress had set February 29 as the last day for paying the three-hundred-dollar bounty, and on that day thirty men signed up at the Lancaster office. The next day only two came in, after which recruiting was "a dead letter" despite local bounties. Captain Stevens informed his influential uncle of the situation, evidently to stimulate action, but a joint resolution extending the bounty offer had already passed both houses.[62]

While all those new regiments and recruits for old regiments were preparing to leave their home-state rendezvous, the governors of five Western states pressed upon the president an offer of 100,000 volunteers for a hundred days of service that summer. They envisioned using those men to guard prisoners and lines of communications, thereby releasing veteran troops for use in offensive operations, but they also offered them for employment "wherever else their services may be required." Obviously the hope was that those 100,000 and the new levies of three-year men would overwhelm Confederate forces before autumn. Lincoln passed the proposal on to Edwin Stanton, but he immediately handed it off to Ulysses Grant, who had taken command of all Union armies with the revived rank of lieutenant general. Like most professionally trained soldiers,

Grant had little use for short-term troops, except perhaps as home-front substitutes for experienced soldiers, but he betrayed his own overconfidence with his qualified assent. He would soon write of chasing down Lee's army "if it takes all summer," and he was not thinking beyond a decisive summer campaign when he speculated that the hundred-day men might be mobilized at a juncture that would make them "of vast importance." With that, Lincoln approved the plan.[63]

The hundred-day troops were to draw no bounties and count against no recruiting quotas, but the governors may have hoped to draw out many of the men who would only pay commutation or hire substitutes anyway. They could wear uniforms, taste a bit of camp life, and tell old-age stories of serving in the great war of their generation, all with as little risk as a cruise to California. After all, the brevity of the term implied that there would be no time for training, and the original proposal had specifically suggested them for use "in fortifications."[64] Their enlistment also protected them from conscription into more deadly service until the end of their term, which coincided with what promised to be a brutal campaign season. A captain in a seasoned Iowa regiment expected the summer soldiers would "take a great deal of credit to themselves for being willing to go for 100 days with the understanding that they will not be placed where there is any danger of their seeing a rebel!"[65] A sergeant in the armies operating against Atlanta remarked that his comrades "failed to see the bravery or patriotism of men enlisting for *100 days,* when there was such a prospect for a draft. When they thought the war was just ending; expecting no fighting, but simply guarding forts." He assured his mother, "we do not, cannot recognize them as brother soldiers."[66]

Indiana, Illinois, Iowa, and Wisconsin raised far fewer hundred-day men than their governors had anticipated: the four had collectively planned to contribute 55,000 men, but they were only able to produce twenty-eight regiments at the minimum complement, totaling less than half the number of troops they had promised. Ohio only exceeded its projected 30,000 men by calling out forty-two National Guard regiments organized the year before for local defense and other duties. Even with seventeen regiments from New York, New Jersey, Pennsylvania, and Massachusetts, the envisioned hundred-day army fell short by a good 20,000 troops overall.[67]

The hundred-day regiments betrayed more than a hint of wealth and a degree of privilege that was consistent with an image of men otherwise disconnected from the war. Senator Ben Wade's niece remarked that when the 29th Ohio National Guard left Cleveland, it carried away "the better class of young men." It was "an aristocratic regiment," she conceded, enumerating a host of clerks who disappeared from the city's businesses when the regiment departed.[68] Near Cincinnati, one woman welcomed the deployment: "We got rid of some of the 'stayathomes' by the calling out of the National Guard," she wrote, noting that even a fop she ridiculed as "the exquisite 'Awnderson'" had had to shoulder a musket.[69] Another woman in a town west of Columbus felt a touch of pity for those called up, remembering that the regiments had been composed of men—many of them married, with families—who had joined them as a military alternative to the draft that would allow them to stay home. An unusual number of young boys went with those units, having persuaded their parents how innocuous the hundred-day service would be. To the distress of some of those novices, a few of their regiments were sent to guard railroads and supply depots uncomfortably close to Confederate lines, where Union veterans greeted them with mock sympathy.[70]

Investigation of the wealth represented by the rosters of the hundred-day regiments only confirms the observations of the women who watched them muster and march away. To an even greater degree than the nine-month regiments of 1862, the hundred-day men reversed the almost invariable tendency among the three-year regiments toward a majority of men from the poorer half of each state's population. The sample companies from seven of the ten states that raised hundred-day troops show sizable majorities of men from households possessed of greater-than-median wealth; in Indiana, Massachusetts, and New York, more than two-thirds of the sampled soldiers ranked above the median. In nine of the ten states, the proportion of poorer soldiers in the hundred-day regiments fell significantly below the lowest percentage of poor in the same state's three-year regiments. Only 31 percent of the identified hundred-day men in Company A of the 132nd Indiana represented families of less-than-median wealth: the lowest proportion in any of Indiana's sampled three-year regiments had been 61 percent. The hundred-day men from Company A of the 60th Massachusetts included only 33 percent below median wealth, while none of that state's sampled three-year regiments produced less than 71 percent.[71]

Edwin Van Cise, the twenty-two-year-old son of a doctor in Mount Pleasant, Iowa, typified the hundred-day man. He passed his one martial season guarding a length of the Memphis and Charleston Railroad while writing atrocious doggerel that he dedicated to various young ladies. He felt himself "away out in the midst of danger and death," but his regiment never lost a man to hostile fire, and he shared the impatience of his comrades when the army kept him three days over what he calculated as the end of his enlistment. When Van Cise went home, he went for good.[72]

For the most part, those wealthier warriors enjoyed the safe and pleasant excursion they had counted on. In eighty-seven regiments comprising upward of eighty thousand men, exactly one hundred were killed by the enemy—most of them during three raids in Maryland, Kentucky, and Tennessee. A few hundred more died of disease, including several dozen prisoners who perished at Andersonville, but the rest lived to go home: most of them, or their survivors, eventually drew pensions for their service.[73]

The hundred-day men were packing up to go home and the two largest Confederate armies had been backed up to Atlanta and Petersburg when President Lincoln called for another half-million men at the height of summer in 1864. The Northern states had only recently held draft lotteries to provide for the deficiencies on the recruiting calls of the previous winter, and commutation had once again so diminished the number of men pressed into uniform that the provost marshal general advised repealing it. Congress obliged, and a new conscription bill became law in the final moments of the session on July 4, limiting drafted men to personal service or hiring substitutes if they could not meet any of the specific categories for exemption. Any men whose towns failed to fill their quotas with volunteers by September 5 would face that daunting prospect.[74]

The mere news that a bill to repeal commutation was on its way to the president bred a mild panic among wealthy men who had been content to wait and see if they would be drafted. A shortage of substitutes might have forced many of them to shoulder rifles, and they started hiring substitutes ahead of time just in case. Francis Brooks, a nominal lawyer and practicing gentleman from Medford, Massachusetts, authorized his selectmen to hire a substitute for him, to be counted against the town's quota. He expected the fee to exceed $650, but with his abundant resources he was willing to pay whatever it took; Brooks indicated that more than a dozen of his relatives and friends were doing the same thing. In New York, George Templeton Strong paid out $1,100 for the enlistment of "a big 'Dutch' boy," which assured that his periodic complaints about the president not drafting enough men would not be addressed by dragging Strong himself into the army. In Washington substitute prices doubled and kept on going from there, rising from $600 in July to $1,200 and $1,500 by late August, as the due date for volunteers grew near.[75]

The meteoric increase in the cost of substitutes lent much credence to the idea of commutation as a check-rein on those prices. The economic burden of its repeal fell on individuals and on communities, which had to match such premiums for volunteers and so raised the highest bounties of the entire war. A sudden abundance of potential substitutes implied that many had been holding back for the repeal so they could start raising their asking price.[76]

The patriot-drained town of Conway, New Hampshire, had to nearly triple its bounty offer to fill its quota, and it required special effort even at that amount. Only three men enlisted before the September 5 deadline, leaving a quota of twenty-six before two more local boys straggled in over the next week, along with a pair of nonresident substitutes. The draft was scheduled in Portsmouth for September 19, and on that very day a special meeting in Conway approved a bounty of eight hundred dollars. The provost marshal sent up the names of fifty potential conscripts, but the county sheriff—a draft-age citizen of the town—apparently held off delivering those notices until William Allen, another eligible resident, made one last pitch for volunteers. Allen spent the day and evening of September 21 roaming the hills and the villages, reiterating the financial advantages of enlistment, often to men whose names had already been drawn for conscription. Combined with a prorated federal bounty set at one hundred dollars, the county and state bounties, the town offer of eight hundred dollars, monthly pay of at least sixteen dollars, and family subsidies as high as twelve dollars, most Conway volunteers would realize the equivalent of three or four years' income for a year of service. With a new infantry regiment to join that would probably not see action for the rest of the year, that much money was difficult to refuse: the next morning twenty-two men between the ages of eighteen and forty-two met Allen at a local hotel to board the stagecoach for Concord.[77]

This was by far the wealthiest contingent of recruits to come from Conway during the war. Of those who appeared on the 1860 census, 54 percent of the September soldiers could claim property at or above the median, compared to the 81 percent who had fallen below the median among 1861 volunteers; moreover, nearly half of those who were counted below the median came in just below and owned property equal to at least three-quarters of it. An abundance of wealthier citizens remained in town to answer whatever calls the president might issue, and bounties had finally grown so extravagant that many who had previously avoided service were tempted to enlist. Ormand Merrill, one of those last-minute Conway volunteers, came from a reasonably comfortable family but had still received $300 from the town when he was drafted in June, using it to pay for commutation, so in him the community provided a single soldier for

$1,100. He and his comrades also enjoyed the most salubrious and uneventful service of any of the townsmen who preceded them, losing only one of their number to typhoid fever.[78]

Volunteers for the 1st New Hampshire Cavalry earned the additional benefit of a $300 special state bounty. With such an inviting incentive, the governor was trying to make up a recruiting shortfall caused by false announcements that he and the War Department had issued on the eve of the 1864 state elections, hoping to sway the results by purporting that the state's draft quota had been met. New Hampshire paid its bounties in cash, ostensibly on the spot, and most of the recruits for that big new mounted regiment refused to muster in until they saw the money. With the best offer of cash on the barrelhead within several states, the only regiment of Granite State horsemen attracted a disproportionate number of bounty jumpers, who contributed substantially to its 32-percent desertion rate.[79]

Between desertion and disqualifying physical defects, five hundred substitutes and well-paid volunteers bound for one of the Eastern divisions serving with Sherman dwindled to two hundred by the time they reached their destination. Of a hundred sent from New Haven to the 8th Connecticut, only fifty-six remained upon delivery. Many of those who had slipped away had no doubt gone back to try the same trick again in another location before the draft deadline put an end to the bounties. A Massachusetts captain on staff duty under Sherman could not fathom the government's reluctance to eliminate the substitution loophole before imposing mandatory service. "This dallying with hundred days men and imbeciles does not pay," he mused.[80]

Excessive remuneration was all that overcame citizen reluctance in that last late-summer recruiting effort. With less than three weeks left before the quota was due, a Maine man described his town doing all it could to raise enough volunteers and avoid a draft, but he characterized it as "mighty hard" attracting men, even at phenomenal bounties.[81] One farmer in rural Maine who was supporting several orphaned siblings had to pay $750 out of his own pocket for a substitute. Vermont towns that could afford it offered $800 for each volunteer, and a few paid $1,000 apiece, drawing men away from poorer communities and thus reducing the potential pool of substitutes, which in turn brought their prices higher. On the eve of the deadline, men in Orange County had to pay $1,200 for substitutes—if they could find them.[82] A Brookfield man whose only eligible son was already in the army complained that his share of the town debt for bounties would be $75: "There is no patriotism left," he grumbled. "'Tis all for money now & those towns that pay the most soonest fill their quota."[83]

The veterans who greeted recruits to their units in the autumn assumed that they had all come for the money, whether they were recently arrived aliens, urban hoodlums, or friends and neighbors from back home. Democrats who were opposed to the war had filled so many vacancies in one New York battery that the captain credited their presence to the size of the bounties, which he assumed overcame their political objections.[84]

A lust for money, or at least a visible giddiness at having profited so handsomely, did seem to infect the new levies. In New York, family men who had never thought to enlist before could not turn down invitations to serve as substitutes for $1,000 apiece. New troops arriving in the Army of the Potomac frequently let it be known that they had taken in $1,000 or more for their one-year enlistment, and if they did not admit it, their relatives at home did. Many of those recruits soon wound up on the sick list as a result of preexisting infirmities or malingering, and months later a New York soldier observed that the hospitals were filled with "1000 Dollar men who have never done an hours duty nor never will." Expressing surprise that they were almost invariably native-born Americans, he added that those mercenaries boasted openly of how they had swindled the principals for whom they had enlisted, or the communities for which they had volunteered. Even when they were discharged within weeks, bounty men kept their local money and whatever federal installments they had collected. Most of a Pennsylvania hundred-day company reenlisted for an additional year for only $600 in local bounties, but they did so on the disingenuous promises that their summer service would count against the year and that they would remain on guard duty within the state. Amid all these exorbitant incentives, a young Massachusetts man who had been rejected for his delicate constitution grieved for months over the money he had missed and vowed to repeat the attempt if another draft sent bounties soaring again.[85]

To reduce the expense, municipalities and individuals resorted to more distant sources of substitutes and volunteers, although transporting human beings across state lines or international borders for that purpose could risk a sizable fine and a jail sentence. Another shipment of German volunteers brought across the Atlantic by Boston's Foreign Emigrant Society passed through Washington in early September, arousing recollections of the slave trade for one conservative resident of the capital.[86]

Men who had only recently been freed from actual slavery became popular marks as substitutes. An agent for a Connecticut broker visiting Ohio found prospective substitutes available there for anywhere from $500 to $700, noting that "colored subs" were cheapest of all.[87] A young Cleveland bank officer who had gone off as a lieutenant in a six-month regiment in 1862 (predicting that he would come home "a tough boy") sent an employee down to Knoxville looking for a handful of "negro substitutes" for himself and others. He also suggested a business arrangement for a friend by which he could bring some of those freedmen back to Ohio at about $300 apiece and clear as much as $450 from each of them.[88] An officer at the headquarters of the Commission for the Organization of Colored Troops in Nashville wrote to the judge advocate for the Department of Missouri—an abolitionist and Radical Republican—about "buying" black men from the contraband camp in St. Louis. In what he clearly intended as a clandestine enterprise, he suggested paying the superintendent of the camp $10 to $25 apiece and taking the men East to peddle as substitutes, where they would bring as much as $750 each.[89]

The magnetism of cash, more than a lack of manpower, accounted for the extremes of youth and age that tested the resolve of examining surgeons that season. A woman who watched the green recruits of the 31st Michigan stop for a meal in Flint saw one old man in uniform, but many of the rest seemed as young as fifteen or sixteen. A sixty-five-year-old man in southern New Hampshire seriously considered enlisting in the state's new heavy-artillery regiment after his town voted to pay a $600 bounty. One of the October recruits in the 1st Minnesota Heavy Artillery, Albert Woolson, was still a few months short of his fifteenth birthday when he enlisted as a drummer boy. Woolson was not only young but also desperately poor, with a dying father, a sickly younger brother, and a mother who worked as a domestic servant in another household. Even that far west the local bounties were reaching $350 and $400, and to the scattered, scraping Woolson family, that was too generous to pass up. It was as much as a district attorney in that region might earn in a year.[90]

The bounties filtered from the hands of the volunteers to their families, and from there into the communities, fueling inflation and worsening the plight that many of the recruits had meant to alleviate by their sacrifice. "I can see nothing ahead but high prices and hard times," remarked a worried Wisconsin captain who was paying a dollar a day for unsatisfactory board. At home, business had never been better for retailers, and calculating merchants laid up inventory on speculation that prices would rise even further. Impoverished families left behind waited anxiously for their soldiers to send home some money, but late pay and devalued currency wrought worse havoc than ever before. Rising prices afflicted the country from one end to the other: a New Yorker noted the phenomenon at the fringe of civilization in Council Bluffs, Iowa, and innocently pinpointed the cause when he noticed how much cash was accumulating there from pilgrims headed across the plains.[91]

Conservative politicians and bankers had worried about the inflationary effect of simply printing more currency. At one point in the fall of 1864, it cost one soldier $2.85 in greenbacks to buy a dollar in gold. At the end of the fall recruiting drive, a Maine man pined for some gold coin in his neighborhood that he could hoard, cursing the profusion of increasingly worthless "Lincoln skins." To help reduce the flood of currency, the Treasury even tried paying soldiers in small-denomination government bonds that would not come to maturity for five years. Eleutheros Cooke, whose son Jay had been the government's agent for selling Treasury bonds, tried to cash his in early to reduce his loss to inflation. Local and state bounties, meanwhile, all came in cash—either in greenbacks, the new national bank notes, or the less-negotiable local bank notes that the government was taxing out of circulation. That created an acute, artificial prosperity. A few weeks after his son recruited enough men to fill the quota of their town in northern New Hampshire, merchant Richard Kent recorded a week's sales of $700; between the indulgence of the war weary and those momentarily flush with funds, his receipts on Christmas Eve set a one-day record of $341, with $175 of it in cash. Kent collected on one long-overdue account by buying the town's promissory note to a volunteer whose family owed him $100, deducting the debt before he handed the balance of the bounty to the soldier's wife. He also earned interest on the note.[92]

From the beginning of conscription to the bitter end of the conflict, the effort to satisfy one levy had no sooner been concluded than the president issued another. The War Department announced a new draft of 300,000 more men only days before Christmas, 1864, with February 15, 1865, as the cutoff date for reducing the quota with volunteers. The cycle of pleading followed by paying thereupon repeated itself. Legislatures that had not yet established a state bounty began doing so, or at least discussing one, and as usual those in the East paid more to bring anyone in. Editors regurgitated the same appeals to pocketbook they had been plying since 1861, garnishing them with headlines predicting "The End is Approaching" and "Discord and Despair in Dixie."[93]

Even with the Confederacy teetering toward collapse, most eligible civilians declined generous bounties and paid handsomely to avoid service if they could raise the money. A young Ohioan hired a substitute for $800, while a Vermonter working for the Quartermaster Department in Arkansas vowed that if he were drafted he would find someone to serve for him if he had to pay $1,000—although he supposed he could hire a freedman for a fraction of that.[94] A resident of Pike County, Missouri, apprised an absent neighbor how much the county had appropriated for substitutes, noting that the judges had gone to St. Louis laden with plenty of "Greens" to avoid having citizens drafted.[95] Reading of the sums offered and paid, a Massachusetts soldier wrote a friend back home that the patriotic air had changed from "We are coming Father Abraham, 300,000 more" to "Who is the man that will go for me, $300 more?"[96]

There were, however, many who would take the money, including the very young and the hard pressed. Often they were men already in the army, or just out of it. Exaggerated tales of the bounties offered for reenlisting in the Regular Army sparked considerable excitement in January, 1865, among young men who had not yet been volunteers for a year: one heard that $600 of a $1,000 bounty came in gold, and another understood that a three-year enlistment yielded $1,300 while a five-year recruit would get $1,800. Neither was true, so neither soldier made the leap. A Vermont sergeant promoted to lieutenant in the 24th U.S. Colored Troops had to reenlist for three years anyway to accept the commission, and he sent his mustering papers back to his home town to collect the bounty there; he told his father that if the selectmen would not give him the money to take the papers to another town and credit him to the draft quota there.[97]

Some discharged veterans had not blended back into society very well and began scanning recruiting advertisements again when they had reached the limits of economic desperation. Would-be poet John A. Dickie had joined an Ohio regiment in 1861 and served out his term, coming home in July of 1864, a few weeks after his twentieth birthday. That summer he made some money painting a house, but—as many laborers learned that year—his wages barely kept up with his expenses. He had been scribbling verse that he considered everlasting and, when cold weather precluded further outdoor occupation, he paid a printer to run off enough of his poetry in pamphlet form to fill a suitcase. Intending to make a living by selling his rhymes and lecturing, Dickie started across Ohio around Christmas, peddling his booklets among soldiers at Camp Dennison and at the doors of houses along the road. The lack of interest pained him deeply, for he was sure he had "the genius," and his diary dripped with self-pity because no one else recognized it. Late in January he spent his last dollar on part of his room rent, leaving his broadcloth coat as collateral for the rest, and headed for Cincinnati with forty cents in his pocket. As much as he had hated the army, he started to shop the recruiting offices as soon as he arrived. He tried for a civilian job, too, visiting an employment agency, but his lack of skills and finicky temperament hampered him. "O dear me," he mourned on January 31, 1865, "I wish something would turn up so that I could keep out of the army." Nothing did, and Dickie only avoided reenlisting in the army by joining the navy two days later.[98]

Abram Parmenter had completed his enlistment in the 12th Michigan one week into the new year, returning to his wife and children in Cass County, Michigan. He had received no bounty in 1861 and collected only the one-hundred-dollar federal discharge bonus when he came home, but his lot had improved on three years of regular pay and the fifteen-dollar monthly family supplement from Michigan. He owned a home, albeit with a mortgage, and by reenlisting he could retire that debt, restore his wife's "state pay," and put some money away. Ten weeks after he came home he reenlisted in Winfield Hancock's new corps of veterans, for which recruits received a special three-hundred-dollar bounty in addition to all others.[99]

Expediency moved Henry Rinker to enlist for the first time in the final weeks of the war. At the age of forty and as an ordained Presbyterian minister with a wife and two children at home, he need not have feared conscription, but things seemed not to be going well for him. He had no parish and may not have had one for some time when, early in March of 1865, he enlisted as a private in a New Jersey regiment. Reverend Rinker drew a substantial bounty, although how much is uncertain. He assured his wife that if he lived he would have a commission "without fail," and while he would prefer to be a chaplain, "a lieutenancy would be quite as desirable." Rinker certainly had an eye for opportunity, for within three months he was appointed chaplain of the 86th New York. The war had ended by then, and he was mustered out four weeks later, but in 117 days of service he had achieved his main goal. "I think I have made a pretty good haul thus far this year," he confessed, while speculating whether he could improve on that income with an appointment in a black regiment or the Freedmen's Bureau.[100]

Back in that Copperhead community of Conway, New Hampshire, the last men to apply themselves to the town quota were Jesse Watson, a thirty-year-old bachelor known as a "loafer" in the family he lived with, and Moses Bean, a fifty-year-old farmer down on his luck. Watson had spent his life as a hired hand. He was personally acquainted with several young men who had been killed in the summer of 1864, and he had not responded to the town's eight-hundred-dollar bounty offer in September. By late March the end of the war lay in sight, and he was one of few eligible men left on Conway's enrollment list when he accepted five hundred dollars from the town for a year's enlistment. Bean, the father of seven children, worked as a laborer on other men's farms: he was well past draft age, but he was broke, having long since sold off the last of his own property. This pair enlisted on March 28, with Bean shaving about seven years off his age.[101]

From Concord, Bean and Watson were sent to Galloup's Island in Boston Harbor to camp and train until their company could be filled. They were still there when Robert E. Lee surrendered, twelve days later, and on May 6 a boat carried them and most of the other recruits on the island back to the wharf in Boston, landing them with their discharge papers. Bean and Watson returned home before their uniforms began to fade—the last poor men from their town who had taken advantage of a financial opportunity by risking the fortunes of war in place of those who could afford to avoid it.[102]

9

THE NEEDY HERO

Demobilization spread joy, sadness, and anxiety through the army camps as the pleasure of going home alternated with emotional farewells to comrades and nagging uncertainty over the chances of making a living in civilian society. That uncertainty would have weighed more heavily on those whose economic positions had been particularly precarious when they enlisted, and especially for those who had enlisted precisely to rectify financial difficulties.

Some private soldiers had improved their fortunes tremendously, at least for the immediate future, by speculating in merchandise, lending money, buying recruits' bounty certificates at cash discounts, or simply sending all their bounties and pay home. Others who had hoped to restore their fortunes in the army found themselves no better off—or even further behind—in 1865 than they had been when they went to war. Onley Andrus, a newlywed whose in-laws frowned on his spasmodic industry and his economic prospects, had left his bride and infant daughter in 1862 with the consolation that at least he was finally making money and could save a stake for their future. As a senior noncommissioned officer he earned more than a private soldier, but he essentially acknowledged after the end of the war that his critics had judged him well. He still owned no home, had little money, and could not say what his future would be.[1]

Soldiers had been worrying about their civilian employment prospects since long before the shooting stopped. Enlisted men nearing the ends of their terms had inquired among army contractors about jobs in construction and railroad maintenance, or considered working for their regimental sutlers or as teamsters and wagon masters with the army's trains. Officers had written home about business opportunities or positions as clerks and bookkeepers, hoping to line something up against the tidal wave of unemployed men who would be inundating their communities when the armies disbanded. Hundreds of thousands of those men had entered the army without skills, had learned nothing useful during their service, and faced an increasingly demanding job market.[2]

Most officers earned more from the army than they could have at home. Competition with a jobless mob would only have worsened their chances for any satisfactory livelihood, and many of them therefore hoped to keep their commissions as long as possible. That prospect specifically worried Captain Henry Brown of the 1st U.S. Colored Troops as he observed Confederate surrender negotiations in North Carolina: "I do not wish to be thrown suddenly out of employment with the two or three hundred thousand others that will also be relieved," he told his mother. "I hope to stay until affairs get settled & I can perhaps save a few dollars & be able to find some employment." The same thought struck Major James Madison Bowler of the 113th U.S. Colored Troops, who had entered the army unemployed in 1861. "From this day on every day in the service will pay me more than I could otherwise gain," he explained to his wife, who pressured him to resign and come home. Bowler expected his regiment, like most of the newer black regiments, to be held in service the longest, and he wished to remain on duty at least until he had accumulated some savings.[3]

Those of more exalted rank felt the same threat. Brigadier General Adin Underwood, who had been crippled by a leg wound, continued to draw his salary as he sat on court-martial duty in Washington. His wife worried about the rising cost of living and what he would do if he were discharged, accusing him of always being dissatisfied with whatever occupation he followed. Thinking about the cost of educating their children, she consented to his remaining in the service as long as he could, remarking that she had married him for better or worse—as though she felt it had come to worse. Ultimately he was mustered out in August, albeit with a brevet promotion to major general, but he partially recouped the loss of his general's salary with a federal appointment as surveyor of the port of Boston.[4]

From his Milwaukee headquarters the commander of the Department of the Northwest, Major General Samuel Curtis, reminded his own wife that they would also see an inevitable decline in their standard of living. "We must keep the matter of the reduction of the army in view," he cautioned her, "and prepare for the cessation of our present ample income by strict economy."[5]

The war had absorbed vast legions of the nation's poor and unemployed, and it spit them back out so abruptly that many of them returned to the same conditions that had led them to enlist. Wartime attrition had depleted the labor force, but immigration filled that void, and on leaving the army many a foreign-born soldier found employment that put him in a far better financial position than he had ever previously known.[6] After the initial glut of returning veterans had dissipated, industrial development employed hundreds of thousands whose incomes had been interrupted or whose businesses had been ruined by the recession of the early war. Others headed west to booming new cities, or to homesteads on the plains.[7] The expanding federal bureaucracy absorbed a great many of them through post offices and customhouses, but there were always more applicants than positions.[8]

Eventually most veterans found adequate employment, at least for a time, in an era fraught with financial panic. They came to see themselves on a separate plane from their fellow citizens, and most seemed to embrace an independent spirit best signified and maintained by economic self-sufficiency. A burgeoning corporate economy often impeded their quest for financial security, thereby eroding the ideal of personal independence. A liberal pension law undermined that culture of self-reliance a little further by rekindling the common wartime notion that the government could provide a source of income as a last resort. The monthly benefit must have paled alongside the cost in pride, at least at first, but sooner or later most veterans applied.[9]

The public image of the veteran suffered from those who secured undeserved pensions, and few exemplified such opportunists better than Newton T. Colby. That gun-shy New York officer exemplified the Union volunteer whose actions during and after the war were motivated entirely by self-interest. He had taken a commission in the army when his search for a secure, salaried position in Washington had failed. After the terror of Antietam, he risked staying with his regiment through winter, well behind the front lines, and in that quiet posting the resignations of others brought him the rank of lieutenant colonel. Colby found the salary and emoluments unbearably attractive until, in the spring of 1863, his regiment entered the four days of fighting at Chancellorsville. He manufactured an excuse to slip out of the fight early, asking his colonel's permission on Saturday morning, May 2, to go back to the field hospital to check on a wounded officer. The colonel contemptuously described Colby "promising faithfully not to be gone over half an hour," adding "I did not see him again until Tuesday."[10]

So conspicuously damning a commentary in the colonel's official report of the battle ended Colby's usefulness with the regiment, so he reported himself sick, staying in the hospital until he was discharged for disability on September 5. Only sixteen days later Colby wrote to his father asking him to obtain "the strongest certificate" of disability he could get (obviously without any physical examination) from a doctor they knew on the draft enrollment board. He needed the certificate to apply for a commission in the Invalid Corps, where he could still draw full pay but would have to perform nothing more dangerous than administrative functions. He soon resumed his rank of lieutenant colonel in that light-duty service, holding on to it until his regiment was disbanded in the summer of 1866. With the fighting over, he deemed himself fit for the field again and tried for a commission in the U.S. Army, but there were not enough commissioned billets for those officers who had distinguished themselves, let alone for the likes of Colby.[11]

For some years Colby floundered about as an unsuccessful merchant, insurance agent, and bank clerk. Then, early in 1879, Congress modified the 1862 pension law with the Arrears Act, reopening the period in which veterans could apply for pensions and allowing them to collect retroactive benefits in a lump sum from their original date of discharge. Applicants no longer needed medical records to prove their claims, either, but could simply submit a couple of affidavits from friends who had served with them. Colby was among the first in the country to apply, a few weeks after the bill became law. In his original submission he estimated, with patently strategic inaccuracy, that he had been stricken with typhoid fever about "March or April 1863—because the regiment went on the Chancellorsville Campaign not long thereafter." He claimed that he tried to keep up when the regiment marched, but only overtook it at its next camp, after the battle, where he lay "sick and delirious" when the unit moved again, after which he said he never saw it again. By such circumlocution did Colby imply that he had never been at Chancellorsville at all, besides giving himself an excuse for having left the battle if someone brought up his embarrassing disappearance from that field. His application passed a perfunctory examination process despite contradictory records and surviving comrades who (like his former colonel in the 107th New York) might have scuttled his hopes in a sentence or two.[12]

Colby collected thousands of dollars in back pay and drew a considerable monthly stipend for more than twenty-six years longer, in addition to whatever civilian salaries he was able to earn. He persistently appealed for a federal appointment through powerful friends in Washington—primarily Senator Zebulon Vance, a former Confederate governor whose gratitude he had engendered while commanding the guards where Vance was held prisoner. Those political connections finally won Colby the government sinecure he had been looking for since before the war. He spent the last dozen years of his working life as a pension examiner, certifying the applications of other veterans, some of whom had also submitted claims of doubtful merit, and at least a few of whom were gaming the system as blatantly as he was.[13]

The Pension Bureau originally applied stringent criteria in an effort to limit its distribution of very modest sums to disabled veterans or their survivors, but that changed dramatically in the quarter century after the war. As the Grand Army of the Republic grew in political strength, it edged away from the spirit of independence and self-sufficiency so many veterans had embraced or pursued, turning instead to the goal of public relief for veterans. The Arrears Act of 1879 had marked the first step in that relief. In 1890 a bill called the Dependent Pension Act slipped through with a provision to allow pensions for disabilities resulting from ailments and injuries altogether unrelated to military service. Along with a later provision for increasing monthly allotments for age alone, the 1879 and 1890 laws begat a flood of applications. In 1878, the last full year before the Arrears Act, government outlays for pensions totaled $26,844,000; in 1880, the first full year of its operation, the total came to $57,240,000. More than twice as many applicants filed for pensions in June of 1880 alone as had in all of 1877. Payments first exceeded $100 million a year in 1890, and the number of pensioners grew nearly eightfold between 1866 and 1902, when there were just under a million recipients on the rolls.[14]

Even under the more rigorous control of the 1862 law, pensions had occasionally been granted for ludicrous reasons: one Maine cavalryman won a discharge and pension for having been "moonstruck" while lying on the open ground on a certain night in 1862. With the later legislation, fraud grew more frequent. Some men who had suffered genuine wounds exaggerated the disabling effects, while some falsified the circumstances of their injuries. Misrepresentation became fairly common among those pensioned for illness—as the especially glaring example of Colby illustrates. Veterans who boasted at regimental reunions of their successful professional practices presented themselves to pension examiners as indigent and debilitated. A comrade's recollection of an applicant's cold or cough during the war might become the basis of a claim for consumption contracted after the war, or explain chronic lung disorders more attributable to smoking. Tens of thousands of men who had served only in the bucolic encampments of ninety-day and hundred-day regiments prepared their stories and lined up to collect the same annuity as men who had spent years in uniform and fought in a dozen battles or lost limbs.[15]

Abuse of the system and the extension of benefits to the undeserving severely tainted the public's once-reverent opinion of those who had rallied to the colors. In an open letter to *Century Magazine* intended to elicit pity for veterans and garner support for the 1890 pension law, a former captain in the Pennsylvania Reserves inadvertently pinpointed why so many veterans swallowed their pride and asked for public assistance. Frank Bell had lost part of his right leg at Gettysburg, and since then he had simultaneously drawn a disability pension and a succession of government salaries from the Veteran Reserve Corps, the Treasury Department, the Land Office, and finally the Pension Department, where by 1891 he was a special examiner—and undoubtedly a sympathetic one. He presented the average veteran as economically handicapped on his return from the army, although Bell himself personified the hiring preference accorded to veterans. He conceded that the 1890 law allowed pensions for men suffering no disability from their service, and he admitted taking a disability pension himself when he was not at all disabled from the full-time work he pursued. Yet he still defended the law, believing it just because, as he put it, "the large majority of our old comrades are poor men."[16]

With that phrase Bell touched on a significant, forgotten factor in Union recruiting. His assertion that most Civil War veterans occupied the poorer half of society may have been accurate, and it would have been perfectly logical because that was the population that produced a solid majority of Union volunteers. Poor men were heavily overrepresented in the regiments that lost most heavily on the battlefield, and in those that suffered disproportionately from disease. Almost invariably, when men from the upper economic strata composed the majority of any regiment, it was one recruited for a short term—ninety days, one hundred days, or nine months—and more often than not they did not see the arduous, deadly service of the less affluent three-year men. Still, the poor were so numerous that their greater mortality would not have significantly reduced their proportion among the survivors of the two economic classes. If they continued to exhibit a degree of economic motivation as pension applicants, in most cases it would have been for the same reason so many of them had enlisted in the first place: they were driven to the decision by financial need.[17]

Albert Hard was not yet eighteen when he enlisted in the 32nd New York one month after the firing on Fort Sumter. As the son of a moderately prosperous farmer, he does not appear to have been among those who enlisted from pressing economic necessity. Prompted by the one-year limit of the Arrears Act, he nevertheless applied for a pension on March 19, 1880, when he was only thirty-six. Likely he sought compensation for whatever sent him to army hospitals through May and June of 1862 and again from October 29 of that year into the winter of 1863. The nature of his ailment is now lost—apparently through government misplacement of his pension records—but malaria was a common complaint, and Hard first entered an army hospital on the mosquito-infested Virginia Peninsula. His application would have resulted in back payments dating from his discharge in 1863, and he collected that benefit seventy-three years longer. After the relaxation of eligibility and documentation requirements in 1890, he retired from manual labor to act as an agent for other veterans seeking pensions and continued to make his living in that way into his late seventies, buying his first home early in the new century. He lived on his own into his nineties, and only after he had been collecting his pension for more than forty years did he appear to really need it—a circumstance that would have given pension reformers fits during the Cleveland administrations. In return for his two years of service, Hard drew a government stipend covering nine decades, from the payments backdated to his discharge in June of 1863 until his death on March 12, 1953, at the age of 109. No other man collected compensation so long for having carried a rifle in Lincoln's army—or probably in any army.[18]

Hard's demise left a single pensioner from the Union army. Hard and Albert Woolson shared a first name, memories of boyhood in central New York, late-life prominence in the Grand Army of the Republic, and an addiction to cigars. Until his last few years, however, Woolson never knew the security Hard usually enjoyed. As a boy Woolson had lived with his married older sister while his mother worked as a domestic servant and a younger brother boarded with a third family. His father, Willard Woolson, had gone to Minnesota, perhaps to start a new home where his health might improve, but he enlisted in the 4th Minnesota when the war broke out, only to be discharged after a few months in worse condition than before. The elder Woolson was dying by the autumn of 1864, and with him would die any hope of family income, so fourteen-year-old Albert enlisted as a drummer boy six months before Lee's surrender. By then the minimum age for enlistment had been reduced to sixteen with parental permission, but he still had to lie about his age, just as Hard had in 1861. Woolson was only fifteen when he came home the next year, finding himself the family breadwinner.[19]

Woolson married young—at nineteen—and begat a large family. He worked on steam engines and boilers in various mills for more than half a century, raising seven children with one wife and three more with another, but comfort eluded him. When the Dependent Pension Act became law, he quickly took advantage of it, filing for relief in 1891, when he was only forty-one. In 1907 the law was amended again to provide additional compensation for veterans who reached the age of sixty-two, and on February 19, 1909, he filed for that increase. He would not really have turned sixty-two until 1912, but he spent more than half of 1909 out of work and had already begun a second family with a Norwegian girl in her early twenties, who was pregnant again when he applied. So great was his need for money that he continued working into his seventies as a mechanic at a Duluth iron works: Woolson never bought a home, and in his nineties he was still paying twenty-five dollars in rent every month. By then his pension provided most, if not all, of his income.[20]

After the death of his second wife, Woolson moved in with his youngest daughter's family. It was while living in their home, in 1953, that he became a national celebrity as the last survivor of all those who had worn the blue, and while he surely never thought of it that way, he was also the last of Lincoln's mercenaries. He had donned a uniform in a state of extreme financial want, and that same want returned to him in middle age, as it did to so many other veterans. In both instances it was service in the Union army that saved him from destitution.[21]

In his familiarity with financial hardship, Albert Woolson was more typical of his comrades in arms than not. Two-thirds of Union soldiers represented the poorer half of their states' populations. Those who, like Woolson's father, answered the call at the outset of the war—the men historically regarded as the most patriotic—reflected the most widespread economic distress of all. For most of them, the altruistic motives for which they are now congratulated were often equaled or overshadowed by acute or even chronic pecuniary plight.

Soldiers who wrote home crediting their enlistments to patriotic impulses might well have felt those emotions at the time. Especially following the attack on Fort Sumter, nationalist hysteria quickened the pulse of millions. Tens of thousands of men flocked to the colors, and the excitement and variety of their new experience may have distracted many from noticing that the modest emoluments of military service had eased or solved their personal financial woes. Others did recognize the salutary effects of army pay and family subsidies, and some enlisted precisely to benefit from them, but understandably few admitted being attracted by monetary incentives. There was, after all, great honor attached to fighting for one's country, and intense opprobrium associated with fighting for profit: much of the public and many in the army stood ready to condemn soldiers who went to war for money. Allegations of mercenary motivation surfaced in the summer of 1862, as soon as large sums of cash became necessary to lure volunteers. Repressive measures incorporated in the Militia Act amendments that summer indicated that the government anticipated that imputation, which it silenced with an alacrity that illustrated how deeply such rhetoric was feared as an effective curb on recruiting.

James McPherson's extensive survey of the correspondence of Union soldiers revealed that two-thirds of them made some expression of patriotic motive. Almost exactly the same proportion of Union soldiers came from the poorer half of Northern society. Few of them admitted the attraction of financial incentives, but so disreputable was financial motivation and so revered was the impulse to defend the flag that professions of patriotism would inevitably have outweighed any admissions of mercenary impulse. However sincere those expressions may usually have been, the man who insisted most vehemently that he was impelled by duty or nationalist indignation was not always able to convince his own neighbors or family members. Quantifying the respective frequency of such claims in contemporary correspondence is not likely to produce reliable conclusions about motive, and a similar effort among memoirs would likely be even more misleading. In the first place, there is no way to assure how accurately surviving manuscripts reflect overall sentiment among Union soldiers, or even among all Union soldiers who kept diaries and wrote letters, since most such written records have probably been lost. Patriotically inspiring missives would have been more likely to be preserved—partly because of the content but also because soldiers who felt especially patriotic were so often killed. Conspicuous accounts of battles, or the letters of a brother or father who died in the war, were far less likely to be lost or discarded.[22]

Most veterans, meanwhile, might reasonably have been expected to destroy correspondence as compromising as Newton Colby left behind, betraying his extreme self-interest. Such direct evidence of mercenary intent usually survives only by oversight, accident, or through a combination of avarice and diligence in the same candid veteran. Not many a soldier would admit, as Vermonter Philip Arsino did, that he had only enlisted "for twenty dollars per month," but many of them—like Arsino—kept their side of the bargain even at the cost of their lives.[23] Plenty of equally dutiful soldiers left indirect epistolary evidence of their economic preoccupation, but that alone is no more reliable for gauging motivation throughout the Union army than are the most movingly patriotic letters.

The strongest indication that money provided a significant attraction for Union soldiers is to be found in the relative poverty from which most of them came. A sample of the 1860 census finally allows a meaningful assessment of the distribution of wealth among Union soldiers by establishing median wealth for each state. That a large majority of soldiers represented families whose worldly property amounted to less than the median suggests an obvious inference about motivation.[24]

Well over 64 percent of all the volunteers surveyed in Table 1 fell below the median wealth in their home states. The ninety-day soldiers who began the war presented the heaviest concentrations, 71 percent of them volunteering from the poorer half of the population. The two- and three-year regiments raised in 1861 reflected only slightly less poverty, drawing 70 percent of their initial recruits from the humbler classes, and 67 percent of the three-year men of 1862 came from that same cohort. In the nine-month regiments of 1862, however, only 57 percent of the average complement was composed of men from families below the median wealth, and two-fifths of the sampled nine-month units had a sizable majority from above the median. The hundred-day volunteers of 1864, whom the fighting men regarded as no soldiers at all, produced the most conspicuously affluent results, with an average of only 45 percent of poor men in their ranks: wealthier volunteers outnumbered them by substantial majorities in most of the hundred-day regiments, often exceeding two-thirds of each roster.

The reason for such an overwhelming majority of economically disadvantaged men in the three-month regiments is obvious. Secession bred consumer boycotts, debt repudiation, a cotton embargo, and currency disruption that initiated severe commercial stagnation, extensive unemployment, and widespread desperation for cash. That economic turmoil spawned throngs of unoccupied men eager for regular pay, perhaps especially if it involved a little adventure against those they deemed responsible for their financial predicament. That same idle multitude contributed heavily to the longer-term regiments that followed the militia call during the war's first year, which explains the similar proportion of men from households of more modest resources. In the 1861 regiments generally, men from the poorer half of society outnumbered their comrades from the wealthier half by more than two to one. Clearly something drew them that held less attraction for the more comfortable, and in many cases that "something" was simply basic subsistence.

The pool of unemployed had shrunk considerably by the summer recruiting drive of 1862. The bounties raised to satisfy the new military quotas nevertheless exerted their greatest influence on those who enjoyed the least wealth, helping to attract disproportionately high ratios of volunteers from the lower end of the economic scale. Most of the nine-month regiments organized toward the end of 1862 also fielded a majority of poorer men, but the proportion fell sharply, perhaps partly because so much of that population had just enlisted in three-year regiments. The 1862 militia call also brought the first threat of compulsory service, and men of somewhat better means who would not have considered a three-year term may have been willing to risk the relatively short enlistment.

Conscription for the more arduous three-year service followed in 1863, but the wealthy and much of the middle class avoided that through the options of commutation or substitution. The very nature of the substitute exchange assured that poorer men would almost always don the uniform, often wholly or partially at the expense of clients who were better off. That contributed to a slight jump in the ratio of poorer men in the three-year regiments raised between the fall of 1863 and the spring of 1864, back to 70 percent of the sampled units.

Most of the hundred-day regiments raised in the spring of 1864 revealed the opposite economic composition, consisting chiefly of men who had accumulated more than the median amount of wealth—or the sons of such men. It could have been predicted that those regiments would attract far fewer of the poor because they counted against no quotas, and therefore no bounties of any kind were offered for those volunteers. The hundred-day troops also understood that they would probably not be put in harm's way, which attracted great numbers of richer men who could escape the draft but sought token participation with little risk or commitment. The hundred-day misadventure demonstrated both how much more easily poor men were drawn into the army by money and how determined wealthier men were to avoid more serious military service.

After the repeal of the commutation clause during the summer of 1864, substitute prices and bounties both soared, but they never rose high enough to tempt the established professional or successful businessman. A struggling tradesman or frugal farmer might weigh potential substitute costs against bounty offers and conclude that he could better afford to enlist than stay home, but that was about as rich a recruit as financial incentives secured for the army. Such personal calculations, combined with shrinking pools of draft-eligible males, accounted for a slight drop in the percentage of poorer volunteers among the one-year regiments recruited in the last six months of the conflict. Still, to the very last it was poor men who, by heavy majorities, dominated the regiments that bore the brunt of the conflict.

Addressing a question of class long asked by Civil War historians, the calculations in Table 1 show that in the Union army—as in today's volunteer army—economic condition was a principal factor determining whether someone enlisted.[25] From first to last, the forces that brought the Confederacy to its knees drew the lion's share of their recruits from the poorer half of the population. However he felt about the Union, republican government, or slavery, and whether or not he yearned for adventure, wished to prove himself, or consciously enlisted for money, a man or boy was twice as likely to serve in Lincoln's army if he was poor.

NOTES

ABBREVIATIONS

AAS	American Antiquarian Society
AHEC	Army Heritage and Education Center
BGSU	Bowling Green State University
BL	Bentley Library, University of Michigan
BPL	Boston Public Library
CCHS	Chautauqua County Historical Society
CG	U.S. Congress, *Congressional Globe*
CHS	Connecticut Historical Society
CinHS	Cincinnati Historical Society
CL	Clements Library, University of Michigan
CPL	Conway Public Library
CSR	Compiled Service Records of Volunteer Union Soldiers Who Served in Organizations from the State of Missouri (M405)
DC	Dartmouth College
HSCC	Historical Society of Cheshire County
IHS	Indiana Historical Society
IPUMS-USA	Ruggles, Steven, Katie Genadek, Ronald Goeken, Josiah Grover, and Matthew Sobek. *Integrated Public Use Microdata Series: Version 6.0* [Machine-readable database]. Minneapolis: University of Minnesota, 2015.
ISL	Indiana State Library
IU	Indiana University
IWA	Iowa Women's Archives, University of Iowa
KSHS	Kansas State Historical Society
LC	Library of Congress
MEHS	Maine Historical Society

MHS	Massachusetts Historical Society
MNBP	Manassas National Battlefield Park
MNHS	Minnesota Historical Society
MOHS	Missouri Historical Society
MSSM	*Massachusetts Soldiers, Sailors, and Marines in the Civil War*
NA	National Archives
ND	University of Notre Dame
NHDRMA	New Hampshire Department of Records Management and Archives
NHHS	New Hampshire Historical Society
NHSL	New Hampshire State Library
NIU	Northern Illinois University
NYSL	New York State Library
OHS	Ohio Historical Society
OR	*War of the Rebellion: A Compilation of the Official Records of the Union and Confederate Armies.* All citations from series 1 unless otherwise stated.
PEM	Peabody Essex Museum
PPL	Providence Public Library
RBHPL	Rutherford B. Hayes Presidential Library
RG	Record Group
RIHS	Rhode Island Historical Society
RJCCW	*Report of the Joint Committee on the Conduct of the War*
SHC	Southern Historical Society, University of North Carolina
SHSI-DM	State Historical Society of Iowa, Des Moines
SHSI-IC	State Historical Society of Iowa, Iowa City
UIA	University of Iowa
UNH	University of New Hampshire
UVM	University of Vermont
VAHS	Virginia Historical Society
VHS	Vermont Historical Society
VPI	Virginia Polytechnic Institute and State University
WCNB	Wilson's Creek National Battlefield
WHMC	Western Historical Manuscripts Collection, State Historical Society of Missouri
WHS	Wisconsin Historical Society
WRHS	Western Reserve Historical Society

PREFACE

1. McPherson, *Battle Cry of Freedom,* 602–3; McPherson, *For Cause and Comrades,* 101–2.

2. Gallman, *North Fights the Civil War,* 56–57; Mitchell, *Civil War Soldiers,* 11–15, 32–34.

3. Sheehan-Dean, *View from the Ground,* 9.

4. Margo, "Wages and Prices during the Antebellum Period," 193–94, 196; Monkkonen, *Walking to Work;* Clement, "Transformation of the Wandering Poor," 65.

5. Spall, "Foreigners in the Highest Trust," 340–41; Fabre, "In Defence of Mercenarism," 540 (also cited in Spall); Washington, *Papers,* 8:525.

6. James McPherson concluded that those late-war soldiers "were motivated marginally if at all by ideology or patriotism." *What They Fought For,* 42.

7. Lutz, "Who Joins the Military?," 184–85.

8. Lee, "Socioeconomic Differences in the Health of Black Union Army Soldiers," separates former slaves economically by the type and size of plantation they came from, but that relationship seems rather tenuous.

9. Glatthaar, *Soldiering in the Army of Northern Virginia,* 11; Glatthaar, "'Touched with Fire," 19.

10. Rothman, "Slavery, the Civil War, and Reconstruction," 83–84.

INTRODUCTION

1. Snell, "'If They Would Know What I Know,'" 80, 113.

2. Kemp, "Community and War," 59, 65–66. Kemp evidently calculated individual rather than family wealth.

3. Hoptak, "Influence of Socio-economic Background," 53.

4. Ledman, *A Maine Town Responds,* 122, 212–15.

5. Duerkes, "I for One Am Ready," 325–27.

6. Buck, "'A Contest in Which Blood Must Flow Like Water,'" 13–14. My sampling of DuPage County recruits was taken from *Report of the Adjutant General of the State of Illinois,* 6:486–97.

7. Vinovskis, "Have Social Historians Lost the Civil War?," 17–20.

8. Ibid., 20.

9. Lee, "Selective Assignment of Military Positions," 75.

10. Thomas, "For the Union, Not for Glory," 44.

11. Rorabaugh, "Who Fought for the North," 698–701.

12. Shannon, "Mercenary Factor"; Blair, "We Are Coming, Father Abraham," 194.

13. The comment was made by Clayne L. Pope in Gallman, *American Economic Growth,* 170.

14. Vinovskis, "Have Social Historians Lost the Civil War?," 14; Hoptak, "Influence of Socio-economic Background," 11.

15. Robert Margo noted that immigrants tended to have less wealth than the native born "and thus were more vulnerable to economic distress." *Wages and Labor Markets,* 152.

16. *OR,* ser. 3, 5:519.

CHAPTER ONE

1. *New York Times,* Oct. 12, 1857; *New York Herald,* Oct. 11, 1857.

2. Nevins and Thomas, *Diary of George Templeton Strong,* 2:359.

3. Wainwright, *Philadelphia Perspective,* 279, 281.

4. *New York Herald,* Oct. 12, 1857; Nevins and Thomas, *Diary of George Templeton Strong,* 2:359; *New York Tribune,* Oct. 12, 1857.

5. *New York Herald,* Aug. 25, Oct. 15, 1857; *Cincinnati Daily Enquirer,* Aug. 28, 1857; *New York Tribune,* Sept. 28, 1857; *Boston Post,* Oct. 15, 1857; *New Orleans Bee,* Oct. 12, 16, 1857; *Louisiana*

Courier (New Orleans), Oct. 18, 1857; *Highland Weekly News* (Hillsborough, Ohio), Mar. 31, 1859. James Huston, *The Panic of 1857,* remains the most detailed work on the third of America's cyclical financial crises, but Kenneth Stampp provides a convenient synopsis in *America in 1857,* 221–30.

6. *New York Herald,* Nov. 3, 6, 12, 1857 (quotation); *New York Tribune,* Nov. 7, 12, 1857.

7. Kiesling and Margo, "Explaining the Rise in Antebellum Pauperism," 405–8; Margo, *Wages and Labor Markets,* 152.

8. Sklansky, *Soul's Economy,* 80–84; Wainwright, *Philadelphia Perspective,* 259; *Daily Union* (Washington, D.C.), Sept. 15, 1855; Glickstein, *American Exceptionalism,* 222–23; Mintz, *Moralists and Modernizers,* 83–85.

9. *New York Herald,* Dec. 22, 1854, Dec. 2, 1855; *Indiana American* (Brookville), Aug. 24, 1855; Sokoloff, "Productivity Growth," 23, 29; Weiss and Schaefer, *American Economic Development,* 2; Margo, *Wages and Labor Markets,* 144, 148–53.

10. Fogel, *Without Consent or Contract,* 355–57; Schaefer, "U.S. Immigration," 56; Fogel, "Toward a New Synthesis of the Role of Economic Issues," 203; *Plymouth (Ohio) Advertiser,* Dec. 1, 1854; *Grand River (Mich.) Times,* Dec. 27, 1854; *Daily Evansville (Ind.) Journal,* Mar. 28, 1855. For "The One-Acre Farm," see, for instance, *Western Reserve Chronicle* (Warren, Ohio), Jan. 17, 1855; *Jackson Standard* (Jackson Court House, Ohio), Mar. 1, 1855; *Vermont Watchman and State Journal* (Montpelier), Mar. 30, 1855; *Bradford Reporter* (Towanda, Pa.), Apr. 7, 1855; and *Sunbury (Pa.) American* Aug. 25, 1855.

11. Fogel, "Toward a New Synthesis of the Role of Economic Issues," 204; Margo, *Wages and Labor Markets,* 149–51; Ferrie, "Rich and the Dead," 36; Long, *Revival of 1857–58,* 32, 35, 51. In their survey of antebellum economics, Mark Thornton and Robert Ekelund seem to discount one hypothesis for a slump in real wages that is based on a reduction in the average height of men who grew up in the 1850s, indicating malnutrition; in fact, immigration could have affected average heights as readily as nutrition, but Thornton and Ekelund also appear to reject the idea of any decline in real wages during this period, although that decline appears to be corroborated by the profusion of references to "hard times" in contemporary newspapers and correspondence. See *Tariffs, Blockades, and Inflation,* 8.

12. *Lansing (Mich.) State Republican,* Mar. 1, 1859; *Ashtabula (Ohio) Weekly Times,* June 4, 1859; *Red Wing (Minn.) Sentinel,* Dec. 24, 1859; Fogel, "Toward a New Synthesis of the Role of Economic Issues," 204.

13. *Meigs County Telegraph* (Pomeroy, Ohio), Jan. 17, 1854; *Ottawa (Ill.) Free Trader,* Apr. 29, 1854.

14. Blanche Hazard estimated that 1,354 shoemaking factories in Massachusetts employed an average of forty-six people apiece in 1860 (or one person in twenty) and acknowledged that women did much of the stitching. *Organization of the Boot and Shoe Industry,* 113–14. In the town of Essex, for example, nearly 12 percent of the total male population and 10 percent of the female population worked at shoemaking. Eighth Census (1860), Essex, Essex County, Mass., Dwellings 1–348, RG29, NA.

15. Faler, "Cultural Aspects of the Industrial Revolution," 372–73, 389, 393; *Haverhill (Mass.) Gazette,* Feb. 24, Mar. 2, 16, 30, 1860; *Boston Post,* Feb. 22, 24, 27, Mar. 7, 8, 1860; *Democratic Mirror* (Leesburg, Va.), Mar. 14, 1860. Blanche Hazard documented higher wages before the Panic of 1857 but cited the piecework earnings of fully employed experts in specialty crafts. *Organization of the Boot and Shoe Industry,* 87–89. Average Massachusetts board is recorded in *Statistics of the United States,* 512.

16. *Cheshire Republican* (Keene, N.H.), Jan. 2, 1861; *Manchester (N.H.) Democrat,* Jan. 17, 1861; *Shoe and Leather Reporter,* quoted in the *Dover (N.H.) Sentinel,* Jan. 4, 1861.

17. *Haverhill (Mass.) Gazette,* Mar. 1, 8, 15, 1861.

18. For a few examples showing the extent of lawsuits and attachments, see *True American* (Steubenville, Ohio), July 14, 21, 1858; *Meigs County Telegraph* (Pomeroy, Ohio), Dec. 14, 1858; *Randolph County Journal* (Winchester, Ind.), Feb. 10, 1859; and *Cincinnati Daily Press,* Jan. 16, 1861. On state laws regarding collection of debt, see *New York Herald,* Apr. 21, 1859, and *Orleans Independent Standard* (Irasburgh, Vt.), Dec. 21, 1860. Robert Fogel classed the petty merchant with his nonnative, laboring-class customer in *Without Consent or Contract,* 355. Edward Balleisen addressed the innocence and incompetence of mercantile entrepreneurs in *Navigating Failure,* 50–52.

19. *Fort Dodge (Iowa) Republican,* Nov. 28, 1860; *Weekly Racine (Wis.) Advocate,* Feb. 27, 1861; *Bureau County Republican* (Princeton, Ill.), Feb. 28, 1861; *Mankato (Minn.) Semi-Weekly Record,* Mar. 15, 1861; Throne, "Iowa Farm Letters," 79–81.

20. Peter Wolford to "Dear Brother," Apr. 14, 1861, MNHS; *Fort Dodge (Iowa) Republican,* Nov. 28, 1860; *Cedar Valley Times* (Cedar Rapids, Iowa), Dec. 6, 1860; *St. Cloud (Minn.) Democrat,* Nov. 29, Dec. 13, 1860.

21. *Stillwater (Minn.) Messenger,* Dec. 25, 1860; *Wabashaw Semi-Weekly County Herald* (Read's Landing, Minn.), Mar. 23, 1861; *Red Wing (Minn.) Sentinel,* Dec. 19, 1860; *Mankato (Minn.) Semi-Weekly Record,* Feb. 5, 8, 12, 15, 19, Mar. 15, Apr. 5, 1861; *Rochester (Minn.) City Post,* Mar. 30, Apr. 20, 27, 1861; *Bureau County Republican* (Princeton, Ill.), Mar. 28, Apr. 4, 11, 1861; *Daily Democratic Union* (Peoria, Ill.), Jan. 8, 9, 22, 25, Feb. 2, 1861.

22. Bek, "Civil War Diary of John T. Buegel," 308; *Quincy (Ill.) Herald,* Jan. 15, Feb. 15, 1861; *Weekly Racine (Wis.) Advocate,* Feb. 27, Mar. 6, 1861; *Freeborn County (Minn.) Standard,* Mar. 27, Apr. 10, 17, 1861; *Green Bay (Wis.) Advocate,* Apr. 4, 1861 (quotation); Quaife, "Diary of Harvey Reid," 42–44, 48.

CHAPTER TWO

1. Horatio Nelson Taft Diary, Apr. 18–25, 1861, LC; Burlingame and Ettlinger, *Inside Lincoln's White House,* 5, 11; Memorial of E. McDonald, James Wren, et al., n.d., Reel 6, Cameron Papers, LC; *OR,* 2:7, ser. 3, 1:67–68; Favill, *Diary of a Young Officer,* 12.

2. *New York Times,* Apr. 9, 10, 16, 21, 22, 1861; *New York Herald,* Apr. 22, 1861.

3. *Weekly Iowa State Reporter* (Iowa City), Apr. 24, 1861; *Muscatine (Iowa) Weekly Journal,* Apr. 26, 1861; *Roster and Record of Iowa Soldiers,* 1:12–83; Briggs, "Enlistment of Iowa Troops," 335–36. The *Waterloo (Iowa) Courier* of May 7, 1861, republished an unofficial claim by the *Chicago Journal* that enlisted men would get 160 acres and officers more. A million acres in land was assigned to Mexican War veterans in 1861 alone under an 1847 act of Congress that many expected to see repeated. Oberly, *Sixty Million Acres,* 106–10, 114.

4. *Linn County Hawk-Eye* (Mount Vernon, Iowa), Apr. 23, 1861; *Roster and Record of Iowa Soldiers,* 1:12–83; Lambert A. Martin to "Sister Martha," May 12, 1861, Yale University.

5. *Daily Democrat and News* (Davenport, Iowa), Apr. 20, 1861; *Roster and Record of Iowa Soldiers,* 1:12–83. This percentage includes men later rejected for service. Of all the officers and men who could be identified on the 1860 census, 72.3 percent fell below median wealth. For the methodology behind these calculations, see the Introduction.

6. *Prairie Farmer* (Chicago), Apr. 18, 25, May 2, 9, 16, 23, 30, 1861; *Report of the Adjutant General of the State of Illinois,* 1:274, 6:675; William N. Bullard to "Dear Father," June 21, 1861; and Bullard to "Dear Brother," Sept. 9, Oct. 20, 1861, AHEC.

7. *Ottawa (Ill.) Free Trader,* Apr. 20, 1861; *Winona (Minn.) Daily Republican,* Apr. 24, 1861; *Keene (N.H.) Sentinel,* Apr. 18, 1861; *Union and Advertiser* (Rochester, N.Y.), Apr. 19, 1861; *Cheshire Republican* (Keene, N.H.), Apr. 24, 1861; *Compiler* (Gettysburg, Pa.), Apr. 22, 1861; *Peterborough (N.H.) Transcript,* Apr. 27, 1861; *Daily Gazette and Courier* (Northampton, Mass.), Apr. 25, 1861; *Daily Toledo (Ohio) Blade,* Apr. 26, 1861.

8. Based on median wealth calculated from *IPUMS-USA* data. See Table 1.

9. *MSSM,* 1:148–65, 169; Seventh Census (1850), Hanson, Plymouth County, Mass., Dwelling 54; Eighth Census (1860), Plympton, Plymouth County, Mass., Dwellings 1–174; Halifax, Plymouth County, Mass., Dwellings 1–157; and Hanson, Plymouth County, Mass., Dwellings 1–266, RG29, NA. In Halifax 71 of 216 men worked as shoemakers exclusively, and 2 claimed to be both shoemakers and farmers; in Hanson 181 of 387 men called themselves shoemakers, with one farmer-shoemaker. In Plympton shoemakers accounted for 103 of that town's 270 employed males in 1860.

10. *Haverhill (Mass.) Gazette,* Mar. 1, 8, 15, 1861; *Boston Evening Transcript,* Apr. 16, 19, 1861.

11. Trimble, *Brothers 'til Death,* 4; Franz Schwenzer to "Liebt Frau Anna," Sept. 22, 1861, AHEC; Luther Van Buren Furber to "Dear Mother," Apr. 20, 23, 1861, Maryland Historical Society; *OR,* ser. 3, 1:153.

12. *MSSM,* 1:71–147, 617–81. At Hazard's highest estimate of 62,000 workers, shoemaking employed 5 percent of the state's entire 1860 population—men, women, and children. *Organization of the Boot and Shoe Industry,* 113–14.

13. *MSSM,* 5:575–91. Lause, *Free Labor,* 41–42.

14. Mark Lause argued that union members enlisted en masse at the outset of the war because they considered it essential to free labor, implying that they saw it as a war against slavery long before the first hint of emancipation policy. *Free Labor,* 42. He also seemed to credit unsubstantiated postwar statements made by Knights of Labor leader T. V. Powderly in a history designed to improve the image of his union.

15. Alexander S. Webb to "My dear Sister," Oct. 24, 1861, SHC.

16. Scott, *Fallen Leaves,* 30–33; Howe, *Touched with Fire,* 3–19, 90–91. Lorien Foote discusses the rather condescending sense of duty exhibited by the Brahmin officers of Massachusetts regiments. "Rich Man's War," 272–77.

17. Hesseltine, *Lincoln and the War Governors,* 146–53; Harris, *Lincoln and the Union Governors,* 15–18; Engle, *Gathering to Save a Nation,* 47, 48, 52–53, 99; Joseph H. Gilmore to Joseph A. Gilmore, Apr. 19, 1861, NHHS; Nevins and Thomas, *Diary of George Templeton Strong,* 2:133; Gurowski, *Diary,* 30, 40; *Burlington (Vt.) Free Press,* Apr. 26, 1861; *Daily Green Mountain Freeman* (Montpelier, Vt.), Apr. 24, 1861; *Grand Rapids (Mich.) Eagle,* quoted in *Lansing (Mich.) State Republican,* Apr. 24, 1861.

18. Hess, *Liberty, Virtue, and Progress,* 8; Paludan, *"A People's Contest,"* 22, 150; Lawson, *Patriot Fires;* Marten, *Children for the Union,* 45.

19. Hess, *Union Soldier in Battle,* 141; McPherson, *What They Fought For,* 35; McPherson, *For Cause and Comrade,* 17.

20. Frank, *With Ballot and Bayonet,* 57–58.

21. Mitchell, *Vacant Chair,* 154; Gallagher, *The Union War,* 5, 61. Lesley Gordon, for example, attributed enlistments in the 16th Connecticut to such factors as "pure patriotism," impulse (but patriotic impulse), a sense of duty and tradition, devotion to familial connections, and the desire for a commission, but downplayed mercenary intent. *A Broken Regiment,* 13–18. The 16th was

organized at Hartford when state and city bounties and subsidies totaled as much as $447 for the first year of service, nearly quadrupling the income of an army private.

22. Motivational analysts often accept allusions to patriotic motive at face value and thereby probably exaggerate its actual extent. One dissertation laden with citations asserting patriotic motive (Luebke, "Shattering the Slave Power") is remarkable in depending entirely on published materials, including regimental histories and memoirs. Many of the published diaries and letters were revised, edited, or expanded after the war, and even those more objectively edited were sometimes chosen for publication precisely because of features such as the extent or eloquence of patriotic content—yielding disproportionate emphasis on that sentiment compared to what might be found among more mundane manuscripts.

23. Thomas T. Taylor to Margaret A. Taylor, May 23, June 18, 1861; and "Netta" to Thomas Taylor, Sept. 14, 1861, OHS; *Official Roster of the Soldiers of the State of Ohio,* 4:389; Walter Q. Gresham to Matilda Gresham, Apr. 28, 1861, LC; Eighth Census (1860), Harrison, Harrison County, Ind., Dwelling 533; Pleasant, Brown County, Ohio, Dwelling 377; and Ninth Census (1870), New Albany, Floyd County, Ind., Dwelling 398, RG29, NA.

24. Alvah C. Trueblood Diary, Apr. 19, 23, 1861, KSHS; Eighth Census (1860), Salem, Washington County, Ind., Dwelling 154; and Otisfield, Cumberland County, Maine, Dwelling 159, RG29, NA; George E. Andrews to "Dear friends," n.d. [early May 1861], AHEC. Marvin Cain acknowledged the personal motives that often dominated the decision to enlist, and he particularly noted how soldier's accounts of their motives for enlisting change over time. "A 'Face of Battle' Needed," 13, 26–27.

25. *St. Cloud (Minn.) Democrat,* May 2, 1861; *Indiana State Sentinel* (Indianapolis), May 15, 1861; *Green Mountain Freeman* (Montpelier, Vt.), Aug. 18, 1862; *Bedford (Pa.) Gazette,* Aug. 29, 1862. The concepts of manliness and courage are addressed in Linderman, *Embattled Courage,* 8, 16, 296; Mitchell, *Vacant Chair,* 7–17; and more generally Foote, *Gentlemen and the Roughs.*

26. Samuel J. Alexander to Agnes G. Alexander, Sept. 1, 1861, AHEC; Southwick, *A Duryee Zouave,* 27–28; Seventh Census (1850), New York City Ward 12, N.Y., Dwelling 1047; and Eighth Census (1860), New York City Ward 19, Dist. 2, N.Y., Dwelling 218, RG29, NA; Foote, *Gentlemen and the Roughs,* 2 (quotes Southwick memoir).

27. Eighth Census (1860), Howard, Parke County, Ind., Dwelling 721, RG29, NA; McClure, *Hoosier Farm Boy,* 14–17, 44, 54, 56, 57; Mitchell, *Vacant Chair,* 4–5.

28. Wilkie, *Pen and Powder,* 13.

29. Ibid., 14–15.

30. *Hartford (Conn.) Weekly Times,* Mar. 2, 1861; *Indiana State Sentinel* (Indianapolis), May 1, 1861.

31. George C. Burmeister Diary, Apr. 18–20, 1861, AHEC; Foroughi, *Go If You Think It Your Duty,* 28.

32. Sears, *For Country, Cause & Leader,* 1, 5, 6.

33. Sauers, *Civil War Journal of Colonel Bolton,* 13–14.

34. Bek, "Civil War Diary of John T. Buegel," 307–9, 528–30.

35. Gustav Hammerstein to Bailey & Woodward, Nov. 28, 1864, Lucien Eaton Papers, MOHS; files of Gustav, August, Frederick, and Julius Hammerstein, CSR, Reels 367, 370, RG94, NA.

36. Eighth Census (1860), Philadelphia Ward 8, Pa., Dwelling 1091, RG 29, NA; Athearn, *Soldier in the West,* 22, 28, 50–51; Bates, *History of Pennsylvania Volunteers,* 1:159, 165; Heitman, *Historical Register,* 1:544.

37. Eighth Census (1860), Yellow Springs, Greene County, Ohio, Dwelling 53, RG29, NA; Becker and Thomas, *Hearth and Knapsack,* xii–xv, 2–3; *Official Roster of the Soldiers of the State of Ohio,* 1:343, 6:238; Heitman, *Historical Register,* 1:611.

38. *Daily Ohio Statesman* (Columbus), May 19, 1861; *OR,* ser. 3, 1:153. "Bounty" was the term usually applied to money paid to recruits at the time of enlistment, either in full or in installments, in addition to regular pay and benefits. In the era before generous state and local enlistment bounties, most soldiers also referred to the $100 federal discharge payment as a bounty, but the legislation approving it did not characterize it as one. Ibid., 382. Except for a portion of it that was paid in advance after the late summer of 1862, that money served essentially as a "bonus" for those who completed their terms or received honorable discharges for service-connected disabilities.

39. *Farmers' Cabinet* (Amherst, N.H.), May 17, 1861; *Delphi (Ind.) Weekly Times,* May 11, 1861; *Randolph County Journal* (Winchester, Ind.), May 16, 1861; *Green Bay (Wis.) Advocate,* May 2, 1861; *Lawrence (Kans.) Republican,* June 6, 1861. Wealth statistics for soldiers in sample companies from the earliest regiments of each state indicate that anywhere from 62 percent to 89 percent of recruits came from families owning less than their respective state's median real and personal property. See Table 1.

40. Dyer, *Annual Report of the Adjutant General,* 1:1, 65; *Providence (R.I.) Evening Press,* Apr. 18, 1861. Rhode Island's median wealth was established through the *IPUMS-USA* sampling of the 1860 census; 55.1 percent of households claimed no property.

41. *Providence (R.I.) Evening Press,* May 30, 1861; Sarah Fales to Edmund Fales, May 4, 1861, RIHS.

42. *New Hampshire Patriot and State Gazette* (Concord), May 1, 1861; Ayling, *Revised Register,* 3–23; *OR,* ser. 3, 2:278. The wealth of those volunteers was derived from Eighth Census (1860), New Hampshire, RG29, NA. Only five of eighty enlisted men were farmers or farm laborers.

43. *Daily Green Mountain Freeman* (Montpelier, Vt.), Apr. 29, 30, 1861.

44. *OR,* ser. 3, 1:145–46, 161; Tappan to Goodwin, May 7, 1861, NHHS. On the relation of the state governors to mobilization, see Stephen D. Engle's impressively expansive study, *Gathering to Save a Nation.*

45. Robertson, *Civil War Letters of General Robert McAllister,* 31–32.

46. *OR,* 3:408; *South Danvers (Mass.) Wizard,* July 17, 1861; William Branson Diary, July 22, 1861, WHMC; Poole Diary, June 26–29, 1861, WCNB.

47. Easley, "Journal of the Civil War in Missouri," 19; Bek, "Civil War Diary of John T. Buegel," 308.

48. *OR,* 3:72, 81, 408; Lavant L. Jones to "My Dearest," Aug. 8, 1861, Herbert S. Hadley Papers, MOHS; Poole Diary, Aug. 9–12, 1861, WCNB. Bates, who was thirty years old, saw no further service, and his name appears in the *OR* only to note his absence from the battle.

49. *OR,* 2:167–69, 170, 172; *RJCCW,* 2:141–42; Memorial of E. McDonald et al., n.d., Reel 6, Cameron Papers, LC.

50. Luther Van Buren Furber to "Dear Mother," Apr. 20, 1861, Maryland Historical Society; *South Danvers (Mass.) Wizard,* May 8, 1861; Duncan, *Blue-Eyed Child of Fortune,* 75.

51. *Daily Democrat and News* (Davenport, Iowa), Aug. 8, 1861; and *Emporia (Kans.) News,* Aug. 17, 1861, both quoted in Piston and Hatcher, *Wilson's Creek,* 130–31; Poole Diary, July 23, 1861, WCNB (quotation); Ware, *Lyon Campaign,* 240–41; *OR,* 3:407.

52. Abbott, *First New Hampshire,* 137–38, 157, 162 (quotation); 1st New Hampshire Court-Martial Records, Box 10, RG12, NHDRMA; Ayling, *Revised Register,* 12, 16, 18, 19, 22.

53. James J. Gillette to "Dear Mother," July 14, 1861; and Gillette to "Dear Father," July 15, 1861, LC; Sears, *For Country, Cause & Leader,* 51–52; Samuel P. Heintzelman Journal, July 19, 1861, LC; Roelker, "Civil War Letters of William Ames," 90.

54. *RJCCW,* 2:20; Simpson and Berlin, *Sherman's Civil War,* 119.

55. *OR,* 2:325, 745.

56. Ibid., 353, 389; *RJCCW,* 2:214–15; Charles E. Bowers to Lydia Bowers, July 26, 1861, MHS.

57. *OR,* 2:351, 404; Basler, *Collected Works of Abraham Lincoln,* 5:167. Brig. Gen. Charles P. Stone repeatedly found fault with Tompkins and the 2nd N.Y.S.M. later in 1861, after which Tompkins and his officers started offering themselves as witnesses for the Radical effort to paint Stone as disloyal.

58. *New Hampshire Patriot and State Gazette* (Concord), Aug. 7, 1861; Tappan to Goodwin, May 7, 1861, NHHS; Ayling, *Revised Register,* 3–23.

59. Ayling, *Revised Register,* 3–23.

60. Oscar Frink to "My own wife and friend," Jan. 21, 1863, HSCC; Ayling, *Revised Register,* 51, 1048.

61. Abby Rogers to "ever dear husban," May 5, 1861; and Dr. Alphonso Bickford to Tappan, May 15, 1861, Correspondence, Box 8, RG12, NHDRMA; Ayling, *Revised Register,* 18, 263.

62. Eighth Census (1860), Dover Ward 3, Strafford County, N.H., Dwelling 830, RG29, NA. In 1860 Rogers owned no real estate and claimed only fifty dollars' worth of personal property; according to calculations of reported wealth derived from *IPUMS-USA,* only 14.9 percent of heads of households in New Hampshire reported fifty dollars or less in total property.

63. Disbursements of Aid for Soldiers' Families, Keene City Records, HSCC; Catherine McGovern relief voucher, Oct. 3, 1861, Otis Norcross Recruitment Papers, MHS; *OR,* ser. 3, 1:234–35, 402.

CHAPTER THREE

1. *OR,* ser. 3, 1:700–701, 5:730; Dyer, *Compendium,* 1008–1673. See Table 1 for the economic status of samples of soldiers for each of the Northern states.

2. *Randolph County Journal* (Winchester, Ind.), May 16, 1861; William Trites to "My Dear Uncle," Oct. 18, 1861, AHEC; John Wilmot to Sophronia Ann Prescott, Mar. 5, 1862, VHS; Charles Mumford to Clarissa Mumford, Dec. 24, 1862, Feb. 1, 1863, WHS; *Rochester (Ind.) Mercury,* Apr. 25, 1861; *Lewiston (Maine) Daily Evening Journal,* Apr. 22, 23, 1861; *Daily Toledo (Ohio) Blade,* Apr. 26, 1861; *Rutland (Vt.) Herald,* June 13, Aug. 1, 1861; *Provincetown (Mass.) Banner,* May 9, 1861; *Peterborough (N.H.) Transcript,* May 18, 1861; *Winona (Minn.) Daily Republican,* Apr. 24, 25, 1861; *Cincinnati Daily Gazette,* May 28, 1861.

3. Carroll E. Kingsley to "Dear Mother," Apr. 30, 1861, AHEC; *OR,* ser. 3, 1:383–84; Joseph Leach to "Dear Sister," Oct. 24, 1861, CL.

4. *OR,* ser. 3, 1:383–84; Norris, "Northern Businessman," 140 (quotation); *Cincinnati Daily Press,* Mar. 19, 26, Apr. 16, 19, 27, 1861; *Daily Evansville (Ind.) Journal,* Mar. 13, Apr. 10, 20, May 11, 1861; *Mankato (Minn.) Semi-Weekly Record,* June 21, July 2, 1861; *Daily Gate City* (Keokuk, Iowa), Feb. 11, 1861; *Vermont Phoenix* (Brattleboro), Feb. 28, 1861. *Hartford (Conn.) Weekly Times,* Feb. 9, 1861. The first Kansas regiment raised during the war was mustered for three years: in the sample from that regiment, 87 percent of recruits hailed from families reporting less than the median Kansas wealth of $550.

5. *Oxford Democrat* (Paris, Maine), Oct. 11, 1861; *Aroostook Herald* (Presque Isle, Maine), May 25, 1861; R. P. Bush to "Friend Jim," Aug. 30, 1861, SHC; [Lusk], *War Letters,* 72–75.

6. Haynes, *History of the Second Regiment,* 54; *Report of the Adjutant-General of the State of New-Hampshire for the Year Ending June 1, 1868,* 372; Eighth Census (1860), Portsmouth Ward 1, Rockingham County, N.H., Dwelling 237, RG 29, NA; Ayling, *Revised Register,* 83.

7. *OR,* ser. 3, 1:73, 187, 203–4; Haynes, *History of the Second Regiment,* 4; Ai B. Thompson to "Dear Father and Mother," May 21, 1861, MNBP; Haynes, *Minor War History,* 5.

8. Ayling, *Revised Register,* 52; George W. Gordon to "Dear Wife," July 22, 1857, Sept. 23, 1860, May 22, 1861, NHHS.

9. Ai B. Thompson to J. H. Thompson, July 24, 27, 30, 1861, MNBP; Samuel Burnham to "My Dear Mother," Aug. 12, 1861, NHHS.

10. Haynes, *Minor War History,* 5; Haynes, *History of the Second Regiment,* 54; Ayling, *Revised Register,* 83, 1013; Original claim, William O. Sides Pension Certificate 134, RG15, NA; *OR,* 40(3):741, ser. 2, 7:98; Ninth Census (1870), Portsmouth Ward 2, Rockingham County, N.H., Dwelling 477, RG 29, NA.

11. Ayling, *Revised Register,* 52; George W. Gordon to "Dear Wife," Sept. 26, Oct. 21, 1861, Jan. 21, Mar. 3, 1862, July 4, 1863, NHHS; Angeline B. Gordon headstone, Head Cemetery, Hooksett, N.H.

12. *OR,* ser. 3, 1:153, 402.

13. *Boston Post,* July 11, 1861; *Lafayette (Ind.) Daily Courier,* July 31, Aug. 9, 1861; *Daily Gate City* (Keokuk, Iowa), July 19, 1861; *Mankato (Minn.) Semi-Weekly Record,* June 21, July 2, 1861; Louis Morrison to Rebecca Morrison, July 13, 1861, May 25, 1862, SHC (first two quotations); Francis Bowman to "My Dear Wife," Mar. 2, 1862, NIU (third quotation); James Turner to "My dear Parents and Sisters," Jan. 2, May 2, 1862, NYSL (final quotation).

14. Sandage, *Born Losers,* 16, 190–91 (quotation); *CG,* 38th Cong., 1st sess., 2636–38; *Dubuque (Iowa) Herald,* Sept. 14, 1861.

15. *Beardstown (Ill.) Democrat,* Aug. 22, 1861; *Rutland (Vt.) Herald,* Sept. 26, 1861.

16. Schuyler P. Coe to "Dear Mother," Sept. 18, 1861, AHEC; *Council Bluffs (Iowa) Bugle,* May 1, 8, 1861; *Ottumwa (Iowa) Courier,* Apr. 24, May 1, 1861; John Brandon to William Brandon, Oct. 6, 1861, AHEC; Hodge, *Civil War Letters of Perry Mayo,* 180; Robertson, *Michigan in the War,* 22, 120.

17. Joseph Lester to "My Dear Father and Sister," June 5, 1864, LC.

18. Eighth Census (1860), Warren, Joe Daviess County, Ill., Dwelling 2638, RG29, NA; Luther Cowen to Harriet Cowen, Dec. 9, 1861, Jan. 4, 29, Feb. 4, Mar. 8, 23, 1862; and Luther Cowen to Mary E. Cowen, Jan. 21, May 3, 1862, Galena Public Library; Cowen Diary, Feb. 6, 1862, Galena Public Library; Ninth Census (1870), Warren, Joe Daviess County, Ill., Dwelling 131, RG29, NA; Mary E. Cowen to Pension Bureau, Nov. 19, 1913, Harriet Cowen Widow's Certificate 17859, RG15, NA.

19. Eighth Census (1860), Upper Paxton, Dauphin County, Pa., Dwelling 74, RG29, NA; Samuel Thoman to "Dear Wife," Oct. 19, Nov. 30, 1861, Apr. 13, 1862, AHEC; Original claim, Sarah Thoman Pension Certificate 84969, RG15, NA.

20. Eighth Census (1860), Temperanceville, Allegheny County, Pa., Dwelling 763, RG29, NA; Bates, *History of Pennsylvania Volunteers,* 2:463; Samuel J. Alexander to Agnes G. Alexander, Sept. 13, 20, 24, Nov. 3, 1861, AHEC.

21. Jordan, *Civil War Journals of John Mead Gould,* 9; *Report of the Adjutant General of the State of Maine,* 36; *Eastern Argus* (Portland, Maine), July 27, Dec. 10, 1861 (quotation).

22. Original claim, Lydia Manchester Pension Certificate 99434, RG15, NA; *Lewiston (Maine) Daily Evening Journal,* May 2, 1861; Manchester, *Joseph K. Manchester,* 28, 36–38; Ninth Census (1870), Windham, Cumberland County, Maine, Dwelling 52, RG29, NA.

23. Original claim, Washington Carlton Pension Certificate 146513, RG15, NA; Simon Carlton to Washington Carlton, Sept. 22, 23, Nov. 21, 1861, Sept. 5, 1862, AHEC. The original Carlton letters are in the pension file, while AHEC has transcripts, at least one of which is misdated.

24. John O. Stevens to "Dear Father," July 24, 1862, NHHS; Affidavits of J. Everett Sargent, George Simpson, A. G. Hammond, and G. S. Dean, Apr. 3, 1868, Louisa Stevens Pension Certificate 115090, RG15, NA.

25. *OR,* ser. 3, 1:153, 234, 383, 402–3; *CG,* 37th Cong., 1st sess., 448.

26. Original declaration and Sylvanus Bartlett affidavit, Eliza Plummer Pension Certificate 39706, RG15, NA. Roughly speaking, the 1861 dollar was worth about twenty-eight 2015 dollars. Depending on whether the base year of 1860 is calculated in conjunction with base years 1913 or 1967 for the Consumer Price Index, inflation-adjusted values range from $26.34 against the estimated 2015 CPI to $28.98 for 2016 on the inflation calculator of the Bureau of Labor Statistics. Those estimates are based on averages that do not take into account disproportionate upward or downward trends of individual commodities. To illustrate the disparities that such calculations can distort or disguise, the base pay for a U.S. Army recruit is now nearly 120 times what it was after the 1861 increase, and comparing the value of specific items can inflate that comparison even more: the value of a slave as a measure of economic status, for instance, can equate to nearly 500 times as many dollars in modern money; as a measure of economic power (i.e., a percentage of gross domestic product) that value can be the equivalent of 3,250 times as many modern dollars. See those and other similar comparisons in Williamson and Cain, "Measuring Slavery in 2016 Dollars."

27. Eighth Census (1860), Howell, Monmouth County, N.J., Dwelling 380, RG29, NA; Trimble, *Brothers 'til Death,* 4–5.

28. Frederick W. Clark to Lizzie Clark, Sept. 16, 1861, DU; *Granite State News* (Wolfeborough, N.H.), Oct. 9, 1861. For a discussion of the effects on real wages, see Kessel and Alchian, "Real Wages in the North," 107, 111.

29. Day, *My Diary,* 5; Eighth Census (1860), Milford, Worcester County, Mass., Dwelling 1021, RG29, NA; *MSSM,* 3:12; Original claim, David L. Day Invalid Pension Certificate 473588, RG15, NA.

30. *MSSM,* 3:9; Stearns, *Narrative,* 5–6.

31. Eighth Census (1860), Auburn, Androscoggin County, Maine, Dwelling 103, RG29, NA; *Lewiston (Maine) Daily Evening Journal,* May 29, 1861; Marshall Phillips to "Dear Wife," Aug. 29, Oct. 3, Nov. 23, 1861, MEHS.

32. Eighth Census (1860), Hampstead, Rockingham County, N.H., Dwelling 456, RG29, NA; Ayling, *Revised Register,* 175; Leander Harris to Emily Harris, Feb. 5, 1863, Jan. 6, Feb. 7, 1864, UNH.

33. Original declaration, Sarah J. Upton Widow's Certificate 42966, RG15, NA; George Upton to Sarah Upton, July 17, Dec. 2, 1862, Jan. "18" [25?], Feb. 28, June 19, Dec. 13, 1863, NHHS.

34. *Manchester (N.H.) Democrat,* Feb. 7, 1861; *New Hampshire Statesman* (Concord), Feb. 9, 1861; *Keene (N.H.) Sentinel,* June 6, 1861; *Dollar Weekly Mirror* (Manchester, N.H.), May 11, June 22, 1861; *Providence (R.I.) Evening Press,* May 30, 1861; *Daily American* (Manchester, N.H.), July 10, Aug. 9–14, Sept. 7, 10, 21, 1861; *Eastern Argus* (Portland, Maine), Aug. 16, 1861; John H. Norton to "Dear Sister," May 1, 1861, CHS.

35. *Providence (R.I.) Daily Post,* Aug. 3, 1861, quoted in *Hartford (Conn.) Weekly Times,* Aug. 10, 1861.

36. *Boston Journal,* July 11, 1861; *New York Times,* July 13, 1861; *Boston Evening Transcript,* July 12, 16, 1861 (quotation).

37. Lyman Hapgood to Thomas Vincent, Aug. 16, 1861, File H522, 1861; and Hapgood to B. W. Brice, Feb. 17, 1865, File H221, 1865, Letters Received by the Office of the Adjutant General, RG94, NA; W. E. Webster, S. B. Stebbins, Charles B. Hall, Albert J. Wright, Thomas Gaffield, John S. Keyes, et al. to Charles Sumner, July 25–Aug. 9, 1865; and Lyman Hapgood to Sumner, Aug. 21, 1865, File H1353, 1865, Letters Received by the Commission Branch, RG94, NA; Eighth Census (1860), Boston Ward 5, Suffolk County, Mass., Dwelling 1221; and Ninth Census (1870), Boston Ward 12, Suffolk County, Mass., Dwelling 255, RG29, NA.

38. *Boston Evening Transcript,* Aug. 20, 1861; *Report of the Adjutant-General of the State of New-Hampshire for the Year Ending June 1, 1866,* 2:473, 508; *Daily Morning Chronicle* (Portsmouth, N.H.), Aug. 10, 28, 1861; 1st New Hampshire Battery, Enlistment Papers, NHDRMA. The governor's bounty proclamation is reproduced in Eldredge, *Third New Hampshire,* 6.

39. Alfred Wheeler to Alonzo Wheeler, Apr. 4, "1860" [1861]; and Alfred Wheeler to "Dear Mother," Aug. 1861, AHEC; *Philadelphia Inquirer,* Feb. 22, 1861; Bates, *History of Pennsylvania Volunteers,* 2:810.

40. Orr, *Last to Leave the Field,* 7–11; Bates, *History of Pennsylvania Volunteers,* 1:449.

41. Original declaration, Nancy Marietta White Widow's Certificate 830, RG15, NA; Alfred M. White to "Dear Etta," Oct. 28, 1860, MHS; *MSSM,* 1:99; Eighth Census (1860), Marlborough, Cheshire County, N.H., Dwelling 575, RG29, NA. In June of 1860 White was a farm laborer in Marlborough, New Hampshire; in October he was working in Holyoke, Massachusetts; and when he enlisted on May 9, 1861, he listed himself as a weaver in West Boylston, Massachusetts.

42. Herbert Willand Journal, Apr. 15–Oct. 11, 1861, NHSL.

43. *MSSM,* 1:696; Frederick W. Clark to Lizzie Clark, July 22, Aug. 4, Sept. 16, 1861, DU. A year into his enlistment Clark would slip away from an early battle, coming back after the fight with a suspicious pistol wound in the hand that resulted in his discharge. Blight, *When This Cruel War Is Over,* 168. His failure to seek a pension for the resulting disability suggests that Clark suspected his desertion would be reported by any comrades from whom he solicited a corroborating affidavit.

44. *Atlas and Argus* (Albany, N.Y.), Sept. 4, 1861; *New York Journal of Commerce,* quoted in Scarborough, *Diary of Edmund Ruffin,* 1:504; *New York Times,* Apr. 21, 22, 1861; *New York Herald,* Apr. 22, 1861.

45. Muster roll of the field and staff, 42nd New York, Sept. 1, 1861, Timothy O'Meara Military Service Record, RG94, NA; Affidavits of John Fogarty and Michael Whelan, Mother's Pension Certificate 39332, RG15, NA; Thomas McDermott to "Dear Mother and Brothers," Dec. 10, 1861, Civil War Letters, Thomas Balch Memorial Library.

46. *Boston Journal,* quoted in *Dover (N.H.) Gazette,* June 29, 1861; Longacre, *From Antietam to Fort Fisher,* 23.

47. Seventh Census (1850), New Haven, New Haven County, Conn., Dwelling 808; and Eighth Census (1860), New Haven Ward 2, New Haven County, Conn., Dwelling 2166, RG29, NA; William Willoughby to Nancy, Aug. 1862, AAS; *Hartford (Conn.) Weekly Times,* Sept. 7, 1861.

48. Cassedy, *Dear Friends at Home,* v–vi, 21, 38, 58, 63, 65, 73, 197, 221, 237, 450–51; *New York Herald,* Aug. 8, 1861; *Brockport (N.Y.) Republic,* Aug. 8, 15, 1861; *Freeman's Journal (Cooperstown, N.Y.),* Aug. 16, 1861.

49. Eighth Census (1860), Albany, Orleans County, Vt., Dwelling 1153, RG29, NA; Peck, *Revised*

Roster of Vermont Volunteers, 193, 432; Seth Bumps to "Father," Nov. 11, 1861, and "dear mother sister and brother," Nov. 24, 1861, Hunter Family Letters, AHEC.

50. Eighth Census (1860), Mount Holly, Rutland County, Vt., Dwelling 881, RG 29, NA; Ai B. Thompson to J. H. Thompson, July 15, 1861, MNBP; Wilson, *Shouts and Whispers,* 26; Manchester, *Joseph K. Manchester,* 28.

51. *Daily Green Mountain Freeman* (Montpelier, Vt.), Apr. 29, 1861; Spalding, *Tuf as a Boiled Owl,* 1, 4–5, 17, 22.

52. Foster, *New Jersey and the Rebellion,* 776; Bilby, "Give My Love to All," 37, 42.

53. Eighth Census (1860), Northampton, Hampshire County, Mass., Dwelling 1132, RG29, NA; *MSSM,* 1:695; Blight, *When This Cruel War Is Over,* 33, 40, 67, 78, 150.

54. Fred Lyman to "Dear Brother and Sister," Dec. 8–9, 1861, VPI.

55. Eighth Census (1860), Lawrence, Douglas County, Kans., Dwelling 90, RG29, NA; Lavant L. Jones to "My Dearest," Aug. 8, 1861, Herbert S. Hadley Papers, MOHS; Original claim, Harriet E. Jones Widow's Pension Certificate WC20, RG15, NA.

56. *Eighth Census* (1860), Corning, Steuben County, N.Y., Dwelling 778, RG 29, NA; Hughes, *Civil War Papers of Lt. Colonel Newton T. Colby,* 7, 10, 19, 126.

57. Eighth Census (1860), Gorham, Cumberland County, Maine, Dwelling 544, RG29, NA; Frederic Speed to "Dear ones at Woodburn," Aug. 3, Nov. 2, 1861; Frederic Speed to "Dear Mother," Mar. 11, Apr. 2, 1862, Feb. 26, 1863; and Frederic Speed to "Dear Father," May 26, 1863, CL. In 1865 Speed was court-martialed and convicted of complicity in the overloading of the transport *Sultana,* on which hundreds of Union soldiers died when it exploded and burned, but the conviction was inexplicably overturned by Judge Adv. Gen. Joseph Holt, whose specious grounds for reversing the decision contradicted the evidence in the case.

58. Mushkat, *A Citizen-Soldier's Civil War,* 6–7; *Summit County Beacon* (Akron, Ohio), Dec. 13, 20, 1860; *Steubenville (Ohio) Weekly Herald,* Dec. 26, 1860; Eighth Census (1860), Akron, Summit County, Ohio, Dwelling 240, RG29, NA; *Official Roster of the Soldiers of the State of Ohio,* 3:382, 5:565. The base pay of a lieutenant colonel when Alvin Voris enlisted was $181 per month.

59. *Cincinnati Daily Enquirer,* Apr. 27, 30, 1861; *Ohio State Journal* (Columbus), Apr. 17, 1861; *Marietta (Ohio) Intelligencer,* May 1, 1861; *Springfield (Ohio) Evening News,* Aug. 5, 6, 8, 9, Oct. 3, 1861; *Daily Toledo (Ohio) Blade,* Apr. 26, 1861; *Holmes County Republican* (Millersburg, Ohio), May 23, 1861; *OR,* ser. 3, 1:384.

60. Eighth Census (1860), Fremont, Sandusky County, Ohio, Dwelling 334, RG29, NA; Carlisle Journal, May 12–June 2, 1861, and Memoir, AHEC.

61. *Holmes County Farmer* (Millersburg, Ohio), June 20, 1861; *Cleveland Morning Leader,* Aug. 6, 1861; *Weekly Lancaster (Ohio) Gazette,* May 9, 1861; *Daily Dayton (Ohio) Journal,* May 16, 1861; *Belmont Chronicle* (St. Clairsville, Ohio), May 9, 1861; *Cincinnati Daily Gazette,* May 28, 1861; *Spirit of Democracy* (Woodsfield, Ohio), May 29, 1861.

62. *Daily Evansville (Ind.) Journal,* June 10, July 13, 1861; *Indiana State Sentinel* (Indianapolis), July 3, 1861; *Weekly Racine (Wis.) Advocate,* July 31, 1861; *Appleton (Wis.) Crescent,* Aug. 31, 1861; *People's Friend* (Covington, Ind.), Oct. 2, 1861; *Morning Star* (Dover, N.H.), Nov. 20, 1861; *Putnam Republican Banner* (Greencastle, Ind.), July 11, 1861; Quinn, *Military History of Wisconsin,* 46; Allen Church to "My Dear wife," Aug. 23, 1862, WHS; Samuel Thoman to "Dear Wife," Apr. 13, 1862, AHEC; William Otto to "Dear Charlotte," Nov. 12, 1861, AHEC; Joseph Rutherford to "Dear Wife," Dec. 18, 1862, UVM.

63. *Daily Evansville (Ind.) Journal,* Sept. 2, 1861; *Putnam Republican Banner* (Greencastle, Ind.), July 11, 1861; *Marshall County Republican* (Plymouth, Ind.), Aug. 8, 22, 1861 (quotations on bounty-land bill); *Plymouth (Ind.) Weekly Democrat,* June 20, Sept. 12, 1861.

64. *Wayne County Democrat* (Wooster, Ohio), June 6, 1861; *Prairie Farmer* (Chicago), June 20, 27, 1861 (quotation); *Ottawa (Ill.) Free Trader,* Aug. 3, 1861.

65. *Indiana State Sentinel* (Indianapolis), May 1, 1861; *Joliet (Ill.) Signal,* July 9, 1861; *Lafayette (Ind.) Daily Courier,* July 31, 1861; *Wolverine Citizen* (Flint, Mich.), June 22, 1861. Wayne Duerkes did not consider the depressed commercial climate in Illinois in 1861 and credited St. Charles merchant Francis Bowman with accepting a captain's commission in the 52nd Illinois out of irresistible patriotic fervor. "I for One Am Ready," 319. Bowman revealed in a March 1862 letter that his business partnership was not nearly as "prosperous" as Duerkes assumed. See Bowman to "My Dear Wife," Mar. 2, 1862, NIU.

66. *Appleton (Wis.) Crescent,* June 22, 1861; *Prairie Farmer* (Chicago), June 27, 1861; *Ottawa (Ill.) Free Trader,* June 29, 1861; *Wolverine Citizen* (Flint, Mich.), June 29, 1861.

67. *Appleton (Wis.) Crescent,* June 8, July 20, Sept. 21, 1861; *Weekly Racine (Wis.) Advocate,* Sept. 4, 1861; *St. Paul (Minn.) Pioneer and Democrat,* July 11, 1861.

68. *Appleton (Wis.) Crescent,* June 29, 1861; *Illinois State Journal* (Springfield), July 17, 1861 (quotation); *Prairie Farmer* (Chicago), June 27, 1861; *Ottawa (Ill.) Free Trader,* June 29, 1861; Basler, *Collected Works of Abraham Lincoln,* 4:381; *Wolverine Citizen* (Flint, Mich.), Sept. 14, 1861; *St. Charles City (Iowa) Republican Intelligencer,* Aug. 29, 1861.

69. *Detroit Advertiser,* quoted in the *Daily Gate City* (Keokuk, Iowa), July 19, 1861; *Appleton (Wis.) Crescent,* Aug. 24, 1861; *Chicago Tribune,* quoted in the *Daily Gate City* (Keokuk, Iowa), July 9, 1861; *Weekly Racine (Wis.) Advocate,* Aug. 21, 1861.

70. *Wolverine Citizen* (Flint, Mich.), Aug. 3, 10, 1861; *Springfield (Ohio) Evening News,* Aug. 9, 11, 15, 1861; *Putnam Republican Banner* (Greencastle, Ind.), Aug. 15, 1861.

71. George W. Young (17th Indiana) to "Dear father," June 26, 1861, AHEC.

72. Daniel Wooten to Miriam W. Green, July 11, 1861, IHS (quotation); Eighth Census (1860), Bureau, Bureau County, Ill., Dwelling 4593, RG29, NA; Webster W. Moses Diary, Mar. 14, Sept. 2, 1861, KSHS; George B. Lower to Henry Saner, July 21, 1861, AHEC; Rundell, "'Despotism of Traitors,'" 333; *Weekly Racine (Wis.) Advocate,* Aug. 21, 1861.

73. *Official Records of the Union and Confederate Navies.* ser. 1, 22:278–81; Branch, "Proposed Calendar," 21; Alice Cayton to "My dear Brother," May 12, 1861, Badger Collection, MOHS; Richard Johnson Diary, May 11, 1861, MOHS.

74. *Daily Gate City* (Keokuk, Iowa), June 1, 1861 (quotation); *Dubuque (Iowa) Herald,* July 11, 1861; *Daily Evansville (Ind.) Journal,* July 13, 1861.

75. *OR,* ser. 3, 1:384; Easley, "Journal of the Civil War in Missouri," 19 (quotation).

76. James Draper to "Dear Sister," Aug. 18, 1861, WHMC.

77. Neal, *Illustrated History of the Missouri Engineer and 25th Infantry Regiments,* 9–14 (quotation); CSR, Reels 765, 766, RG94, NA. Bissell had ostensibly gone to St. Louis from New York with plans for building a suspension bridge over the Mississippi. Barnes, "Bridging the Lower Falls," 14; *Union and Advertiser* (Rochester, N.Y.), Feb. 21, 1857.

78. Branch, *Mark Twain's Letters,* 1:121–22; James H. Guthrie Diary, June 13–16, 1861, KSHS; *Daily Messenger* (Hannibal, Mo.), June 13, 14, 1861.

CHAPTER FOUR

1. Arvilla Thompson to "Dear Children," Jan. 7, 1862, Aldrich-Thompson Family Papers, NHHS.

2. Quinn, *Military History of Wisconsin,* 74; Fish, "Social Relief in the Northwest," 313–16; *Journal of the House of Representatives of the State of Indiana,* 18, 32, 52, 57, 64–65; *Wayne County Democrat* (Wooster, Ohio), Mar. 13, 1862; *Lansing (Mich.) State Republican,* May 15, 1861; *East Saginaw (Mich.) Courier,* Jan. 28, 1862.

3. Disbursements of Aid for Soldiers' Families, Keene City Records, HSCC; Receipts of Silas Brown, Eliza J. Potter, Calvin Hatch, and Jonah Hamilton, Pauper File, 1862, Old Town Records Collection, CPL.

4. *Bangor (Maine) Daily Whig and Courier,* May 26, 1862; George M. Redlon to "Dear Father," Apr. 13, 1862, MEHS; Charles R. Johnson to "Dear Nellie," Oct. 5, 1861, AHEC; Fish, "Social Relief in the Northwest," 314.

5. Emily Harris to Leander Harris, fragment, n.d., [early 1862], DC.

6. Harris and Niflot, *Dear Sister,* 3; Rhodes, *History of Battery B,* 3; *Cincinnati Daily Gazette,* May 28, Oct. 19, 1861; Samuel J. Alexander to "My Dear," Nov. 3, 1861, AHEC.

7. *Dubuque (Iowa) Herald,* Apr. 21, 22, Oct. 3, Nov. 22, 1861, Jan. 8, 1862. Russell L. Johnson examined Dubuque's care of soldiers' families in "'A Debt Justly Due.'"

8. *New York Tribune,* Aug. 8, 1861 (Greeley quotation); Nevins and Thomas, *Diary of George Templeton Strong,* 3:132, 143, 163 (second quotation); *New York Herald,* Jan. 8, 1862.

9. *Plymouth (Ind.) Weekly Democrat,* Sept. 12, 1861; *Daily Evansville (Ind.) Journal,* Sept. 2, 1861, Jan. 10, 1862; letter to *Louisville (Ky.) Anzeiger,* Sept. 12, 1861, quoted in Reinhart, *August Willich's Gallant Dutchmen,* 26 (quotation). For such failures in Indiana, see, for instance, Morgan, "Responsibilities of a Community at War," and Marshall, "Aid for Union Soldiers' Families."

10. Richard M. Lay receipt, Feb. 18, 1863; and Declaration of J. R. Thompson and Daniel B. Merrill, Apr. 18, 1863, 1863 Pauper File, CPL.

11. *Boston Evening Traveler,* May 23, 1861; Franz Schwenzer to "Liebt Frau Anna," Sept. 22, 24, 1861, AHEC; John McCoy to "Dear Martha," June 25, 1864, DC; John Peirce to Clarissa Peirce, Jan. 3, June 23, 1864, PEM; John Viles to Frances Viles, Aug. 11, 15, 1861, AHEC.

12. Disbursements of Aid for Soldiers' Families, Keene City Records, HSCC.

13. *Nashua (N.H.) Gazette and Hillsborough County Advertiser,* Jan. 30, 1862; Eighth Census (1860), Hartland, Windsor County, Vt., Dwelling 868, RG29, NA; John Gilbert to Ellen Gilbert, Jan. 23, 1862; and John Gilbert to Edward A. Wardner, Feb. 4, Apr. 11, 1862, NHHS.

14. Foote, *Gentlemen and the Roughs,* 130. Geary's letter scorning the economic motivation of the new men included an unintentionally ironic postscript in which he told his wife he had sent her another $350—nearly as much as many substitutes received for a three-year enlistment. Blair, *Politician Goes to War,* 110.

15. Harris, "Sons and Soldiers," 160; Eighth Census (1860), Deerfield, Franklin County, Mass., Dwelling 997; and Greenfield, Franklin County, Mass., Dwellings 261, 372, RG29, NA. Massachusetts farm laborers earned an average of $15.34 per month and board. *Statistics of the United States,* 512.

16. Harris, "Sons and Soldiers," 160; Eighth Census (1860), Rowe, Franklin County, Mass., Dwelling 287; Deerfield, Franklin County, Mass., Dwelling 493; Barre, Worcester County, Mass.,

Dwelling 43; Easthampton, Hampshire County, Mass., Dwelling 979; and Conway, Franklin County, Mass., Dwelling 114, RG29, NA.

17. Clark Carr to Caroline Carr, Dec. 13, 1861, Jan. 4, Feb. 11, Apr. 13, July 7, 1862, HSCC.

18. Ameur, *Voyage en Amérique,* 421.

19. Of the letters and diaries consulted for this study, the majority testify to men sending their pay home: Peter Abbott to "Friends at Home," Sept. 23, Dec. 15, 1862, VHS; David Ackerman to "Dear Brother," May 10, 1863, AHEC; Samuel Alexander to "My Dear Wife," Sept. 24, 1861, AHEC; Shannon, *Civil War Letters of Sergeant Onley Andrus,* 17; John Barney to "Dear Father," Oct. 5, 1862, WHS; Augustus Barr to "My Wief [sic]," Sept. 18, 1862, AHEC; Elijah Barstow to "Dear Uncle," July 20, Aug. 4, Dec. 22, 1864, AHEC; Lyman Beebe to "Mother," Oct. 22, 1862, AHEC; Elizur Belden Diary, Aug. 26, 27, 1862, CHS; Fleetwood Benson to "Dear wife," Feb. 26, 1865, AHEC; Cora Benton to Charles Benton, Oct. 26, 1862, ND; Aaron Blake to "Dear Sister," Oct. 5, 1862, AHEC; Henry Bobinhouse to William Bobinhouse, Sept. 20, 1862, SHSI-DM; Hughes and Althouse, *Civil War Letters of John A. Boon,* 5–6; Clement Boughton to Esther Boughton, Apr. 23, Aug. 16, 1862, Mar. 17, 1863, CL; Cassedy, *Dear Friends at Home,* 132; Addison Boyce to "Dear Mary," Jan. 12, 1864, BL; William Boyce to "Dear Parents," Mar., 1862, AHEC; Bohrnstedt, *While Father Is Away,* 97; Jerry Brakeman to "Dear Mary Ann," Oct. 19, 1862, AHEC; Truxall, *"Respects to All,"* 40, 94; George Bronson to "Dear Mary," Jan. 20, 1862, AHEC; Harvey Brooks to "Dear Father," Jan. 16, 1865, AHEC; Thomas Brown to Horace Brown, Sept. 25, 1862, VHS; George Buffum to "Dear Wife and Family," n.d., [late summer 1864], WHS; William Bullard to "Dear Brother," Oct. 20, 1861, AHEC; William Burbank to "Dr. Mother," Dec. 7, 1862, CL; John P. Burnell to Alanson Burnell, Dec. 1, 1861, AHEC; Eben Calderwood to "Dear Wife," Feb. 13, 1863, MEHS; Charles Caley to Juliett Caley, Aug. 26, 1862, ND; Simon Carlton to "Dear farther" [sic], Sept. 5, 22, 1861, AHEC; Levi Carr to "Dear Sister," Dec. 26, 1862, AHEC; Alanson Chandler to Frances Chandler, Aug. 28, 1862, Miller Family Correspondence, ND; George Chapin to John Chapin, June 22, 1863, IHS; Menge and Shimrak, *Civil War Notebooks of Daniel Chisholm,* 103, 118, 130; Hiram Clay to "Dear wife," Mar. 9, 1864, AHEC; Samuel Claytor to "My kind and affectionate wife," Dec. 14, 1862, AHEC; Mary Houston to "My Dear Brother," Jan. 21, 1863, William Coates Letters, Yale University; Merit Cole to "Dear sister and friends," Mar. 7, 1864, AHEC; Frank Collins to "Dear Father," June 25, 1864, SHSI-IC; Josiah Corban to "Dear Wife and Children," Apr. 15, July 10, 1863, CHS; William Cotton to "Dear Mother," Apr. 12, July 2, 1862, SHSI-IC; William Croop to "Dear Father," June 17, 1862, AHEC; Newton H. Culver Diary, July 30, Aug. 1, Sept. 28, 1862, WHS; Horace Currier Diary, Dec. 19, 1862–June 22, 1863, WHS; George DeHart to "Dear Sister," Mar. 15, 1863, SHSI-IC; Elisha Douglass to "Dear Wife," Apr. 11, 1864, NHHS; Silas Fales to "Dear Mary," Feb. 18, May 20, 1863, SHC; Robert Forbes to "Dear Father," Jan. 5, 1865, AHEC; James Forbis to "My Dear Companion," Jan. 11, 1863, AHEC; Jacob Gauchnauer to "Dear Wife and Mother and Benny," Mar. 17, 1865, AHEC; Henry Gay to "Dear Father," Dec. 25, 1863, and to "Dear Father and Mother," July 11, 1864, AHEC; George Gordon to "Dear wife," Nov. 26, 1861, NHHS; Harris and Niflot, *Dear Sister,* 23; Michael Green to "My Dear Wife," June 4, Dec. 10, 1863, SHS; Metzger, *Griffith Letters,* 88; Albion Gross to "Dear Wife," Feb. 21, 1864, AHEC; Edward Hall to "My dear Susan," Jan. 19, Dec. 2, 1862, NHHS; George Hall to "Dear Father," Sept. 24, 1864, UIA; Lucy Hayes to Rutherford Hayes, Aug. 12, 1863, Sept. 8, 1864, RBHPL; William Haynes to "Dear wif [*sic*]," May 8, 1863, KSHS; Charles Hewitt to "Dear Brother and Sister," Feb. 27, 1862, SHC; Charles Hewitt to "Dear Parents," Apr. 29, Aug. 28, 1862, SHC; John Hilton to "Dear Wife," Oct. 10, 1862, VPI; James Howes to "My Dear Wife," Jan. 29, 1863, NHHS; Lewis Jones

to "Dear wife," Nov. 15, 1861, AHEC; John Kerwecker to "Dear Father," Apr. 17, 1863, BGSU; Frederick Kehrwecker to "Dear Brother," Nov. 27, 1861, AHEC; Elisha Kempton to "Dear Folks at Home," Apr. 23, 1863, NHHS; Ezra Kidder to "Dear Wife," Jan. 30, 1864, AHEC; John Kline to "Dear Wife," Oct. 17, 1861, AHEC; Joseph Kohout to "Dear Father and Mother," Feb. 27, 1863, UIA; Frederick Kronenberger to "Dear Parents and Sister," Dec. 14, 1863, Feb. 9, Mar. 28, 1864, Gettysburg College; John Lake to "Dear Friends at home," Jan. 5, 1862, HSCC; Joseph Harrison Law to "Dear Mary," Sept. 4, 12, 1862, AHEC; Jacob Lester to "Dear Mother," Nov. 1, 30, 1863, AHEC; Thomas Jefferson Lewis to "My Dear Wife," Mar. 23, 1863, SHSI-DM; William Lowe to "Dear Father," Dec. 11, 1861, AHEC; Charles Lutz to "Dear Brother," Oct. 23, 1861, AHEC; Charles Marples to "Dear Wife," Mar. 15, 1865, MNHS; Hodge, *Civil War Letters of Perry Mayo,* 173, 177, 188, 211, 217; Robert McCreight to "Dear Mother," July 26, 1861, AHEC; Sylvester McElheney to "Dear Wife," Mar. 20, 1865, AHEC; McKitrick, *Civil War Letters,* 19; Robert McNeal to "Father," Feb. 17, 1863, AHEC; Alanson Miller to Frances Miller, Dec. 6, 1862, ND; Patrick and Willey, *Fighting for Liberty and Right,* 12, 112, 195, 269; Benjamin Morse to "Dear Rosina," July 4, 7, 1862, Gale-Morse Family Papers, VHS; James Mulligan to "My Dear Wife," Feb. 5, 1864, AHEC; Charles Mumford to "Dear Wife," Apr. 27, 1862, WHS; Burr Murdock to "Dear Sister," Nov. 5, 1862, AHEC; William Murray to "Dear Wife and Children," June 19, 1861, AHEC; Joseph Neff to "Dear Wife and Children," Mar. 24, 1864, AHEC; David Nichol to "Dear Father," Aug. 21, 1863, AHEC; Steensma, *Drifting to an Unknown Future,* 27, 32, 66, 76, 81; Michael O'Brien to "Dear and Affectionate Wife and Children," Apr. 15, 1863, AHEC; James Albert Osborne Diary, Jan. 7, 1863, MHS; William Otto to "Dear Charlotte," Nov. 12, 1861, AHEC; Tabor Parcher to "Dear Sarah," "September" [Aug.] 31, 1862, UVM; Francis Patrick to "Dear wife and child," Oct. 16, 1864, AHEC; Gavin, *Infantryman Pettit,* 7; Alonzo Pierce to "Dear Uncle," Sept. 30, 1862, NHHS; Jacob Powell to "Dear Mother," Nov. 6, 1861, AHEC; Albert Rake to "Dear Lucy," Nov. 27, 1861, Apr. 15, 1862, AHEC; Harrison Randall to "Dear Father & Mother," Dec. 29, 1862, ND; Cornelius T. Richmond to "My Dear Wife," Sept. 23, 1862, AHEC; Isaac Richardson to "Dear Esther," May 26, 1865, SHC; Jonathan Rickett to Peter Mowrer, Apr. 25, July 28, Sept. 1, 1862, Ellen Mowrer Miller Collection, IWA; Bruen and Fitzgibbons, *Through Ordinary Eyes,* 54, 87; Abram Rowell to "Dear Wife," Oct. 24, 1862, UVM; Ozias Sanford to "Dear Father," Jan. 13, 1863, Sheldon Museum; George Sargent to "Dear Mother," June 13, 1862, NHHS; Franz Schwenzer to "Liebt Frau Anna," Sept. 22, 24, 1861, AHEC; Charles Scott to "Dear Annie," Jan. 13, 1862, AHEC; Hampton Sloane to "My Dear Wife," Oct. 18, 1862, AHEC; Joseph Spafford to "Dear Sister," Oct. 24, 1862, VHS; Andrew Sproul to "Dear Fanney," Mar. 15, Apr. 27, 1863, SHC; Samuel Steiner to "Dear Brother," Nov. 4, 1861, AHEC; Frank Sterns to "Dear Parents," ca. Feb. 24, 1863, CL; Jeremiah Stetson to Abbie Stetson, Dec. 29, 1861, May 6, 1863, SHC; James Stoddard to Cynthia Stoddard, June 12, 1862, VHS; Merritt Stone to his father, Oct. 18, 1862, VHS; Alderson and Alderson, *Letters Home to Sarah,* 36, 42; George Telling to "Dear Brother," Jan. 20, Mar. 8, 1863, AHEC; Willard Thayer to Esther Thayer, Sept. 17, 1862, VHS; George Thomas to Minerva Thomas, Mar. 17, 1863, ND; Charles Tillison to Dudley Tillison, May 31, 1863, VHS; Nathaniel Truell to "Dear Mother," Feb. 11, 1862, NHHS; James Turner to "My dear Parents and Sisters," May 1, July 29, 1862, Mar. 10, 1863, NYSL; Timothy Vedder to "Dear Sister," Oct. 15, 1861, June 9, Sept. 21, 1862, AHEC; John Viles to Francis Viles, Aug. 11, 15, Sept. 9, 1861, AHEC; Michael Vreeland to "Dear Mother," June 25, Aug. 7, 1862, AHEC; Burgess, *Uncommon Soldier,* 24, 25, 28, 40; Charles Walbridge to George Walbridge, Oct. 21, 1862, Apr. 21, May 24, 1863, NYSL; Alfred Waldo Diary, Aug. 13, 14, 1862, Stoughton Historical Society; David West to "Dear Father," Sept. 19, 1862, SHSI-DM; Charles Wilcox to Mrs. E. B.

Wilcox, Sept. 21, 1862 and "No. 6," n.d., HSCC; John Wilmot to "Dear Ann," Nov. 12, 1862, VHS; William Winship to "Dear Mother," May 5, 1863, CHS; Hunley, *14th U.S. Infantry,* 47–48; Thomas Zanhiser to John Zanhiser, Jan. 24, 1862, AHEC.

20. Richard P. Kent Diary, Oct. 12, 1861, Oct. 28, 1862, NHHS (for a general merchant's report of surprisingly good sales just after local volunteers would have received their first pay and their state or local bounty money); *Keene (N.H.) Sentinel,* June 6, Oct. 17, Nov. 7, 1861; *Daily American* (Manchester, N.H.), July 10, Aug. 9–14, Sept. 7, 10, 21, 1861; *Aegis and Transcript* (Worcester, Mass.), Sept. 21, 1861; *Boston Journal,* Sept. 24, Oct. 3, 1861; Charles Scott to "Dear Annie," Jan. 13, 1862, AHEC. For the forgotten importance of the concept of Union to Civil War soldiers, see Gary W. Gallagher, *The Union War.* For more general motivations, including patriotism and devotion to comrades, see McPherson, *For Cause and Comrades,* esp. 17–19, 27–29, 101–2. Chandra Manning's *What This Cruel War Was Over,* meanwhile, focuses heavily on initial or eventual opposition to slavery as a compelling motivation.

21. Seth Bumps and Hiram Hunter to assorted correspondents, Nov. 11, 24, Dec. 9, 20, 1861, Hunter Family Letters, AHEC; Eighth Census (1860), Albany, Orleans County, Vt., Dwellings 1020, 1153, RG29, NA; William T. H. Brooks to "Dear Father," Dec. 25, 1861, AHEC.

22. Foroughi, *Go If You Think It Your Duty,* 27–36, 296, 306; *Minnesota in the Civil and Indian Wars,* 188, 725.

23. Patrick and Willey, *Fighting for Liberty and Right,* 2, 3, 7–10. Miller acted as a hospital steward during part of his enlistment and spent his last half century as a druggist.

24. William Montgomery to "Dear Sister," Feb. 7, 1862, Ann Sturtevant Collection, AHEC; Joseph Knowlton to "Dear Sir," Apr. 7, 1861, Letters Received by the Confederate Secretary of War, Reel 1, RG109, NA; Ayling, *Revised Register,* 181, 1060.

25. Eighth Census (1860), Boscawen, Merrimack County, N.H., Dwelling 872, RG29, NA; Henry W. Baker to "Dear Sister," Oct. 12, 1861, AAS; Ayling, *Revised Register,* 396.

26. Ferdinand Davis to Raymond Davis, Sept. [28], 1861, BL.

27. Eighth Census (1860), Cabot, Washington County, Vt., Dwelling 2291, RG29, NA; Marriage license and birth record, Harriet Scott Widow's Certificate 124749, RG15, NA; Luther Scott to "Father," Oct. 19, 1861, UVM.

28. Flannery and Oomens, *Well Satisfied with My Position,* 1–2, 108–9; Eighth Census (1860), Philadelphia Ward 7, Pa., Dwelling 1663, RG29, NA. A sketch in a genealogical compendium that was probably based on Bonsall's secondhand war stories reported that he served as a first lieutenant *before* becoming a hospital steward—which would have reflected a significant demotion—and that he was injured at Gettysburg when his horse was shot and fell on him. Jordan, *Colonial and Revolutionary Families of Pennsylvania,* 3:1348. The editors of Bonsall's journal apparently credited those undocumented, inconsistent, and improbable claims, besides offering special pleading for his desertion.

29. James E. Mitchell letter fragment, [Sept. 9, 1862], AHEC; Heitman, *Historical Register,* 1:716.

30. The estimates of wintertime mobilization are based on organizational dates in Dyer, *Compendium,* 1006–1681. New Jersey supplied no new units that season, and Minnesota raised only two artillery batteries.

31. Ellis to "Dear Sister," May 23, 1862; and Ellis to "Dear Nephew," n.d. (ca. Feb. 1, 1863), AHEC.

32. *Eastern Argus* (Portland, Maine), Mar. 6, 1861; *Bangor (Maine) Daily Whig and Courier,* Jan. 4, 1862 (quotations); *Portland (Maine) Advertiser,* Dec. 5, 1861; *Kennebec Journal* (Augusta, Maine), Jan. 15, 1862.

33. [Sawyer], *Civil War Letters of Captain John Franklin Godfrey,* 5; *Report of the Adjutant General of the State of Maine,* 36–37.

34. Ameur, *Voyage en Amérique,* 241–42.

35. McPherson and McPherson, *Lamson of the Gettysburg,* 197; Hill, *Civil War Sketchbook of Charles Ellery Stedman,* 117; *Providence (R.I.) Evening Press,* May 30, 1861.

36. Eighth Census (1860), Exeter, Rockingham County, N.H., Dwelling 1394, RG29, NA; Wainwright Journal, Nov. 21, 26, 1861, Mystic Seaport Museum; Charles Pickering to George Pearson, Feb. 3, 1862; and Pearson to Gideon Welles, Feb. 4, 1862, Pickering Letterbooks, NHHS.

37. Poole, "Journal," Nov. 27, 28, Dec. 2, 11, 1861, Mystic Seaport Museum; Charles Pickering to George Pearson, Feb. 3, 1862; and Gideon Welles to Pickering, n.d., NHHS.

38. Eighth Census (1860), Portsmouth Ward 1, Rockingham County, N.H., Dwelling 523, RG29, NA; DeWit Journal, 1, 4, 8, Mystic Seaport Museum.

39. *Daily Morning Chronicle* (Portsmouth, N.H.), Dec. 30, 1861, Jan. 1, 10, 14, 15, 17, 1862.

40. Eighth Census (1860), New York City Ward 20, Dist. 1, N.Y., Dwelling 82; and Troy Ward 4, Rensselaer County, N.Y., Dwelling 1438, RG29, NA; Original declaration, Martha Geer Navy Widow's Pension Certificate 9508, RG15, NA; George S. Geer to Martha Geer, "February" [Mar.] 2, Mar. 10, 24, May 20, 1862, Mariners Museum.

41. Greene, "In the 'Monitor' Turret," 719; George Geer to Martha Geer, Apr. 16, May 15, 1862, Mariners Museum.

42. George Geer to Martha Geer, Mar. 18, Apr. 27, May 20, June 4, July 20, 29, Sept. 24, 1862, Mariners Museum.

43. Geer to Martha Geer, June 9, July 15, Nov. 29, 1862, ibid.

44. Unknown to "My Dear Sir," Nov. 19, 1862, John Brislin Letters, AHEC; *Daily Evening Courier* (Madison, Ind.), Apr. 21, 1862.

45. Josyph, *Wounded River,* 3, 41.

46. Dyer, *Compendium,* 1006–1681; Buckingham, *All's for the Best,* 6–9.

47. Buckingham, *All's for the Best,* 12; *Lewiston (Maine) Daily Evening Journal,* Feb. 1, 4–8, 1862.

48. *Camden (N.J.) Democrat,* Feb. 22, 1862.

49. Ibid., Mar. 22, 1862 (both quotations); *Lansing (Mich.) State Republican,* Mar. 5, 1862; *New York Herald,* Mar. 26, 1862; *Lancaster (Ohio) Gazette,* Mar. 20, 1862; *Raftsman's Journal* (Clearfield, Pa.), Mar. 5, 1862.

50. *OR,* ser. 3, 2:2–3, 28–29; Stanton to Irenius Prime, Mar. 26, 1862, Gratz Collection, Historical Society of Pennsylvania; Burlingame, *Dispatches from the White House,* 70. I am not the only person to suggest, as I did in *Lincoln's Autocrat* (356), that the interruption of recruiting prolonged the war: Alpert and Kauffman came to the same conclusion, citing a general malaise in recruiting, in "Economics of the Union Draft," 105.

51. Bela St. John Diary, Apr. 6, 7, 1862, LC; William Stimson to "Dear Wife and little Children," Apr. 10, 1862, LC; Andrew F. Davis to "Dear Brother," Apr. 21, 1862, AHEC; Samuel M. Buford to Charles Buford, Apr. 21, 1862, LC; Jacob Behm to "Dear Brother & Sister," Apr. 27, 1862, AHEC; *Camden (N.J.) Democrat,* Apr. 12, 1862.

52. Mary Jane Vaughn Clark to "Dear Sister," May 9, 1862, WHMC; Harwell, *Kate,* 14; Josyph, *Wounded River,* 48; *Evening Argus* (Rock Island, Ill.), Apr. 14, 1862; *Cleveland Morning Leader,* Apr. 10, 16, 1862; *Daily Ohio Statesman* (Columbus), Apr. 15, 1862; *Daily Evansville (Ind.) Journal,* Apr. 15, 1862; *Cadiz (Ohio) Democratic Sentinel,* Apr. 23, 1862; *Keene (N.H.) Sentinel,* May 1, 1862; *New York Herald,* Apr. 15, 22, 1862.

53. Henry Franklin Huffer to "Dear wife and children," Apr. 13, 1862, AHEC; *Evening Star* (Washington, D.C.), May 1, 1862; *OR,* ser. 3, 2: 28–29.

54. Augusta Kidder to Olivia Brown, May 18, 1862, Hazeltine Papers, WHS; Rundell, "'Despotism of Traitors,'" 334.

55. Ray, *Diary of a Dead Man,* 33–38.

56. *OR,* ser. 3, 2:61.

57. Ibid., 44–49, 61–63.

58. *OR,* 12(3):216–17, 219–23, ser. 3, 2:62–65, 68–70; Niven, *Chase Papers,* 1:345–46; *RJCCW,* 1:684.

59. Henry L. Dawes to Ella Dawes, May 29, 1862, LC.

60. Edwin Stanton to Horace Binney, June 2, 1862, LC; Niven, *Chase Papers,* 3:205–6; *New York Herald,* May 25, 29, 1862; *Bangor (Maine) Daily Whig and Courier,* May 27, 1862; *Cleveland Morning Leader,* June 13, 1862 (quotation); *Illinois State Journal* (Springfield), June 9, 1862; *Urbana (Ohio) Union,* June 4, 1862; *Chicago Tribune,* Apr. 18, 1862; Catherine M. Snedeker to Catherine E. L. Snedeker, May 14, 1862, IWA; Ayling, *Revised Register,* 1089–95.

61. Thomas Blanchard to Sarah Walker, June 15, 1862, ND.

62. *Lamoille Newsdealer* (Hyde Park, Vt.), May 30, 1862; *Indiana State Sentinel* (Indianapolis), June 9, 1862; Unidentified brother to Leander Harris, July 29, 1862, UNH; Henry Fowler to Henry P. Fowler, Sept. 29, 1862, PEM; Henry Rogers Smith to "Dear Father," Dec. 10, 1862, AAS; *Smoky Hill and Republican Union* (Junction City, Kans.), June 26, 1862.

63. *Cleveland Morning Leader,* June 4, 1862; *Daily Morning Chronicle* (Portsmouth, N.H.), May 30, 1862; *Carroll County Register* (Ossipee, N.H.), June 12, 1862; *New Hampshire Patriot and State Gazette,* (Concord), Aug. 27, 1862; Albert Merrill's roll of recruits, Alton-Conway folder, Recruiting Station Records, RG12, NHDRMA; *Record of Service of Connecticut Men,* 552–85.

64. Hughes, *Civil War Papers of Lt. Colonel Newton T. Colby,* 126–31.

65. *OR,* ser. 3, 2:80–81, 226; Benedict, *Vermont in the Civil War,* 2:183–84; *Green Mountain Freeman* (Montpelier, Vt.), June 19, 24, 1862; *Orleans Independent Standard* (Irasburgh, Vt.), June 27, 1862.

66. *OR,* ser. 3, 2:179–80, 181, 186, 198–200.

67. *New Hampshire Argus and Spectator* (Newport), July 11, 1862; *OR,* ser. 3, 2:182, 186.

68. *Civilian and Telegraph* (Cumberland, Md.), July 17, 1862; *Cleveland Plain Dealer,* July 7, 1862.

69. Steensma, *Drifting to an Unknown Future,* 35; *Cleveland Plain Dealer,* July 10, 1862; *Chicago Tribune,* July 9, 15, 1862.

70. *Hartford (Conn.) Courant,* July 10, 11, 14, 28, 1862; *Hartford (Conn.) Weekly Times,* July 19, 1862.

71. *Lewistown (Pa.) Gazette,* July 23, 1862 (quotation); *Goodhue (Minn.) Volunteer,* July 30, 1862; *Vermont Phoenix* (Brattleboro), July 24, 1862; *Cleveland Morning Leader,* July 31, 1862; *Bradford Reporter* (Towanda, Pa.), July 31, 1862; *Cleveland Plain Dealer,* July 22, 24, 1862.

72. Charles Reed to "Dear Sister," July 25 [1862], LC.

73. *Cleveland Plain Dealer,* July 26, 1862; *Nashua (N.H.) Gazette and Hillsborough Advertiser,* Sept. 25, 1862.

CHAPTER FIVE

1. *CG,* 37th Cong., 2nd sess., pt. 4, 3178, 3197–3207, 3397–98, 3404; *OR,* ser. 3, 2:280–82.

2. Shannon credited the "horror of drafting" to the stigma of being drafted, which was a factor,

but most citizens obviously feared being forced into unpleasant and dangerous service. "Mercenary Factor," 527–28.

3. *Daily Wabash Express* (Terre Haute, Ind.), July 19, 1862; Josyph, *Wounded River,* 50; *Daily Evening Courier* (Madison, Ind.), Apr. 21, 1862; *Waterloo (Iowa) Courier,* July 30, Aug. 6, 1862 (quotation); Elder, *Damned Iowa Greyhound,* 8.

4. *Door County Advocate* (Sturgeon Bay, Wis.), Aug. 2, 1862; *Lansing (Mich.) State Republican,* Aug. 6, 1862; *Jasper (Ind.) Weekly Courier,* Aug. 6, 1862; *Der Lecha Caunty Patriot* (Allentown, Pa.), Aug. 13, 1862; *Marshall County Republican* (Plymouth, Ind.), Aug. 14, 1862; *Cleveland Morning Leader,* Aug. 20, 1862. The only free federal land made available to Union soldiers came through the Homestead Act, and a civilian had more opportunity than a soldier to stake such a claim.

5. *OR,* ser. 3, 2:270–73.

6. *Lansing (Mich.) State Republican,* Aug. 6, 1862; *Cleveland Morning Leader,* Aug. 20, 1862. Russell Johnson first pointed out the apparently deliberate efforts to confuse the mandatory element of the militia draft with the three-year levy as well as the false newspaper claims about the lower pay and other disadvantages that would be inflicted on the drafted man. See "'Volunteer While You May.'"

7. *Hillsdale (Mich.) Standard,* July 29, 1862; *Daily Whig and Republican* (Quincy, Ill.), July 29, 1862; *Ottawa (Ill.) Free Trader,* Aug. 2, 1862; *Nashua (N.H.) Gazette and Hillsborough County Advertiser,* Sept. 25, 1862.

8. *Daily Evansville (Ind.) Journal,* July 26, 1862; *St. Cloud (Minn.) Democrat,* July 31, 1862; *Rochester (Minn.) City Post,* Aug. 2, 1862; *Mankato (Minn.) Semi-Weekly Record,* July 30, 1862.

9. *Dubuque (Iowa) Herald,* July 23, 1862; *Cass County Republican* (Dowagiac, Mich.), July 31, 1862; *Grand Haven (Mich.) News,* July 30, 1862; *Hillsdale (Mich.) Standard,* Aug. 26, 1862; *East Saginaw (Mich.) Courier,* Aug. 5, 1862. "Citizens' Bounty" is alluded to in the last three newspapers cited.

10. *Daily Gate City* (Keokuk, Iowa), July 29, 1862; *Cedar Valley Times* (Cedar Rapids, Iowa), July 31, 1862; *Lancaster (Ohio) Gazette,* Aug. 7, 1862; *Jasper (Ind.) Weekly Courier,* Aug. 6, 1862 (quotation).

11. Edward Klein to "Dear Brother," July 24, 1862, BPL; *Nantucket (Mass.) Inquirer,* July 16, 23, 1862 (quotation); *Barnstable (Mass.) Patriot,* July 22, 1862; *Boston Evening Transcript,* July 19, 1862; *New York Times,* July 20, 1862; *Goodhue (Minn.) Volunteer,* July 23, 1862; *Cambridge (Mass.) Chronicle,* July 19, Aug. 2, 1862.

12. *Daily Morning Chronicle* (Portsmouth, N.H.), July 23, 1862; *Providence (R.I.) Daily Journal,* Aug. 5, 1862; *Goodhue (Minn.) Volunteer,* July 23, 30, 1862; *Report of the Adjutant General of the State of Maine,* 37; *Kennebec Journal* (Augusta, Maine), Aug. 8, 1862; Kallgren and Crouthamel, *"Dear Friend Anna,"* 25; *Daily Evansville (Ind.) Journal,* July 23, 1862; *Bradford Reporter* (Towanda, Pa.), July 31, 1862; *Atlas and Argus* (Albany, N.Y.), July 25, Aug. 1, 1862; *OR,* ser. 3, 2:202; *Peninsula News and Advertiser* (Milford, Del.), July 18, Aug. 1, 1862; *Delaware Journal* (Wilmington), July 29, 1862.

13. *National Eagle* (Claremont, N.H.), July 17, 1862; *Vermont Phoenix* (Brattleboro), July 24, 1862; *Burlington (Vt.) Free Press,* July 25, 29, 31, Aug. 1, 1862; *Green Mountain Freeman* (Montpelier, Vt.), July 29, Aug. 1, 1862; *Orleans Independent Standard* (Irasburgh, Vt.), Aug. 1, 1862.

14. *Hartford (Conn.) Courant,* July 28, 1862.

15. Henry Halleck to Edwin Stanton, Aug. 3, 1862, LC; *OR,* ser. 3, 2:291–92.

16. Carolyn Barrett White Diary, Aug. 4, 9, 12, 1862, AAS ("astonishing"); *Pioneer,* Aug. 23, 1862; Charles Woodwell Diary, Aug. 20, 23, 25–29, 1862, LC; Lucy Larcom Diary, Aug. 21, 1862, MHS (other quotations).

17. Edward Hall to "Dear Susan," Sept. 16, 1862, NHHS.

18. Marshall Phillips, draft of a letter to the editor (apparently never published), n.d. [Aug. 1862], MEHS.

19. John W. Ames to "My dear Mother," July 21, 1862, AHEC; Coco, *From Ball's Bluff to Gettysburg,* 117 (Bowen quotation); Francis Skillin to "Dear Farther [sic]," Sept. 9, 1863, AHEC.

20. *Barnstable (Mass.) Patriot,* Aug. 19, 1862; *Hartford (Conn.) Courant,* Aug. 22, 1862.

21. *New Haven (Conn.) Daily Palladium,* Aug. 20, 1862; Ezra Sanborn Diary, Aug. 7, 1862, NHHS.

22. *Housatonic Republican* (Falls Village, Conn.), Aug. 16, 1862. The men appear in the Eighth Census (1860), Canaan, Litchfield County, Conn., Dwellings 74–283, RG29, NA.

23. *OR,* ser. 3, 2:380–81; *Providence (R.I.) Daily Journal,* Aug. 5, 1862; *St. Cloud (Minn.) Democrat,* Aug. 14, 1862; *Peterborough (N.H.) Transcript,* Aug. 9, 16, 1862; *Hartford (Conn.) Courant,* Aug. 6, 16, 1862; *Chicago Evening Journal,* quoted in *Dubuque (Iowa) Herald,* Aug. 8, 1862; *Vinton (Iowa) Eagle,* Aug. 27, 1862; *Atlas and Argus* (Albany, N.Y.), Aug. 28, 1862.

24. *New Haven (Conn.) Daily Palladium,* Aug. 19, 20, 1862 (quotations); *Housatonic Republican* (Falls Village, Conn.), July 26, 1862; *New York Herald,* Aug. 18, 1862; *Cleveland Morning Leader,* Aug. 20, 1862.

25. *Portland (Maine) Advertiser,* Aug. 15, 28, 30, Sept. 1, 1862; *Kennebec Journal* (Augusta, Maine), Aug. 8, 1862. Several examples of such posters are owned by different Maine historical societies or museums.

26. *Cambridge (Mass.) Chronicle,* Aug. 9, 16, 23, 30, 1862; *Boston Evening Transcript,* Aug. 18, 1862; Margaretta Harris to Leander Harris, Aug. 10, 1862, UNH.

27. *OR,* ser. 3, 2:240; *Boston Evening Transcript,* July 22, 23, 24, 1862. Hitchcock did not formally enlist until early August but noted in a preface to his transcribed wartime journal that he and at least one companion enrolled in an 1861 regiment "on a calm summer's afternoon in July 1862"; he added that his parents had previously denied him permission to enlist. Watson, *From Ashby to Andersonville,* xv. Stanton's reply to Andrew stated that the governor was "authorized to say that new recruits for old regiments will be mustered with the regiment," omitting the word "out." *OR,* ser. 3, 2:240. Stanton, whose perennial guile gives the omission an air of design, might later have claimed that he had only meant to say the recruits would be mustered *in* with the regiment. Some Vermont recruits in old regiments were deceived in that same promise.

28. *Republican Journal* (Belfast, Maine), Aug. 15, 1862; brief in *Burrill vs. City of Boston,* Charles Burrill Papers, MHS; Hammer, *Frederic Augustus James's Civil War Diary,* 23.

29. *Cheshire Republican* (Keene, N.H.), Aug. 13, 20, 1862; *Daily Morning Chronicle* (Portsmouth, N.H.), Aug. 14, 15, 1862; Emily Harris to Leander Harris, Aug. 16, 1862, UNH; *Winnipisaukee Gazette* (Wolfeborough, N.H.), Aug. 30, 1862; *Boston Evening Transcript,* Aug. 18, 1862; *Carroll County Register* (Ossipee, N.H.), Sept. 18, 1862.

30. *Cleveland Morning Leader,* Aug. 20, 1862; Sarah Fales to Edmund Fales, Aug. 6, 13, 1862, RIHS. Fred Shannon doubted that any towns offered higher bounties than $350 during this draft, but he relied exclusively on New York newspapers for New England information. *Organization and Administration of the Union Army,* 1:59.

31. Peck, *Revised Roster of Vermont Volunteers,* 382, 407.

32. *Green Mountain Freeman* (Montpelier, Vt.), Aug. 15, 1862 (quotations); Eighth Census (1860), Berlin, Washington County, Vt., Dwellings 405–729, RG29, NA; Peck, *Revised Roster of Vermont Volunteers,* 44–46, 670, 673.

33. *Vermont Watchman and State Journal* (Montpelier), Aug. 29, 1862; *Green Mountain Freeman* (Montpelier, Vt.), Aug. 19, 1862; *Lamoille Newsdealer* (Hyde Park, Vt.), Aug. 22, 29, 1862; *Vermont Phoenix* (Brattleboro), Aug. 21, 1862; Joel Glover to "Dear Wife," Nov. 23, 30, 1862, Jan. 16, 1863, UVM; Richard J. Irwin to "Dear Mother & Sister," Dec. 8, 1862, UVM.

34. *Fort Scott (Kans.) Bulletin,* Aug. 16, 1862 (first quotation); *Kansas Chief* (White Cloud), Aug. 7, 1862 (second quotation); *Appleton (Wis.) Crescent,* Aug. 9, 1862; *OR,* ser. 3, 3:741–65, 812.

35. *Door County Advocate* (Sturgeon Bay, Wis.), July 19, Aug. 9, 1862; *Appleton (Wis.) Crescent,* Aug. 9, 16, 23, 30, 1862; *Weekly Racine (Wis.) Advocate,* Aug. 6, 13, 1862; Minutes of War Meeting, Aug. 20, 1862, John T. Clark Papers, WHS (quotation).

36. *Goodhue (Minn.) Volunteer,* July 23, 30, Aug. 13, 1862; *Mankato (Minn.) Semi-Weekly Record,* Aug. 9, 1862; *Hillsdale (Mich.) Standard,* Aug. 5, 12, 1862.

37. *Vinton (Iowa) Eagle,* Aug. 13, 1862, Sept. 10, 1862; *Daily Gate City* (Keokuk, Iowa), Aug. 13, 21, 28, 1862; *Waterloo (Iowa) Courier,* Aug. 6, 13, 1862; *Council Bluffs (Iowa) Bugle,* Aug. 6, 1862; *Ottumwa (Iowa) Courier,* Aug. 9, 1862.

38. *East Saginaw (Mich.) Courier,* Aug. 5, 1862; *Holmes County Farmer* (Millersburg, Ohio), Aug. 7, 1862; *St. Paul (Minn.) Pioneer and Democrat,* Aug. 2, 1862; *Daily Ohio Statesman* (Columbus), Aug. 7, 1862; *Wyandot Pioneer* (Upper Sandusky, Ohio), Aug. 15, 22, 1862.

39. *Hancock Jeffersonian* (Findlay, Ohio), Aug. 8, 1862; *Delaware (Ohio) Gazette,* Aug. 8, 1862; *Daily Toledo (Ohio) Blade,* Aug. 11, 1862; *Urbana (Ohio) Union,* Aug. 6, 1862; *Marshall County Republican* (Plymouth, Ind.), Aug. 14, 1862; *Daily Evansville (Ind.) Journal,* Aug. 12, 1862; *Council Bluffs (Iowa) Bugle,* Aug. 13, 1862; *Gallipolis (Ohio) Journal,* Aug. 28, 1862; *Goodhue (Minn.) Volunteer,* Aug. 20, 1862. In Terre Haute's *Daily Wabash Express,* for instance, every issue of late July and early August carried recruiting ads with bold heads offering "$50 BOUNTY," which added Vigo County's $10 contribution to the $40 in government cash.

40. *Highland Weekly News* (Hillsborough, Ohio), Aug. 14, 1862; Henry Carroll to "Dear Father," Aug. 31, 1861, AHEC.

41. *Ottawa (Ill.) Free Trader,* July 26, Aug. 9, 16, 30, 1862; *Chicago Tribune,* Aug. 10, 1862; Bohrnstedt, *Soldiering with Sherman,* 36.

42. See Table 1 and Introduction.

43. Bohrnstedt, *Soldiering with Sherman,* 50–51.

44. Hosea Smith to "Dear Mother," Dec. 18, 1862, AHEC.

45. *Dubuque (Iowa) Herald,* Sept. 14, 1861; *Holmes County Farmer* (Millersburg, Ohio), July 31, 1862; *Belmont Chronicle* (St. Clairsville, Ohio), Aug. 7, 1862; Snell, "'If They Would Know What I Know,'" 72, 81 (and *York Democratic Press,* Oct. 1, 1861, quoted therein); Jacob Haas to "My Dear Bro.," Dec. 18, 1862, Jan. 3, 1863, AHEC; *Fairfield (Iowa) Constitution,* quoted in *Fairfield (Iowa) Ledger,* July 31, 1862.

46. *Lansing (Mich.) State Republican,* Aug. 6, 13, 1862; Eighth Census (1860), Lansing, Ingham County, Mich., Dwelling 365, RG29, NA.

47. *Vinton (Iowa) Eagle,* Aug. 6, 1862; Eighth Census (1860), Taylor, Benton County, Iowa, Dwelling 723, RG29, NA.

48. *Cambridge (Mass.) Chronicle,* Aug. 2, 16, 1862 (quotation); *MSSM,* 4:24; Samuel Storrow to "My dear Father," Oct. 12, 1862, MHS; Adams, *Education,* 129; Elizabeth Matson to William L. Matson, Sept. 27, Nov. 11, 1862, CHS. On Andrew using his appointment power to salt Massachusetts regiments with the scions of elite families, see Miller, "Brahmin Janissaries."

49. Chapman, *Sketches of the Alumni of Dartmouth College,* 289–470; Ayling, *Revised Register,* 1093–95. By contrast, five Dartmouth graduates fought for the Confederacy, of whom three were killed and one died of disease. Richard Miller, in *Harvard's Civil War,* referred to the thirty-four alumni who died in uniform between July of 1862 and July of 1863, but did not provide total mortality figures or calculate either the percentage of graduates of military age who served or the mortality rate among them. Miller earlier wrote that "using Harvard affiliation as a rough indicator of Brahmin status, the number of patricians among the ten Massachusetts regiments that suffered the most combat casualties in the war is striking," but he offered no numbers or proportions to support that assertion. "Brahmin Janissaries," 232.

50. Marvel, "A Poor Man's Fight," 37–39; Ledman, *A Maine Town Responds,* 215, 217. The national statistics are based on a white-male population of 5,738,258 between the ages of ten and fifty in 1860 in the Northern states, plus one-half the population of 1,613,848 among the same demographic in the Border States and Upper South, against estimated white mortality of 299,956 and estimated Union enlistments of 2,489,836, rounded down to 2,000,000 to reflect black soldiers and multiple enlistments by individuals. Population figures are from *Statistics of the United States,* xxxiii. The enlistment estimates are those of the National Park Service, and the mortality figure consists of the NPS estimate of 334,680 Union deaths minus 34,724 deaths among black enlisted men of the U.S. Colored Troops. *OR,* ser. 3, 5:1029–30. The low participation rates in part reflect large numbers of military-age males who were exempt from service for one reason or another.

51. Richard Cary Morse Jr. to Richard Cary Morse Sr., July 8, 1862, with reply of same date; and Cornelius L. Kitchel to Morse Jr., Sept. 5, 1862, CL.

52. *OR,* ser. 3, 2:45 (Andrew quotation); Blight, *When This Cruel War is Over,* 181; Henry Tisdale Diary, July 30, 1862, BPL (quotation on motive). Fred Shannon remarked that "all the foot-free willing prospects had been recruited in 1861," as though the volunteers of 1861 had enlisted for the adventure of it, but he did not consider that many of the 1861 volunteers had also been economically motivated, and perhaps a bit more so than those of 1862. *Organization and Administration of the Union Army,* 1:12. The cumulative average of below-median wealth among three-year volunteers in 1862 was 67 percent, but in 1861 it had been 70 percent.

53. Basler, *Collected Works of Abraham Lincoln,* 6:445.

54. Eighth Census (1860), Prairie du Chien, Crawford County, Wis., Dwelling 100, RG29, NA; *Prairie Du Chien Courier,* July 17, 24, 1862.

55. *Chicago Times,* quoted in *Indiana State Sentinel* (Indianapolis), July 28, 1862; *Eastern Argus* (Portland, Maine), July 21, 1862.

56. Letter published in *Caledonian* (St. Johnsbury, Vt.), Aug. 8, 1862.

57. *McArthur (Ohio) Democrat,* Aug. 7, 1862.

58. *Boston Journal,* Aug. 13, 1862.

59. Eighth Census (1860), Dubuque, Dubuque County, Iowa, Dwelling 1909, RG29, NA; Dennis Mahony to Charles Mason, Oct. 4, 1862, Mason Papers; and C. C. Flint to Samuel J. Kirkwood, Aug. 14, 1862, Disloyal Sentiments File, Adjutant General's Correspondence, SHSI-DM; *Dubuque (Iowa) Herald,* July 2, Sept. 14, 1861, Aug. 2, 1862 (quotation).

60. H. M. Hoxie to Stanton, Aug. 22, 1862, Case 413, Case Files of Investigations, Reel 14, RG94, NA; *Dubuque (Iowa) Herald,* Aug. 6, 1862 (quotation).

61. Affidavits of Arthur McCame, n.d., and Frank M. Robinson and H. A. Wiltse, Aug. 13, 1862, with H. M. Hoxie to Stanton, Aug. 22, 1862, Case 413, Case Files of Investigations, Reel 14, RG94, NA.

62. *Dubuque (Iowa) Daily Times,* Aug. 20, 1862, cited in Johnson, "'Volunteer While You May,'" 46. The surveyed soldiers were from Company A, 19th Iowa Volunteers.

63. *Dubuque (Iowa) Herald,* Aug. 23, 1862; *Fort Dodge (Iowa) Republican,* Sept. 16, 1862.

64. *Dubuque (Iowa) Herald,* July 16, 18, 19, 1862; *New York Herald,* Aug. 9, 1862; *Cadiz (Ohio) Democratic Sentinel,* July 16, 1862; *Daily Ohio Statesman* (Columbus), July 6, 1862.

65. *Jasper (Ind.) Weekly Courier,* Aug. 6, 1862.

66. *Minnesota Staats-Zeitung* (St. Paul), Aug. 2, 1862. The *Staats-Zeitung* was a German-language newspaper, but it is not clear if the workers themselves were German.

67. Petition of Gardner Durgin et al., Aug. 28, 1862; Jonathan Ela to Levi C. Turner, Aug. 30, 1862; and Joseph Holt endorsement of Sept. 9, 1862, Case 200, Case Files of Investigations, Reel 8, RG94, NA.

CHAPTER SIX

1. Lassen, *Dear Sarah,* 1–2, 40, 53 (quotations); Robertson, *Michigan in the War,* 30; *Cass County Republican* (Dowagiac, Mich.), July 31, 1862; *Detroit Free Press,* July 31, 1862; *Caledonian* (St. Johnsbury, Vt.), Aug. 8, 1862.

2. *Detroit Free Press,* Aug. 6, 28, 30, 1862; Lassen, *Dear Sarah,* 9, 14, 62, 112, 117, 120, 124, 126, 127; Original declaration, Sarah Pardington Widow's Certificate 12653, RG15, NA.

3. See Table 1. Company A of the 24th Michigan provided the sample for Michigan's three-year recruits for 1862 in row 8, column 3.

4. Eighth Census (1860), Centreville, St. Joseph County, Mich., Dwelling 1006, RG29, NA; Beasecker, *I Hope to Do My Country Service,* 10, 13, 18, 20, 22, 32, 46–48, 54, 57, 68, 87 (quotations); Joseph Rutherford to "My Dear Wife," Jan. 25, 1863, UVM.

5. Child, *Letters from a Civil War Surgeon,* 17; Rutherford to Hannah Rutherford, Nov. 25, Dec. 18, 1862, Jan. 13, 25, 1863, UVM; Eighth Census (1860), Derby, Orleans County, Vt., Dwelling 181, RG29, NA.

6. A. A. Bean to family, Oct. 7, Dec. 20, 1862, Jan. 4, Mar. 14, 1863; John V. Bean to "Dear Father," Dec. 27, 1862; Mary P. Bean to "Dr. Bean," Nov. 19, 1862, Jan. 12, 1863; and F. W. Brigham to Mary Bean, Apr. 26, 1863, UIA; *OR,* ser. 3, 2:145.

7. Throne, "Iowa Doctor in Blue," 99–100, 139.

8. Myron Underwood to Sophia Underwood, Sept. 14, 1862, Feb. 8, 1863, UIA.

9. Eighth Census (1860), Exeter, Penobscot County, Maine, Dwelling 334, RG29, NA; John B. Wilson to "My Darling," May 30, June 9, 1864, AHEC.

10. B. N. Bond to Trumbull, Apr. 18, 1862, Reel 12, Trumbull Papers, LC; muster-in roll, Nov. 8, 1862, 27th Missouri Infantry, Benjamin N. Bond file, CSR, Reel 594, RG94, NA. Trumbull fielded numerous requests from avowedly fervent Republicans for appointments under the tax law, especially after passage of the new law on July 1, 1862. See Reels 12 and 13, Trumbull Papers, LC.

11. Charles Bowers to "Dear Lydia," Nov. 27, [1863], MHS.

12. Josiah Fuller to "My Dear Wife," Dec. 7, 1862, MHS; John Owen Jr. to "My Dear Mother," July 4, 1864, MHS.

13. William Lambert to "Dear George," Sept. 9, 1862, AHEC.

14. Jones, "Letters of Lauren Elmer Bent," 37.

15. Zerah Coston Monks to "My Dear Hattie," Oct. 9, 1864, WRHS.

16. Underhill, *"Your Soldier Boy Samuel,"* 15–17; *MSSM,* 3:806.

17. Goldin and Lewis, "Economic Cost of the American Civil War," 304.

18. Philip Arsino to "Dear Mother," Jan. 7, 1863, VHS.

19. George H. Caverly Diary, Aug. 9–12, 1862, NHHS. George Caverly was the only one of the three to come home alive: Mason Caverly and Albert Corson were both killed in 1864.

20. John Jenks to Almina Jenks, Dec. 29, 1859, Oct. 3, 1862, Jan. 25, 1863, UNH; *Keene (N.H.) Sentinel,* Sept. 13, 1860–June 26, 1862, Aug. 21, 1862; *Cheshire Republican* (Keene, N.H.), Sept. 12, 1860–June 25, 1862, Aug. 20, 1862; Eighth Census (1860), North Brookfield, Worcester County, Mass., Dwelling 408, RG29, NA; Certified birth record of Henry C. Jenks, Almina Jenks Widow's Certificate 70512, RG15, NA; Disbursements of Aid for Soldiers' Families, Keene City Records, HSCC.

21. John Jenks to Almina Jenks, Oct. 3, 1862, July 22, 1863, UNH.

22. Eighth Census (1860), Winchester, Cheshire County, N.H., Dwellings 116, 118, 158; and Ninth Census (1870), Winchester, Cheshire County, N.H., Dwelling 306, RG29, NA; Ayling, *Revised Register,* 703; *Cheshire Republican* (Keene, N.H.), Aug. 13, 1862; William Combs to Eliza Combs, Feb. 15, 27, "1862" [1863], Mar. 21, 1865, ND.

23. Priest, *John T. McMahon's Diary,* 5, 23, 31.

24. Burgess, *Uncommon Soldier,* 10, 18, 21–25, 28.

25. Eighth Census (1860), Brimfield, Peoria County, Ill., Dwelling 59, RG29, NA; Stockwell Diary, Sept. 1, 1862; and Stockwell to "Dear Parents," Nov. 3, 1862, WRHS; Original declaration, Harriet Stockwell Widow's Certificate 47334, RG15, NA.

26. Fred Kappelman to "Dear Parents," Sept. 2, 1862, Feb. 19, 1863, AHEC.

27. *Jeffersonian Democrat* (Chardon, Ohio), Aug. 1, 1862; Charles Caley to Juliett Caley, Aug. 28, 1862, ND; Ransom Neal Diary, Sept. 28, Oct. 4, 1862, NHSL; *National Eagle* (Claremont, N.H.), Aug. 7, 14, 1862; Lewis Caswell to "Dear Brother," Oct. 14, 1862, PEM (this letter is misdated "October 19, 1863," in Silber and Sievens, *Yankee Correspondence,* 145–46). Neal weighed only 103 pounds and died of diphtheria two months to the day after his wedding.

28. Gilbert Gulbrandson to "Dear Parents," Aug. 20, Sept. 2, 1862, AHEC; M. D. Peak to "Mr. Wood," Mar. 5, 1862, MNHS; Adin Stebbins to "Dear Mother," July 23, 1862, MNHS (quotation); Eighth Census (1860), Hayward, Freeborn County, Minn., Dwelling 742; and Ninth Census (1860), Hayward, Freeborn County, Minn., Dwelling, 17, RG29, NA. The relatively poor Gulbrandsons had grown prosperous by 1870, including Gilbert.

29. A. O. Allen to Agnes Allen, Sept. 12, Oct. 22, 1862; and Agnes Allen to "Orlando" Allen, Sept. 7, Nov. 2, 12, 25, 1862, SHSI-DM; Original declaration, Agnes Allen Widow's Certificate 17423, RG15, NA; *Morning Star* (Dover, N.H.), Nov. 20, 1861.

30. Jacob Hunter to Mary Hunter, Sept. 14, 24, Oct. 15, 28, Nov. 4, 7, 13, 16, 1862; and Peter Kline to Mary Hunter, Apr. 1, 1863, SHSI-DM; Original declaration, Mary Hunter Widow's Certificate 13019, RG15, NA.

31. Woodworth, *Musick of the Mocking Birds,* 117. Although he conceded that "no unequivocal answer is possible," James McPherson felt that patriotic purpose kept men in the ranks through thick and thin, and numerous other scholars have agreed. *For Cause and Comrades,* 114–16. In *Gentlemen and the Roughs,* however, Lorien Foote emphasized that violence, including the threat of death, was freely used to force reluctant soldiers to do their duty.

32. Thomas Sterns to "My dear Wife," Oct. 6, 10, 26, 27, 1862, Apr. 3, 1863; and Sterns's teaching certificate, UIA; Original declaration, Eliza Van Deusen Dependent's Certificate 362390, RG15, NA.

33. Puck, *Sacrifice at Vicksburg,* 8.

34. Kohl, *Irish Green and Union Blue,* 17, 20, 65–67, 69.

35. Eighth Census (1860), Bridgeport, Fairfield County, Conn., Dwelling 1722, RG29, NA; *Housatonic Republican* (Falls Village, Conn.), July 26, Aug. 2, 16, 1862 (quotations); *Record of Service of Connecticut Men,* 758.

36. Edwin Wentworth to Caroline Wentworth, July 20, 21, 1862, LC.

37. Edwin Wentworth to Caroline Wentworth, July 20, Sept. 4, 1862; and Edwin Wentworth to Robert Wentworth, Sept. 17, 1862, ibid.; *MSSM,* 3:817.

38. Mohr, *Cormany Diaries,* 218–29.

39. Ibid., 229–30, 311, 505.

40. Ibid., 217–29, 231, 246–47, 311, 313, 315.

41. Henry V. Christy to J. A. J. Cresswell, Sept. 26, Oct. 4, 15, 22, 1862; and John P. Bennett to Cresswell, July 25, 1862, LC; Bates, *History of Pennsylvania Volunteers,* 2:441, 5:239.

42. W. W. Henry to Mary Jane Henry, July 23, Nov. 24, 1861, Jan. 22, Aug. 18, Nov. 2, 1862, Jan. 11, May 31, 1863; and recommendation of Paul Dillingham et al., Aug. 7, 1862, Henry Papers, VHS.

43. Hughes, *Civil War Papers of Lt. Colonel Newton T. Colby,* 126–33.

44. *OR,* 19(1):198–99, 494–96 (quotation); Hughes, *Civil War Papers of Lt. Colonel Newton T. Colby,* 176.

45. Marvel, *Race of the Soil,* 421, 430, 437, 452, 484. Wayne Duerkes generously interprets one immediate postbattle resignation as an example of an officer who wished to demonstrate his courage before leaving the army, but the evidence more likely suggests a man unnerved by his first battle. Francis Bowman had sold his interest in a struggling business to accept a commission as captain, but he and another captain submitted their resignations within forty-eight hours after their regiment was mauled at Shiloh, Bowman considering it "a wonder to me that I am alive." Their resignations were quickly accepted, suggesting that they had unfavorably impressed their colonel, who usually disapproved resignations except for physical disability. Duerkes, "I for One Am Ready," 323; Bowman to "My Dear Wife," Mar. 2, 6, Apr. 18, May 1, 1862, NIU.

46. Hughes, *Civil War Papers of Lt. Colonel Newton T. Colby,* 176, 183–84.

47. The letter appeared in the *Portland (Maine) Daily Press* on March 6, 1863, perhaps to the surprise of Lieutenant Nichols.

48. Sumner Hurd to "Dear Coz," Jan. 5, 27, Feb. 10, 1863, DC. For the dim view Colonel Cross entertained of Captain Barton, see Cross to J. B. Fry, May 31, 1863, Ira M. Barton Papers, DC.

49. *Roster and Record of Iowa Soldiers,* 1:702, 734; William H. Cotton to "Dear Wife," Apr. 10, May 3, 1862, SHSI-IC; Eighth Census (1860), Bellevue, Jackson County, Iowa, Dwelling 269, RG29, NA. Cotton was wounded and captured at Iuka in September, 1862, and mortally wounded at Milliken's Bend the following summer.

50. [Acton], "Dear Mollie," 18–20.

51. Skipper and Taylor, *Handful of Providence,* 19, 65, 177, 189, 191, 201, 209; Ninth Census (1870), Albany Subdivision 35, Albany County, N.Y., Dwelling 896, RG29, NA.

52. James Law to "Dear Sister," Nov. 19, 1862, CHS; *Daily Morning Chronicle* (Portsmouth, N.H.), Aug. 15, 1862; *Cambridge (Mass.) Chronicle,* Aug. 23, 1862.

53. Charles H. Smith to his wife, Aug. 24, Sept. 8, 1862, AHEC; John Sheahan to "My Dear

Father and Sister Mary," Sept. 22, 1862, MEHS (quotation); *North Branch Democrat* (Tunkhannock, Pa.), Aug. 13, 1862; *Highland Weekly News* (Hillsborough, Ohio), Aug. 21, 1862.

54. *MSSM*, 4:310–44, 6:335–83. On the percentages of men from families below median wealth, see Table 1.

55. Haines, *Letters from the Forty-fourth*, 23; George Troup Diary, Aug. 7, 21, 1862, MHS.

56. See Table 1.

57. Ledman, *A Maine Town Responds*, 118–19, 122–23; Dyer, *Compendium*, 1225, 1227; *OR*, 21:134, 25(1):178, 27(1):178.

58. N. Clifford Bragg to parents, Oct. 17, 1861, AHEC; Mann, *History of the Forty-Fifth*, 48–49, 529–36 (quotation); Oliver Peabody to "My Darling Wife," Sept. 10, 1862, MHS; *Nantucket (Mass.) Inquirer*, July 23, 1862. Peabody, who claimed to be a clerk with no property in 1860, was a partner in a major business and worth $75,000 by 1870. Ninth Census (1870), Milton, Norfolk County, Mass., Dwelling 104, RG29, NA. The "buying" and even the "stealing" of volunteers from other recruiters was also practiced that summer. Hauptman, *A Seneca Indian in the Union Army*, 57.

59. Miller, "Brahmin Janissaries," 229–31; *OR*, ser. 3, 2:595; Dyer, *Compendium*, 1249–50, 1264–66. Some of the regiments sent to Louisiana lost heavily due to disease.

60. Dyer, *Compendium*, 1614–15, 1619–22. On Governor Curtin's resistance to War Department demands for three-year troops in the summer of 1862, see Blair, "We Are Coming, Father Abraham."

61. Robert E. Miller to "Dear Parents," Nov. 2, 1862, CL.

62. Henry Brown to John Lingle, Dec. 16, 1862; and Mary Lingle to John, Jan. 5, 1863, AHEC.

63. John M. Jackson to "My Dear Mother," Oct. 27, 1862, ND.

64. Nathan Gould to "Father," n.d. [early autumn 1862], NHHS.

65. Darius Starr to "Dear Mother," Mar. 18, 1863, Duke University.

66. Johnson and Buel, *Battles and Leaders*, 3:137. A veteran of the 24th Michigan later claimed that the private funds only went to Detroit recruits and that county residents (like Pardington) never drew a cent of it, but a published letter from Detroit in August, 1862, contradicts that statement. Ibid., 142; *Caledonian* (St. Johnsbury, Vt.), Aug. 8, 1862. When Pardington went to war, he left so much cash behind that his father and father-in-law both tried to borrow some of it, and after only nine months of service he had accumulated enough money—after supporting his family—to consider buying a house, indicating that his pay had been supplemented by a good deal more than the $40 federal advance. Lassen, *Dear Sarah*, 14, 117–18, 127.

67. "John" to Alexander Thompson, Sept. 27, [1862], SHC.

68. Calvin Smith to "Dear Mother," Sept. 5, 1862, MHS; George Spinney to "Dear Sister," Nov. 19, 1862, BPL (quotation).

69. George Brown to "Dear Mother," Aug. 24, 1862, AHEC.

70. Joseph Spafford to "Dear Sister," Apr. 19, 1863, VHS.

71. William L. Winship to "My Dear Mother," Aug. 14, 1862, CHS.

72. John Parrish Sheahan to "My Dear Father," Aug. 29, 1862, MHS.

73. Myron Rice Wood to "My dear home," July 30, 1862, MHS.

74. John D. Hill to "Dear Sister," July 3, 1862, AHEC.

75. Delina Hopper to "Dear Sister," n.d. [Oct. 1862]; and Delina Hopper to Daniel Hopper, Mar. 26, Apr. 7, July 13, 1863, May 8, 1864, WRHS; Eighth Census (1860), Youngstown, Mahoning County, Ohio, Dwelling 1017; and Ninth Census (1870), Youngstown Ward 2, Mahoning County,

Ohio, Dwelling 182, RG29, NA; Hopper family headstones, Oak Hill Cemetery, Youngstown, Ohio. In the militia draft of 1862, any able-bodied man could serve as a substitute, as tradition dictated, but the 1863 draft law required that substitutes not be liable to conscription, thus most substitutes were exempt by either age or alienage.

76. Ellsworth Phelps to "My Dear Wife," Oct. 30, 1862, CHS. Phelps's wealth increased from $200 in 1860 to $20,000 in 1870. Eighth Census (1860), Windsor, Hartford County, Conn., Dwelling 349; and Ninth Census (1870), Windsor, Hartford County, Conn., Dwelling 34, RG29, NA.

77. Seventh Census (1850), Eagle Harbor, Houghton County, Mich., Dwelling 54; and Eighth Census (1860), Winona, Winona County, Minn., Dwelling 357, RG29, NA; Louis Morrison to Rebecca Morrison, July 13, 1861, Mar. 20, Apr. 6, May 25, July 20, Oct. 8, 30, 1862, SHC. The Morrison collection includes a photo of Louis in uniform, looking rather portly.

78. Catton, *Glory Road,* 13. That last surviving recruit was James Albert Hard, who enlisted in the 32nd New York in May of 1861 and served in the Army of the Potomac. *New York Times,* Jan. 10, 1953; *Binghampton (N.Y.) Press,* Mar. 13, 1953.

CHAPTER SEVEN

1. Minerva Thomas to George Thomas, July 6, 1862, ND; Olive Steele to William Steele, Oct. 8, Nov. 16, 1862; Ebenezer Steele to William Steele, Nov. 16, 1862; and Inventory of William Steele's estate, Feb. 2, 1863, IHS; Charles Tillison to Dudley Tillison, Feb. 27, 1863, VHS; John Amidon to "Dear Wife and Children," Nov. 8, 1863, Jan. 16, 1864, UVM (quotation); Hoover, Neiterman, and James, *From Your Loving Son,* 1, 25, 34.

2. John Viles to Frances Viles, Aug. 11, 15, Sept. 9, 1861, AHEC; Francis Boland to John Brislin, Nov. 11, 1862, AHEC; Allen Church to "My Dear Wife," Aug. 23, 1862, WHS; Clarkson Butterworth Diary, Aug. 5, 1862, Earlham College; David Werking to "Dear Wife," Mar. 4, 1863, IHS; McKitrick, *Civil War Letters,* 4, 5; Hunley, *14th U.S. Infantry,* 8; Albert Huntington to "Dear Sister Sue," n.d. (summer 1863), UR; Francis Reges to "Dear Wife," Oct. 6, 1863, AHEC; Edwin Horton to "Dear Ellen," Oct. 18, 1863, Apr. 6, Nov. 6, 1864, Apr. 20, 1865, VHS; Metzger, *Griffith Letters,* 105, 260; Thomas Hyatt to "Dear Wife," Aug. 19, 1864, WRHS; Charles Marples, letter fragment, late 1864; and to "Dear Wife and Children," Mar. 6, 1865, MNHS; Chester Evans to his wife, Mar. 13, 1865, MNHS. On inflation increasingly outpacing wages, see Fite, *Social and Industrial Conditions,* 183–84; and Sharkey, *Money, Class, and Party,* 180–81.

3. Willis Pomeroy to "Dear Mother," July 6, 1861, AHEC; William L. Broaddus to "Dear Wife," Aug. 8, 1861, Duke University; Charles Johnson to "Dear Nellie," Oct. 5, 1861, AHEC; George M. Redlon to "Dear Father," Apr. 13, 1862, MEHS; Manny Austin to "Dear Aunt," Apr. 15, 1862, AHEC; James Turner to "My dear Parents and Sisters," May 1, 1862, NYSL; William Sayre to Ziba Sayre, Aug. 6, 1862, AHEC; Spalding, *Tuf as a Boiled Owl,* 22; William Thompson to Jane Thompson, Sept. 18, Nov. 3, Dec. 3, 22, 1862, Feb. 2, Mar. 10, 1863, SHSI-DM; "John" to Alexander E. Thompson, Sept. 27, [1862], SHC; Robert Shortelle to "Dear Sister," Oct. 14, 1862, LC; George Chapin to Ella Chapin, Oct. 14, 1862, IHS; Joseph Cross to Deborah Cross, Oct. 23, Nov. 30, 1862, AAS; Thomas Brown to "Dear wife," Oct. 23, 1862, VHS; George Randall to "Dear Joey," Oct. 31, 1862, PPL; John Turner Wood to "My dear mother," Nov. 8, 1862, AHEC; William Russell to "Dear Col," Nov. 16, 1862, UIA; Abram Rowell to "Dear Wife," Nov. 23, 1862, UVM; George Wallace Newcomb to "My Dear Wife,"

Nov. 24, 1862, AHEC; Francis Boland to John Brislin, Dec. 2, 1862, AHEC; Benjamin Ashenfelter to "Father Churchman," Dec. 23, 1862, AHEC; William Presley to "Dear Father," Dec. 23, 1862, AHEC; Cassedy, *Dear Friends at Home,* 129, 216, 232; James Brown to "Dear Friends at Home," Dec. 30, 1862, MEHS; Adoniram Withrow to Libertatia Withrow, Jan. 3, 1863, SHSI-IC; Levi Shell to "Dear Brother," Jan. 5, 1863; and Levi Shell to "Dear Mother," Jan. 26, 1863, WHS; McKitrick, *Civil War Letters,* 7; Grimsley and Miller, *The Union Must Stand,* 75, 89; Elijah Cavins to "Dear Ann," Jan. 18, 1863, IHS; Charles Littlefield to "Dear Wife," Jan. 24, Feb. 1, 1863, AHEC; William Barnes to "my loving wife," Feb. 4, 1863, SHSI-DM; Popchock, *Soldier Boy,* 30; William Winship to "Dear Mother," Mar. 6, May 5, 1863, CHS; Daniel Faust to "Dear Mother," Mar. 14, 1863, AHEC; Darius Starr to "Dear Mother," Mar. 18, 1863, Duke University; George Rowell to "Dear Parents," Mar. 18, "1862" [1863], NHHS; Mannis and Wilson, *Bound to Be a Soldier,* 152; Marion Ward to "Home Friends," Mar. 21, 1863, WRHS; Jasper Mabie to Angeline Mabie, Apr. 17, 1863, NYSL; Charles Walbridge to George Walbridge, Apr. 21, 1863, NYSL; Abram Bogart to Mary Bogart, Apr. 23, 1863, NYSL; James Adams to "Dear Father," May 7, 1863, IHS; Theodore Tillison to "Dear Brother," May 24, 1863, VHS; Charles Hill to "My Very Dear Martha," Mar. 19, 1863, Federal Soldiers' Letters, SHC; Bohrnstedt, *While Father Is Away,* 96, 98, 294; Patrick and Willey, *Fighting for Liberty and Right,* 269.

4. George Fluent to William McClain, Aug. 26, 1864, UIA; Burr Murdock to "Dear Sister," Apr. 27, 1863, AHEC; Eugene Hadley to "My Dear Wife," Oct. 2, 1864, George O. Jewett Papers, LC; Orra Bailey to Sophia Bailey, Mar. 25, 1863, CHS; Orra Bailey to Sophia Bailey, May 15, June 6, July 31, Aug. 25, 31, Sept. 10, 1864, LC; John Carvel Arnold to "Dear wife and family," July 26, 1864, LC.

5. Hunley, *14th U.S. Infantry,* 46; Jonathan Remington to "Friend Thell," Jan. 9, 1864, UVM; Mushkat, *A Citizen-Soldier's Civil War,* 101; A. P. Davies to Sarah Davies, Feb. 29, 1864, MNHS; John Carvel Arnold to "Dear wife and family," Mar. 8, 1864, LC; William Doyle to "My Dear Wife," Mar. 10, 1864, MNHS; George Benson Fox to "My Dear Father," Mar. 12, 1863, CinHS; Edmund Townsend to Samuel Townsend, May 16, 1864, CL; W. B. Fox to Robert Crouse, June 8, 1864, BL; Elmer Wallace to "My Dear Mother," June 19, 1864, BL; Benjamin Wright to "My Dear Abbie," June 19, 1864, WHS; Lyman Williams to "Dear Sister Lois," June 25, 1864, VHS; Aaron Overstreet to "Dear Wife and Children," June 30, 1864, AHEC; Frank Morse to "My dear Nellie," June 30, 1864, MHS; Valentine Barney to "My Dear Maria," July 3, 1864, VHS; William Bryant Adams to "Dear Father," July 12, 1864; and Adams Diary, July 12, 1864, MEHS ("greenbacks"); Mary Simpson to "Francis Simpson," Sept. 7, 1864, CHS; Harrison Nesbitt to "Dear Wife," Sept. 30, 1864, AHEC; George Buffum to "Dear wife and fammoly," Dec. 8, 1864, WHS.

6. Niven, *Chase Papers,* 3:358, 363–65, 4:127; *CG,* 37th Cong., 3rd sess., 381; Beale, *Diary of Edward Bates,* 292; Kohl, *Irish Green and Union Blue,* 88.

7. Isaac Webb to "Dear Father," Feb. 18, "1862" [1863], MEHS; Mary Dunham to Thaddeus Stevens, Mar. 28, 1864, LC; Charles Gould to "Dear Mother," Nov. 7, 1864, UVM; Adjutant General to George Oscar French, Jan. 18, 1865, VHS; Kamphoefner and Helbich, *Germans in the Civil War,* 287, 289; William A. Day to Andrew Davis, Mar. 9, 1887; and Davis payment notice, Feb. 14, 1889, UIA.

8. Marcellus Darling to "Dear parents, brothers, sisters, friends," Dec. 6, 1862, UIA; Thomas Brown to "Dear wife," Oct. 23, 1862, VHS; Spalding, *Tuf as a Boiled Owl,* 111, 138, 152, 165, 170.

9. Woodworth, *Musick of the Mocking Birds,* 117; Samuel Brooks to "Dear Wife," Sept. 21, 1862, AHEC; William Oberlin to "Dear Annie," Nov. 26, 1862, AHEC; John Frederick to "Dear Wife," Jan. 9, 1863, SHSI-IC; Heber Chase to "Dearest Anne," Aug. 20, 1863, Apr. 11, 1864, AHEC; Charles Chace to "Dear Mother," Dec. 3, 1863, UVM; Harvey Miller to "Dear Hattie," n.d. [Jan. 1864],

AHEC; John McCoy to "Dear Martha," June 25, 1864, DC; John Peirce to "Dear Wife," June 23, 1864, PEM.

10. J. W. Shepard to "Dear Sister," May 16, 1861, AHEC; Joseph D. Baker to "Mother," Nov. 23, 1861, AHEC; William Sayre to Ziba Sayre, Mar. 23, 1862, AHEC; Charles Varnum to "Dear Mother," Sept. 16, 1862, AHEC; Henry Rogers Smith to "Father," Oct. 1, 1862, AAS; Kallgren and Crouthamel, *"Dear Friend Anna,"* 9; Talmadge Wood to "Dear wife and daughters," Dec. 17, 1862, AHEC; John M. Steward to "Dear Abby," Jan. 16, 1864, AHEC; Timothy O'Sullivan to "Dear Mother & Sister," Jan. 11, 1865, CHS; Horace Rugg to "Dear Friends," Dec. 24, 1862, HSCC (quotation).

11. Hosea Towne to "Dear Friends," Dec. 5, 1862, NHHS; James Houlihan to "Deir Brother thoms," July 11, 1862, HSCC; Edward H. C. Taylor to "My dear Sister," Sept. 13, 1863, BL (quotation).

12. George Jones to "Dear Friends at Home," Mar. 3, 1864, UVM; White, *Civil War Diary,* 135; Racine, *Unspoiled Heart,* 112–13; Kohl, *Irish Green and Union Blue,* 139; *OR,* 21:859–60; James Brown to "Dear Friends at Home," Dec. 30, 1862, MEHS; Charles Littlefield to his wife, Feb. 1, 1863, AHEC; William Oberlin to "Annie," May 15, 1863, AHEC; Tatum, "'Please Send Stamps,'" 305; Charles Manson to "Dear Mother," Mar. 2, 1865, UVM; John Boardman to "Father," Apr. 17, 1865, BL; Francis Boland to John Brislin, Dec. 2, 1862, AHEC.

13. Elijah Cavins to "Dear Ann," Aug. 8, 1863, IHS; Elmer Wallace to "Dear Father," Dec. 19, 1864, BL; Peter Abbott to "Friends at Home," Dec. 13, 1862, VHS; Alonzo Jack to "Dear Parents," Sept. 26, 1862, WHS; Gavin, *Infantryman Pettit,* 52; Hiram Barton to Mary Barton, Feb. 22, 1863, VHS; Andrew Linscott to "Dear Parents," July 4, 1864, MHS; Cassedy, *Dear Friends at Home,* 204–5; David Siebert to "Father and all," June 1, 1863, AHEC; Charles Bates to "Dear Parents," Apr. 24, 1864, VAHS; Merritt Stone to "Dear Sister Ella," Apr. 24, 1864, VHS; David Scott to "My Dear Wife," July 2, 18, 1864, IHS; Hosea Towne to "Dear Friends," June 5, 1862, NHHS; Charles Cummings to "My Dear Wife," July 3, 1864, VHS; William Hamilton to "My dear Mother," Mar. 17, 1863, LC; Wesley Shaw to "Dear father & mother," Jan. 15, "1862" [1863], NYSL; J. B. Dawley to "Dear Brother," Jan. 15, "1864" [1865], Yale University; Rufus Mead to "Dear Folks at Home," May 9, Aug. 29, 1863, LC.

14. L. D. MacFarlane to John Schofield, Nov. 23, 1863, Odon Guitar Collection, WHMC; William Wirt Henry to Mary Jane Henry, Jan. 11, 1863, VHS; James Gillette to "Dear Parents," Jan. 14, 1863, LC.

15. Elijah Cavins to "Dear Ann," Oct. 29, 1864, IHS; Henry Grimes Marshall to "My Dear Hattie," Nov. 19, 1864, CL; Robertson, *Civil War Letters of General Robert McAllister,* 472; Benjamin Wright to "My Dear Abbie," June 19, 1864, WHS; [Sawyer], *Civil War Letters of Captain John Franklin Godfrey,* 12–13 (quotation).

16. George Kies to Fannie Kies, Apr. 25, 29, May 13, 14, 1863, CHS.

17. Amanda Chittenden to "My dear husband," June 21, 1863, ISL.

18. Julius Wood to "Dear Ones at Home," Jan. 20, 1863, WRHS; George Ayers to Isaac S. Waterman, Mar. 19, 1863, LC; Samuel Webber to "My dear wife," Aug. 23, 1864, MHS.

19. Greenleaf, *Letters to Eliza,* 112; Emily Harris to Leander Harris, Feb. 23, 1864, UNH; Sarah Upton to "My Dear George," July 29, 1864, NHHS; Blair, *Politician Goes to War,* 178–79; John Arnold to "Dear wife and family," July 7, Aug. 19, 28, 1864, LC; Thomas Brown to "my wife," Feb. "the 30," 1863, VHS.

20. Elmer Wallace to "Dear Parents," Nov. 9, 1864, BL (quotation); James Burrows to Jabez Burrows, Dec. 9, 1863, CCHS; "Father and Mother" to William Rigby, July 26, 1863, Feb. 2, 1864, Mar. 5, 1865, UIA; Lawrence Joyce to "My Dear wife and children," May 30, 1864, MEHS; Eighth Census

(1860), Brunswick, Cumberland County, Maine, Dwelling 384; and Ninth Census (1870), Brunswick, Cumberland County, Maine, Dwelling 404, RG29, NA; Alfred Keith to "My Dear Sister," June 2, 1863, VHS; William Wirt Henry to "My own darling wife," July 25, 1864, VHS. The "five-twenty" government bonds sold to finance the war were redeemable after five years and matured at twenty years.

21. Eben Calderwood to "Dear Wife," Apr. 15, 1863, MEHS; James Howes to "My Dear Wife," May 21, 1863, NHHS; Edward H. C. Taylor to "My dear Lottie," Sept. 29, 1863, BL.

22. Amos Noyes Currier to "My Dear Friend," Jan. 1, 1864, SHSI-IC.

23. *Portland (Maine) Daily Press,* Mar. 6, 1863; Burgess, *Uncommon Soldier,* 37; Joseph Kohout to "Dear Father and Mother and Sister," Mar. 4, 1863, UIA; John Barney to "All at Home," "December" [Jan.] 2, 1863, WHS; Christopher Keller to "Dear Carrie," Jan. 18, 1863, CL; Lucius Wood to "Dear Ones at Home," Jan. 20, 1863, WRHS; Walter E. Gardiner to "My dear Friend," Nov. 25, 1862, PPL; John D. Wilkins to "My Dearly beloved wife," Mar. 29, 1863, CL (quotation); William T. H. Brooks to "Dear Father," Apr. 28, 1861, AHEC; William B. Franklin to Fitz John Porter, Apr. 7, 1863, Reel 3, Porter Papers, LC.

24. Lewis Fales to Silas Fales, Mar. 15, 1863, SHC; Houston, *Keep Up Good Courage,* 49.

25. Abram Bogart to Mary Bogart, May 28, 1863, NYSL.

26. Horace Hooker to Susan Hooker, Feb. 26, Apr. 3, 1863, Huntington-Hooker Papers, UR.

27. Cook, *Quiet Corner of the War,* 48; *OR,* 23(2):323–24; Albert Rogall Diary, June 14, 1864, OHS; Houston. *Keep Up Good Courage,* 63 (quotation).

28. Priest, *John T. McMahon's Diary,* 60; Eighth Census (1860), Lima, Livingston County, N.Y., Dwelling 440, RG29, NA.

29. Ayling, *Revised Register,* 607; Joseph F. Lovering Diary, Apr. 2–13, 1865, IU.

30. Clark Carr to "My Dear Wife," Nov. 10, 1862, HSCC.

31. George Gordon to "Dear Wife," July 19, 1862, NHHS; George Chapin to Rev. John Chapin, Feb. 17, 1863, IHS (quotation).

32. Silas Fales to unknown, May 31, 1863, SHC.

33. Ransom Neal Diary, Oct. 12, 1862, NHSL; William Boston to "Dear Aunt," Jan. 24, 1865, BL; Jonas Howe to "Dear Aunt," Apr. 30, 1865, MNHS.

34. Francis Crowninshield Journal, May 8, 1864, PEM.

35. Ellen Emerson to "My dear Papa," Jan. 12–15, 1865, AAS.

36. Charles Coit to "Dear All," June 4, 1862; and Coit to unknown, Sept. 18, 1862, Yale University; Wilkie, *Pen and Powder,* 14–15.

37. Charges and specifications, Feb. 24, 1862, Rufus King Papers, WHS; Eighth Census(1860), Poughkeepsie Ward 2, Dutchess County, N.Y., Dwelling 1641; and Milwaukee Ward 7, Wis., Dwelling 805, RG29, NA; *Roster of Wisconsin Volunteers,* 1:346; Heitman, *Historical Register,* 1:681. On Richmond's past, see Onderdonk, *Letter to the Rev. James C. Richmond,* and Richmond, *Reply.*

38. Thomas Scott to Edwin Stanton, Feb. 12, 1862; James Todd to Edwin Stanton, Feb. 12, 1862; and John H. Mulkey to Montgomery Meigs, Feb. 11, 1862, Stanton Papers, LC; Basler, *Collected Works of Abraham Lincoln,* 4:461, 5:116, 177 (quotation). Hatch was implicated in the fatal overloading of the *Sultana,* which raised suspicions of kickbacks from the boat owners. In that case he again avoided prosecution, while Capt. Frederic Speed (whose correspondence revealed a casual attitude toward bribery) was convicted only of incompetence, and even that was later overturned by Judge Adv. Gen. Joseph Holt. This aspect of the *Sultana* tragedy is described more fully in Marvel, *Tarnished Victory,* 339–43, 419nn43–46.

39. Lewis Fales to Silas Fales, Mar. 15, 1863, SHC; *Louisville (Ky.) Daily Democrat,* Aug. 4, 7, 1863; *Cincinnati Daily Commercial,* Apr. 23, 1863; *Crisis* (Columbus, Ohio), July 29, 1863; *Ohio Democrat* (New Philadelphia), July 31, 1863; Charles Dana to Edwin M. Stanton, Sept. 8, 1863, LC; Niven, *Chase Papers,* 4:210–11; Pease and Randall, *Diary of Orville Hickman Browning,* 1:652, 657; Edwin M. Stanton to Joshua Speed, Feb. 18, 1864, LC; Speed to Joseph Holt, Sept. 8, 12, 1864; H. W. Allen to Holt, Sept. 11, 1864; and William Rosecrans to Holt, Sept. 14, 1864, LC; Herman Biggs to Montgomery Meigs, Nov. 5, 1864, LC.

40. Bohrnstedt, *While Father Is Away,* 18–19, 29, 96–98, 118; *Star and Herald* (Dwight, Ill.), Nov. 17, 1900; William Bradbury to "Dear Frederic," June 28, 1864, LC.

41. Williard Templeton to "Dear Brother James," Feb. 17, 1863, NHSL; Sparks, *Inside Lincoln's Army,* 276, 331, 350; James Brown to "Dear Brother," Apr. 13, 1864, MEHS.

42. *New Orleans Daily Crescent,* Oct. 20, 1860; *Newbern (N.C.) Weekly Progress,* Dec. 4, 1860; *Lancaster (Ohio) Ledger,* Feb. 6, 1861; Stephen Hurlbut to "Dear William," May 31, 1863, CL; Judson Bemis to Stephen Bemis, Oct. 17, 1863, MOHS; Charles Dana to Edwin M. Stanton, Sept. 8, 1863; and Phelps's unsigned report, Oct. 20, 1862, Stanton Papers, LC.

43. Christopher Keller to "Dear Carrie," Jan. 18, 1863, CL; Joseph Kohout to "Dear Father and Mother and Sister," Mar. 4, 1863, UIA; Marcus P. Wheeler to Gideon Winan Allen, Mar. 10, 1863, WHS; John Barney to "All at Home," "December" [Jan.] 2, 1863, WHS; Horace Hooker to Susan Hooker, Dec. 24, 1862, UR.

44. *OR,* 22(2):106.

45. Hunley, *14th U.S. Infantry,* 16; Walter Roberts to "Dear Bro.," Nov. 24, 1862, Earlham College; Julia Day to Henry C. Wright, Feb. 9, 1863, Harvey Letters, Earlham College.

46. Ransom Sargent to "Dear Maria," Sept. 28, 1862, DC; John Burrill to "Dear Parents," Jan. 1, Feb. 6, 1863, AHEC; Fitz John Porter to Manton Marble, Sept. 30–Oct. 3, 1862, Marble Papers, LC.

47. Scott, *Fallen Leaves,* 161 (quotation); William Barrus to "Dear Brother," May 10, 1863, UNH; Claude Goings to Mary Goings, Jan. 20, Mar. 25, 1863, DC; Marion Ward to "Home Friends," Mar. 21, 1863, WRHS; Richard Irwin to "Dear Mother & Sister," May 30, 1863, UVM; Eben Roberts to "Kind Cousin," Apr. 16, 1863, Calderwood Letters, MEHS; John Buck to Albert Fletcher, Dec. 30, 1862, Sheldon Museum; Jacob Haas to "My Dear Bro.," Jan. 3, 1863, AHEC.

48. Joel Fales to "Dear Brother," Feb. 1, 1863; and Lewis Fales to "Dear Brother," Nov. 12, 1862, SHC.

49. *Mankato (Minn.) Semi-Weekly Record,* Feb. 8, Apr. 9, May 17, June 14, Nov. 15, 1861, July 16, Aug. 9, 1862; *Winona (Minn.) Daily Republican,* Apr. 27, 1861; Thomas Stebbins to "dear mother," Jan. 5, 1862; and Stebbins to "Dear Father and Mother," Oct. 18, 1863, MNHS; Peter Wolford to "Dear Brother," Apr. 30, 1862, Jan. 29, Mar. 2, 1863, MNHS; Sewell Farwell to "Dear Brother," Aug. 6, 1862, SHSI-IC; Thomas Barnett Diary, Aug. 14, 1863, Earlham College.

50. Thomas Stebbins to "dear mother," Jan. 5, 1862; Stebbins to "Dear father and mother," Oct. 18, 1863; and Jonas Stebbins to "Dear Father & Mother," Jan. 27, 1862, MNHS; Joel Fales to "Dear Brother," Feb. 1, 1863; and Charles B. Lowell to "Dear Brother," Mar. 1, 1863, Fales Papers, SHC; Kiper, *Dear Catherine,* 92, 121; Sallie Miller to "Dear Brother Clason," May 7, 1863, CinHS; Isaac Morrow to "Dear Brother," Feb. 18, 1863, AHEC; Mary Bean to Asa Bean, Nov. 19, 1862, UIA.

51. Cora Benton to Charlie Benton, Oct. 1, 1862, ND; Lewis Caswell to "Dear Brother," Oct. 14, 1862, PEM.

52. "Mary" to "My Dear Sister," Apr. 25, 1864, Savage Family Papers, UVM; Matthew Askew to "Dear Brother," Jan. 21, 1863, BGSU; Edward Waite to "Dear Father," Apr. 27, 1864, MEHS.

53. Wesley Shaw to "Dear Brother," Dec. 24, 1861; and Shaw to "Dear father & mother," Jan. 15, "1862" [1863], NYSL; Merritt Stone to his father, Oct. 18, 1862, VHS; George Upton to Sarah Upton, Jan. 18, 1863, NHHS; William Hamilton to "My dear Mother," Mar. 17, 1863, LC; Edward R. Joslyn to "Dear Parents," May 6, 1864, AAS; Elisha Douglass to "Dear Wife," Mar. 20, 1864, NHHS; Willard Templeton to "Dear Friends at Home," July 20, 1864, NHSL; Charles Littlefield to his wife, Feb. 1, 1863, AHEC; Timothy O'Sullivan to "Dear Mother & Sister," Jan. 11, 1865, CHS; Matthew Askew to "Dear Brother," Jan. 21, 1863, BGSU; Mathew Hopkins to Albert Fletcher, Apr. 27, 1862, Sheldon Museum; Hosea Towne to "Dear Friends," Oct. 10, 1862, NHHS; Peter Faulk to "Dear Sister," Dec. 26, 1862, BGSU; Stephen Pingree to "Cousin Augustus," July 18, 1863, Lyndon State College Collection, VHS; Augustus Phetteplace to "Dear Father," June 16, 1863, CCHS; William Hogan to "Dear Son," Nov. 16, 1863, VHS.

54. *CG*, 37th Cong., 2nd sess., pt. 1, 763, 803–4, 881–86, 899–900, 929, 938–39; J. A. Fischer to William Lehmann, Aug. 7, 1862, WHS. On the currency bill, see Mitchell, *History of the Greenbacks*, 44–78; and Sharkey, *Money, Class, and Party*, 29–46.

55. *CG*, 37th Cong., 3rd sess., pt. 1, 705, 739; pt. 2, 976, 981, 984, 999–1000, 1002, 1293. On the passage of the Enrollment Act, see Geary, *We Need Men*, 49–64.

56. *OR*, ser. 3, 3:88–89, 551; *CG*, 37th Cong., 3rd sess., pt. 2, 981–84; *Eastern Argus* (Portland, Maine), Mar. 3, 1863; *Detroit Free Press*, July 18, 1863; *Crisis* (Columbus, Ohio), Mar. 4, 1863; *New Hampshire Patriot and State Gazette* (Concord), July 29, 1863; James Law to "Dear Sister Agnes," Mar. 4, 1863, CHS; Robert Findlay to Robert Crouse, July 27, 1863, BL; Blight, *When This Cruel War Is Over*, 247 (quotation).

57. *OR*, ser. 3, 3:90–91.

58. *Urbana (Ohio) Union*, June 3, 1863; *Grand Haven (Mich.) News*, July 1, 1863; *Raftsman's Journal* (Clearfield, Pa.), July 8, 1863; *Peterborough (N.H.) Transcript*, Sept. 12, Nov. 7, 1863; *OR*, ser. 3, 3:484. One loophole in the draft law seems to have gone unexploited. The introductory section declared men "between the ages of twenty and forty-five years" eligible for conscription, but Section 8 divided them into two classes, defining the second class as those "above the age of thirty-five and under the age of forty-five." Strictly speaking, the use of "between" in the first section could have been interpreted to mean that only those aged twenty-one to forty-four were eligible, whereas the word "under" in Section 8 explicitly (if unintentionally) exempted those who had turned forty-five. Ibid., 88–89. The law was nonetheless applied against those aged twenty and forty-five, apparently without challenge.

59. *OR*, ser. 3, 3:89; Palmer and Ochoa, *Selected Papers of Thaddeus Stevens*, 1:420–21; Richard W. Thompson Sr. to Richard W. Thompson Jr., Dec. 7, 1863, IU.

60. *OR*, ser. 3, 3:104–5, 113–14, 170–71, 5:544–46, 549, 552.

61. Thomas Barnett Diary, June 10–19, 1863, Earlham College; *OR*, ser. 3, 3:462–64.

62. *Providence (R.I.) Daily Post*, July 8, 1863; *OR*, ser. 3, 3:482, 5:730 (quotation).

63. William W. Chapin Diary, July 15–17, 1863, RIHS.

64. *New York Times*, July 13–17, 1863; *New York Herald*, July 14–17, 1863; Nevins and Thomas, *Diary of George Templeton Strong*, 3:335–39; Helen McCalla Diary, July 17, 1863, LC; John A. Parker to Richard Lathers, July 18, 1863, LC; *Boston Journal*, July 15, 16, 1863; Adelaide Fowler to "Dear Brother," July 19, 1863, PEM; *Daily Morning Chronicle* (Portsmouth, N.H.), July 14–18, 1863; Joseph Ricketson to Deborah Weston, July 19, 1863, Chapman Family Papers, BPL; Edwin S. Barrett to Joseph Gilmore, July 13, 14, 16, 1863, NHHS; Frank Howe to Joseph Gilmore, July 14, 1863, Executive

Correspondence, NHDRMA; *OR,* ser. 3, 3:534–35. For divergent interpretations of the cause of the New York riot, see McCague, *Second Rebellion,* and Bernstein, *New York City Draft Riots.*

65. *Portland (Maine) Daily Press,* July 3, 1863; *Carroll County Register* (Ossipee, N.H.), July 30, 1863; J. L. Barton Affidavit, Feb. 3, 1864, Cary Library; Richard Kent Diary, Aug. 6, 1863, NHHS; *Keene (N.H.) Sentinel,* Aug. 20, 27, 1863; *Daily Morning Chronicle* (Portsmouth, N.H.), Aug. 18, 21, 1863; Emily Harris to Leander Harris, Sept. 11, 1863, UNH.

66. *OR,* ser. 3, 5:730.

67. Ameur, *Voyage en Amérique,* 241–42. The comte de Paris recorded reading heavy-artillery recruiting posters in Auburn, New York, in January of 1862 that were emblazoned with these assurances of comfort and ease.

68. *OR,* 27(3):206 (quotation); Ayling, *Revised Register,* 907, 913.

69. Holden, Ross, and Slomba, *Stand Firm and Fire Low,* 141.

70. Ayling, *Revised Register,* 914; Jones, "Letters of Lauren Elmer Bent," 143; Benjamin Marshall to "Dear Sister," n.d. [summer 1863], AHEC; Original declaration, Mary Marshall Widow's [i.e., Mother's] Certificate 97775, RG15, NA.

71. Numerous heavy artillery regiments were assigned to the Army of the Potomac as infantry in 1864, and Maj. Gen. Ambrose Burnside reported that those in his corps all appeared to be shirking battle, remarking, "they didn't enlist to fight and it is unreasonable to expect it of them." Lowe, *Meade's Army,* 211.

72. *Alexandria (Va.) Gazette,* July 28, 1863 (p. 2, marked July 27); *New York Tribune,* Aug. 4, 1863; *Cleveland Morning Leader,* Aug. 12, 1863; Francis Miller to Alanson Miller, Oct. 26, 1862, ND; James Law to "Dear Sister Agnes," Mar. 18, 1863, CHS; Henry Robinson to "My dear and affectionate wife and children," Apr. 26, 1863, IHS.

73. Emily Harris to Leander Harris, Sept. 11, 1863, UNH; Solomon Grannis Diary, Oct. 8, 1863, NHHS; C. D. Longfellow to Charles Sherman, Oct. 6, 1863, CHS; *OR,* ser. 3, 5:735; Lester Fales to Richard Taft, Jan. 21, 1865, RIHS.

74. *Cleveland Morning Leader,* Apr. 4, 1863; *Alleghanian* (Ebensburg, Pa.), Apr. 16, 1863; *Hancock Jeffersonian* (Findlay, Ohio), Apr. 19, 1863; *Jeffersonian Democrat* (Chardon, Ohio), May 8, 1863; *OR,* ser. 3, 3:88–89.

75. Kamphoefner and Helbich, *Germans in the Civil War,* 69, 284, 289; Emily Harris to Leander Harris, Sept. 11, 1863, UNH; Henry Converse to Mary Haralson, Dec. 12, 1863, VPI.

76. *Oxford Democrat* (Paris, Maine), Aug. 7, 1863; James Easton to "Dear Brother," Feb. 7, 1864, OHS; *Lansing (Mich.) State Republican,* Aug. 19, 1863 (quotation).

77. *Oxford Democrat* (Paris, Maine), Sept. 11, 1863; *Dakotian* (Yankton, Dak. Terr.), July 28, Aug. 18, Nov. 23, Dec. 8, 1863; Jacob Giffen to "Dear Father," June 20, 1864, OHS; N. B. Cobb to "Brother Walter," Sept. 18, 1864, UVM; B. F. and Josie Knowles to Moses Southard, Nov. 20, 1864, Moses Letters, MEHS; E. P. Feaster to W. W. Wadsworth, Mar. 9, 1864, WHMC.

78. George Miles to Frank Miles, Aug. 6, 1863, Boardman and Miles Family Papers, VHS; *Crisis* (Columbus, Ohio), Apr. 15, 1863; *Stanstead (C.E.) Journal,* Aug. 27, Nov. 26, 1863.

79. Elizabeth Matson to William L. Matson, Jan. 23, July 17, 1863, CHS.

80. Laas, *Wartime Washington,* 307; Racine, *Unspoiled Heart,* 63; Charles Coit to "Dear all," Aug. 4, 1863, Yale University; Marcellus Darling to "Dear Mother," Sept. 2, 1863, UIA; Bradford Sparrow to "Father," Sept. 1, 1863, UVM; Andrew Stone to "brother Wes," Sept. 27, 1863, NHHS; Greenlief Foster to "Dear Brother," Sept. 12, 1863, MEHS; Charles Chase, letter fragment, n.d.

[1863], UVM; Samuel Howe to William Kinerson, Oct. 12, 1863, UVM; Edwin Horton to "Dear Wife," Sept. 28, 1863, VHS; John Henry Jenks to "Dear Wife," Nov. 8, 1863, UNH; Nevins, *Diary of Battle,* 279 (final quotation).

81. Roth, *Well Mary,* 39 (quotation); Stephen Green to "Dear Wife," Aug. 8, 1863, CCHS; Racine, *Unspoiled Heart,* 63; Stephen Pingree to "Cousin Augustus," Oct. 2, 1863, Lyndon State College Collection, VHS; Aldridge, *No Freedom Shrieker,* 191–92.

82. Peck, *Revised Roster of Vermont Volunteers,* 111–41.

83. Substitute affidavits, Alexandria Recruiting Records, NHHS; Nevins, *Diary of Battle,* 319; Curtis T. Woodruff to Charles E. Sherman, Dec. 11, 1863, CHS; Felix Voltz to "Dear Brothers," May 20, 1865, VPI.

84. Curtis T. Woodruff to Charles E. Sherman, Dec. 11, 1863; Charles G. Wilson's receipt, Sept. 9, 1863; and Sherman's certificate of exemption, Sherman Collection, CHS. When Davis's widow applied for a pension in 1889, she identified his real name as Samuel F. Rundlett. Original declaration, Widow's Certificate 375379, RG15, NA.

85. Horrocks, *My Dear Parents,* 21, 23–25.

86. Original declaration, Douce Johnson Widow's Certificate 46872, RG15, NA; Jordan, *Civil War Journals of John Mead Gould,* 287.

87. *OR,* ser. 3, 3:414–16; Frank Daniels to Frederick Pratt, May 29, 1863, AAS; Jordan, *Civil War Journals of John Mead Gould,* 287 (quotation); *Report of the Adjutant General of the State of Maine,* 37; Original declaration, Douce Johnson Widow's Certificate 46872, RG15, NA.

88. Peter Wolford to "Dear Brother," Mar. 4, 1864, MNHS; T. W. Stebbins to "Dear father and mother," Oct. 18, 1863; and Stebbins to "Dear mother," Feb. 7, 1864, MNHS; James Nichol to "Dear Brother John," Nov. 10, 1863, David Nichol Papers, AHEC.

89. Emily Harris to Leander Harris, Aug. 24, 1862, Aug. 16, 1863, UNH.

CHAPTER EIGHT

1. Balace, *Recrutements en Belgique,* 2; *Cleveland Morning Leader,* Aug. 23, 1862; *Daily Intelligencer* (Wheeling, Va.), Aug. 30, 1862; *Ashtabula (Ohio) Weekly Telegraph,* Sept. 8, 1862.

2. Bigelow, *Retrospections of an Active Life,* 1:538–39, 547.

3. Balace, *Recrutements en Belgique,* 2; Cullop, "Unequal Duel," 106.

4. Balace, *Recrutements en Belgique,* 2, 5; Cullop, "Unequal Duel," 101–2; *New York Herald,* Jan. 6, 1864.

5. *Eastern Townships Gazette and Shefford County Advertiser* (Granby, C.E.), May 1, 1863; Elvira Aplin to George Aplin, Mar. 16, 1863, CL; Frederick Bill to H. C. Holmes, Aug. 2, 1864, CHS; *Stanstead (C.E.) Journal,* Feb. 4, Mar. 24, 31, 1864. On this recruiting tack, see Hamer, "Luring Canadian Soldiers into Union Lines."

6. *Foreign Emigrant Society,* 1–2; *Portland (Maine) Daily Press,* Mar. 28, 1864; *Portland (Maine) Advertiser,* Apr. 2, 14, 1864; *Boston Daily Advertiser,* Apr. 25, 1866; Pearson, *Life of John A. Andrew,* 2:138–40; *MSSM,* 2:504–22. The story of this not-so-secret operation was minutely reconstructed by Michael E. Hager in "Massachusetts's German Mercenaries," 20–24.

7. *OR,* ser. 3, 3:89, 621, 5:731. In the July draft of 1863, 5,723 drafted veterans were exempted for having been in the service on March 3, 1863. Ibid., 5:731. This little-known detail has been over-

looked by historians, but it was occasionally mentioned in soldiers' letters at the time the law was passed. The loophole was never closed, perhaps to avoid having to admit that it had been unintended, and the reenlistment program may have been meant, at least partly, to compensate for the consequences.

8. *OR,* ser. 3, 3:414–16; Marion Ward to "Home friends," Aug. 1, 1863, WRHS; Thomas Brown to his wife, Oct. 22, 1863, VHS; James Nesbitt to "Dear Sisters," Nov. 4, 1863, WRHS; William R. Barnes to "Dear wife and children," Dec. 9, 1863, SHSI-DM.

9. *OR,* ser. 3, 3:785; Downing, *Civil War Diary,* 156–57; John F. Lester Diary, Jan. 5, 1864, IHS; Nelson Chapin to "My Dear Wife," Jan. 6, "1863" [1864], AHEC; Flavius Bellamy to "Dear Father," Oct. 17, 1863, ISL; William Combs to Eliza Combs, Jan. 8, 1864, ND; Gavin, *Infantryman Pettit,* 124; Jabez Burrows Diary, Oct. 10, 1863, CCHS; Osborne, *Private Osborne,* 181; John Boyer to "Dear father & mother," Dec. 21, 1863, AHEC; Charles E. Bates to "Dear Parents," Jan. 24, 1864, VAHS; John Yowell to Caleb Core, Dec. 3, 1863, OHS; Christopher Keller to "Dear Parents & Friends at Home," Aug. 14, 1863, Jan. 12, 1864, BL; Joseph Barton to "Dearest Wife," Jan. 17, 1864; Messent and Courtney, *Civil War Letters of Joseph Hopkins Twitchell,* 291; Lucy Webb Hayes to "My dear Mother," Oct. 1, [1863], RBHPL.

10. Luther Lawrence to "Dear Brother," June 2, 1863, North Yarmouth Historical Society; Spalding, *Tuf as a Boiled Owl,* 108; George Stearns to "Dear Mother," July 25, 1864, NHHS (quotation).

11. Downing, *Civil War Diary,* 157, 161; William Jackman to "Dear Nancy," Dec. 24, 1863, RBHPL; W. C. Patton Diary, Nov. 15, 1863, IHS; Albert Luther to James Luther, Oct. 25, 1863, Mar. 7, Apr. 27, 1864, ISL; Henry Keiser Diary, Feb. 4–10, 1864, AHEC; Blight, *When This Cruel War Is Over,* 273; Cummings, *No Regrets,* 159–61; Day, *My Diary,* 110–11; Basile, *Civil War Diary of Amos E. Stearns,* 28, 29, 31–32; Wilbur Fisk Diary, Nov. 25, 1863, LC; Elijah Cavins to "Dear Ann," Dec. 19, 28, 1863, IHS; Stephen Pingree to "Cousin Augustus," Oct. 8, 1863, Lyndon State College Collection, VHS; Edwin Wentworth to "My dear Wife," Dec. 16, 1864, LC; Henry Robinson to "My very dear and affectionate wife and children," Aug. 17, 1863, IHS; Clement Hoffman to "Dear Mother," Jan. 6, 1864, AHEC; James Giauque to "Brother Alf," Dec. 31, 1863, UIA.

12. James Brown to "Dear Friends," Oct. 13, 1863, Jan. 9, 1864, MEHS.

13. Woodworth, *Musick of the Mocking Birds,* 117; David Leigh to Herman Drumgold, Feb. 1, 1864, DC; Levi Perry to "Dear Mother," Nov. 3, 1863, Mar. 1, 1864, MEHS; Peter Abbott to "Dear Mother," Feb. 21, 1864, VHS; James Holmes to Abbie Homer, Nov. 6, 1863, MHS; George Brigham to "Dear Sister," [Jan.?] 22, 1864, AAS; Hodge, *Civil War Letters of Perry Mayo,* 242; Augustus Paddock to "Dear Brother Eph," Jan. 17, 1864, UVM; Leonard Valentine to "Dear Father and Mother," June 3, 1863, MEHS; George Sargent to "Dear Mother," Jan. 1, 1864, NHHS; David Werking to "Dear Becca," Apr. 3, 1864, IHS; Loving, *Civil War Letters of George Washington Whitman,* 129; William Thompson to "Dear Father," Jan. 2, 1864, AAS; Robert Shortelle to unknown, June 4, 1863, LC.

14. George Jewett to "Dear Dick," Mar. 6, 1865, LC.

15. John Cuddy to "Dear Parents," Mar. 29, Apr. 11, 1864, Dickinson College; William Stow to "Dear Mother," Apr. 14, 1864, UVM.

16. John V. Yowell to Caleb Core, Jan. 18, 1864, OHS; Ninth Census (1870), Summit, Marion County, Iowa, Dwelling 8, RG29, NA; Silas Sadler to "Dear Father and Mother," n.d. [ca. Mar. 1864], BL.

17. Addison S. Boyce to "Dear Mary," Feb. 26, 1864, BL.

18. Susan E. Miller to "Dear Parents," Apr. 10, 1864, James T. Miller Letters, CL.

19. Emily Harris to Leander Harris, Dec. 6, 1863, Feb. 23, 1864; and Leander Harris to Emily Harris, Jan. 6, Feb. 7, 1864, UNH.

20. Edward H. C. Taylor to "My dear Lottie," Sept. 29, 1863; and Taylor to "Dear Will," Jan. 11, 1864, BL; Nathaniel Parmeter Diary, Jan. 5–26, 1864, OHS; *Roster of Ohio Soldiers,* 3:371; Charles Howe to "Dear Sister," Mar. 30, 1864; Register of Enlistments, Reel 78, 29, RG94, NA.

21. John Wilmot to Sophronia Ann Prescott, Mar. 5, 1862, Dec. 19, 1863, VHS; Robert Cowden Diary, Mar. 20–25, 1864, CCHS.

22. Spalding, *Tuf as a Boiled Owl,* 3, 108–9.

23. Martin L. Clark to Wealthy Field, Mar. 6, 1864, VHS; Osborne, *Private Osborne,* 181.

24. Charles Maxim to "Dear Father," Dec. 2, 1863, Sturtevant Papers, DC; Maxim to "Dear Brother," July 31, 1864; and Maxim to "Dear Mother," Nov. 11, 1864, CL. The letter of December 2, 1863, is the only one from Maxim in the Sturtevant Papers, and how it came to be there is a mystery as there was no apparent connection between the two men.

25. Thomas Covert to "My Dear Wife," July 8–11, 17, 1864, WRHS.

26. Edwin Wentworth to "My dear Wife," Dec. 20, 1863, Jan. 3, 17, 31, 1864, LC.

27. Rufus Mead to "Dear Folks at Home," Jan. 4, 7, 1864, LC; *Hartford (Conn.) Weekly Times,* Jan. 16, 1864.

28. Rosenblatt and Rosenblatt, *Hard Marching Every Day,* vii, 186; Fisk Diary, Dec. 25, 29, 1863, LC.

29. Augustus Paddock to "Dear Friends at Home," Apr. 21, 1864, UVM; Elmer Wallace to "Dear Parents," Feb. 15, 1864, BL; Chester Leach to unknown, Feb. 21, 1864, UVM; Peck, *Revised Roster of Vermont Volunteers,* 33–66; Bates, *History of Pennsylvania Volunteers,* 3:409; *OR,* ser. 3, 3:414–15, 4:189–90, 5:678.

30. E. N. Gilpin Diary, July 21, 1864, LC; Hazard Stevens to "Dear Mother," June 28, 1864, LC (quotation).

31. *OR,* ser. 3, 4:190, 5:600, 651. Bruce Catton wrote that "probably slightly more than half the total number whose terms were expiring" reenlisted. *Stillness at Appomattox,* 35. Reid Mitchell remarked that "when the three-year men's enlistments ran out, most veterans of the Union cause chose to remain in the army." *Civil War Soldiers,* 182. James McPherson also deemed the 136,000 who reenlisted to be "more than half of those whose terms expired in 1864." *For Cause and Comrades,* 173. Those observations not only imply a significant underestimate of the number of men eligible to reenlist but also inaccurately suggest that the 136,000 who did reenlist would all have been due to go home in 1864. The reenlistments actually included tens of thousands of the nine-month and two-year veterans who were mustered out in 1863 as well as many thousands of others who would not have been discharged until well into 1865.

32. The reenlistment offer remained open after March 31, 1864, for three-year men who had completed two years of their commitment, although with the federal bounty reduced to $100. *OR,* ser. 3, 4:190.

33. The samples were drawn from the companies in the column for 1861 three-year enlistments in Table 1. The only contemporary source Catton used to assess reenlistment motive was Edwin O. Wentworth's letters, which are now held by the Library of Congress. Although Wentworth made clear that money was the main attraction for him, Catton discounted that incentive. *Stillness at Appomattox,* 35, 395–96n26. Also relying almost exclusively on memoirs and regimental histories, Gerald Linderman followed Catton's lead, citing and evidently adopting his interpretation that the reenlistment furlough posed the greatest incentive. *Embattled Courage,* 261–64. As is usually the

case, contemporary sources tell a different story. In two detailed statistical studies of reenlistments by men from Massachusetts, Wisconsin, and Pennsylvania, John Gordon Robertson deemed patriotism a less significant factor and economic status more significant. See "Re-Enlistment Patterns of Civil War Soldiers," esp. 25; and "Rich Man's War, Poor Man's Opportunity?"

34. *OR,* ser. 3, 3:892.

35. John Worthington Ames to "My dear Mother," July 21, 1862, AHEC; Sallie Miller to "My dear Brother," July 21, 1864, CinHS; Catherine Fisk to "Dear Cousin," May 16, 1864, Schwab Letters, CinHS.

36. William Jackman to "Dear Nancy," Jan. 1, 1864, RBHPL (quotation); Robert Findlay to Robert Crouse, July 27, 1863, BL; Guilford Mace to "Dear Uncle," Jan. 28, 1863, AHEC.

37. Elizabeth Matson to William L. Matson, Feb. 20, Mar. 10, Apr. 2, May 12, Aug. 4, 1863, CHS.

38. Lizzie Corning Diary, Oct. 15, Nov. 12, 1862, Mar. 4, May 10, 24, 1863, Apr. 30, May 2, 1864, NHHS; Moskow, *Emma's World,* xix, 173, 179. Among the innumerable men whose eligible sons never served were Edward Everett, who delivered the longer of the two Gettysburg addresses (he had three sons), wartime New Hampshire governor Joseph Gilmore (who had four), and John Barbour, the deputy collector of internal revenue at Cambridge, Massachusetts (with three sons—and two daughters, including the Emma of the last-named source).

39. *OR,* ser. 3, 3:892.

40. Mary Grant to Claudius Grant, Nov. 21, 1863, BL; *OR,* ser. 3, 3:828; 4:59, 181; Thomas Barnett Diary, Feb. 24, 1864, Earlham College; Robert E. Miller Sr. to James T. Miller, Jan. 2, 1864, CL; Elisha Cowan to "Dear Brother," May 24, 1864, MNHS; Hiram Jones to "Dear Wife & Children," Dec. 28, 1863, UVM.

41. *OR,* ser. 3, 3:828, 993–94, 995–97.

42. *Daily Morning Chronicle* (Portsmouth, N.H.), May 27, 1861; Town Clerk's Records, 6:63–64, Conway Town Hall; Bounties Paid to Volunteers, 1863 and 1864, Old Town Records Collection, CPL; Ayling, *Revised Register,* 463, 481, 495. In local records Heath's first name is invariably spelled "Marcus."

43. Oscar Robinson to "Dear Mother," Jan. 5, 1864, DC.

44. William I. Brown to George H. Chandler, Mar. 13, 1864, NHHS; Edwin Turner to "My Dear Addie," Feb. 1, 1864, VHS; Moses Parker to "Friend Eliza," Sept. 16 [1864], UVM; James Helme Rickard to "Dear Sister Lizzie," Sept. 11, 1864, AAS; Norman Carr to "Dear Parents," Feb. 16, 1865, UR; Fred Phillips to "Dear Sister," Mar. 3, 1865, CL.

45. Edward Waite to "Dear Father," Mar. 26, 1864, MEHS; Burgess, *Uncommon Soldier,* 21, 22; Frederick Kronenberger to "Dear Parents," Jan. 30, 1864, Gettysburg College.

46. Muster-roll entry of Co. D, 9th N.H. Vols., Jan.–Feb., 1864, Daniel Babb Military Service Record, RG94, NA; Albert Stearns to "Dear Sister," Jan. 11, 1864, NHHS; Henry J. Vaughn to Volney Vaughn, July 24, 1863, VHS; Edward Waite to "Dear Father," Mar. 26, 1864, MEHS; Elvira Aplin to "My Dear Son George," May 21, 1863, CL.

47. Rachel Aldrich to Asa Aldrich, Apr. 29, 1864, Orrin Brownson Papers, NHHS; Cora Benton to Charles Benton, June 5, Dec. 6, 1863, Jan. 31, Feb. 12, 1864, ND; Nevins, *Diary of Battle,* 320.

48. Flavius Bellamy to "Dear Parents," Oct. 24, 1863, ISL; George Jones to "Dear Friends at Home," Feb. 7, 1864, UVM; Barnes, *Medical and Surgical History,* 1:452–55; *Stanstead (C.E.) Journal,* Feb. 11, 1864; *Orleans Independent Standard* (Irasburgh, Vt.), Feb. 12, 1864; *OR,* ser. 3, 4:1149–51, 5:892, 894, 901.

49. Andrew Knox to "My Dear Wife," Aug. 21, 1862, AHEC; Charles Chace to "Dear Mother," Oct. 19, 1863, UVM; William Thompson to "Dear Father," Jan. 2, 1864, AAS; Philip Arsino to "Dear Mother," Feb. 16, 1864, VHS; George E. Parker to "My Dear sister Eliza," Feb. 18, 1864, Calvert-Parker Letters, VHS; John Sheahan to "My Dear Father," undated [ca. Feb., 1864], MEHS; Alonzo Cushman to "Dear Sister," Apr. 28, 1864, AAS; William C. Weeks to "Dear Father," Sept. 10, 1864, IU; Bender, *Like Grass before the Scythe,* 122.

50. *Prairie du Chien (Wis.) Courier,* Dec. 31, 1863, Jan. 7, 1864.

51. Karl Wesslau to his brother, Sept. 28, 1864, quoted in Kamphoefner and Helbich, *Germans in the Civil War,* 284; "Lizzie" to Mary E. Richards, Oct. 2, 1864, MNHS; Emma Mitchell to John H. Mitchell, Nov. 20, 1864, MNHS.

52. *Appleton (Wis.) Crescent,* Dec. 19, 26, 1863; David Coon to "Dear Wife and Children" and "Dear Wife," Feb. 28, Mar. 2, 11, Apr. 6, 16, 30, 1864, LC; *OR,* ser. 3, 5:748.

53. Menge and Shimrak, *Civil War Notebooks of Daniel Chisholm,* xi, 103, 117, 118–19, 130, 135, 161–62; Eighth Census (1860), Union, Fayette County, Pa., Dwelling 560; and Ninth Census (1870), Uniontown West Ward, Fayette County, Pa., Dwelling 8, RG29, NA.

54. Meshack Larry to "Dear Sister Phebe," Jan. 26, 1864, MEHS.

55. Frederick Hooker to "Dear mother and wife," Feb. 4, 1864; and Hooker to "der mother," Apr. 14, 1864, CHS (quotations); Original declaration, Nancy M. Hooker Widow's Certificate 65152, RG15, NA; Ninth Census (1870), New Haven Ward 7, New Haven County, Conn., Dwelling 495, RG29, NA.

56. John Carvel Arnold to Mary Ann Arnold, Mar. 8, 10, May 19 and "—th," June 5, July 7, 13, 26, Aug. 2, 12, 1864, LC.

57. John M. Jackson to "Dear Mother," Nov. 15, 1863, ND; Houston, *Thirty-second Maine,* 486; Ninth Census (1870), Lewiston Ward 1, Androscoggin County, Maine, Dwelling 982, RG29, NA.

58. Wilbur Huntington Proctor Diary, Mar. 6–27, 1864, LC.

59. Edward Van Deusen to "Dear Friends," July 10, 1864, Papers of the Sterns Family, UIA; Affidavits of B. F. and J. B. Mathews, Aug. 20, 1891, Eliza Van Deusen Widow's [i.e., Mother's] Certificate 362,390, RG15, NA.

60. John Rowe to "Dear Sister," Apr. 18, Nov. 1, 1864; and A. D. J. Heastings to "Mrs Rowe," n.d., AHEC.

61. Gilbert Gulbrandson to "Brother Hans," Nov. 15, 1864, AHEC; D. C. Hulburd to Benjamin Hulburd, Oct. 16, 1864, VHS; Hodge, *Civil War Letters of Perry Mayo,* 245; Menge and Shimrak, *Civil War Notebooks of Daniel Chisholm,* 132; Dennis Townsend to "Dear Parents, Brothers & Sisters," Jan. 10, 1865, VHS; Birt Scott to "Dear Brother," Sept. 9, 1863, IHS; James Burrows to "Dear Brother," June 17, 1864, CCHS; Timothy Stevens to "Dear Sister," Nov. 22, 1862; and William Stevens to "My Dear Sister," Mar. 26, 1864, Sheldon Museum; John W. Miner to "Dear Wife," July 4, 1864, Gettysburg College; Artemus Cook to Curtis Babbitt, Jan. 21, 1864, Charles Babbitt Letters, RBHPL.

62. Thaddeus Stevens Jr. to Thaddeus Stevens, Mar. 6, 1864, LC; *OR,* ser. 3, 4:154.

63. *OR,* 36(1):4, ser. 3, 4:237–39.

64. *OR,* ser. 3, 4:238.

65. Ibid., 406, 410–11; Larimer, *Love and Valor,* 271.

66. Bohrnstedt, *Soldiering with Sherman,* 124.

67. *OR,* ser. 3, 4:237. The hundred-day regiments are enumerated in Dyer, *Compendium.*

68. Maggie Wade to "My Dear Aunt," May 13, 1864, LC.

69. Sallie Miller to "My dear Brother," July 21, 1864, CinHS.

70. Catherine Fisk to "Dear Cousin," May 16, 1864, Schwab Letters, CinHS; E. A. Miller to "My dear Clason," May 15, 1864, CinHS; William Fast to Amanda Fast, May 7, 1864, BGSU; Christopher Keller to "Dear Parents," May 22, 1864, CL; Britton and Reed, *To My Beloved Wife,* 240; George Codman to "Dear Sister," June 28, 1864, DC; Henry Marshall to "Dear Folks at Home," Sept. 11, 1864, CL.

71. The statistics are taken from Table 1.

72. Edwin Van Cise Diary, May 15–Sept. 24, 1864 (esp. July 2, Sept. 4), LC.

73. Edgar Chandler to "Dear Sister Helen," Sept. 13, Oct. 16, 1864, UR; William Barrus to "Dear Brother," July 15, 1864, UNH; Henry Winterstein to "Dear Clinton," Aug. 15, 1864, OHS. Casualties are tallied from regimental summaries in Dyer, *Compendium,* 1101–1688. Van Cise's Company A, 45th Iowa, never fired a shot but accounted for 92 pension applications (including his) out of 103 officers and men; in few companies from three-year regiments did that many even live long enough to collect service pensions.

74. *OR,* ser. 3, 4:421, 515–16; *CG,* 38th Cong., 1st sess., pt. 4, 3547.

75. Francis Brooks Diary, June 29, 1864, MHS; Nevins and Thomas, *Diary of George Templeton Strong,* 3:450, 479; William Owner Diary, Aug. 24, 1864, LC.

76. *OR,* ser. 3, 5:675; Shannon, "Mercenary Factor," 536.

77. *Daily Morning Chronicle* (Portsmouth, N.H.), Sept. 20, Oct. 4, 1864; Town Clerk's Records, 6:89–90, Conway Town Hall; "Copy of Returns to Provost Marshall [sic], 1863 & 1864," Old Town Records Collection, CPL; *New Hampshire Statesman* (Concord), Oct. 7, 1864; *Carroll County Register* (Ossipee, N.H.), Oct. 6, 13, 1864.

78. Ayling, *Revised Register,* 804–26, 932, 943; Eighth Census (1860), Conway, Carroll County, N.H., Dwelling 82, RG29, NA.

79. *OR,* ser. 3, 4:232; John L. Thompson to "Dear Father," Aug. 4, 1864, Thompson Family Papers, NHHS; Ayling, *Revised Register,* 890.

80. Henry Comey to "Dear Father," Aug. 13, 1864, AAS (quotation); Charles Coit to "Dear All," Aug. 10, 1864, Yale University.

81. James A. Milliken to "Dear Charles," Aug. 17, 1864, MEHS.

82. B. F. Knowles to Moses Southard, Nov. 20, 1864, Moses Letters, MEHS; Valentine Barney to Maria Barney, July 31, 1864, VHS; Mary Jane Henry to William Henry, Aug. 18, 1864, VHS; Ann Hibbard to "My dear Uncle and Aunt," Sept. 4, 1864, Beard Family Papers, VHS.

83. Silas Hall to Edwin C. Hall, Aug. 17, 1864, VHS.

84. Maria Sargent to Ransom Sargent, Sept. 8, 1864, DC; George Anthony to "Kind Brother," Oct. 24, 1864, CL.

85. "Jane" to "Dear Cousin," Dec. 11, 1864, Fellows Family Papers, UR; John Campbell to "Dear Father," Oct. 4, 1864, AHEC; James Moore to "My Kind Friend," Apr. 16, 1865, Fellows Family Papers, UR (quotation); "Lizzie" to Mary Richards, Oct. 2, 1864, MNHS; Charles Hadsall Diary, May 5, 1864, Nebraska State Historical Society; Bentley Kutz to "Dear Parents," Aug. 29, Sept. 8, 1864, AHEC; Edward Penney to "Dear Friends," Dec. 5, 1864, Jewett Papers, LC.

86. "Andrew" to Warren S. Barrows, July 15, 17, 1864, AHEC; William Owner Diary, Sept. 7, 1864, LC.

87. Frederick Bill to H. C. Holmes, Aug. 2, 1864, CHS.

88. Virgil C. Taylor to Andrew Foster, July 25 (two letters of that date), Aug. 2, 1864, Alexander Bunt Family Papers, WRHS.

89. John B. White to Lucien Eaton, Aug. 8, 1864, MOHS.

90. Sarah Aplin to "Brother George," Oct. 9, 1864, CL; Albert Putnam to Eleazer Putnam, Sept. 2, 1864, DC; *Minnesota in the Civil and Indian Wars,* 623; Eighth Census (1860), Antwerp, Jefferson County, N.Y., Dwellings 389, 409, RG29, NA; *Goodhue (Minn.) Volunteer,* Aug. 31, 1864; *St. Cloud (Minn.) Democrat,* Oct. 20, 1864; Gideon Allen to "My darling little girl," Dec. 5, 1864, WHS.

91. Henry Young to "Dear Father," Sept. 19, 1864, WHS (quotation); Menge and Shimrak, *Civil War Notebooks of Daniel Chisholm,* 118; Parker Pillsbury to "My Dear Friend," July 17, 1864, BPL; Helen Wordsworth to "Dear Juliette," July 31, 1864, Fellows Family Papers, UR; Sarah Upton to "My Dear George," July 29, 1864, NHHS; Elvira Aplin to "Dear Son George," Jan. 14, 1865, CL; Mary B. Dodge to "Ever dear friend," Jan. 23, 1865, Ball Family Papers, Aldrich Public Library; "Mary" to "My Dear Sister," Apr. 25, 1864, Savage Papers, UVM; Richard Kent Diary, June 15, 1864, NHHS; Rachel Woods to "Beloved Father and Mother," Jan. 17, 1865, Beard Family Papers, VHS; Charles Cummings to "My Dear Wife," July 14, 1864, VHS; George Southard to "Brother Moses," Jan. 20, 1865, Moses Letters, MEHS; A. Washburne to Edward Washburne, Sept. 19, 1864, CL.

92. John Elewell to Thaddeus Stevens, Apr. 30, 1864, LC; James Gallatin to James Doolittle, May 10, 1864, WHS; Joseph Leighty to "Dear Brother," Apr. 9, 1865, University of Kansas; B. F. Knowles to Moses Southard, Nov. 20, 1864, Moses Letters, MEHS (quotation); W. P. Gould to William Pitt Fessenden, Sept. 16, 1864, CL; Eleutheros Cooke to Jay Cooke, July 12, Aug. 5, 1864, RBHPL; N. B. Cobb to Walter Cobb, Dec. 29, 1864, UVM; Richard Kent Diary, Sept. 3–5, Oct. 22, Dec. 5, 24, 1864, NHHS.

93. *OR,* ser. 3, 4:1002–3; *New York Herald,* Jan. 8, 1865; *Weekly Register* (Point Pleasant, Ohio), Jan. 26, 1865; *Grand Haven (Mich.) News,* Feb. 8, 1865; *Cecil Whig* (Elkton, Md.), Feb. 18, 1865; *Highland Weekly News* (Hillsborough, Ohio), Mar. 9, 1865; *Keene (N.H.) Sentinel,* Jan. 26, Feb. 9, 16, 1865 (quotations).

94. John Giffen to "Dear Father," Feb. 20, 1865, OHS; Albert Harris to "Mother and All," Jan. 25, 1865; and Albert Harris to "Dear Brother," Feb. 19, 1865, VHS.

95. D. L. Caldwell to Henry Carroll, Mar. 13, 1865, AHEC.

96. Lyman F. Holyoke to Samuel James Henderson, Jan. 15, 1865, MHS.

97. Fred Phillips to "Dear Sister," Mar. 3, 1865, CL; Nettie Brown to "Dear Aunt & Uncle," Mar. 24, 1865, Hubert and Laura Tupper Brown Letters, VHS; Alderson and Alderson, *Letters Home to Sarah,* 193, 214; William Phillips to "Dear Father and Mother," Jan. 31, 1865, WHS; William Proctor to "Father," Mar. 14, 1865, Fairbanks Museum.

98. John N. Dickie Diary, Aug. 10–16, Sept. 7, 30, Dec. 23, 1864–Feb. 2, 1865, CL; *Roster of Ohio Soldiers,* 3:204.

99. Abram Parmenter Diary, Mar. 20–22, May 11, 1865, LC; Eighth Census (1860), Milton, Cass County, Mich., Dwelling 1564, RG29, NA.

100. Henry Rinker to "My Dear Mary," Mar. 26, Apr. 9, June 17, 1865, AHEC.

101. Ayling, *Revised Register,* 804, 826; Eighth Census (1860), Jackson, Carroll County, N.H., Dwelling 600; and Ninth Census (1870), Fryeburg, Oxford County, Maine, Dwelling 219; and Conway, Carroll County, N.H., Dwelling 203 (in which Watson is described as a "Loafer"), RG29, NA.

102. Ayling, *Revised Register,* 804, 826.

CHAPTER NINE

1. Joseph Lester to "My Dear Father and Sister," June 5, 1864, LC; Irvin W. Spooner to "Aunt Saley," Mar. 12, 1865, VHS; William Willoughby to "My Dear Wife," May 22, Sept. 23, 1864, AAS; Harvey Warner to "Dear Father and Mother," Aug. 14, 1863, BL; Shannon, *Civil War Letters of Sergeant Onley Andrus,* 48, 136.

2. George W. Young (2nd Pennsylvania Cavalry) to "Dear friend," Feb. 10, 1862, AHEC; Cassedy, *Dear Friends at Home,* 548, 555; Albion Tourgée to "Darling Wife," Nov. 29, 1863, CCHS; David F. Cheney to Lyman Cheney, Dec. 10, 1863, AHEC; Benjamin T. Wright to "My Dear Abbie," July 31, 1864, WHS; S. Y. Webster to "Brother Chas.," Jan. 8, 1865, AHEC; Abram Bogart to Mary Bogart, Mar. 28, 1865, NYSL; Marten, *Sing Not War,* 55–56, 233; Wecter, "The Veteran Wins Through," 85.

3. Henry Brown to "dear Mother," Apr. 22, 1865, CHS; Foroughi, *Go If You Think It Your Duty,* 293.

4. Jane Underwood to "My dear Adin," June 25, 1865, MHS; Adin B. Underwood to Lorenzo Thomas, Nov. 17, 1866, Letters and Their Enclosures Received by the Commission Branch of the Adjutant General's Office, Reel 304, RG94, NA.

5. Samuel Ryan Curtis to "My dear wife," May 3, 1865, Yale University.

6. Lawrence Kreiser identified a trend toward economic improvement among foreign-born veterans in "Socioeconomic Study of Veterans of the 103rd Ohio," 179.

7. See Lee, "Military Service and Economic Mobility."

8. Emerson Fite cited laws giving disabled veterans hiring preference for government jobs in a chapter entitled "Charity." See *Social and Industrial Conditions in the North,* 287.

9. On the reintegration of veterans, their self-perception, and pensions, see Marten, *Sing Not War,* 55–56, 233–34, 180; and Casey, *New Men,* 19–34, 49–63, 106–10.

10. Hughes, *Civil War Papers of Lt. Colonel Newton T. Colby,* 212, 217–23; *OR,* 25(1):718 (quotation). Colby's great-great-grandson edited his papers, interpreting the unflattering implications of his military record with extraordinary sympathy.

11. Hughes, *Civil War Papers of Lt. Colonel Newton T. Colby,* 233, 240–41.

12. Ibid., 316–21.

13. Ibid., 322–24; Drop order, Newton T. Colby Invalid Pension Certificate 276420, RG15, NA.

14. Glasson, *Federal Military Pensions,* 174–75, 234–37, 248–49, 273; McConnell, *Glorious Contentment,* 143–53.

15. Tobie, *History of the First Maine Cavalry,* 572; Original declaration, Bailey T. Royal Invalid Certificate 94908, RG15, NA ("moonstruck" claim cited in both sources). Consider the contradictory claims of Col. and Bvt. Brig. Gen. Herbert B. Titus, who represented himself to his regimental historian as a successful lawyer and to the pension bureau as nearly an invalid, dependent on his pension. See History of claim and Titus's affidavits, Mar. 16, 1893, Dec. 4, 1894, Mar. 6, 1899, Invalid Certificate 882050, RG15, NA; and Lord, *History of the Ninth New Hampshire,* 743. Union soldiers' pensions were extensively discussed in McConnell, *Glorious Contentment* and Jordan, *Marching Home.* Jordan evinced much sympathy for the veterans' side of the pension debate, while McConnell approached the subject with judicious skepticism.

16. Bell, "Question of Pensions," 791 (quotation); Bates, *History of Pennsylvania Volunteers,* 1:931; Barnes, *Medical and Surgical History,* 12:494.

17. Chulhee Lee found that household wealth exerted "no clear effect" on the chances of dying from disease in a sample of Ohio recruits. "Socioeconomic Background, Disease, and Mortality among Union Recruits," 36. The sampling in Table 1, however, is based on companies rather than individuals, and the companies composed of more men from households that enjoyed above-median wealth tended to suffer lower overall mortality.

18. Index card for James A. Hard's Invalid Pension Certificate 273398, Organization Index to Pension Files of Veterans, Reel 319, RG15, NA; Muster-roll entries for Co. E, 32nd N.Y. Volunteers, Albert Hard Military Service Record, RG94, NA; Eighth Census (1860), Windsor, Broome County, N.Y., Dwelling 946; Twelfth Census (1900), Rochester Ward 19, Monroe County, N.Y., Dwelling 31; Thirteenth Census (1910), Rochester Ward 19, Dist. 195, Monroe County, N.Y., Dwelling 77; Fourteenth Census (1920), Rochester Ward 19, Dist. 236, Monroe County, N.Y., Dwelling 190; and Fifteenth Census (1930), Rochester Ward 19, Dist. 157, Dwelling 185, RG29, NA; *Binghampton (N.Y.) Press,* Mar. 13, 1953. According to an 1893 note from the Pension Office in his military file, Hard enlisted as Albert Hard, although his birth name was James Albert Hard. Like several of the last Civil War veterans, Hard misremembered his birthdate late in life, but in 1900 he gave it as July of 1843, and the censuses of 1850 and 1860 agree. He inflated his age two years when he enlisted to avoid being rejected, which probably accounts for his reported age of 111 when he died. In response to two Freedom of Information Act requests made since 2003, the Bureau of Veterans Affairs informed the author that it no longer has Hard's pension file; it should have been deposited with the National Archives after Hard's death, but requests there produced only the reference to presumed VA possession. Supervisory Archivist Eric V. Voelz to the author, Sept. 25, 2014.

19. Eighth Census (1860), Antwerp, Jefferson County, N.Y., Dwellings 389, 409; Gouverneur, Saint Lawrence County, N.Y., Dwelling 166; and Oshawa, Nicollet County, Minn., Dwelling 884, RG29, NA; Willard P. Woolson Invalid Pension Application 61679 (incomplete), RG15, NA; Muster-roll entries for Cos. C and D, 1st Minn. Heavy Artillery, Albert Woolson Service File, RG94, NA; Ohio Provost Marshal's Papers, 262, OHS (for the reduced age limits). Woolson also padded his age over the years, in later life claiming that he was seventeen when he enlisted. The Seventh Census ([1850], Champion, Jefferson County, N.Y., Dwelling 13) lists Henry Albert Woolson (he later reversed his first and middle names) as six months old in August of 1850, indicating that he was born in February of that year; in 1900 he said he was born in February of 1848, but in April of 1910 he reported himself as only sixty, consistent with a birth date in February of 1850; thereafter he gave his birthday as February 11, 1847, probably to comport with his 1909 application for a pension increase on the grounds of having turned sixty-two.

20. Tenth Census (1880), Saint Peter, Nicollet County, Minn., Dwelling 358; Twelfth Census (1900), Great Bend, Dist. 77, Cottonwood County, Minn., Dwelling 347; Thirteenth Census (1910), Duluth Ward 6, Saint Louis County, Minn., Dwelling 75; Fourteenth Census (1920), Duluth Dist. 121, Saint Louis County, Minn., Dwelling 34; Fifteenth Census (1930), Duluth Dist. 57, Saint Louis County, Minn., Dwelling 71; and Sixteenth Census (1940), Duluth Dist. 88–46A, Saint Louis County, Minn., Dwelling 269, RG29, NA.

21. *Duluth (Minn.) News-Tribune,* Aug. 3, 1956.

22. McPherson, *For Cause and Comrades,* 100–101. See also McPherson's persuasive reflections on family preservation of veterans' papers (ix–x) as well as his comment that he was "less interested in the motives of skulkers who did their best to avoid combat." Skulkers and shirks would certainly be of no use in illustrating the patriotism of Union soldiers, but they are very pertinent in assessing

the extent of mercenary motivation; many perfectly conscientious men were drawn into the army by economics as well.

23. Philip Arsino to "Dear Mother," Jan. 7, 1863, VHS.

24. *IPUMS-USA*.

25. See Lutz, "Who Joins the Military?," 184–85.

BIBLIOGRAPHY

MANUSCRIPTS

Aldrich Public Library, Barre, Vt.
- Ball Family Papers

American Antiquarian Society, Worcester, Mass.
- Henry W. Baker Letters
- George Taylor Brigham Letters
- Civil War Collection
  - Alonzo S. Cushman Letters
  - Correspondence of William Thompson
- Comey Family Papers
- Joseph Cross Letters
- Ellen Tucker Emerson Letters
- Joslyn-Burditt Family Papers
- Frederick Sumner Pratt Letters
- James Helme Rickard Letters
- Henry Rogers Smith Letters
- Carolyn Barrett White Diary
- William A. Willoughby Papers

Army Heritage and Education Center, Carlisle, Pa.
- William T. H. Brooks Papers
- Civil War Documents Collection
  - David H. Ackerman Letters
  - Samuel J. Alexander Correspondence
  - George E. Andrews Correspondence
  - Manny Austin Correspondence

Joseph D. Baker Letters
Augustus Barr Letters
Warren S. Barrows Correspondence
Elijah W. Barstow Letters
Lyman Beebe Letters
Fleetwood Benson Letters
Aaron K. Blake Letters
William H. Boyce Letters
Bragg Family Papers
Jerry Brakeman Letters
John Brandon Letters
George Bronson Letters
Harvey P. Brooks Letters
Samuel Brooks Letters
George F. Brown Letter
William N. Bullard Letters
George C. Burmeister Diary
John P. Burnell Letters
John Preston Campbell Letters
Hugh T. Carlisle Journal and Memoir
Simon B. Carlton Letters
Levi L. Carr Letters
Heber Chase Letters
Hiram Clay Letters
Samuel C. Claytor Letters
Schuyler P. Coe Letters
Merit N. Cole Letters
Ellis-Marshall Family Papers
James Forbis Letters
Henry W. Gay Letters
Albion Gross Letters
John D. Hill Letter
Hunter Family Letters
Lewis H. Jones Collection
Frederick Kehrwecker Letters
Ezra Kidder Letters
Carroll E. Kingsley Letters
John Kline Letters
William H. Lambert Letters
Joseph Harrison Law Correspondence

Jacob Lester Letters
John C. Lingle Letters
Charles H. Littlefield Correspondence
William B. Lowe Letters
George B. Lower Letters
Charles Lutz Correspondence
Guilford D. Mace Letter
Robert McCreight Correspondence
Sylvester McElheney Letters
Robert Bruce McNeal Letter
Benjamin "J." [F.] Marshall Papers
Harvey M. Miller Letters
James E. Mitchell Letters
James W. Mulligan Letters
Burr Murdock Correspondence
William C. Murray Letters
Joseph Neff Letters
Harrison Nesbitt Letters
George Wallace Newcomb Letters
William Penn Oberlin Papers
Michael O'Brien Letters
William W. Otto Letters
Aaron Overstreet Letters
Francis Patrick Letters
Willis A. Pomeroy Letters
Jacob Powell Letters
Rake Family Letters
Francis A. D. Reges Letters
Cornelius T. Richmond Letters
John "A." [P.] Rowe Correspondence
William Moore Sayre Letters
Franz Schwenzer Correspondence
Charles N. Scott Correspondence
J. W. Shepard Letter
Francis M. Skillin Correspondence
Hampton P. Sloane Correspondence
Charles H. Smith Correspondence
Hosea H. Smith Letters
Samuel C. Steiner Letters
John M. Steward Letters

Ann Sturtevant Collection
George Telling Letters
Samuel Thoman Letters
William H. Trites Letter
Varnum Family Correspondence
Timothy Vedder Correspondence
John Viles Correspondence
S. Y. Webster Letter
Alfred Wheeler Letters
Thomas Williams Collection
Robert A. Forbes Correspondence
John B. Wilson Correspondence
John Turner Wood Correspondence
Talmadge Wood Correspondence
George W. Young Correspondence (17th Indiana)
George W. Young Letter (2nd Pennsylvania Cavalry)
Thomas C. Zanhiser Letter
Civil War Times Illustrated Collection
Jacob Behm Correspondence
John Burrill Letters
Nelson Chapin Letters
William Henry Croop Letters
Andrew F. Davis Letter
Friedrich P. Kappelman Letters
Harrisburg Civil War Round Table Collection
John Worthington Ames Papers
Benjamin F. Ashenfelter Letters
Joseph Barton Letters
John Boyer Letters
John Brislin Letters from the 96th Pennsylvania
Henry Carroll Papers
Daniel Faust Letters
Jacob Gauchnauer Letter
Gilbert Gulbrandson Letters
Jacob W. Haas Papers
Clement Hoffman Letters
Henry Franklin Huffer Letters
Henry Keiser Diary
Andrew Knox Letters
Bentley Kutz Letters

Isaac and Joseph Morrow Letters
David Nichol Papers
William Presley Letters
Henry Rinker Letters
David S. Siebert Papers
William Prince Collection
David F. Cheney Papers
Charles R. Johnson Letters
Michael J. Vreeland Papers
Thomas Balch Memorial Library, Leesburg, Va.
Civil War Letters
Boston Public Library, Boston, Mass.
Chapman Family Papers
Edward Klein Letters
Parker Pillsbury Letter
George A. Spinney Letters
Henry W. Tisdale Diary
Bowling Green State University, Bowling Green, Ohio
Askew Family Correspondence
Fast Family Letters
Peter Faulk Letters
Kerwecker Family Papers
Cary Library, Houlton, Maine
J. L. Barton Affidavit
Chautauqua County Historical Society, Westfield, N.Y.
James Burrows Letters
Robert I. Cowden Diary
Stephen P. Green Letters
Augustus Phetteplace Letters
Albion W. Tourgée Letters
Cincinnati Historical Society, Cincinnati, Ohio
George Benson Fox Letters
Miller Family Collection
Mathias Schwab Letters
Connecticut Historical Society, Hartford
Orra B. Bailey Letters
Elizur D. Belden Diary
Frederick Bill Letter
Henry H. Brown Papers
Josiah B. Corban Letters

Frederick Hooker Letters
George Kies Letters
James B. Law Letters
Mrs. William Newton Matson Letters
John H. Norton Letters
Timothy O'Sullivan Letters
Ellsworth N. Phelps Letters
Charles E. Sherman Collection
Francis Simpson Papers
William L. Winship Letters
Conway Public Library, Conway, N.H.
Old Town Records Collection
Conway Town Hall, Center Conway, N.H.
Town Clerk's Records
Dartmouth College, Hanover, N.H.
Ira M. Barton Papers
George Benton Codman Letters
Claude Goings Letters
Leander and Emily Harris Letters
Sumner F. Hurd Letters to Ira M. Barton
David Leigh Letters
John McCoy Letters
Albert M. Putnam Letters
Oscar D. Robinson Papers
Ransom F. Sargent Papers
John W. Sturtevant Papers
Dickinson College, Carlisle, Pa.
John Taylor Cuddy Letters
Duke University, Durham, N.C.
William L. Broaddus Papers
Frederick W. Clark Papers
Darius Starr Papers
Earlham College, Richmond, Ind.
Thomas W. Barnett Diary
Clarkson Butterworth Diary
John Harvey Letters
Walter Roberts Letters
Fairbanks Museum, St. Johnsbury, Vt.
William Henry Proctor Papers
Galena Public Library, Galena, Ill.

Luther Cowen File
Gettysburg College, Gettysburg, Pa.
Frederick H. Kronenberger Papers
John W. Miner Letters
Rutherford B. Hayes Presidential Library, Fremont, Ohio
Charles Babbitt Letters
Cooke Family Papers
Lucy Webb Hayes Letters
William Jackman Letters
Historical Society of Cheshire County, Keene, N.H.
Clark H. Carr Letters
Disbursements of Aid for Soldiers' Families, Keene City Records
Oscar T. Frink Letters
James Houlihan Letters
Lake Family Civil War Letters
Horace Kendall Rugg Letters
Charles W. Wilcox Papers
Historical Society of Pennsylvania, Philadelphia
Simon Gratz Collection
Indiana Historical Society, Indianapolis
James A. Adams Letters
Elijah H. C. Cavins Papers
Chapin Family Papers
Miriam W. Green Papers
John F. Lester Diary
W. C. Patton Diaries
Henry A. Robinson Letters
Birt Scott Letter
David S. Scott Letters
William Steele Letters
David Werking Letters
Indiana State Library, Indianapolis
Flavius Bellamy Diary
Chittenden Papers
James H. Luther Collection
Indiana University, Bloomington
Joseph F. Lovering Diary
Thompson Manuscripts
Weeks Family Manuscripts
Kansas State Historical Society, Topeka

James H. Guthrie Diary
William Casper Haynes Papers
Webster W. Moses Diaries
Alvah Curtis Trueblood Diary
Library of Congress, Washington, D.C.
John Carvel Arnold Papers
George R. Ayers Letter
Orra B. Bailey Papers
William H. Bradbury Papers
Charles Buford Papers
Simon Cameron Papers
David Coon Letters
John A. J. Cresswell Papers
Henry L. Dawes Papers
Wilbur Fisk Diary
James J. Gillette Papers
E. N. Gilpin Diary
Walter Quintin Gresham Papers
William Hamilton Papers
Samuel P. Heintzelman Journal
Joseph Holt Papers
George O. Jewett Papers
Richard Lathers Papers
Joseph Lester Papers
Manton Marble Papers
Helen Varnum Hill McCalla Diary
Rufus Mead Papers
Montgomery Meigs Papers
William Owner Diary
Abram V. Parmenter Diary
Fitz John Porter Papers
Wilbur Huntington Proctor Diary
Charles W. Reed Collection
James Edward Shortelle Papers
Edwin M. Stanton Papers
Hazard Stevens Family Papers
Thaddeus Stevens Papers
William R. Stimson Letters
Bela T. St. John Papers
Horatio Nelson Taft Diary

Lyman Trumbull Papers
Edwin A. Van Cise Papers
Benjamin Wade Papers
George Washington Papers
Edwin O. Wentworth Papers
Charles H. Woodwell Diary
Maine Historical Society, Portland
William Bryant Adams Papers
James Brown Papers
Eben S. Calderwood Letters
Greenlief P. Foster Letters
Lawrence Joyce Papers
Meshack P. Larry Letters
James A. Milliken Collection
Carl Knowles Moses Letters
Perry Family Correspondence
Marshall Phillips Correspondence
George M. Redlon Papers
John Parris Sheahan Correspondence
Leonard Valentine Correspondence
Edward F. Waite Correspondence
Isaac Webb Letters
Manassas National Battlefield Park, Manassas, Va.
Ai B. Thompson Letters
Mariners Museum, Newport News, Va.
George S. Geer Letters
Maryland Historical Society, Baltimore
Luther Van Buren Furber Collection
Massachusetts Historical Society, Boston
Charles E. Bowers Papers
Francis Brooks Diary
Charles Burrill Papers
Josiah C. Fuller Papers
Henderson Family Papers
Holmes Family Papers
Lucy Larcom Diaries
Andrew H. Linscott Papers
Frank C. Morse Papers
Otis Norcross Recruitment Papers
James Albert Osborne Diary

John Owen Jr. Letters
Oliver W. Peabody Papers
Calvin W. Smith Papers
Samuel Storrow Papers
Troup Family Papers
Adin Ballou Underwood Letters
Webber Family Correspondence.
Alfred Metcalf White Letters
Myron Rice Wood Letters

Minnesota Historical Society, St. Paul
"Letters Written by Elias and Elisha Cowan" (typescript)
A. P. Davies Letters
William Doyle Letter
Chester E. Evans Letters
Jonas Holland Howe and Family Papers
Charles Marples and Family Correspondence
John H. Mitchell and Family Papers
M. D. Peak Letters
Mary E. Richards and Family Papers
Stebbins Family Papers
Peter Wolford Letters

Missouri Historical Society, St. Louis
Badger Collection
Bemis Family Papers
Lucien Eaton Papers
Herbert S. Hadley Papers
Richard Marshall Johnson Diaries

Mystic Seaport Museum, Mystic, Conn.
Carsten DeWit Journal
Charles A. Poole, "Journal of the Cruis of the U.S.S. Kearsarge in Serch of Rebel Privateers"
William Wainwright Journal

National Archives, Washington, D.C.
Records of the Veterans Administration, RG15
Individual Pension Files
Navy Widow's Certificates (M1279)
Organization Index to Pension Files of Veterans Who Served between 1861 and 1900 (T289)
Bureau of the Census, RG29
Seventh Census of the United States (M432)

Eighth Census of the United States (M653)
Ninth Census of the United States (M593)
Ninth Census of Minnesota (T132)
Twelfth Census of the United States (T623)
Thirteenth Census of the United States (T624)
Fourteenth Census of the United States (T625)
Fifteenth Census of the United States (T626)
Records of the Adjutant General, RG94
Case Files of Investigations by Levi C. Turner and Lafayette C. Baker, 1861–66 (M797)
Compiled Service Records of Volunteer Union Soldiers Who Served in Organizations from the State of Missouri (M405)
Individual Military Service Records
Letters and Their Enclosures Received by the Commission Branch of the Adjutant General's Office, 1863–70 (M1064)
Letters Received by the Office of the Adjutant General, Main Series, 1861–70 (M619)
Register of Enlistments in the U.S. Army, 1798–1914 (M233)
War Department Collection of Confederate Records, RG109
Letters Received by the Confederate Secretary of War (M437)
Nebraska State Historical Society, Lincoln
Charles Hadsall Diaries
New Hampshire Department of Records Management and Archives, Concord
Enlistment Papers
Executive Correspondence
Military Records, RG12
Court-Martial Records, Box 10
Correspondence, Box 8
Recruiting Station Records
New Hampshire Historical Society, Concord
Aldrich-Thompson Family Papers
Alexandria Recruiting Records
Orrin Brownson Papers
Burnham-Stearns Family Papers
George H. Caverly Diary
George Henry Chandler Papers
Lizzie Corning Diary
Elisha and Samuel Douglass Papers
John Gilbert Letters
Joseph Gilmore Papers

George W. Gordon Letters
Solomon Grannis Diary
Edward F. Hall Letters
Charles Emerson Howe Letters
James S. Howes Letters
Elisha M. Kempton Papers
Richard Peabody Kent Diary
Charles Whipple Pickering Letterbooks
Alonzo F. Pierce Letters
George H. P. Rowell Letters
Ezra Sanborn Diary
George H. Sargent Letters
Albert B. Stearns Letters
George Stearns Letters
John O. Stevens Letters
Andrew J. Stone Papers
Mason Weare Tappan Papers
Thompson Family Papers
Hosea Towne Papers
Nathaniel Truell Letters
George E. Upton Letters

New Hampshire State Library, Concord
Ransom Merritt Neal Diary
Willard J. Templeton Letters
Herbert J. Willand Journal

New York State Library, Albany
Abram Bogart Letters
Jasper Mabie Letter
Wesley H. Shaw Letters
James B. Turner Papers
Charles E. Walbridge Letters

Northern Illinois University, DeKalb
Francis H. Bowman Collection

North Yarmouth Historical Society, North Yarmouth, Maine
Luther Lawrence Letters

Ohio Historical Society, Columbus
Core-Porter Letters
Joseph Easton Papers
Joseph and John Giffen Papers
Ohio Provost Marshal's Papers

Nathaniel L. Parmeter Diary
Albert Rogall Papers
Thomas Thomson Taylor Papers
Clinton B. Winterstein Papers
Peabody Essex Museum, Salem, Mass.
Lewis R. Caswell Letters
Francis Crowninshield Papers
Fowler Family Manuscripts
John Peirce Papers
Providence Public Library, Providence, R.I.
Letters of Charlotte Dailey, Albert Dailey, and Walter Gardiner
George Randall Letters
Rhode Island Historical Society, Providence
William W. Chapin Diary
Edmund W. Fales Family Papers
Lester P. Fales Papers
Sheldon Museum, Middlebury, Vt.
Albert Fletcher Correspondence
Sanford Family Collection
William B. Stevens's Civil War Letters, Rokeby Museum
State Historical Society of Iowa, Des Moines
Adjutant General's Correspondence
Disloyal Sentiments File
Amasa Orlando Allen Papers
William R. Barnes Letters
Henry Bobinhouse Letters
Jacob Hunter Papers
Thomas Jefferson Lewis Papers
Charles Mason Papers
William and Jane Thompson Letters
David West Papers
State Historical Society of Iowa, Iowa City
Frank Collins Letters
William H. Cotton Letters
Amos Noyes Currier Letters
George DeHart Letters
S. S. Farwell Collection
John M. Frederick Letters
Adoniram Judson Withrow Letters
State Historical Society of Missouri, Columbia

Western Historical Manuscripts Collection
William W. Branson Diary
Mary Jane Vaughn Clark Letter
Draper-McClurg Family Papers
Odon Guitar Collection
Henry Wadsworth Letters
Stoughton Historical Society, Stoughton, Mass.
Alfred Edward Waldo Diary
University of Iowa, Iowa City
Papers of the Bean Family
Marcellus W. Darling Papers
Andrew F. Davis Papers
Giauque Family Papers
Papers of George F. Hall
Iowa Women's Archives
Catherine Snedeker Hill Collection
Ellen Mowrer Miller Collection
Joseph Kohout Papers
Byron McClain Letters
Papers of William and Titus Rigby
Russell Family Papers
Papers of the Sterns Family
Papers of Myron Underwood
University of Kansas, Lawrence
Joseph Henry Leighty Collection
University of Michigan, Ann Arbor
Bentley Library
Boardman Family Papers
William Boston Papers
Addison S. Boyce Letters
Robert Crouse Papers
Raymond Cazallis Davis Papers
Claudius Buchanan Grant Papers
Edward Henry Courtney Taylor Correspondence
Elmer D. Wallace Letters
Harvey L. Warner Letters
Clements Library
George Tobey Anthony Letters
Aplin Family Papers
Clement Abner Boughton Papers

Burbank Brothers Papers
John N. Dickie Diary
William Pitt Fessenden Papers
Stephen A. Hurlbut Letter
Christopher Keller Letters
Joseph H. Leach Letter
Henry Grimes Marshall Letters
Charles M. Maxim Letters
James T. Miller Letters
Miller Brothers Letters
Richard Cary Morse Letters
Fred [Ferdinand] H. Phillips Letter
William and Frederic Speed Letters
Frank H. Sterns Letters
Edmund Townsend Papers
Washburne Family Letters
John Darrah Wilkins Letters
University of New Hampshire, Durham
Barrus Family Papers
Leander Harris Letters
John Henry Jenks Papers
University of North Carolina, Chapel Hill
Southern Historical Collection
R. P. Bush Letter
Silas E. Fales Papers
Federal Soldiers' Letters
Michael Green Letters
Charles L. Hewitt Letters and Notebook
Louis Phillip Morrison Papers
Isaac C. Richardson Letters
Andrew J. Sproul Papers
Jeremiah Stetson Papers
Letters Addressed to Alexander E. Thompson
Webb Family Papers
University of Notre Dame, Notre Dame, Ind.
Benton-Beach Family Correspondence
Blanchard-Walker Letters
Caley Family Correspondence
William Combs Letters
John M. Jackson Letters

Miller Family Correspondence
Harrison E. Randall Letters
Thomas Family Correspondence
University of Rochester, Rochester, N.Y.
Norman B. Carr Papers
Lyman Chandler Family Papers
Fellows Family Papers
Huntington-Hooker Papers
University of Vermont, Burlington
John Q. Amidon Letters
Charles E. Chace Letters
Cobb Family Papers
Joel Glover Letters
Charles Gilbert Gould Letters
Richard J. Irwin Letters
George M. Jones Papers
Kinerson Family Papers
Chester K. Leach Papers
Charles Manson Letters
Augustus Paddock Letters
Tabor H. Parcher Letters
Parker Family Papers
Jonathan Remington Papers
Abram Rowell Letters
Joseph C. Rutherford Papers
Savage Family Papers
Scott Letters
Bradford P. Sparrow Papers
William Stow Letters
Vermont Historical Society, Barre
Peter M. Abbott Letters
Philip Arsino Letters
Valentine G. Barney Papers
Barton Family Papers
Beard Family Papers
Boardman and Miles Family Papers
Hubert and Laura Tupper Brown Letters
Thomas H. Brown Letters
Calvert-Parker Letters
Charles Cummings Papers

Letters to Miss Wealthy Field
George Oscar French Letters
Gale-Morse Family Papers
Edwin C. Hall Letters
Albert Harris Papers
William Wirt Henry Papers
William Hogan Letters
Edwin Horton Papers
Benjamin F. Hulburd Letters
Alfred Horton Keith Papers
Lyndon State College Collection
Middlesex Papers
Henry J. Vaughn Letters
Joseph Spafford Letters
Irvin W. Spooner Correspondence
James F. Stoddard Letters
Merritt H. Stone Letters
Esther M. Thayer Correspondence
Dudley Tillison Letters
William Townsend Family Papers
"Letters of the Samuel Cook Turner Family" (typescript)
Lyman Williams Papers
John Wilmot Letters

Virginia Historical Society, Richmond
Charles Edward Bates Papers

Virginia Polytechnic Institute and State University, Blacksburg
Henry A. Converse Letter
John Hilton Collection
Fred Lyman Letter
Felix Voltz Letters

Western Reserve Historical Society, Cleveland
Alexander Bunt Family Papers
Thomas A. Covert Papers
Daniel D. Hopper Papers
Hyatt Family Papers
Zerah Coston Monks Family Papers
James Nesbitt and Isaac P. C. Raub Letters
Cyrus H. Stockwell Papers
Marion D. Ward Letters
E. G. Wood Papers

Wilson's Creek National Battlefield, Republic, Mo.
 Horace Poole Diary
Wisconsin Historical Society, Madison
 Gideon Winan Allen Letters
 John J. Barney Papers
 George W. Buffum Letters
 Allen Church Letter
 John T. Clark Papers
 Newton H. Culver Diary
 Horace Currier Diary
 James Rood Doolittle Papers
 Olivia Brown Hazeltine Papers
 Alonzo Gilbert Jack Letters
 Rufus King Papers
 Lehmann Family Papers
 Charles N. Mumford Letters
 William L. Phillips Letters
 Levi Shell Letters
 Benjamin T. Wright Correspondence
 Henry F. Young Papers
Yale University, New Haven, Conn.
 Beinecke Library
  William Coates Letters
  Samuel Ryan Curtis Papers
  Lambert A. Martin Diary and Letters
 Sterling Library
  Charles Morgan Coit Papers
  J. B. Dawley Correspondence

PUBLISHED WORKS

Abbott, Stephen G. *The First New Hampshire Volunteers in the Great Rebellion.* Keene, N.H.: Sentinel, 1890.

[Acton, Edward A.]. "'Dear Mollie': Letters of Captain Edward A. Acton to His Wife, 1862." *Pennsylvania Magazine of History and Biography* 89, no. 1 (January 1965): 3–51.

Adams, Henry. *The Education of Henry Adams: An Autobiography.* 1918. Reprint with an introduction by D. W. Brogan. Boston, Mass.: Houghton Mifflin, 1961.

Alderson, Kevin, and Patsy Alderson, eds. *Letters Home to Sarah: The Civil War Letters of*

Guy C. Taylor, Thirty-sixth Wisconsin Volunteers. Madison: University of Wisconsin Press, 2012.

Aldridge, Katherine M., ed. *No Freedom Shrieker: The Civil War Letters of Union Soldier Charles Biddlecom.* Ithaca, N.Y.: Paramount Market, 2012.

Alpert, Cady, and Kyle D. Kauffman. "The Economics of the Union Draft: Institutional Failure and Government Manipulation of the Labor Market during the Civil War." *Essays in Economic and Business History* 17 (1999): 89–107.

Ameur, Farid. *Voyage en Amérique, 1861–1862: Un prince français dans la guerre de Sécession.* Paris: Perrin/Fondation Saint-Louis, 2011.

Annual Report of the Selectmen of the Town of Conway, N.H. Concord, N.H.: various printers, 1855–65.

Athearn, Robert G., ed. *Soldier in the West: The Civil War Letters of Alfred Lacey Hough.* With an introduction by John Newbold Hough. Philadelphia: University of Pennsylvania Press, 1957.

Ayling, Augustus D. *Revised Register of the Soldiers and Sailors of New Hampshire in the War of the Rebellion, 1861–1866.* Concord, N.H.: Ira C. Evans, 1895.

Balace, Francis. *Recrutements en Belgique pour les troupes fédérales, 1864–1865: En marge de la Guerre de Sécession.* Brussels: Center for American Studies, 1970.

Balleisen, Edward J. *Navigating Failure: Bankruptcy and Commercial Society in Antebellum America.* Chapel Hill: University of North Carolina Press, 2001.

Barnes, Joseph K. *The Medical and Surgical History of the War of the Rebellion (1861–65).* 15 vols. 1870. Reprint, Wilmington, N.C.: Broadfoot, 1990.

Barnes, Joseph W. "Bridging the Lower Falls." *Rochester History* 36, no. 1 (January 1974): 1–24.

Basile, Leon, ed. *The Civil War Diary of Amos E. Stearns, a Prisoner at Andersonville.* Rutherford, N.J.: Fairleigh Dickinson University Press, 1981.

Basler, Roy P., ed. *The Collected Works of Abraham Lincoln.* 9 vols. New Brunswick, N.J.: Rutgers University Press, 1953.

Bates, Samuel P. *History of Pennsylvania Volunteers, 1861–5.* 5 vols. Harrisburg, Pa.: B. Singerly, 1869–71.

Beale, Howard K., ed. *The Diary of Edward Bates.* Washington, D.C.: Government Printing Office, 1933.

Beasecker, Robert, ed. *I Hope to Do My Country Service: The Civil War Letters of John Bennitt, M.D., Surgeon, 19th Michigan Infantry.* Detroit, Mich.: Wayne State University Press, 2005.

Becker, Carl M., and Ritchie Thomas, eds. *Hearth and Knapsack: The Ladley Letters, 1857–1880.* Athens: Ohio University Press, 1988.

Bek, William G., trans. "The Civil War Diary of John T. Buegel, Union Soldier." *Missouri Historical Review* 40, no. 3 (April 1946): 307–29; no. 4 (July 1946): 503–30.

Bell, Frank [J]. "The Question of Pensions: A Soldier's View." *Century Magazine* 42, no. 5 (September 1891): 790–92.

Bender, Robert Patrick, ed. *Like Grass before the Scythe: The Life and Death of Sgt. William Remmel, 121st New York Infantry.* Tuscaloosa: University of Alabama Press, 2007.

Benedict, G. G. *Vermont in the Civil War: A History of the Part Taken by the Vermont Soldiers and Sailors in the War for the Union, 1861–5.* 2 vols. Burlington, Vt.: Free Press, 1886, 1888.

Bernstein, Iver. *The New York City Draft Riots: Their Significance for American Society and Politics in the Age of the Civil War.* New York: Oxford University Press, 1990.

Bigelow, John. *Retrospections of an Active Life.* 5 vols. Garden City, N.Y.: Doubleday, Page, 1913.

Bilby, Joseph. "Give My Love to All: A Lieutenant's Letters Told the Story of the 3d New Jersey Infantry." *Civil War Times Illustrated* 28 (May 1989): 36–43.

Blair, William. "We Are Coming, Father Abraham—Eventually: The Problem of Northern Nationalism in the Pennsylvania Recruiting Drives of 1862." In *The War Was You and Me: Civilians in the American Civil War,* edited by Joan E. Cashin. Princeton, N.J.: Princeton University Press, 2002.

Blair, William Alan, ed. *A Politician Goes to War: The Civil War Letters of John White Geary.* University Park: Pennsylvania State University Press, 1995.

Blight, David W., ed. *When This Cruel War Is Over: The Civil War Letters of Charles Harvey Brewster.* Amherst: University of Massachusetts Press, 1992.

Bohrnstedt, Jennifer Cain, ed. *Soldiering with Sherman: Civil War Letters of George F. Cram.* With an Introduction by Orville Vernon Burton. DeKalb: Northern Illinois University Press, 2000.

———, ed. *While Father Is Away: The Civil War Letters of William H. Bradbury.* Lexington: University of Kentucky Press, 2003.

Branch, Edgar M. "A Proposed Calendar of Samuel Clemens's Steamboats, 15 April 1857 to 8 May 1861, with Commentary." *Mark Twain Journal* 24, no. 2 (Fall 1986): 2–27.

Branch, Edgar Marquess, et al., eds. *Mark Twain's Letters.* 6 vols. Berkeley: University of California Press, 1988–2002.

Briggs, John Ely. "The Enlistment of Iowa Troops during the Civil War," *Iowa Journal of History and Politics* 15 (July 1917): 323–92.

Britton, Anne Hartwell, and Thomas J. Reed, eds. *To My Beloved Wife and Boy at Home: The Letters and Diaries of Orderly Sergeant John F. L. Hartwell.* Madison, N.J.: Fairleigh Dickinson University Press, 1997.

Bruen, Ella Jane, and Brian M. Fitzgibbons, eds. *Through Ordinary Eyes: The Civil War Correspondence of Rufus Robbins, Private, 7th Regiment, Massachusetts Volunteers.* Lincoln: University of Nebraska Press, 2005.

Buck, Stephen J. "'A Contest in Which Blood Must Flow like Water': Du Page County and the Civil War." *Illinois Historical Journal* 87, no. 1 (Spring 1994): 2–20.

Buckingham, Peter H., ed. *All's for the Best: The Civil War Reminiscences and Letters of Daniel W. Sawtelle,* Eighth Maine Volunteer Infantry. Knoxville: University of Tennessee Press, 2001.

Burgess, Lauren Cook, ed. *An Uncommon Soldier: The Civil War Letters of Sarah Rosetta Wakeman, Alias Private Lyons Wakeman, 153rd Regiment, New York State Volunteers.* Pasadena, Md.: Minerva Center, 1994.

Burlingame, Michael, ed. *Dispatches from Lincoln's White House: The Anonymous Civil War Journalism of Presidential Secretary William O. Stoddard.* Lincoln: University of Nebraska Press, 2002.

Burlingame, Michael, and John R. Turner Ettling, eds. *Inside Lincoln's White House: The Complete Civil War Diary of John Hay.* Carbondale: Southern Illinois University Press, 1997.

Cain, Marvin R. "A 'Face of Battle' Needed: An Assessment of Motives and Men in Civil War Historiography." *Civil War History* 27, no. 1 (March 1982): 5–27.

Casey, John A. Jr. *New Men: Reconstructing the Image of the Veteran in Late-Nineteenth-Century American Literature and Culture.* New York: Fordham University Press, 2015.

Cassedy, Edward K., ed. *Dear Friends at Home: The Civil War Letters and Diaries of Sergeant Charles T. Bowen, Twelfth United States Infantry, 1861–1864 (Army of the Potomac).* Baltimore, Md.: Butternut and Blue, 2001.

Catton, Bruce. *Glory Road.* Garden City, N.Y.: Doubleday, 1952.

———. *A Stillness at Appomattox.* Garden City, N.Y.: Doubleday, 1956.

Chapman, George T. *Sketches of the Alumni of Dartmouth College, from the First Graduation in 1771 to the Present Time, with a Brief History of the Institution.* Cambridge, Mass.: Riverside, 1867.

Child, William. *Letters from a Civil War Surgeon.* Solon, Maine: Polar Bear, 2001.

Clement, Priscilla Ferguson. "The Transformation of the Wandering Poor in Nineteenth-Century Philadelphia." In *Walking to Work: Tramps in America, 1790–1935,* edited by Eric H. Monkkonen. Lincoln: University of Nebraska Press, 1984.

Coco, Gregory A., ed. *From Ball's Bluff to Gettysburg . . . and Beyond: The Civil War Letters of Private Roland E. Bowen, 15th Massachusetts Infantry, 1861–1864.* Gettysburg, Pa.: Thomas, 1994.

Cook, Judy, ed. *A Quiet Corner of the War: The Civil War Letters of Gilbert and Esther Claflin, Oconomowoc, Wisconsin.* Madison: University of Wisconsin Press, 2013.

Cullop, Charles P. "An Unequal Duel: Union Recruiting in Ireland, 1863–1864." *Civil War History* 13, no. 2 (June 1967): 101–13.

Cummings, Pamela, ed. *No Regrets: The Civil War Diary of David Day.* N.p.: AmberQuill, 2003.

Day, D[avid] L. *My Diary of Rambles with the 25th Mass. Volunteer Infantry, with Burnside's Coast Division; 18th Corps, and Army of the James.* Milford, Mass.: King & Billings, 1884.

Downing, Alexander G. *Downing's Civil War Diary.* Des Moines: Historical Department of Iowa, 1916.

Duerkes, Wayne N. "I for One Am Ready to Do My Part: The Initial Motivations That Inspired Men from Northern Illinois to Enlist in the U.S. Army, 1861–1862." *Journal of the Illinois Historical Society* 105, no. 4 (Winter 2012): 313–32.

Duncan, Russell, ed. *Blue-Eyed Child of Fortune: The Civil War Letters of Colonel Robert Gould Shaw.* Athens: University of Georgia Press, 1992.

Dyer, Elisha, comp. *Annual Report of the Adjutant General of the State of Rhode Island and Providence Plantations for the Year 1865.* 3 vols. Providence, R.I.: E. L. Freeman & Son, 1893–95.

Dyer, Frederick H. *A Compendium of the War of the Rebellion.* 1908. Reprint, with an introduction by Lee A. Wallace Jr., Dayton, Ohio: Morningside, 1978.

Easley, Virginia, ed. "Journal of the Civil War in Missouri: 1861, Henry Martyn Cheavens." *Missouri Historical Review* 56, no. 1 (October 1961): 12–25.

Elder, Donald C., III, ed. *A Damned Iowa Greyhound: The Civil War Letters of William Henry Harrison Clayton.* Iowa City: University of Iowa Press, 1998.

Eldredge, D[aniel]. *The Third New Hampshire and All about It.* Boston: E. B. Stillings, 1893.

Engle, Stephen D. *Gathering to Save a Nation: Lincoln and the Union's War Governors.* Chapel Hill: University of North Carolina Press, 2016.

Fabre, Cécile. "In Defence of Mercenarism." *British Journal of Political Science* 40, no. 3 (July 2010): 539–59.

Faler, Paul. "Cultural Aspects of the Industrial Revolution: Lynn, Massachusetts Shoemakers and Industrial Morality, 1826–1860." *Labor History* 15, no. 3 (Summer 1974): 367–94.

Favill, Josiah M. *The Diary of a Young Officer Serving with the Armies of the United States during the War of the Rebellion.* Chicago: R. R. Donnelley & Sons, 1909.

Ferrie, James P. "The Rich and the Dead: Socioeconomic Status and Mortality in the United States, 1850–1860." In *Health and Labor Force Participation over the Life Cycle,* edited by Dora L. Costa. Chicago: University of Chicago Press, 2003.

Fish, Carl Russell. "Social Relief in the Northwest during the Civil War." *American Historical Review* 22, no. 2 (January 1917): 309–24.

Fite, Emerson David. *Social and Industrial Conditions in the North during the Civil War.* 1910. Reprint, Williamstown, Mass.: Corner House, 1976.

Flannery, Michael A., and Katherine H. Oomens, eds. *Well Satisfied with My Position: The Civil War Journal of Spencer Bonsall.* Carbondale: Southern Illinois University Press, 2007.

Fogel, Robert William. "Toward a New Synthesis of the Role of Economic Issues in the Political Realignment of the 1850s." In *American Economic Development in Historical Perspective,* edited by Thomas Weiss and Donald Schaefer. Stanford, Calif.: Stanford University Press, 1994.

———. *Without Consent or Contract: The Rise and Fall of American Slavery.* New York: W. W. Norton, 1989.

Foote, Lorien. *The Gentlemen and the Roughs: Manhood, Honor, and Violence in the Union Army.* New York: New York University Press, 2010.

———. "Rich Man's War, Poor Man's Fight: Class, Ideology, and Discipline in the Union Army." *Civil War History* 51, no. 3 (November 2005): 269–87.

Foreign Emigrant Society. [Boston]: Prentiss and Deland, n.d.

Foroughi, Andrea R., ed. *Go If You Think It Your Duty: A Minnesota Couple's Civil War Letters.* St. Paul: Minnesota Historical Society Press, 2008.

Foster, John Young. *New Jersey and the Rebellion, a History of the Services of the Troops and People of New Jersey in Aid of the Union Cause.* Newark, N.J.: Martin R. Dennis, 1868.

Frank, Joseph Allan. *With Ballot and Bayonet: The Political Socialization of American Civil War Soldiers.* Athens: University of Georgia Press, 1998.

Gallagher, Gary W. *The Union War.* Cambridge, Mass.: Harvard University Press, 2011.

Gallman, J. Matthew. "Entrepreneurial Experiences in the Civil War: Evidence from Philadelphia." In *American Economic Development in Historical Perspective,* edited by Thomas Weiss and Donald Schaefer. Stanford, Calif.: Stanford University, 1994.

———. *The North Fights the Civil War: The Home Front.* Chicago: Ivan R. Dee, 1994.

Gallman, Robert E., ed. *American Economic Growth and Standards of Living before the Civil War.* Chicago: University of Chicago Press, 1992.

Gavin, William Gilfillan, ed. *Infantryman Pettit: The Civil War Letters of Corporal Frederick Pettit.* New York: Avon Books, 1990.

Geary, James W. *We Need Men: The Union Draft in the Civil War.* DeKalb: Northern Illinois University Press, 1991.

Glasson, William H. *Federal Military Pensions in the United States.* New York: Oxford University Press, 1918.

Glatthaar, Joseph T. *Soldiering in the Army of Northern Virginia: A Statistical Portrait of the Troops Who Served under Robert E. Lee.* Chapel Hill: University of North Carolina Press, 2011.

———. "'Touched with Fire': Uncommon Soldiers of the Civil War." *Organization of American Historians Magazine of History* 26, no. 2 (April 2012): 19–24.

Glickstein, Jonathan A. *American Exceptionalism, American Anxiety: Wages, Competition, and Degraded Labor in the Antebellum United States.* Charlottesville: University of Virginia Press, 2002.

Goldin, Claudia D., and Frank D. Lewis. "The Economic Cost of the American Civil War: Estimates and Implications." *Journal of Economic History* 35, no. 2 (June 1975): 299–326.

Gordon, Lesley J. *A Broken Regiment: The 16th Connecticut's Civil War.* Baton Rouge: Louisiana State University, 2014.

Greene, Samuel Dana. "In the 'Monitor' Turret." In Buel and Johnson, *Battles and Leaders of the Civil War,* 1:719–29.

Greenleaf, Margery, ed. *Letters to Eliza from a Union Soldier.* Chicago: Follett, [1970].

Grimsley, Mark, and Todd D. Miller, eds. *The Union Must Stand: The Civil War Diary of John Quincy Adams Campbell, Fifth Iowa Volunteer Infantry.* Knoxville: University of Tennessee Press, 2000.

Gurowski, Adam. *Diary from March 4, 1861, to November 12, 1862.* Boston, Mass.: Lee and Shepard, 1862.

Hager, Michael E. "Massachusetts's German Mercenaries in the Civil War." *New England Ancestors* 8, no. 2 (Spring 2007): 20–24.

[Haines, Zenas T.]. *Letters from the Forty-fourth Regiment, M.V.M.: A Record of the Experience of a Nine Months' Regiment in the Department of North Carolina in 1862–3, by "Corporal."* Boston: Herald Job Office, 1863.

Hamer, Marguerite B. "Luring Canadian Soldiers into Union Lines during the War between the States." *Canadian Historical Review* 27, no. 1 (March 1946): 150–62.

Hammer, Jefferson J., ed. *Frederic Augustus James's Civil War Diary: Sumter to Andersonville.* Rutherford, N.J.: Fairleigh Dickinson University Press, 1973.

Harris, Emily J. "Sons and Soldiers: Deerfield, Massachusetts and the Civil War." *Civil War History* 30, no. 2 (June 1984): 157–71.

Harris, Robert F., and John Niflot, eds. *Dear Sister: The Civil War Letters of the Brothers Gould.* Westport, Conn.: Praeger, 1998.

Harris, William C. *Lincoln and the Union Governors.* Carbondale: Southern Illinois University Press, 2013.

Harwell, Richard Barksdale, ed. *Kate: The Journal of a Confederate Nurse.* Baton Rouge: Louisiana State University Press, 1959.

Hauptman, Laurence M., ed. *A Seneca Indian in the Union Army: The Civil War Letters of Sergeant Isaac Newton Parker, 1861–1865.* Shippensburg, Pa.: Burd Street, 1995.

Haynes, Martin A. *A History of the Second Regiment, New Hampshire Volunteer Infantry, in the War of the Rebellion.* Lakeport, N.H.: privately printed, 1896.

———. *A Minor War History Compiled from a Soldier Boy's Letters to "The Girl I Left behind Me," 1861–1864.* Lakeport, N.H.: privately printed, 1916.

Hazard, Blanche. *The Organization of the Boot and Shoe Industry in Massachusetts before 1875.* Cambridge, Mass.: Harvard University Press, 1921.

Heitman, Francis B. *Historical Register and Dictionary of the United States Army, from its Organization, September 29, 1789, to March 2, 1903.* 2 vols. Washington, D.C.: Government Printing Office, 1903.

Hess, Earl J. *Liberty, Virtue, and Progress: Northerners and Their War for the Union.* New York: New York University Press, 1988.

———. *The Union Soldier in Battle: Enduring the Ordeal of Combat.* Lawrence: University Press of Kansas, 1997.

Hesseltine, William B. *Lincoln and the War Governors.* New York: Alfred A. Knopf, 1948.

Hill, Jim Dan, ed. *The Civil War Sketchbook of Charles Ellery Stedman, Surgeon, United States Navy.* San Rafael, Calif.: Presidio, 1976.

Hodge, Robert W., ed. *The Civil War Letters of Perry Mayo.* East Lansing: Michigan State University, 1967.

Holden, Walter, William E. Ross, and Elizabeth Slomba, eds. *Stand Firm and Fire Low: The Civil War Writings of Colonel Edward E. Cross.* Hanover, N.H.: University Press of New England, 2003.

Hoover, Mary Ellen, and Elin Williams Neiterman, and E. Dianne James, eds. *From Your Loving Son: Civil War Correspondence and Diaries of Private George F. Moore and His Family.* Bloomington, Ind.: iUniverse, 2011.

Horrocks, James. *My Dear Parents: The Civil War as Seen by an English Union Soldier.* Edited by A. S. Lewis. New York: Harcourt Brace Jovanovich, 1982.

Houston, Alan Fraser, ed. *Keep Up Good Courage: A Yankee Family in the Civil War.* Portsmouth, N.H.: Peter E. Randall, 2006.

Houston, Henry C. *The Thirty-second Maine Regiment of Infantry Volunteers.* Portland, Maine: Southworth Brothers, 1903.

Howe, Mark DeWolfe, ed. *Touched with Fire: Civil War Letters and Diary of Oliver Wendell Holmes, Jr. 1861–1864.* 1947. Reprint, New York: Da Capo, 1969.

Hughes, Ruth Lauer, and Jerry A. Althouse, eds. *The Civil War Letters of John A. Boon.* Lincoln, Neb.: privately printed, 1994.

Hughes, William E., ed. *The Civil War Papers of Lt. Colonel Newton T. Colby, New York Infantry.* Jefferson, N.C.: McFarland, 2003.

Hunley, C. Russell, ed. *The 14th U.S. Infantry in the American Civil War: John Young Letters.* Shippensburg, Pa.: Burd Street, 2000.

Huston, James L. *The Panic of 1857 and the Coming of the Civil War.* Baton Rouge: Louisiana State University Press, 1987.

Johnson, Robert U., and Clarence C. Buel, eds. *Battles and Leaders of the Civil War,* 4 vols. New York: Century, 1884–88.

Johnson, Russell L. "'A Debt Justly Due': The Relief of Civil War Soldiers and Their Families in Dubuque." *Annals of Iowa* 55, no. 3 (Summer 1996): 207–38.

———. "'Volunteer While You May': Manpower Mobilization in Dubuque, Iowa." In *Union Soldiers and the Northern Homefront: Wartime Experiences, Postwar Adjustments,* edited by Paul A. Cimbala and Randall M. Miller. New York: Fordham University Press, 2002.

Jordan, Brian Matthew. *Marching Home: Union Veterans and Their Unending Civil War.* New York: Liveright, 2014.

Jordan, John W., *Colonial and Revolutionary Families of Pennsylvania.* 4 vols. New York: Lewis, 1911.

Jordan, William B., ed. *The Civil War Journals of John Meade Gould, 1861–1866*. Baltimore, Md.: Butternut and Blue, 1997.

Josyph, Peter, ed. *The Wounded River: The Civil War Letters of John Vance Lauderdale, M.D.* East Lansing: Michigan State University Press, 1993.

Journal of the House of Representatives of the State of Indiana, during the Special Session of the General Assembly, Commencing April 24, 1861. Indianapolis: Berry R. Sulgrave, 1861.

Kallgren, Beverly Hayes, and James L. Crouthamel, eds. *"Dear Friend Anna": The Civil War Letters of a Common Soldier from Maine*. Orono: The University of Maine Press, 1992.

Kamphoefner, Walter D., and Wolfgang Helbich, eds. *Germans in the Civil War: The Letters They Wrote Home*. Translated by Susan Carter Vogel. Chapel Hill: University of North Carolina Press, 2006.

Kemp, Thomas R. "Community and War: The Civil War Experience of Two New Hampshire Towns." In *Toward a Social History of the American Civil War: Exploratory Essays*, edited by Maris A. Vinovskis. Cambridge, Eng.: Cambridge University Press, 1990.

Kessel, Reuben A., and Armen A. Alchian. "Real Wages in the North during the Civil War: Mitchell's Data Reinterpreted." *Journal of Law and Economics* 2 (October 1959): 95–113.

Kiesling, Lynne L., and Robert A. Margo. "Explaining the Rise in Antebellum Pauperism: New Evidence." *Quarterly Review of Economics and Finance* 37, no. 2 (Summer 1997): 405–17.

Kiper, Richard L., ed. *Dear Catherine, Dear Taylor: The Civil War Letters of a Union Soldier and His Wife*. Lawrence: University Press of Kansas, 2002.

Kohl, Lawrence Frederick, ed. *Irish Green and Union Blue: The Civil War Letters of Peter Welsh*. New York: Fordham University Press, 1986.

Kreiser, Lawrence A., Jr. "A Socioeconomic Study of Veterans of the 103rd Ohio Volunteer Infantry Regiment after the Civil War." *Ohio History* 107, no. 3–4 (Summer–Autumn 1998): 171–84.

Laas, Virginia Jeans, ed. *Wartime Washington: The Civil War Letters of Elizabeth Blair Lee*. Urbana: University of Illinois Press, 1991.

Larimer, Charles F., ed. *Love and Valor: The Intimate Civil War Letters between Captain Jacob and Emeline Ritner*. Western Springs, Ill.: Sigourney, 2000.

Lassen, Coralou Peel, ed. *Dear Sarah: Letters Home from a Soldier in the Iron Brigade*. Bloomington: Indiana University Press, 1999.

Lause, Mark A. *Free Labor: The Civil War and the Making of an American Working Class*. Urbana: University of Illinois Press, 2015.

Lawson, Melinda. *Patriot Fires: Forging a New American Nationalism in the Civil War North*. Lawrence: University Press of Kansas, 2002.

Ledman, Paul J. *A Maine Town Responds: Cape Elizabeth & South Portland in the Civil War.* Cape Elizabeth, Maine: Next Steps, 2003.

Lee, Chulhee. "Military Service and Economic Mobility: Evidence from the American Civil War." *Explorations in Economic History* 49, no. 3 (July 2012): 367–79.

———. "Selective Assignment of Military Positions in the Union Army: Implications for the Impact of the Civil War." *Social Science History* 23, no. 1 (Spring 1999): 67–97.

———. "Socioeconomic Background, Disease, and Mortality among Union Army Recruits: Implications for Economic and Demographic History." *Exploration in Economic History* 34, no. 1 (January 1997): 27–55.

———. "Socioeconomic Differences in the Health of Black Union Army Soldiers." *Social Science History* 33, no. 4 (Winter 2009): 427–57.

Linderman, Gerald F. *Embattled Courage: The Experience of Combat in the American Civil War.* New York: Free Press, 1987.

Long, Kathryn Teresa. *The Revival of 1857–58: Interpreting an American Religious Awakening.* New York: Oxford University Press, 1998.

Longacre, Edward G., ed. *From Antietam to Fort Fisher: The Civil War Letters of Edward King Wightman, 1862–1865.* Rutherford, N.J.: Fairleigh Dickinson University Press, 1985.

Lowe, David W., ed. *Meade's Army: The Private Notebooks of Lt. Col. Theodore Lyman.* Kent, Ohio: Kent State University Press, 2007.

Lord, Edward O. *History of the Ninth New Hampshire Volunteers in the War of the Rebellion.* Concord, N.H.: Republican Press Assoc., 1895.

Loving, Jerome M., ed. *Civil War Letters of George Washington Whitman.* Durham, N.C.: Duke University Press, 1975.

[Lusk, William Thompson]. *War Letters of William Thompson Lusk, Captain, Assistant Adjutant General, United States Volunteers, 1861–1863.* New York: privately printed, 1911.

Lutz, Amy. "Who Joins the Military?: A Look at Race, Class, and Immigration Status." *Journal of Political and Military Sociology* 36, no. 2 (Winter 2008): 167–88.

Manchester, Carol H., ed. *Joseph K. Manchester: Northern Son in the South, 1861–1863, His Letters, Family, and Friends.* Rockland: Maine Authors, [2012].

Mann, Albert W. *History of the Forty-Fifth Regiment Massachusetts Volunteer Militia, "The Cadet Regiment."* Jamaica Plain, Mass.: privately printed, 1908.

Manning, Chandra. *What This Cruel War Was Over: Soldiers, Slavery, and the Civil War.* New York: Alfred A. Knopf, 2007.

Mannis, Jedediah, and Galen R. Wilson, eds. *Bound to Be a Soldier: The Letters of Private James T. Miller, 111th Pennsylvania Infantry, 1861–1864.* Knoxville: University of Tennessee Press, 2001.

Margo, Robert A. *Wages and Labor Markets in the United States, 1820–1860.* Chicago: University of Chicago Press, 2000.

———. "Wages and Prices during the Antebellum Period: A Survey and New Evidence." In *American Economic Growth and Standards of Living before the Civil War,* edited by Robert E. Gallman. Chicago: University of Chicago Press, 1992.

Marshall, Joan E. "Aid for Union Soldiers' Families: A Comfortable Entitlement or a Pauper's Pittance? Indiana, 1861–1865." *Social Service Review* 78, no. 2 (June 2004): 207–42.

Marten, James [Alan]. *Children for the Union: The War Spirit on the Northern Home Front.* Chicago: Ivan R. Dee, 2004.

———. *Sing Not War: The Lives of Union and Confederate Veterans in Gilded Age America.* Chapel Hill: University of North Carolina Press, 2011.

Marvel, William. *Lincoln's Autocrat: The Life of Edwin Stanton.* Chapel Hill: University of North Carolina Press, 2015.

———. "A Poor Man's Fight: Civil War Enlistment Patterns in Conway, New Hampshire." *Historical New Hampshire* 43, no. 1 (Spring 1988): 21–40.

———. *Race of the Soil: The Ninth New Hampshire Regiment in the Civil War.* Wilmington, N.C.: Broadfoot, 1988.

———. *Tarnished Victory: Finishing Lincoln's War.* Boston: Houghton Mifflin Harcourt, 2011.

Massachusetts Soldiers, Sailors, and Marines in the Civil War. 8 vols. Norwood: Massachusetts Adjutant General, 1932.

McCague, James. *The Second Rebellion: The New York City Draft Riots of 1863.* New York: Dial, 1968.

McClure, John R. *Hoosier Farm Boy in Lincoln's Army: The Civil War Letters of Pvt. John R. McClure.* N.p.: privately printed, 1971.

McConnell, Stuart. *Glorious Contentment: The Grand Army of the Republic, 1865–1900.* Chapel Hill: University of North Carolina Press, 1992.

McKitrick, John. *The Civil War Letters of John McKitrick to His Wife Sophia.* Lincoln, Neb.: privately printed, 1982.

McPherson, James M. *Battle Cry of Freedom: The Civil War Era.* New York: Oxford University Press, 1988.

———. *For Cause and Comrade: Why Men Fought in the Civil War.* New York: Oxford University Press, 1997.

———. *What They Fought For, 1861–1865.* Baton Rouge: Louisiana State University Press, 1994.

McPherson, James M., and Patricia R. McPherson, eds. *Lamson of the Gettysburg: The Civil War Letters of Lieutenant Roswell H. Lamson, U.S. Navy.* New York: Oxford University Press, 1997.

Menge, W. Springer, and J. August Shimrak, eds. *The Civil War Notebooks of Daniel Chisholm: A Chronicle of Daily Life in the Union Army, 1864–1865.* New York: Ballantine Books, 1989.

Messent, Peter, and Steve Courtney, eds. *The Civil War Letters of Joseph Hopkins Twichell: A Chaplain's Story.* Athens: University of Georgia Press, 2006.

Metzger, Joan, ed. *The Griffith Letters: The Story of Frank Griffith and the 116th New York Volunteer Infantry in the Civil War.* Westminster, Md.: Heritage Books, 2004.

Miller, Richard F. "Brahmin Janissaries: John A. Andrew Mobilizes Massachusetts Upper Class for the Civil War." *New England Quarterly* 75, no. 2 (June 2002): 204–34.

———. *Harvard's Civil War: A History of the Twentieth Massachusetts Volunteer Infantry.* Hanover, N.H.: University Press of New England, 2005.

Minnesota in the Civil and Indian Wars, 1861–1865. St. Paul, Minn.: Pioneer, 1891.

Mintz, Stephen. *Moralists and Modernizers: America's Pre-Civil War Reformers.* Baltimore: Johns Hopkins University Press, 1995.

Mitchell, Reid. *Civil War Soldiers.* New York: Viking, 1988.

———. *The Vacant Chair: The Northern Soldier Leaves Home.* New York: Oxford University Press, 1993.

Mitchell, Wesley Clair. *A History of the Greenbacks, with Special Reference to the Economic Consequence of Their Issue: 1862–65.* Chicago: University of Chicago Press, 1903.

Mohr, James C., and Richard E. Winslow III, eds. *The Cormany Diaries: A Northern Family in the Civil War.* Pittsburgh: University of Pittsburgh Press, 1982.

Monkkonen, Eric H., ed. *Walking to Work: Tramps in America, 1790–1935.* Lincoln: University of Nebraska Press, 1984.

Morgan, Anita. "The Responsibilities of a Community at War." *Indiana Magazine of History* 113, no. 1 (March 2017): 48–77.

Moskow, Shirley Blotnick, [ed.]. *Emma's World: An Intimate Look at Lives Touched by the Civil War Era.* Far Hills, N.J.: New Horizon, 1990.

Mushkat, Jerome, ed. *A Citizen-Soldier's Civil War: The Letters of Brevet Major General Alvin C. Voris.* DeKalb: Northern Illinois University Press, 2002.

Neal, William A. *An Illustrated History of the Missouri Engineer and 25th Infantry Regiments.* Chicago: Donohue and Henneberry, 1889.

Nevins, Allen, ed. *A Diary of Battle: The Personal Journals of Colonel Charles S. Wainwright, 1861–1865.* New York: Harcourt, Brace & World, 1962.

Nevins, Allan, and Milton Halsey Thomas, eds. *The Diary of George Templeton Strong.* 4 vols. New York: Macmillan, 1952.

Niven, John, ed. *The Salmon P. Chase Papers.* 5 vols. Kent, Ohio: Kent State University Press, 1993–98.

Norris, James V. "A Northern Businessman Opposes the Civil War: Excerpts from the Letters of R. G. Dun." *Ohio History* 71, no. 2 (July 1962): 138–47.

Oberly, James W. *Sixty Million Acres: American Veterans and the Public Lands before the Civil War.* Kent, Ohio: Kent State University Press, 1990.

Official Records of the Union and Confederate Navies in the War of the Rebellion. 31 vols. Washington, D.C.: Government Printing Office, 1894–1927.

Official Roster of the Soldiers of the State of Ohio in the War of the Rebellion, 1861–1866. 12 vols. Cincinnati: State of Ohio, 1886.

Onderdonk, Benjamin T. *A Letter to the Rev. James C. Richmond, Presbyter of Rhode Island, and by His Own Showing, Principal Agent of the Conspirators, in the Recent Combination to Destroy the Bishop of New-York.* New York: Jones & Welsh, 1845.

Orr, Timothy J., ed. *Last to Leave the Field: The Life and Letters of First Sergeant Ambrose Henry Hayward, 28th Pennsylvania Volunteer Infantry.* Knoxville: University of Tennessee Press, 2011.

Osborne, Frederick M. *Private Osborne, Massachusetts 23rd Volunteers: Burnside Expedition, Roanoke Island Expedition, Second Front against Richmond.* Gretna, La.: Pelican, 2002.

Palmer, Beverly Wilson, and Holly Byers Ochoa, eds. *The Selected Papers of Thaddeus Stevens.* 2 vols. Pittsburgh: University of Pittsburgh Press, 1997–98.

Paludan, Phillip Shaw. *"A People's Contest": The Union and Civil War, 1861–1865.* New York: Harper & Row, 1988.

Patrick, Jeffrey L., and Robert J. Willey, eds. *Fighting for Liberty and Right: The Civil War Diary of William Bluffton Miller, First Sergeant, Company K., Seventy-fifth Indiana Volunteer Infantry.* Knoxville: University of Tennessee Press, 2005.

Pearson, Henry Greenleaf. *The Life of John A. Andrew, Governor of Massachusetts, 1861–1865.* 2 vols. Boston: Houghton Mifflin, 1904.

Pease, Theodore Calvin, and James G. Randall, eds. *The Diary of Orville Hickman Browning.* 2 vols. Springfield: Illinois State Historical Library, 1927, 1933.

Peck, Theodore S., comp. *Revised Roster of Vermont Volunteers and Lists of Vermonters Who Served in the Army and Navy of the United States during the War of the Rebellion, 1861–1866.* Montpelier, Vt.: Watchman, 1892.

Piston, William Garrett, and Richard W. Hatcher III. *Wilson's Creek: The Second Battle of the Civil War and the Men Who Fought It.* Chapel Hill: University of North Carolina Press, 2000.

Popchock, Barry, ed. *Soldier Boy: The Civil War Letters of Charles O. Musser, 29th Iowa.* Iowa City: University of Iowa Press, 2008.

Priest, John Michael, ed. . *John T. McMahon's Diary of the 136th New York, 1861–1864.* Shippensburg, Pa.: White Mane, 1992.

Puck, Susan T., ed. *Sacrifice at Vicksburg: Letters from the Front.* Shippensburg, Pa.: Burd Street, 1997.

Quaife, Milo M. "The Diary of Harvey Reid: Kept at Madison in the Spring of 1861." *Wisconsin Magazine of History* 1, no. 1 (September 1917): 35–63.

Quinn, E. B. *The Military History of Wisconsin.* Chicago: Clarke, 1866.

Racine, Phillip N., ed. *Unspoiled Heart: The Journal of Charles Mattocks of the 17th Maine.* Knoxville: University of Tennessee Press, 1994.

Ray, Jean P., ed. *The Diary of a Dead Man: Letters and Diary of Private Ira A. Pettit.* [Conschohocken, Pa.]: Acorn, 1979.

Record of Service of Connecticut Men in the Army and Navy of the United States during the War of the Rebellion. Hartford, Conn.: Case, Lockwood, & Brainard, 1889.

Reinhart, Joseph R. *August Willich's Gallant Dutchmen: Civil War Letters from the 32nd Indiana Infantry.* Kent, Ohio: Kent State University Press, 2006.

Report of the Adjutant General of the State of Illinois. 7 vols. Springfield: Baker, Bailhache, 1867.

Report of the Adjutant General of the State of Maine for the Years 1864 and 1865. Augusta: Stevens & Sayward, 1866.

Report of the Adjutant-General of the State of New-Hampshire for the Year Ending June 1, 1866. 2 vols. Concord: George E. Jenks, 1866.

Report of the Adjutant-General of the State of New-Hampshire for the Year Ending June 1, 1868. Manchester: John B. Clarke, 1868.

Report of the Joint Committee on the Conduct of the War. 3 vols. Washington, D.C.: Government Printing Office, 1863.

Rhodes, John H. *The History of Battery B, First Regiment Rhode Island Light Artillery.* Providence, R.I.: Snow & Farnham, 1894.

Richmond, James Cook. *Mr. Richmond's Reply to the "Statement" of the Late Bishop of New York.* New York : Burgess, Stringer, 1845.

Robertson, James I., Jr., ed. *The Civil War Letters of General Robert McAllister.* 1965. Reprint, Baton Rouge: Louisiana State University Press, 1998.

Robertson, John. *Michigan in the War.* Lansing, Mich.: W. S. George, 1882.

Robertson, John Gordon. "Re-Enlistment Patterns of Civil War Soldiers." *Journal of Interdisciplinary History* 32, no. 1 (Summer 2001): 15–35.

Roelker, William Greene. "Civil War Letters of William Ames: From Brown University to Bull Run." *Rhode Island Historical Society Collections* 33, no. 4 (October 1940): 73–92.

Rorabaugh, W. J. "Who Fought for the North in the Civil War? Concord, Massachusetts, Enlistments." *Journal of American History* 73, no. 3 (December 1986): 695–701.

Roster and Record of Iowa Soldiers in the War of the Rebellion. 6 vols. Des Moines: Emory H. English, 1908–1911.

Roster of Wisconsin Volunteers, War of the Rebellion, 1861–1865. 2 vols. Madison, Wis.: Democrat Printing, 1886.

Roth, Margaret Brobst, ed. *Well Mary: Civil War Letters of a Wisconsin Volunteer.* Madison: University of Wisconsin Press, 1960.

Rothman, Adam. "Slavery, the Civil War, and Reconstruction." In *American History Now,* edited by Eric Foner and Lisa McGirr. Philadelphia: American Historical Association, 2011.

Ruggles, Steven, Katie Genadek, Ronald Goeken, Josiah Grover, and Matthew Sobek. *Integrated Public Use Microdata Series: Version 6.0* [Machine-readable database]. Minneapolis: University of Minnesota, 2015.

Rundell, Walter, Jr. "'Despotism of Traitors': The Rebellious South through New York Eyes." *New York History* 45, no. 4 (October 1964): 331–67.

Sandage, Scott A. *Born Losers: A History of Failure in America.* Cambridge, Mass.: Harvard University Press, 2005.

Sauers, Richard A., ed. *The Civil War Journal of Colonel Bolton, 51st Pennsylvania, April 20, 1861–August 2, 1865.* Conshohocken, Pa.: Combined Publishing, 2000.

[Sawyer, Candace, ed.]. *Civil War Letters of Captain John Franklin Godfrey.* Portland, Maine: [Candace Sawyer], 1993.

Scarborough, William Kauffman, ed. *The Diary of Edmund Ruffin.* 3 vols. Baton Rouge: Louisiana State University Press, 1972–89.

Schaefer, Donald. "U.S. Immigration, 1850–59." In *American Economic Development in Historical Perspective,* edited by Thomas Weiss and Donald Schaefer. Stanford, Calif.: Stanford University Press, 1994.

Scott, Robert Garth, ed. *Fallen Leaves: The Civil War Letters of Major Henry Livermore Abbott.* Kent, Ohio: Kent State University Press, 1991.

Sears, Stephen W., ed. *For Country, Cause & Leader: The Civil War Journal of Charles B. Haydon.* New York: Ticknor & Fields, 1993.

Shannon, Fred A., ed. *The Civil War Letters of Sergeant Onley Andrus.* Urbana: University of Illinois Press, 1947.

———. "The Mercenary Factor in the Creation of the Union Army." *Mississippi Valley Historical Review* 12, no. 4 (March 1926): 523–49.

———. *The Organization and Administration of the Union Army, 1861–1865.* 2 vols. 1928. Reprint, Gloucester, Mass.: Peter Smith, 1965.

Sharkey, Robert P. *Money, Class, and Party: An Economic Study of Civil War and Reconstruction.* Baltimore: Johns Hopkins University Press, 1959.

Sheehan-Dean, Aaron, ed. *The View from the Ground: Experiences of Civil War Soldiers.* Lexington: University Press of Kentucky, 2007.

Silber, Nina, and Mary Beth Sievens, eds. *Yankee Correspondence: Civil War Letters between New England Soldiers and the Home Front.* Charlottesville: University Press of Virginia, 1996.

Simpson, Brooks D., and Jean V. Berlin, eds. *Sherman's Civil War: Selected Correspondence of William T. Sherman, 1860–1865.* Chapel Hill: University of North Carolina Press, 1999.

Skipper, Marti, and Jane Taylor, eds. *A Handful of Providence: The Civil War Letters of Lt. Richard Goldwaite, New York Volunteers, and Ellen Goldwaite.* Jefferson, N.C.: McFarland, 2004.

Sklansky, Jeffrey. *The Soul's Economy: Market Society and Selfhood in American Thought, 1820–1920.* Chapel Hill: University of North Carolina Press, 2002.

Snell, Mark A. "'If They Would Know What I Know It would Be Pretty Hard to Raise One Company in York': Recruiting, the Draft, and Society's Response in York County, Pennsylvania, 1861–1865." In *Union Soldiers and the Northern Homefront: Wartime Experiences, Postwar Adjustments,* edited by Paul A. Cimbala and Randall M. Miller. New York: Fordham University Press, 2002.

Sokoloff, Kenneth L. "Productivity Growth in Manufacturing during Early Industrialization: Evidence from the American Northeast, 1820 to 1860." Working Paper 1685. National Bureau of Economic Research, 1985.

Southwick, Thomas P. *A Duryee Zouave, by Thomas P. Southwick of the Fifth New York Volunteers*. Washington, D.C.: Acme Printing, 1930.

Spalding, Kenena Hansen, comp. *Tuf as a Boiled Owl: The Civil War Letters of Proctor Swallow 7th Vermont Volunteer Regiment*. Bloomington, Ind.: AuthorHouse, 2006.

Spall, Eric. "Foreigners in the Highest Trust: American Perceptions of European Mercenary Officers in the Continental Army." *Early American Studies, An Interdisciplinary Journal* 12, no. 2 (Spring 2014): 338–65.

Sparks, David S., ed. *Inside Lincoln's Army: The Diary of Marsena Rudolph Patrick, Provost Marshal General, Army of the Potomac*. New York: Thomas Yoseloff, 1964.

Stampp, Kenneth M. *America in 1857: A Nation on the Brink*. New York: Oxford University Press, 1990.

Statistics of the United States, (Including Mortality, Property, &c.,) in 1860; Compiled from the Original Returns and Being the Final Exhibit of the Eighth Census. Washington, D.C.: Government Printing Office, 1866.

Stearns, Amos E. *Narrative of Amos E. Stearns, Member of Co. A, 25th Regt. Mass. Vols.* Worcester, Mass.: Franklin P. Rice, 1887.

Steensma, Robert C., ed. *Drifting to an Unknown Future: The Civil War Letters of James E. Northrup and Samuel W. Northrup*. Sioux Falls, S.D.: Center for Western Studies, 2000.

Stryker, William S., comp. *Record of Officers and Men of New Jersey in the Civil War, 1861–1865*. 2 vols. Trenton, N.J.: John L. Murphy, 1876.

Tatum, Margaret Black, ed. "'Please Send Stamps': The Civil War Letters of William Allen Clark." *Indiana Magazine of History* 91, no. 3 (September 1995): 288–320.

Thomas, Teresa A. "For the Union, Not for Glory: Memory and the Civil War Volunteers of Lincoln, Massachusetts." *Civil War History* 40, no. 1 (March 1994): 25–47.

Thornton, Mark, and Robert B. Ekelund, Jr. *Tariffs, Blockades, and Inflation: The Economics of the Civil War*. Wilmington, Del.: Scholarly Resources, 2004.

Throne, Mildred, ed. "An Iowa Doctor in Blue: The Letters of Seneca B. Thrall, 1862–1864." *Iowa Journal of History* 58, no. 2 (April 1960): 97–188.

———. "Iowa Farm Letters, 1856–1865." *Iowa Journal of History* 58, no. 1 (January 1960): 37–88.

Tobie, Edward P. *History of the First Maine Cavalry, 1861–1865*. Boston: First Maine Cavalry Assoc., 1887.

Trefousse, Hans L. *Thaddeus Stevens: Nineteenth Century Egalitarian*. Chapel Hill: University of North Carolina Press, 1997.

Trimble, Richard, ed. *Brothers 'til Death: The Civil War Letters of William, Thomas, and Maggie Jones, 1861–1865*. Macon, Ga.: Mercer University Press, 2000.

Truxall, Aida Craig, ed. *"Respects to All": Letters of Two Pennsylvania Boys in the War of the Rebellion*. Pittsburgh: University of Pittsburgh Press, 1962.

Underhill, Charles S., ed. *"Your Soldier Boy Samuel": Civil War Letters of Lieut. Samuel Edmund Nichols, Amherst, '65, of the 37th Regiment Massachusetts Volunteers.* Buffalo, N.Y.: privately printed, 1929.

U.S. Congress. *Congressional Globe.* 37th and 38th Congresses.

Vinovskis, Maris A. "Have Social Historians Lost the Civil War? Some Preliminary Demographic Speculations." In *Toward a Social History of the American Civil War: Exploratory Essays,* edited by Maris A. Vinovskis. New York: Cambridge University Press, 1990.

Wainwright, Nicholas B., ed. *A Philadelphia Perspective: The Diary of Sidney George Fisher, Covering the Years 1834–1871.* Philadelphia: Historical Society of Pennsylvania, 1967.

Ware, Eugene Fitch. *The Lyon Campaign in Missouri, Being a History of the First Iowa Infantry.* Topeka, Kans.: Crane, 1907.

War of the Rebellion: A Compilation of the Official Records of the Union and Confederate Armies. 128 vols. Washington, D.C.: Government Printing Office, 1880–1901.

Washington, George. *The Papers of George Washington: Revolutionary War Series.* 24 vols. Charlottesville: University Press of Virginia., 1985–2016.

Watson, Ronald G., ed. *From Ashby to Andersonville: The Civil War Diary and Reminiscences of George A. Hitchcock, Company A, 21st Massachusetts Regiment, August 1862–January 1865.* Campbell, Calif.: Savas, 1997.

Wecter, Dixon. "The Veteran Wins Through." In *The Civil War Veteran: A Historical Reader,* edited by Larry M. Logue and Michael Barton. New York: New York University Press, 2007.

Weiss, Thomas, and Donald Schaefer, eds. *American Economic Development in Historical Perspective.* Stanford, Calif.: Stanford University Press, 1994.

White, Russell C., ed. *The Civil War Diary of Wyman S. White, First Sergeant of Company F, 2nd United States Sharpshooter Regiment, 1861–1865.* Baltimore: Butternut and Blue, 1993.

Wilkie, Franc B. *Pen and Powder.* Boston: Ticknor, 1888.

Williamson, Samuel H., and Louis P. Cain. "Measuring Slavery in 2016 Dollars." MeasuringWorth, 2016. https://www.measuringworth.com/slavery.php#textstar.

Wilson, Nancy D., ed. *Shouts and Whispers: The Civil War Correspondence of D. D. Priest of Mount Holly, Vermont.* Manchester Center, Vt.: Shires, 2011.

Woodworth, Steven E., ed. *The Musick of the Mocking Birds, the Roar of the Cannon: The Civil War Diary and Letters of William Winters.* Lincoln: University of Nebraska Press, 1998.

NEWSPAPERS AND PERIODICALS

Aegis and Transcript (Worcester, Mass.)
Alexandria (Va.) Gazette
The Alleghanian (Ebensburg, Pa.)
The Appleton (Wis.) Crescent
Aroostook Herald (Presque Isle, Maine)
Ashtabula (Ohio) Weekly Telegraph
Ashtabula (Ohio) Weekly Times
Atlas and Argus (Albany, N.Y.)
Bangor (Maine) Daily Whig and Courier
Barnstable (Mass.) Patriot
Beardstown (Ill.) Democrat
Bedford (Pa.) Gazette
Belmont Chronicle (St. Clairsville, Ohio)
Binghampton (N.Y.) Press
Boston Daily Advertiser
Boston Evening Transcript
Boston Journal
Boston Post
Bradford Reporter (Towanda, Pa.)
Brockport (N.Y.) Republic
The Bureau County Republican (Princeton, Ill.)
Burlington (Vt.) Free Press
Cadiz (Ohio) Democratic Sentinel
The Caledonian (St. Johnsbury, Vt.)
Cambridge (Mass.) Chronicle
Camden (N.J.) Democrat
Carroll County Register (Ossipee, N.H.)
Cass County Republican (Dowagiac, Mich.)
Cecil Whig (Elkton, Md.)
Cedar Valley Times (Cedar Rapids, Iowa)
Cheshire Republican (Keene, N.H.)
Chicago Evening Journal
Cincinnati Daily Commercial
Cincinnati Daily Enquirer
Cincinnati Daily Gazette
Cincinnati Daily Press
Civilian and Telegraph (Cumberland, Md.)
Cleveland Morning Leader

The Compiler (Gettysburg, Pa.)
Congressional Globe
Council Bluffs (Iowa) Bugle
The Crisis (Columbus, Ohio)
Daily American (Manchester, N.H.)
Daily Dayton (Ohio) Journal
Daily Democrat and News (Davenport, Iowa)
Daily Democratic Union (Peoria, Ill.)
The Daily Exchange (Baltimore, Md.)
Daily Evansville (Ind.) Journal
Daily Evening Courier (Madison, Ind.)
Daily Gate City (Keokuk, Iowa)
Daily Gazette and Courier (Northampton, Mass.)
Daily Green Mountain Freeman (Montpelier, Vt.)
Daily Intelligencer (Wheeling, Va.)
Daily Messenger (Hannibal, Mo.)
Daily Morning Chronicle (Portsmouth, N.H.)
Daily Ohio Statesman (Columbus)
Daily Toledo (Ohio) Blade
The Daily Union (Washington, D.C.)
Daily Wabash Express (Terre Haute, Ind.)
The Daily Whig and Republican (Quincy, Ill.)
The Dakotian (Yankton, Dak. Terr.)
Delaware (Ohio) Gazette
Delaware Journal (Wilmington)
Delphi (Ind.) Weekly Times
Democrat and Sentinel (Ebensburg, Pa.)
Democratic Mirror (Leesburg, Va.)
Dollar Weekly Mirror (Manchester, N.H.)
Door County Advocate (Sturgeon Bay, Wis.)
Dover (N.H.) Gazette
Dover (N.H.) Sentinel
Dubuque (Iowa) Daily Times
Dubuque (Iowa) Herald
Duluth (Minn.) News-Tribune
The Eastern Argus (Portland, Maine)
Eastern Townships Gazette and Shefford County Advertiser (Granby, C.E.)
East Saginaw (Mich.) Courier
Emporia (Kans.) News
Evening Argus (Rock Island, Ill.)

Evening Star (Washington, D.C.)
Fairfield (Iowa) Constitution
Fairfield (Iowa) Ledger
Farmers' Cabinet (Amherst, N.H.)
Fort Dodge (Iowa) Republican
Fort Scott (Kans.) Bulletin
Freeborn County (Minn.) Standard
Freeman's Journal (Cooperstown, N.Y.)
Gallipolis (Ohio) Journal
The Goodhue (Minn.) Volunteer
Grand Haven (Mich.) News
Grand Rapids (Mich.) Eagle
Grand River (Mich.) Times
Granite State News (Wolfeborough, N.H.)
Green Bay (Wis.) Advocate
Green Mountain Freeman (Montpelier, Vt.)
Hancock Jeffersonian (Findlay, Ohio)
Hartford (Conn.) Courant
Hartford (Conn.) Weekly Times
Haverhill (Mass.) Gazette
Highland Weekly News (Hillsborough, Ohio)
Hillsdale (Mich.) Standard
Holmes County Farmer (Millersburg, Ohio)
Holmes County Republican (Millersburg, Ohio)
Housatonic Republican (Falls Village, Conn.)
Illinois State Journal (Springfield)
Indiana American (Brookville)
Indiana State Sentinel (Indianapolis)
Jackson Standard (Jackson Court House, Ohio)
Jasper (Ind.) Weekly Courier
Jeffersonian Democrat (Chardon, Ohio)
Joliet (Ill.) Signal
The Kansas Chief (White Cloud)
Keene (N.H.) Sentinel
Kennebec Journal (Augusta, Maine)
Lafayette (Ind.) Daily Courier
Lamoille Newsdealer (Hyde Park, Vt.)
Lancaster (Ohio) Gazette
Lansing (Mich.) State Republican
Lawrence (Kans.) Republican

Der Lecha Caunty Patriot (Allentown, Pa.)
Lewiston (Maine) Daily Evening Journal
Lewistown (Pa.) Gazette
Linn County Hawk-Eye (Mount Vernon, Iowa)
Louisiana Courier (New Orleans)
Louisville (Ky.) Daily Democrat
Manchester (N.H.) Democrat
Manchester (N.H.) Mirror
Mankato (Minn.) Semi-Weekly Record
Marietta (Ohio) Intelligencer
Marshall County Republican (Plymouth, Ind.)
McArthur (Ohio) Democrat
Meigs County Telegraph (Pomeroy, Ohio)
Morning Star (Dover, N.H.)
Muscatine (Iowa) Weekly Journal
Nantucket (Mass.) Inquirer
Nashua (N.H.) Gazette and Hillsborough County Advertiser
National Eagle (Claremont, N.H.)
Newbern (N.C.) Weekly Progress
New Hampshire Argus and Spectator (Newport)
New Hampshire Patriot and State Gazette (Concord)
New Hampshire Statesman (Concord)
New Haven (Conn.) Daily Palladium
New Orleans Bee
New Orleans Daily Crescent
New York Herald
New York Times
New York Tribune
North Branch Democrat (Tunkhannock, Pa.)
The Ohio Democrat (New Philadelphia)
Ohio State Journal (Columbus)
Orleans Independent Standard (Irasburgh, Vt.)
Ottawa (Ill.) Free Trader
Ottumwa (Iowa) Courier
Oxford Democrat (Paris, Maine)
Peninsula News and Advertiser (Milford, Del.)
The People's Friend (Covington, Ind.)
Peterborough (N.H.) Transcript
Philadelphia Inquirer
Pioneer (New Rochelle, N.Y.)

Plymouth (Ind.) Weekly Democrat
Plymouth (Ohio) Advertiser
Portland (Maine) Advertiser
Portland (Maine) Daily Press
The Prairie Farmer (Chicago)
Providence (R.I.) Daily Journal
Providence (R.I.) Daily Post
Providence (R.I.) Evening Press
Provincetown (Mass.) Banner
Putnam Republican Banner (Greencastle, Ind.)
Quincy (Ill.) Herald
The Raftsman's Journal (Clearfield, Pa.)
Randolph County Journal (Winchester, Ind.)
Red Wing (Minn.) Sentinel
Republican Journal (Belfast, Maine)
Rochester (Ind.) Mercury
Rochester (Minn.) City Post
Rutland (Vt.) Herald
Smoky Hill and Republican Union (Junction City, Kans.)
South Danvers (Mass.) Wizard
The Spirit of Democracy (Woodsfield, Ohio)
Springfield (Ohio) Evening News
Stanstead (C.E.) Journal
Star and Herald (Dwight, Ill.)
St. Charles City (Iowa) Republican Intelligencer
St. Cloud (Minn.) Democrat
Steubenville (Ohio) Weekly Herald
Stillwater (Minn.) Messenger
St. Paul (Minn.) Pioneer and Democrat
The Summit County Beacon (Akron, Ohio)
The Sunbury (Pa.) American
True American (Steubenville, Ohio)
True Northerner (Paw Paw, Mich.)
Union and Advertiser (Rochester, N.Y.)
Urbana (Ohio) Union
Vermont Phoenix (Brattleboro)
Vermont Watchman and State Journal (Montpelier)
Vinton (Iowa) Eagle
Wabashaw Semi-Weekly County Herald (Read's Landing, Minn.)
Waterloo (Iowa) Courier

Wayne County Democrat (Wooster, Ohio)
Weekly Iowa State Reporter (Iowa City)
The Weekly Lancaster (Ohio) Gazette
The Weekly Portage Sentinel (Ravenna, Ohio)
Weekly Racine (Wis.) Advocate
Weekly Register (Point Pleasant, Ohio)
Western Reserve Chronicle (Warren, Ohio)
Winnipisaukee Gazette (Wolfeborough, N.H.)
Winona (Minn.) Daily Republican
Wolverine Citizen (Flint, Mich.)
Wyandot Pioneer (Upper Sandusky, Ohio)

MISCELLANEOUS

Headstone inscriptions, Head Cemetery, Hooksett, N.H.
Headstone inscriptions, Oak Hill Cemetery, Youngstown, Ohio.
Hoptak, John David. "The Influence of Socio-economic Background on Union Soldiers during the American Civil War." Ph.D. diss., Lehigh University, 2003.
Jones, Bruce E. "The Letters of Lauren Elmer Bent." MA thesis, Keene State College. 1976.
Luebke, Peter Clayton. "Shattering the Slave Power: Northern Soldiers Interpret Their Civil War." Ph.D. diss., University of Virginia. 2014.
Robertson, John Gordon. "Rich Man's War, Poor Man's Opportunity? Civil War Reenlistment and the Right to Rise." Ph.D. diss., Carnegie Mellon University, 2009.

INDEX